D0002006

A Tear Is an Intellectual Thing

A Tear Is an Intellectual Thing

The Meanings of Emotion

Jerome Neu

New York   Oxford
Oxford University Press
2000

Oxford University Press

Oxford   New York

Athens   Auckland   Bangkok   Bogotá   Buenos Aires   Calcutta
Cape Town   Chennai   Dar es Salaam   Delhi   Florence   Hong Kong   Istanbul
Karachi   Kuala Lumpur   Madrid   Melbourne   Mexico City   Mumbai
Nairobi   Paris   São Paulo   Singapore   Taipei   Tokyo   Toronto   Warsaw

and associated companies in
Berlin   Ibadan

Published by Oxford University Press, Inc.
198 Madison Avenue, New York, New York 10016

Oxford is a registered trademark of Oxford University Press

Library of Congress Cataloging-in-Publication Data
Neu, Jerome.
A tear is an intellectual thing : the meanings of emotion / Jerome Neu.
p.   cm.
Includes bibliographical references and index.
ISBN 0-19-512337-9
1. Emotions (Philosophy)   I. Title.
B105.E46N48   1999
128'.37—dc21   99-10364

1 3 5 7 9 8 6 4 2

Printed in the United States of America
on acid-free paper

ACKNOWLEDGMENTS

The essays in this book have been written over a period of more than twenty-five years. During that time I have benefited from the support of many institutions and individuals. I wish to gratefully acknowledge fellowships and other material assistance provided by the Rockefeller Foundation, the Stanford Humanities Center, the American Council of Learned Societies, and the National Endowment for the Humanities. Preparation of the manuscript was assisted by Faculty Research Funds granted by the University of California at Santa Cruz, and by the efficient folks at the University's Document Publishing & Editing Center. The places of original publication of the essays are indicated in the references provided at the end of this book, and permission to reprint is here gratefully acknowledged. All of the essays have been revised to some extent. "Mill's Pig" and "Jealous Afterthoughts" are new. I have been sustained in a variety of ways by the people who commented on the essays while they were being written, and to them I am particularly grateful. I dedicate this book to Norman O. Brown, who argued with me every inch of the way.

CONTENTS

A Tear Is an Intellectual Thing

For a tear is an intellectual thing,
And a sigh is the sword of an angel king,
And the bitter groan of the martyr's woe
Is an arrow from the Almighty's bow.

WILLIAM BLAKE

1

MILL'S PIG

An Introduction

"Is it better to be Socrates dissatisfied, or a pig satisfied?" John Stuart Mill's advice on answering his question was: don't ask the pig.[1] He has a point. It is not that pigs should be assumed to be more biased, or less intelligent, or even less experienced (if one is measuring "amount" of experience by length of life, or by events per day, or the like). The point is that the pig's *range* of experience is limited. One can assume that the pig has had all the usual piggy pleasures, but one must recognize that Socrates and humans in general, in addition to enjoying the piggy pleasures, have open to them a whole range of intellectual, spiritual, and "higher" pleasures. And if one is judging between types of pleasures, one ought of course to give greater weight to the person (or creature) of wider experience, the one who has experienced all the relevant types of pleasures.

But then, the question is really more complicated than this. (Of course, one should not assume that Socrates would judge that the pleasures unavailable to the pig immeasurably outweigh those that are.) First, the original question does not call simply for judging between two types of pleasures; it requires one to choose between two types of life. And no one—neither Socrates nor the pig—has experienced two whole lives. And in judging between types of life, it is whole lives that must be compared. Is it better to be Socrates, with all the pains that flesh and spirit are heir to, but with the possibility of philosophical discussion, aesthetic delight, and so on, or to be a pig, full of worldly pleasure, but devoid of "higher" aspirations? One must assume the pig is not aware of what it is missing. With the absence of the intellectual pleasures comes an absence of the sort of self-consciousness that might make one regret their absence. Is a loss still a loss even if one does not feel it? Even if one *could not* feel it? The choice ultimately is between a life with a wide range of experience, but with the discontents of civilization added to the dissatisfactions provided by natural disappointments, and a life of blissful wallowing without any consciousness of what might be missed.

Neither Socrates nor the pig could experience both (whole) lives. Mill is thus wrong to claim that Socrates, unlike the pig, "knows both sides."

There is a second complication. If one narrows the question from comparing whole lives to comparing types of pleasure, or successive styles of life, does experience settle the matter? Are piggy pleasures—bodily, sensual, and so forth—in some sense "lower"? Are Socratic pleasures—intellectual, aesthetic, moral, and so on—in some sense "higher"? And if we give the comparison a sense (say, the more desirable pleasure is the "higher" one) does it follow that any occasion of a higher pleasure must be preferred to any competing occasion of a lower pleasure? If we do not assume that, our criterion for comparing pleasures becomes shaky. Mill tells us that the only test for whether something is desirable is the fact that people do desire it. But what people desire must surely depend on the competing alternatives of the moment, their recent experiences of satisfaction, dissatisfaction, felt lack, and so on, as well as on their general attitudes to different types of pleasure. How then can we ever be sure that a pleasure is "higher" if that judgment depends on its desirability, and that in turn depends on desires that vary with circumstances and individuals? The comparison of types of pleasure may not be much easier than the choice between whole lives.

When Mill tells us that "the sole evidence it is possible to produce that any thing is desirable, is that people do actually desire it" (1961 [1861], 363), what is being measured or shown? Is the point psychological or moral? After all, it can be a surprising lesson to learn just what other people in fact find desirable. The range of sexual interests in particular is extraordinary and it sometimes seems that *anything* one can imagine doing *someone* will want, often passionately, to do. It is one of the many valuable lessons of Freud that reactions of disgust are typically conventional. Thus necrophilia and bestiality and coprophilia may be minority tastes, but there are nonetheless some who find such activities appealing, and their desire is, on Mill's standard, proof of (psychological) desirability. The fact that relatively few have those tastes has some implications, and the question of whether having a particular desire is "good" (moral desirability) remains open. (This is a point much emphasized by G. E. Moore [1903] in his critique of Mill.) On the question of numbers, Mill tells us: "Of two pleasures, if there be one to which all or almost all who have experience of both give a decided preference, irrespective of any feeling of moral obligation to prefer it, that is the more desirable pleasure" (332). This becomes his standard for "quality" of pleasure. But note that what majority rule seems to be settling here—as indicated by the setting aside of "moral obligation"—is a psychological question. How a psychological point, even described as a point about "quality," becomes a moral measure will need clarification. For as I said a moment ago, the question of moral desirability, of the goodness of an object or an activity, does not seem settled by the fact that a few or that many want it. But that a moral measure is what emerges seems essential to utilitarianism as a guide to life.

In the end, when it comes to choosing the best life for human beings (the kind of creature we happen to be), one needs a theory, in particular, a theory of the nature of human nature. To see this, it may be helpful to focus on questions of identity, and show how questions of classification (the kind of creature we happen to be), questions about what counts as good for creatures (or things) of a certain kind, and questions of identity become inextricably entangled.

Philosophers often discuss issues of "personal identity." The questions are typically about the continuity of the self through change and about what constitutes different individual persons at a given point in time. For example, what, if anything, must stay the same over time in order for a two-year-old boy and the eighty-year-old man he becomes to be recognized as the same "person"? Traditionally philosophers have given varying weights to bodily and psychological criteria in order to answer their questions about continuity and individuation. Similar questions of identity can be raised about almost any object, not just persons. Richard Wollheim (1980) distinguishes between this "formal" identity and "ideal" identity, which involves a kind of psychological unity or integrity of the self. I use this second sense of identity when I speak of moral identity, of who one importantly is and feels oneself to be. There are, however, interesting connections between the two sorts of identity.

Many philosophers, looking for an element of continuity between the two-year-old boy and the eighty-year old man, and seeing none, have postulated an unchanging and immortal soul. But the metaphysical move to unchanging substances, whether material or immaterial, to serve as the bearer of the ever-changing properties of things and people is really unnecessary. The notion of substance or of the self as an unchanging substratum is ultimately based on a mistaken notion of identity: for a thing to remain the same thing despite change does not depend on an unchanging substratum (again, whether material or immaterial), but rather on the kind of thing it is and on the limits of change allowed by the concept of the thing. So "the same piece of wax" is soft when heated, hard when cold. Such changing properties under different conditions are part of the essence of a piece of wax. Similarly, we expect rivers to flow (within limits), and boys to develop. It is their nature.

So, to spell out the essence of a thing, one need not reach an unchanging substratum; rather, one needs to spell out what sorts of changes can occur and the thing still be a particular thing of the same type. What sorts of continuities are essential in allowing us to say we and ourselves as children are the same people? The criteria of identity, the limits of change, the conditions of continuity are given by the concept of the thing involved. The question always is how much can a piece of wax, a river, or a person change and be the same piece of wax, river, or person? The essence of a thing depends on how you classify it. This point is spelled out clearly in a passage by W. V. Quine:

The Aristotelian notion of essence was the forerunner, no doubt, of the modern notion of intension or meaning. For Aristotle it was essential in men to be rational, accidental to be two-legged. But there is an important difference between this attitude and the doctrine of meaning. From the latter point of view it may indeed be conceded (if only for the sake of argument) that rationality is involved in the meaning of the word 'man' while two-leggedness is not; but two-leggedness may at the same time be viewed as involved in the meaning of 'biped' while rationality is not. Thus from the point of view of the doctrine of meaning it makes no sense to say of the actual individual, who is at once a man and a biped, that his rationality is essential and his two-leggedness accidental or vice versa. Things had essences, for Aristotle, but only linguistic forms have meanings. Meaning is what essence becomes when it is divorced from the object of reference and wedded to the word. (1961, 22)

Things have an essence only under a heading: what counts as essential depends on how we classify a given thing. (And bear in mind that we may classify things differently given different purposes motivating our classificatory efforts.) Individuals don't have essences, only species or class-terms or individuals under some classification have essences. So when Descartes in his *Meditations* asks, "Who am I?" and goes on to talk about thinking, he is really looking for the essence of mankind, the nature of human nature, not of "I." Descartes's "I" is not a proper heading; it is simply a pronoun standing in for a name or proper description of some individual. He starts by saying "I am a man" and then searches for the essence of man, first considering "rational animal," the traditional Aristotelian answer. Whatever one thinks of his ultimate conclusion that he is essentially only a thing that thinks, a disembodied mind, what he is really asking is who mankind is, not who "I" am. How should one think about the nature of human nature?

When we think about the nature of other things, such as the essence of a chair, we have to recognize that we call all sorts of rather different things by the same name. Chairs may be made from all sorts of different substances or materials (e.g., wood, metal, plastic) and have all sorts of different forms or shapes (backs and even legs are not essential; after all, there are beanbag chairs). Confronted by the vast variety in observable properties of the many diverse items designated as chairs, Plato moved to a supersensible realm of Forms or Ideas. So actual chairs somehow (exactly how was a serious problem) "participated" in the ideal Form of Chair, striving to be like their supersensible model. Later empiricist and rationalist philosophers, troubled by the postulated existence of a world outside experience to give meaning to the words used to describe human experience, suggested that individuals could understand talk about chairs because of common ideas in their heads rather than ideal Ideas in a Platonic heaven. This approach too has its difficulties. Aside from continuing the Platonic assumption that, despite the diversity in the objects designated as chairs, there *must* be something in common in virtue of which they are called chairs, it leaves the nature of the ideas for general kinds unspecified. So the empiricists and rationalists would argue among themselves about, for example, whether general ideas are abstract or particular. (Is the idea of "dog" like a picture of a particular collie, or more like a set of muddy superimposed images of many particular dogs? Is the ideal idea of dog a mongrel mutt?) At any rate, Aristotle had a useful thought early on. Recognizing the vast variety in the many different things called chairs, he pointed out that there was something that they in fact had in common: their function. Chairs are, roughly speaking, things made for sitting on. This works rather nicely for artifacts, which are things made by human beings for human purposes. This makes it easy to determine their function. One need only ask their maker. The criteria of identity also yield, it is significant to note, criteria of goodness. What makes a chair a good chair? It is one that performs its defining function well. A good chair is one that is good for sitting on, just as a good watch is one that tells time accurately.

But this approach runs into problems when one shifts from artifacts to natural kinds. How is one to determine the function of a human being? If one follows the pattern used for chairs, one would ask the maker. But that presumes there is a maker; it presumes the existence of God. And supposing one grants the existence of God (and many do not), how is one to know his purpose in making humans? Direct revelation is rare, and always open to question, and there are many competing authorities that interpret God's supposed purposes in incompatible ways. And even granting both the existence of God and knowledge of his purposes, can we presume that his purposes must be ours? There is a problem of point of view. Chairs do not have a point of view, so their perspective is not being usurped when we turn to the maker of chairs to learn the purpose of such artifacts. But humans do have a point of view of their own, as do other creatures. Supposing a lamb's function from the point of view of the shepherd is to be fatted for slaughter, would it follow that the lamb's function (from its point of view) is to become the best lamb chop possible? If we are to define essence in terms of function, we must determine from whose point of view function is to be specified. Can this difficulty be bypassed?

To get to the essence of his piece of wax, Descartes stripped it of its changeable properties. To get to the essence of human beings, political theorists have often imagined a "state of nature," expecting the nature of humanity would be revealed in such a stripped-down state. These thought experiments generally imagine people in very extreme conditions. Hobbes strips individuals of the authority and protection of the sovereign—the restraints of society—and sees a war of all against all, a state of nature in which life is nasty, brutish, and short. Perhaps the picture is a projection of his own perilous times when highwaymen and sudden death lurked everywhere. (Perhaps those times were not so different from our own.) Locke imagines a more genteel scene: in the state of nature, aside from a few marauding renegades, the loss of the forms of state and of civil society would leave people pretty much as they are. Rousseau sees a very different scene indeed. What for Hobbes are necessary protections, for Rousseau, are distorting chains. They warp the free and happy individual of the state of nature into the miserable creature of society. The noble savage or happy ape in his state of nature looks rather different from the scurrying and clawing rat of Hobbes's world. The bestiaries are different, the masterless humans look different, but the experiment is similar. People will often suggest that one *strip things away*, that one look to extreme conditions (absence of organized society, scarcity of food and means of life) in order to see the true nature of humans. Typically, it is suggested that their mean egotistical motives will be revealed. A modern version of the experiment can be found in William Golding's novel *Lord of the Flies* (1954), in which boys left to themselves revert to primitive savagery. The stories of cannibalism in lifeboats are also occasionally cited.

But one should note how odd this stripping procedure is. We rarely if ever follow it in our efforts to understand other natural kinds. One does not seek to discover the nature of a rose by observing it under arctic conditions. If one did, one would no doubt conclude the rose to be, in its essence, really, a bare twig with thorns. Rather, we put the rose in the best possible conditions, allow it to flourish, and suppose we have discovered its nature only when it has been fulfilled. This approach is not without partisans in the history of political theory. Edmund Burke suggested one could see human nature by looking at people as they are. There is no need to pull away the decent draperies. Of course one would discover nasty things if one scraped away the thin veneer of civilization. But men are what they make themselves—and they make civilization. The accretions of culture do not hide human nature; they express it. The sentiment is perhaps echoed in Oscar Wilde's assertion that nature is artifice.

So there are different experiments and different conclusions even within the same sort of experiment. One approach to the search for human nature seems to yield *basic motives*, the other *fulfilled form*. Yet neither approach is satisfactory. In stripping things away, how can one to be sure that one is discarding only the inessential or distorting conditions? (Consider the rose.) The experiment seems to presuppose its results. And the other approach does not seem to allow sense to "the essential" at all. In accepting everything as it is, nothing is distinguished, and no allowance is made for unfulfilled potential.

Even supposing one could somehow discover which desires are essential to human nature, it is not obvious what one should then do. Isn't it conceivable that, once we discover the nature of human nature, the appropriate response should be to suppress or sublimate part of it rather than to fulfill it all? Put differently, the relationship between human nature and the best life for mankind is not a simple one. Even if one accepts the Aristotelian position that a good chair or human must exemplify to a high degree the special distinctive features of its kind, one may still be troubled by the differences between natural kinds and artifacts that I have already noted. And the Aristotelian position leaves open the question whether a particular kind is good: should there be electric chairs, even (or especially) effective ones? From what point of view do we decide whether it is better to develop our animal or our human nature? (And man as well as being a biped is, after all, an animal.) It is arguable (or at least it has been argued) that those features that distinguish man from animal are burdens and that it is better to be a creature of basic instincts. What does "better" mean here? Its sense cannot come from the category, for here we have a case of conflict between categories. We are stuck with Mill's problem. What do we say of Mill's satisfied pig as opposed to a dissatisfied Socrates, or a dissatisfied lesser man? Mill tells us not to ask the pig, and I have suggested we would not do much better asking the man either, since whole lives are what is at stake here. One could assume the point of view of a particular society, but then mankind will have many natures, and the approach will be no help to the person who wishes to shape his or her life and is prepared to leave his or her own society to seek the best life. How is one to say from which point of view an object is best, or that the point of view from which it is best is the best point of view? May an object strive to change its nature?

Aristotle points out that humans are of a mixed nature. Although he shares Plato's bias in favor of the contemplative life, he insists that we cannot be creatures of pure thought. If we tried, we would fail. While we may have a godlike component to our nature, there are other components that make their own demands and place constraints on contemplative activities. Mill claims that, due to a sense of dignity (as well as a number of contributing lesser factors), no one would choose to move in the reverse direction, choose to abandon higher faculties for swinish pleasures:

> No intelligent human being would consent to be a fool, no instructed person would be an ignoramus, no person of feeling and conscience would be selfish and base, even though they should be persuaded that the fool, the dunce, or the rascal is better satisfied with his lot than they are with theirs. They would not resign what they possess more than he for the most complete satisfaction of all the desires which they have in common with him. If they ever fancy they would, it is only in cases of unhappiness so extreme, that, to escape from it, they would exchange their lot for almost any other, however undesirable in their own eyes. A being of higher faculties requires more to make him happy, is capable probably of more acute suffering, and certainly accessible to it at more points, than one of an inferior type; but, in spite of these liabilities, he can never really wish to sink into what he feels to be a lower grade of existence. (332–33)

In fact, some rather distinguished thinkers have advocated that we give up the discontents of civilization in favor of the polymorphously perverse pleasures of childhood. Some have advocated that we move beyond good and evil and return to the innocence of childhood. What must be recognized, however, is that such moves would have their costs. Childhood is itself mixed, full of contrary and destructive instincts, and so reversion to it (without the controls of adulthood) would lead ultimately to the destruction of the supposedly liberated individuals and those around them. In a world governed by infantile impulses combined with adult powers (and without adult restraints) the darker side of childhood is likely to dominate. While different balances may be reached, we may ultimately have no choice. Given that one's eyes have been opened, perhaps one does not have the option to close them. Our nature places limits on what we can be, and plays a role in establishing the conditions of our happiness.

This is to admit (contrary to certain existentialists and others) that humans do have a nature. To discover that nature one needs what Mill called "experiments in living," and one needs to learn what one can from the experiments of others, from the record of human experience. To understand the nature of other natural kinds, one turns to the relevant science, whether biology and botany in the case of the rose or chemistry and metallurgy in the case of gold. So if we are to understand human nature, we must learn what we can from the natural sciences (including biology), but also from psychology, sociology, anthropology, and history—and literature too (thought experiments can be as revealing in understanding human life as in understanding the universe studied by physics). We need to make use of the best theories available.

In the essays that follow, I pursue a range of questions about what sustains and threatens our identity. Many of the essays tackle the question of the extent to which certain emotions or aspects of emotions (such as particular expressions of emotion) are natural and inevitable. This is because of the centrality of emotions in giving meaning to our lives, and the distinctive way in which mind and body come together in our emotional experience. Many of the essays begin with a puzzle peculiar to a particular emotion: What would we have to give up if we wanted to eliminate jealousy? How can one make sense of hating people because we love them? How are we to understand the possibility of pride, one of the seven deadly sins, also being the theme of identity politics? What would it take to overcome boredom? What makes a sexual desire "perverse," or particular sexual relations (such as incestuous ones) undesirable or even unthinkable? How can one question an individual's understanding of their own happiness or override a society's account of its own rituals? Is it always a good thing to try to cure people of their self-deception? In each case I try to use the resources of the best theory available to me (drawing often from psychoanalysis, often from anthropology) in trying to answer the question.

There are a number of recurring themes. Among them are the relation of the normal and the pathological, the relation of individual development and cultural history, the nature of explanation and evidence, the two faces of many emotions (including jealousy and pride), and the pervasiveness of ambiguity and ambivalence. But perhaps most central is the notion of moral identity, a notion that appears in various guises throughout the essays (including sometimes in terms of integrity, self-esteem, and the superego). These essays are broadly about emotions and the constitution of who we are. The major focus of these essays is not on describing what each particular emotion is, but rather on how emotions are connected to other aspects of human life (for example, to the pursuit of happiness, to socialist political ideals, to pride movements, to the development of identity in early childhood and its maintenance in adulthood).

William Blake understood that, as he put it, "a tear is an intellectual thing." So, in a sense, are all expressions of emotion. So, in a related sense, are all emotions. Because of this fact—the fact that emotions are discriminated from one another on the basis of, and are in part constituted by, thoughts, beliefs, judgments, and the like—changing one's beliefs can be a way of transforming one's emotions. Not that one can simply and directly choose one's beliefs (that is part of the puzzlement of self-deception), but how one conceives, perceives, and understands the world will in large measure determine how one experiences it. And how one understands oneself will affect who one is. While it is not the case that thinking simply makes it so, in the realm of the mental at least, knowledge affects the thing known. This great power of reflexive knowledge is, as Spinoza understood, what makes room for human freedom.

I should perhaps say a bit more about the view of emotions that informs these essays. (It is developed at greater length in Neu 1977.) Emotions are not simple sensations. When we ascribe an emotion to ourselves or others, we are giving an interpretation of complexes of sensation, desire, behavior, and belief, further complicated by contextual factors, both individual and social. Traditionally, there have been two competing points of view about the nature of emotion, one emphasizing feeling and sensation, the other thought and cognition. These differing emphases were recognized by Aristotle, who wrote that "a physicist would define an affection of soul differently from a dialectician; the latter would define e.g. anger as the appetite for returning pain for pain, or something like that, while the former would define it as a boiling of the blood or warm substance surrounding the heart" (On the Soul, 403a). Both emphases are reflected in our ordinary experience and attitudes. Sometimes, when a friend tells us he is angry, we urge him to lie down and rest, in the hope that with time the feeling, like a headache, will pass. Sometimes, however, we ask why he is angry, in the hope that understanding his reasons and discussing them will help; that if, for example, he discovers that his beliefs are ill founded, his feeling will change. Psychoanalysis and other analytic therapies rely on this kind of insight.

The two opposed views toward emotion are developed in philosophical and psychological theories, some treating emotions as essentially feelings, with thoughts and beliefs (if mentioned at all) only incidentally attached.

Some treat thoughts as essential, with feelings and sensations as incidental. To say that thoughts are essential is to say, for example, that what is
most distinctive about my anger is the belief (roughly) that someone has
caused me harm (a belief presupposed by Aristotle's notion of a desire to
"return" pain) and that without that belief my state (no matter what my
sensations) could not be one of "anger" (after all, even if my stomach is
churning in a typically angry fashion, that may be due to what I ate for
lunch). Thoughts (conscious and unconscious) are what differentiate. This
is partly because emotions (unlike headaches) have direction; they take an
object, typically what is believed to be the cause of the emotion. It is difficult to love, hate, or grieve over no one or nothing in particular. (Again, it
does not follow that we are always right about the sources and objects of
our emotions.) Thoughts are crucial not only in giving the direction of a
particular emotion but in distinguishing one type of emotion from another. They make each distinctively what it is. Regret, remorse, shame, embarrassment, and a dozen other related states may all *feel* the same. What
distinguishes each is the precise belief about what has gone wrong, about
whether we are morally or in some other way responsible for it, whether
we think others think less of us, and so on. This makes room for a kind of
understanding and argument about emotions that bare sensations do not
allow. One way to analyze the relations among thought, emotion, and sensation is to consider the *expression* of emotion, which is what I undertake in
the first, the title essay, of this book.

The range of possible feelings depends on our thoughts, and the conceptual distinctions available in different societies will shape and limit
these. (While emotions are an important part of our nature, each emotion
is not itself a natural kind.) To see the dependence of feeling on thought
and language, consider Wittgenstein's question about a dog: "We say a dog
is afraid his master will beat him; but not, he is afraid his master will beat
him tomorrow. Why not?" (1953, §650) Conceptions of time depend on
language, and so a creature without language will lack an emotional life
extended in time, will lack hopes for the distant future or regrets for the distant past. A person who was closed to certain sorts of understanding and
perception would also be closed to certain emotions. Where emotion is essentially characterized through thought, a new way of thinking can also
be a new way of feeling. And feelings as basic and (apparently universal) as
love, at least in certain of its forms, are characterized through thought.
The history of literature can be read as partly the history of changing ideas
and ideals of love, and without the appropriate ideas an individual or a
whole society may simply not be open to the corresponding forms of love,
such as the courtly love of the twelfth-century troubadours. St. Augustine
was not eccentric when he reported in his *Confessions* that in his youth he
had been "in love with love" (1960 [401], 3, §1). The poetic imagination is
what makes certain emotions possible at all.

What are the limits on the emotional life of animals lacking poetic imagination? Can they have emotions not grounded in the simple perception of reality? Do they have the intellectual capacity to be moved by imagined events? The psychological meaning of emotional responses depends on the thoughts that we can plausibly see behind them. So far as those thoughts are limited, so also is the range of emotional experience and emotional expression. We have little trouble ascribing fear and anger to apes, dogs, and certain other animals on the basis of their behavior, because we have little trouble granting them the degree of awareness needed to account for what certainly seems to be fearful or angry behavior in ordinary circumstances. But fear and anger are relatively primitive emotions. Sometimes we project onto animals thoughts and emotions unwarranted by their behavior. We like to think everyone and everything—animals, robots, and even, for children, stuffed toys—is like us. But certain emotions seem to require the kind of self-consciousness only humans have. As Mark Twain wrote, "Man is the only animal that blushes. Or needs to" (1897, 238). Twain's misanthropy aside, other animals are immune to embarrassment—and are shameless—not because their behavior always matches their ideals but because they cannot have the specific thoughts requisite to shame or embarrassment.

The animals' immunity from shame and embarrassment has its cost: while freedom from those painful emotions may seem a benefit, lack of self-awareness is its price. Those who would avoid the fear of loss involved in jealousy must also deny themselves certain forms of passionate attachment with their attendant risks of loss. Love makes us vulnerable in ways that enhance the chance of pain. Emotions have a conceptual structure and there are emotional entailments just as there are emotional entanglements. There is a logic even to our apparently disordered emotional lives. Hume may have misunderstood the nature of emotions when he insisted, "Reason is, and ought only to be the slave of the passions." Conversely, Spinoza may have pointed the way to human freedom which he insisted on an enlarged understanding of those very passions and the role of thought in shaping them. Our animal brethren may have it easier in some ways, but there remain advantages even for a Socrates dissatisfied.

One can do many different things with emotions: have them, express them, cultivate them, repress them, and so on indefinitely. I propose here to think about them, in the belief that thinking about them can transform them. Thinking about emotions is both complicated and enriched by the fact that emotions themselves involve thought, indeed, are themselves a kind of thinking. As a result, as Spinoza understood, reflexive knowledge can in this area have a transformative effect. Thinking about oneself may sometimes have no effect on the object (thinking about one's height does not make one taller). But when the object of knowledge is to some degree constituted by what one believes about it, thinking can change the thing known. We have here another reason for thinking Socrates was right to believe the examined life especially worth living.

2

"A TEAR IS AN
INTELLECTUAL THING"

Why do we cry? My short answer is: because we think. But of course, we may also sometimes cry because we have stubbed our toe or, as in the case of at least one baby I know, because we have gas.[1] And the most natural answer is that we cry because we are sad, or grieving, or ashamed, or otherwise upset—that is, as an expression of emotion—but then one wonders just how the experience of emotions connects to the alternatives already mentioned. Are emotions, as a source of tears, closer to thinking or to gas; are they more like occasions of thought or occasions of physical pain? And why is it that other animals do not cry (assuming for the moment that they do not)? Do they not think? Do they not think sad thoughts? Surely they can suffer, whatever they may or may not think. Is lacrimal secretion a tear only on a human face? My short answer needs elaboration.

Blake refers to the widow's tear and the tear of love and forgiveness.[2] There are tears of sadness and tears of joy and doubtless dozens of other kinds.[3] What differentiates these various kinds of tears? It is not the physiology: all tears look alike. The differences lie in the thoughts that provoke them or that, however inadequately, they express.

Putting the point somewhat differently, there is a difference between a person crying and the eyes watering, between tears of joy and sadness, on the one hand, and tears provoked by an onion, on the other. Emotional tears, unlike mechanically induced or reflex tears, are mediated by thought. This is not to say they are the product of conscious deliberation and calculation, but it is to say that they depend on how we perceive the world, on how we think of it, rather than on how the world simply, in fact, is. They express our nature as well as the nature of the world.

Darwin

There is a chapter on "weeping" in Charles Darwin's *The Expression of the Emotions in Man and Animals* (1965 [1872]). As one might expect, the chapter provides, among other things, an answer in evolutionary terms to the question "Why do we cry?"

Darwin provides first of all a minute physiological description of crying, particularly in infants. He assigns biological functions to various elements of the screaming infant's expression taken individually, for example: "The firm closing of the eyelids and consequent compression of the eyeball . . . serves to protect the eyes from becoming too much gorged with blood" during acts of violent expiration (147, 157). Infants do not actually shed tears or weep (or sob [156]) until after the first few weeks or months of life (152). But aside from that early period, according to Darwin, "Whenever the muscles round the eyes are strongly and involuntarily contracted in order to compress the blood-vessels and thus to protect the eyes, tears are secreted . . . This occurs under the most opposite emotions, and under no emotion at all" (e.g., during violent coughing or vomiting [162]). Given this mechanism, it is not surprising that tears may accompany violent laughter as readily as they may express grief. Indeed, it becomes puzzling how it is that tears come to serve as an expression of grief (unless it is via the effects of grief on respiration). Similarly, while it becomes clear why we can laugh to tears, one still wants to know why amusement should lead to laughter in the first place.[4]

Humans are not the only animals that shed tears or have watery eyes. Darwin reports that "the Indian elephant is known sometimes to weep" (165). Certain species of monkeys are reported to weep (134, 165), and I have seen my own cat's eyes water. This is not to say that tears in animals express the same emotions as in humans, or indeed that they express any emotion.[5] For the lower animals, it is also unclear whether there is a "relation between the contraction of the orbicular muscles during violent expiration and the secretion of tears" (165). But even in humans, though the relation exists, it is not a necessary one.[6] That is, tears can certainly be secreted without the contraction of the muscles around the eye (167). Involuntary and prolonged or energetic contraction of those muscles is one way of exciting the lacrimal glands, but there are others. The question remains, why do we, and perhaps some other animals, cry?

Darwin points to a number of biological functions of crying:

> The primary function of the secretion of tears, together with some mucus, is to lubricate the surface of the eye; and a secondary one, as some believe, is to keep the nostrils damp, so that the inhaled air may be moist, and likewise to favour the power of smelling. But another, and at least equally important function of tears, is to wash out particles of dust or other minute objects which may get into the eyes. (168)

Tears protect the eyes from various forms of irritation. This is doubtless so. And there is doubtless a fuller evolutionary story that would explain why humans have the machinery requisite for producing and shedding tears, for crying. The conditions in the story recur and so will sometimes serve to explain why we cry today (after all, people still get particles of dust in their eyes). But given that we have the machinery, why do we cry when we are in an emotional state?

Some of Darwin's earlier discussion is of use here. Given mechanisms established for one purpose (say the reflex of crying when the surface of the eye is irritated, or the secretion of tears in response to the violent contraction of the muscles around the eyes), these mechanisms will inevitably be activated on other occasions. If peals of loud laughter are accompanied by rapid and violent spasmodic expirations, tears will stream down the face because (to protect the eyes from becoming too engorged with blood) the orbicular muscles contract. Hence one can laugh so hard that one cries. The question now shifts, not to why an emotion may be accompanied by tears, but to why an emotion is accompanied by other physiological states (e.g., violent expiration) that bring tears in their train. The answer to this question could be very neatly provided if emotions simply were physiological states. William James and others have argued for just such an equation. But while physiological states are certainly a part of emotions as experienced by us, I think a relation of simple identity misrepresents the connection. If I am right, understanding the bodily expression of emotions will be more complex than noting a pattern of one physiological state triggering another. Moreover, whether the tears of animals or even of other people express any emotion or the same emotion as in us will not be a matter for simple (or even for deep) physiological observation. We do not regard the tears that accompany violent laughter as tears of amusement, despite the fact that the physiological mechanism that produces them may be the same as in cases of tears of sadness. After all, as Darwin points out, the same mechanism may also produce tears during violent coughing or vomiting.

Before turning to James's theory, we should note that Darwin provides an interesting suggestion about how a bodily activity such as crying, which originally, in the individual or the species, might have been tied to a physiological trigger such as violent expiration, might come in time to be triggered by thoughts alone:

> When complex actions or movements have long been performed in strict association together, and these are from any cause at first voluntarily and afterwards habitually checked, then if the proper exciting conditions occur, any part of the action or movement which is least under the control of the will, will often still be involuntarily performed. The secretion by a gland is remarkably free from the influence of the will; therefore, when . . . the habit of crying out or screaming is restrained, and there is consequently no distension of the blood-vessels of the eye, it may nevertheless well happen that tears should still be secreted. We may see . . . the muscles round the eyes of a person who reads a pathetic story, twitching or trembling in so slight a degree as hardly to be detected . . . If the twitching of the muscles round the eyes . . . had been com-

pletely prevented . . . the lacrymal glands . . . would be eminently liable still to act, thus betraying, though there were no other outward signs, the pathetic thoughts which were passing through the person's mind. (173)

To review the position, what we can usefully take from Darwin so far are two fundamental physiological mechanisms of crying: one involving irritants to the eye, such as dust, which would explain why the eyes tear when we chop onions (onion vapor presumably acting as an irritant), and the other involving spasmodic or violent breathing causing the muscles around the eye to protectively contract to prevent the eyes becoming excessively engorged with blood and so incidentally stimulating the lacrimal glands, which would explain why we can laugh to tears (laugh so hard that we cry) and which might explain why we cry when sad (if grief and other such "pathetic" emotions involve violent or spasmodic breathing). And there is a suggestion in terms of associative habits about how mere thoughts might come to act as triggers to this second mechanism.

James

Williams James's (1884) view is encapsulated in a famous paragraph:

> Our natural way of thinking about . . . standard emotions is that the mental perception of some fact excites the mental affection called the emotion, and that this latter state of mind gives rise to the bodily expression. My thesis on the contrary is that *the bodily changes follow directly the perception of the exciting fact, and that our feeling of the same changes as they occur is the emotion.* Common sense says, we lose our fortune, are sorry and weep; we meet a bear, are frightened and run; we are insulted by a rival, are angry and strike. The hypothesis here to be defended says that this order of sequence is incorrect, that the one mental state is not immediately induced by the other, that the bodily manifestations must first be interposed between, and that the more rational statement is that we feel sorry because we cry, angry because we strike, afraid because we tremble, and not that we cry, strike, or tremble, because we are sorry, angry, or fearful as the case may be. (19)

James's approach has a number of advantages. For one thing, it makes clear one source at least of the felt aspect of emotions, an aspect that helps differentiate them from bare thoughts. This comes from its emphasis on visceral feelings and on the awareness of physiological changes in expressive activities such as running and crying. For another thing, James's approach, through the emphasis on observable expressive activity, makes clearer how our vocabulary for inner states gets a grip on its (on other accounts hidden) referent in a way that allows for interpersonal communication and understanding. And there is of course no mystery on this approach about why we cry when we are sad—the crying is a part of what it is to have the emotion at all.

Nonetheless, despite these advantages (and others), James's approach gives a prominence to isolated physiology that I wish to question. According to him, we do not cry because we are sad; we are sad because we cry. Something happens, we perceive it, our natural response is tears, we notice the tears and thus become aware that we are sad. In effect, the sadness just is the perception of the physiological state. This theory just will not do if some of our most basic beliefs about emotions and some of our most basic emotional discriminations are to make sense. For we believe that emotions can occur independent of their expression, that, for example, we can be sad without crying. While there may be no problem on this approach about why we cry when we are sad, that is only because if we do not cry it does not allow that we are sad—and that is a problem. Moreover, we believe that the same physiological state can express a number of different emotions; so we may cry without being sad, for there can be tears of joy as well as of sadness. As far as the tears go, the physiology is the same. James's approach, referring to physiology alone, leaves the possibility of discrimination unexplained.

James is not left without responses. Where an emotion apparently occurs in the absence of its normal physiological accompaniment, James can insist on incipient tears, on an inclination to the natural expression as the residue that allows us to identify the emotion in the absence of its full expression. And where it appears that two different emotions have the same physiological expression, James can insist on subtle, hidden, physiological differences. Will these responses stand up?

I have already cited Darwin's plausible account of how a residue might trigger an expression in the absence of the full physiological tumult originally involved in the emotion. But it will be recalled that Darwin allows that the residue may be as meager as mere "pathetic thoughts which were passing through the person's mind" (173). Can James maintain his theory when the residue is allowed to shrink so far? I think not. For James the physiological state involved in the expression of the emotion and in the emotion itself are one. If a mere thought is allowed to substitute for the physiological state involved in the emotion itself, the thought then serving (on Darwin's account) to trigger the expression, the unity is lost: it is difficult to see how the emotion itself can be the perception of the expression (which follows it). The person suffering from pathetic thoughts is already sad; they need not wait to cry before being, or noting that they are, sad.

As for subtle physiological differences, there may simply not be enough physiological states to go around. This is the argument of W. B. Cannon, who showed that the same visceral changes occur in a number of otherwise very different emotional states, such as fear and rage: "The responses in the viscera seem too uniform to offer a satisfactory means of distinguishing emotions which are very different in subjective quality" (1968 [1927], 47). If one wishes to argue in response that there may be feelings more subtle than those examined by Cannon, one is shifting away from James's view (which specifies visceral changes as the important ones) and risks shifting into incoherence. For the virtue of James's approach is that it grounds emotion in felt sensation. If one starts appealing to physiological changes too subtle actually to be felt, then the differences in emotions are reduced to differences in unfelt feelings, and it becomes mysterious how we manage to make the emotional discriminations we do in fact make. In any case, it seems wildly implausible to suppose that there is built into our physiological machinery just those differences needed to mark our subtle emotional discriminations (must shame, embarrassment, guilt, regret, remorse, and other emotions in that neighborhood have different *physiological* accompaniments?), and even more implausible to suppose that the machinery marks all the very different differences marked by different societies. This remains true despite a recent, post-Cannon, study that has detected differential skin temperature and heart rate in conjunction with facial expressions characteristic of different emotions.[7] This study suggests emotion-specific activity in the autonomic nervous system for at best only a few (six) emotions. The problem never was that there are *no* physiological differences among emotions; the problem was and remains that there are not enough, or enough of the right kind, to account for our subtle (or even some of our not so subtle) emotion discriminations. And even if physiology is universal across cultures, emotion discriminations are not. Emotions are not natural kinds. They have conventional boundaries. Or at least so I believe. What is the place of nature and convention in emotion and emotional expression?

The Universal and the Local

Biologist that he was, Darwin tended to the view that the basic or "chief" emotions and their expressions are universal and innate. Whatever the explanation for the presumed fact of universality, are emotional expressions in fact universal?

Darwin's book on *The Expression of the Emotions* (1965 [1872]) appeals to a remarkably wide range of evidence: from the observation of animals, infants, children, and the insane, to judgments about art and photographs. But most relevant to our immediate question are his efforts at cross-cultural study. To gather data, Darwin sent out a questionnaire to a number of people with experience of other countries that ultimately contained sixteen questions of the following sort:

1. Is astonishment expressed by the eyes and mouth being opened wide, and by the eyebrows being raised?

2. Does shame excite a blush when the colour of the skin allows it to be visible? and especially how low down the body does the blush extend?

. . . .

12. Is laughter ever carried to such an extreme as to bring tears into the eyes?

13. When a man wishes to show that he cannot prevent something being done, or cannot himself do something, does he shrug his shoulders, turn inwards his elbows, extend outwards his hands and open the palms; with the eyebrows raised? (15–16)

Note that Darwin assumes (e.g., in the first two questions) there is no difficulty in identifying an emotion independently of its expression, even cross-culturally. And he presupposes that emotions, if not their expressions, are universal. The conclusion of his survey is that "the same state of mind is expressed throughout the world with remarkable uniformity" (17), and this despite his including such clearly voluntary and apparently conventional gestures as the shrug of resignation (in question 13). But suppose we, with contemporary researchers, narrow the question to facial expressions, excluding bodily gestures and emblematic (that is, voluntary and conventionally symbolic [Ekman 1973, 181]) expressions; do data such as Darwin's settle the matter?

On the other side we have the reports of cultural variation collected in writings such as Weston LaBarre's much cited "The Cultural Basis of Emotions and Gestures" (1947). LaBarre catalogues societies where the standard head shakes for "yes" and "no" do not obtain, and he notes in relation to laughter "that even if the physiological behavior be present, its cultural and emotional functions may differ. Indeed, even within the same culture, the laughter of adolescent girls and the laughter of corporation presidents can be functionally different things" (52). He concludes that "there is no 'natural' language of emotional gesture" (55). I am in fact reminded of the interpreted character of the apparently natural every time I try to point something out to my cat (the same one whose eyes water) and she sniffs quizzically at the tip of my pointing finger or gazes along the finger and up my arm. The direction of pointing is not given.[8] But do such stories perhaps run together bodily gestures (which may be conventional) and facial expressions (which may be universal)? We will come back to laughter (and crying), but let us first look at the latest twist in the argument.

Paul Ekman reports in *Darwin and Facial Expression* (1973) that certain major or "chief" facial expressions can now be taken *conclusively* as universal. (He singles out six: happiness, disgust, surprise, sadness, anger, and fear.) The anecdotal evidence collected by Darwin may be regarded as open to bias and other problems, as may the equally anecdotal evidence cited by LaBarre and others on the culture side of this nature-culture or universal-variable argument. Seeking to avoid such bias, Ekman relies on "judgment studies" of the face, in which informants in different societies are shown photographs of facial expressions without being told what emotion the investigator thinks the face shows (or much else) and are asked to supply their own interpretations (1973, 174). The results of the completed studies are supposed to show that the societies studied have a shared understanding of certain fixed facial expressions in terms of at least the six basic emotions, and that the emotional facial expressions are in fact universal. Ekman indicates that an effort was made to avoid data contaminated by images disseminated through movies, and the like, by finding visually isolated cultures. He argues that the apparent variations reported by LaBarre and others are to be explained by variation in elicitors, or display rules ("socially dictated obligations which call for the management of facial appearance" [185]), or consequences (195). The studies are serious, and worth careful consideration. The first point to note is that the data for the most visually isolated culture, the Fore in New Guinea, do not exactly show universality, for it is admitted that these people do not distinguish expressions of fear from expressions of surprise.[9] That of course still leaves four, or perhaps five (counting fear/surprise as one), universal expressions.[10] The second point to note is that the subjects were not exactly free to provide their own interpretations. They were shown photographs and asked to select from a short list of emotion words provided in translation by the investigators. Aside from problems of translation, this method does not allow for the possibility that an expression may not be tied to any particular emotion, or that an alternative meaning in that culture might not have been provided among the six choices on the preselected list.[11] But there are deeper difficulties.

Ekman himself notes that "the judgment approach presumes that people can recognize emotion when they view facial expression totally out of context, with no other information available" (191). This presumption is surely false, as shown by Ekman's own appeal to display rules and elicitors and consequences to explain apparent variations. What emotion is felt and exhibited does depend on context. Ekman acknowledges that the same situation may elicit different emotions in different cultures, and that the same emotion may be subject to different display rules (requiring inhibition or masking) in different societies. Nonetheless, he insists that "even though what calls forth a given emotion may differ across cultures, the facial expression for the emotion will be the same" once one takes account of display rules (176). But what is included in the "given emotion"? Of course, if one, like James, uses the expression as the essential criterion for what the emotion is, the same emotion will have the same expression: its having the same expression becomes a condition on our counting it as the same emotion. If one wishes to avoid such a vacuous circle, as I do, one has the burden of specifying what else there is. I would argue that the context matters, in particular the context as understood by the person having the emotion. If display rules may explain divergence in identification, shared beliefs and empirically common contexts may explain convergence in identification—we may not notice this simply because the beliefs and context are often so obvious. We cannot reliably identify others' inner feelings or emotions by direct empathy, by sharing them, but if contextual thoughts and beliefs are given their proper role in discrimination and identification, there is more on which to base an understanding of others' emotions. It is an important fact that one can understand a belief without sharing it (I understand what the flat-earthers believe, even while I don't share their belief). And there is all sorts of evidence, beyond facial expression, for what a person believes. Indeed, even those who would rely on facial expression in the supposedly central cases must themselves turn elsewhere in the absence of such expressions. Darwin pointed out that there does not seem to be any natural expression for jealousy: "Painters can hardly portray suspicion, jealousy, envy, etc., except by the aid of accessories which tell the tale" (79). And it is not clear to me in what sense disgust, which appears on Ekman's list of six basic emotions, is more basic than jealousy (or, for that matter, love). Certainly there are behavioral expressions of jealousy and its associated thoughts even if there is no standard facial expression; it is on such a basis that we readily ascribe jealousy to animals and young children in certain contexts. Ekman has recently claimed "there is a distinctive pan-cultural signal for each emotion"(1984, 330). Where there does not seem to be such a distinctive facial expression, as with contempt and shame (and I, following Darwin, would add jealousy and also love), Ekman proposes that state should not be regarded as an emotion. Whatever the advantages of such an approach for a person interested in facial expressions, it does seem to beg the question.

It should not be surprising (granting for the moment that it is true) that there are some broad cross-cultural uniformities in facial expression, no more surprising than that there may be gross physiological differences (within our culture) for six emotions, as suggested in the study cited earlier. So far as certain types of thoughts (and situations) are universal, there is no reason the associated emotions (and expressions in context) should not be as well. Again, as in my discussion of James, the problem is not that there are no physiological differences among emotions or no facial expression differences among emotions, but that there are not enough to go around, not enough to cover or explain all the discriminations in fact made. And supposing some facial expressions are universal, that is, can be distinguished and recognized across cultures, what does that show? It does not show all emotions are universal. It does not show all expressions are universal. It does not show, even for the allegedly basic six, that the sadness expressed in Fore faces and in American faces is essentially the same emotion. Physiognomical significance may depend on more than the lay of facial muscles.

But suppose an emotion is given, might it still be the case that how that given emotion is naturally exhibited is somehow fixed? Can we make sense of the notion of the "natural expression" of an emotion, short of identifying the emotion with its expression? After all, the interesting underlying suggestion of the recent cross-cultural studies is that (basic) emotions (with any necessary identifying context supplied) have characteristic (facial) expressions.

Natural Expression

I started by asking "Why do we cry?" And I noted that the most natural answer may be "because we are sad." I have also at various points been tempted to press further and ask "Why do we cry when sad?" On at least one very appealing account of the relation of feeling and expression, to ask this further question is "like questioning a tautology" (Hampshire 1972c, 152). Is it?

If bare feelings could be distinguished and identified in total independence from patterns of behavior (which were later found to be merely contingently associated with them), both the feat of identification and then the feat of communication with others about the items identified would be mysterious—in the way much is mysterious on a Cartesian view of the relation of mind and body. By contrast, Stuart Hampshire asks:

> How do we identify a mere something that we feel as anger or as amusement? There is at least one necessary connection that is clear in the normal use of language. If I am amused, I am inclined, or disposed, or have a tendency, to laugh or to smile. If I am angry, I am inclined, or disposed, or have a tendency, to attack or to behave aggressively. Wherever there is this necessary connection between an identifiable feeling or emotion, and the inclination to behave in an identifiable way, the pattern of behaviour may be called the natural expression of the feeling. A certain pattern of behaviour is a natural expression of a certain feeling, if, in distinguishing this feeling from other feelings with which it might be confused, we would specify an inclination towards this particular pattern of behaviour, together with some standard circumstances, actually existing or believed to exist, which provoke the inclination. So in explaining what anger is, as opposed to some other emotion, I would refer to a disposition to attack when the subject has been, or believes that he has been, in some way harmed or hurt. (1972c, 143)

The argument appeals to the conditions for the understanding and learning of language, in which observable behavior must doubtless play a role. On this account, with some similarity to James's, it would appear that there is no anger if there is no inclination to attack. Certainly there is in Hampshire an advance on James: his account of natural expression is in terms of dispositions to behavior rather than actual behavior, and it includes context and beliefs in the specification of an emotion. But the notion that the connection between emotion and expression is necessary or tautologous still needs clarification.

We, in our society, associate crying with sadness. And we also associate crying with happiness. So a single expression may be connected with different emotions. Thus, in these cases, though given a disposition to behavior, no particular emotion may be specified without reference to context and beliefs. We may cry on occasions that have nothing in common but our tears. What about the converse? May a single emotion be connected with different expressions? In a sense, the answer is obviously yes. An angry person might strike or, alternatively, refuse to speak with the presumed offender. If it is true that an inclination to attack is natural (and so in a sense necessary) to anger, what counts as an "attack" will nonetheless be a matter of circumstances and belief (and so in a sense variable and contingent). (Situations may perhaps be more stereotyped for animals— which makes them both easier to read and more limited in range of emotional expression.) A frightened person might run or, alternatively, stand frozen to the spot. (We shall see how Sartre treats both of these as forms of escape.) Thus there may be a number of equally natural expressions for a single emotion.

But could a person express an emotion not by a voluntary action or gesture but by a facial expression naturally tied to another emotion? Once again, the answer seems obvious if one recalls the association of crying with happiness in our society. The happy bride at a wedding can express her joy equally well with smiles or with tears. I can see no reason to assume a one-to-one correlation of emotions with expressions, even basic emotions and natural expressions.

This discussion may not be enough to undermine the tautology claim, but it may be enough to leave room for further questions. Now we cannot say that having in certain circumstances an inclination to cry is what it means to be sad; we have to complicate the connection by referring to an inclination to cry or to do a number of other things. There is not a single unique natural expression for sadness. Once having added the alternatives, one may wonder why an individual (or a society) has an inclination of one kind rather than another.

We are told that the Vietnamese express horror and grief with peals of laughter (Solomon 1978). Ekman would presumably wish to deny the claim, or explain it in terms of display rules, for he believes there is a fixed universal face for sadness. But whether the account in terms of display rules is persuasive depends on the particular situation and story.

> Lafcadio Hearn has remarked that the Japanese smile is not necessarily a spontaneous expression of amusement, but a law of etiquette, elaborated and cultivated from early times. It is a silent language, often seemingly inexplicable to Europeans, and it may arouse violent anger in them as a consequence. The Japanese child is taught to smile as a social duty, just as he is taught to bow or prostrate himself; he must always show an appearance of happiness to avoid inflicting his sorrow upon his friends.

The story is told of a woman servant who smilingly asked her mistress if she might go to her husband's funeral. Later she returned with his ashes in a vase and said, actually laughing, "Here is my husband." Her White mistress regarded her as a cynical creature; Hearn suggests that this may have been pure heroism.[12]

The case of Japanese laughter during grief seems very much a matter of cultivated etiquette, and so appeal to display rules seems appropriate.[13] Similarly, ceremonial weeping does not seem that uncommon (LaBarre 1947, 55). But social display rules do not explain the hysterical laughter that sometimes seems to emerge in grief in our society, and which is perhaps even more common elsewhere. Darwin writes:

> It is scarcely possible to point out any difference between the tear-stained face of a person after a paroxysm of excessive laughter and after a bitter crying-fit. It is probably due to the close similarity of the spasmodic movements caused by these widely different emotions that hysteric patients alternately cry and laugh with violence, and that young children sometimes pass suddenly from the one to the other state. Mr. Swinhoe informs me that he has often seen the Chinese, when suffering from deep grief, burst out into hysterical fits of laughter. (206)

The crucial variable seems to be control. The less controlled the response ("hysterical" laughter is prototypically out of control), the less plausible display rules become.

The relation of emotion and expression begins to look heavily contingent. A person may run when afraid, but equally may stand still. That some may laugh when sad may be no more startling than that some may cry when sad. Darwin concludes his chapter on weeping by noting that his physiological story means "we must look at weeping as an incidental result, as purposeless as the secretion of tears from a blow outside the eye, or as a sneeze from the retina being affected by a bright light" (175).

Sartre: Crying and Action

Is crying an action? This question has a number of different dimensions. Is crying a matter of choice? Is it something we can control? Is it something that just happens to us? These questions are not the same. We can sometimes control involuntary bodily activities that we cannot initiate. In those cases, we do not so much choose them as actions as choose not to stop them once they have started. And sometimes involuntary bodily responses can be actively induced. How they are induced at will is itself an interesting question, sometimes revealing about the normal mechanisms. Actors cultivate various techniques in relation to crying. Many actors cry by turning their thoughts in sad directions. (I am told Shirley Temple used to cry by thinking of her pony.) Children in general quickly learn the instrumental and manipulative uses of crying. Do they use a technique to make themselves cry?

Sartre offers a radical answer to the question of whether crying is an action. His answer is a straight yes. But his answer is made especially radical by the fact that he does not single out crying as an expression of emotion (though he does use it as an example); he believes *all* emotions are actions. This is a reversal of ordinary assumptions as radical as James's. We usually regard emotions as rooted in the body and thus as at least partly passive, as the word *passions* might itself suggest—things that sweep over us without our will or consent.

Sartre, in his *The Emotions: Outline of a Theory* (1948), offers a fascinating account of emotion as action—not, to be sure, as ordinary intentional action, but as a magical attempt to transform the world. He writes:

> When the paths traced out become too difficult, or when we see no path, we can no longer live in so urgent and difficult a world. All the ways are barred. However, we must act. So we try to change the world, that is, to live as if the connection between things and their potentialities were not ruled by deterministic processes, but by magic. Let it be clearly understood that this is not a game; we are driven against a wall, and we throw ourselves into this new attitude with all the strength we can muster. Let it also be understood that this attempt is not conscious of being such, for it would then be the object of a reflection. (58–59)

So a person might faint as an expression of passive fear (62–63). The fainting is an attempt, doubtless an ineffective and in that sense magical attempt, to deal with danger. Fainting does not actually annihilate the dangerous object, but it does eliminate it as an object of consciousness, and so can be seen as a behavior of attempted escape. Especially interesting for our purposes, however, is Sartre's example of crying. He writes of a girl who visits a doctor to tell him of her troubles: "But she is unable to; such social behavior is too hard for her. THEN she sobs. But does she sob BECAUSE she cannot say anything? Are her sobs vain attempts to act, a diffuse upheaval which represents the decomposition of too difficult behavior? Or does she sob precisely IN ORDER NOT TO SAY ANYTHING?" (31). For Sartre the answer is plain: emotion is behavior, an organized system of means aimed at an end (32, 38). The crying is specifically a form of refusal:

> The question is, above all, one of a negative behavior which aims at denying the urgency of certain problems and substituting others. The sick person wanted Janet's feelings to be moved. That means she wanted to replace the attitude of impassive waiting which he adopted by one of affectionate concern. That was what she wanted, and she used her body to bring it about. At the same time, by putting herself into a state which made confession impossible, she cast the act to be performed out of her

range. Thus, as long as she was shaken with tears and hiccups, any possibility of talking was removed . . .

The emotion of active sadness in this case is therefore a magical comedy of impotence; the sick person resembles servants who, having brought thieves into their master's home, have themselves tied up so that it can be clearly seen that they could not have prevented the theft. Only, here, the sick person is tied up by himself and by a thousand tenuous bonds. (66–67)

Here, as everywhere, Sartre gives us a sense of being more responsible for our lives than we might like to believe. But again, as almost everywhere, he here exaggerates. In his effort to portray emotion as action, as chosen, he distorts the notion of action just as he generally distorts the notion of choice. (Sartre tends to say we have a "choice" whenever we can imagine an alternative possibility. But we can always imagine an alternative possibility. So he concludes that we always have a choice. We are condemned to be free. But this neglects the difference between imagining an alternative and an alternative actually being available. Sometimes we are in fact up against a wall and have no real choice.) So while it may be illuminating to suggest that fainting can be understood as a magical attempt to escape, Sartre is carried away by his general theory when he treats running, the expression of active fear, as also a magical attempt. He writes: "Flight is a fainting which is enacted; it is a magical behavior which consists of denying the dangerous object with our whole body by subverting the vectorial structure of the space we live in by abruptly creating a potential direction on the OTHER SIDE. It is a way of forgetting it, of denying it" (63). But running need not be a form of denial. It may be an active recognition of a danger and an appropriate (not magical) response to it. Fainting may never make the danger go away, but running in fact often helps.

The Paradox of Acting

Some bodily states are voluntary, and so especially suitable for the communication of feeling as gestures or facial expressions. Such gestures and expressions can be given culturally variable significance, but because of certain uniformities in our inclinations to respond to standard situations there is some uniformity across cultures.[14] Some bodily states are nonvoluntary, and so while less suitable for the deliberate expression of feeling, they may nonetheless effectively manifest feelings. Indeed, that a certain state cannot be readily called up at will may help it to serve to mark sincerity of feeling. But even nonvoluntary states can often be inhibited at will, and sometimes called up at will. Many states are thus neither simply voluntary nor nonvoluntary. Crying is such a state, smiling is another. We can successfully inhibit a smile, or sometimes we may smile despite ourselves, or, more important for present problems, we may call up a smile for a purpose. The purpose may be personal and social, as in a polite smile at a friend's joke, or even commercial, as in the professional smile of a flight attendant.[15] What does it take to call up a smile or shed a voluntary tear? In particular, does the production of an expression of emotion require or involve the production of the feeling or emotion normally (naturally, nonvoluntarily) expressed?

The method of acting usually attributed to Stanislavski teaches that for an actor to portray emotion convincingly, it is best for him actually to induce the relevant feeling—the appropriate outward expression will then follow. Stanislavski writes: "The great actor should be full of feeling, and especially he should feel the thing he is portraying. He must feel an emotion not only once or twice while he is studying his part, but to a greater or lesser degree every time he plays it, no matter whether it is the first or the thousandth time" (1936, 13). Writing in 1773, several centuries before Stanislavski's work, Diderot provides a powerful argument against such an approach in his book *The Paradox of Acting*. Among other things, Diderot points out that plays often call for rapid shifts in scene and accompanying emotion. It will therefore be difficult for an actor who has worked himself up into a state of intense grief for one scene to transform his state into the lighthearted gaiety required in a scene five minutes later. And night after night, such emotional work, could it be done, would be a terrible drain— one cannot expect consistent strength of performance from those who play from the heart rather than from thought. Diderot writes, "They say an actor is all the better for being excited, for being angry. I deny it. He is best when he imitates anger. Actors impress the public not when they are furious, but when they play fury well" (71). (Theater is not identification, but representation.) Thus the paradox of acting, for Diderot, is that in order better to portray an emotional state it is sometimes best not actually to be in the state.[16]

It is a common observation that forced smiles look different from natural smiles. It is an observation that is confirmed by researchers, who note that deliberate smiles differ from spontaneous smiles in both neural pathways and in extent of asymmetry.[17] It does not follow, however, that the effective actor must actually induce the relevant emotion in order to achieve convincing expression. The distinctive phenomenology of a natural smile gives the actor a target to aim at; what steps are needed to hit it is an empirical question (and the answer may be different for different actors). Similarly, some observers note morphological differences in natural (expressive) crying and instrumental (deliberate) crying (Wolff 1969). And, it may be the case that the chemistry of emotionally induced tears and of tears stimulated by other means is different (Frey 1985). Nonetheless, the squeeze of a concealed onion may be as effective as thinking sad thoughts for the purposes of an actor who wishes to appear to cry tears of sadness.[18] So it remains true that if a person wishes to appear to be in an emotional state at deliberately chosen times, it may be best not actually to be in that state.

But on some theories, notably William James's theory that identifies the emotion with what would usually be taken as its expression, to put on the external form of an emotion is tantamount to experiencing the emotion. James recognizes this corollary of his theory and goes on to draw therapeutic implications from it:

> If our theory be true, a necessary corollary of it ought to be that any voluntary arousal of the so-called manifestations of a special emotion ought to give us the emotion itself . . . Everyone knows how panic is increased by flight . . . Refuse to express a passion, and it dies. Count ten before venting your anger, and its occasion seems ridiculous. Whistling to keep up courage is no mere figure of speech . . . There is no more valuable precept in moral education than this, as all who have experience know: if we wish to conquer undesirable emotional tendencies in ourselves, we must assiduously, and in the first instance cold-bloodedly, go through the *outward motions* of those contrary dispositions we prefer to cultivate. The reward of persistency will infallibly come, in the fading out of the sullenness or depression, and the advent of real cheerfulness and kindliness in their stead. Smooth the brow, brighten the eye, contract the dorsal rather than the ventral aspect of the frame, and speak in a major key, pass the genial compliment, and your heart must be frigid indeed if it does not gradually thaw! (1968 [1884], 27–28)

Would it were so simple. While smiling sometimes helps, it in fact often fails to cheer one up. And repressing unpleasant feelings does not unfailingly make them go away. The problem with the "whistle a happy tune" theory of therapy is that it rarely works. We thus have further reason to doubt the larger theory of which it is a "necessary corollary." (We should note that, whatever *its* problems, Stanislavski's "inside-out" approach to acting does not rely on that theory.)

Emotional Responses to Fictions

What may one say of the responsive tears induced in the audience? Many are moved to tears when reading "pathetic stories," or watching sentimental films, or viewing tragic plays, or when confronted by other works of the imagination that inspire (to omit finer distinctions) sadness or joy. Do emotional reactions to fiction involve "real" emotions? Some would argue that because the relevant beliefs are only make-believe, and because the usual inclinations to action are absent or inhibited, the associated emotions must also be only make-believe (Walton 1978). I do not think that is so. I do not see why we must say the person at a horror movie is only make-believedly afraid. Why cannot a person have a real fear of a make-believe danger?

While there may be no inclination to flee, the physiological responses are real enough, and fear in ordinary circumstances can involve all sorts of different component mixes (including many different types of thoughts). We need not have patently false beliefs in order to be moved by fiction. We need only to let ourselves go.

In addition, in some cases, what may be involved is a refusal to let oneself go. The person at a horror movie, in addition to whatever physiological arousal takes place, may well be inclined to flee the theater, but (recognizing the pointlessness of the inclination) inhibit it. A person who is afraid to fly may nonetheless board a plane, inhibiting their inclination to act on their fear. Fear of fictions need be no less real than irrational fear of flying, despite recognition of the unreality of the underlying thoughts.

One may not believe the actors on stage are really suffering, but one's own sadness may nonetheless be real. That there may not be certain inclinations to action, say to comfort the bereaved actor, does not mean the tears of the audience are false. The thousands who cried at the death of Little Nell were surely saddened by that death, even though action was not in order. Of course, Oscar Wilde was not so moved. According to him, one must have a heart of stone to read the death of Little Nell without laughing (Ford 1965). But his critical view does not depend on the notion that emotional responses are inappropriate, or less than real, when reading fiction. He was differently moved (doubtless more by the manner of description than by the event described). Sticking with more sentimental readers, it would be a mistake to think grief is not "real" unless there is real mourning. The problem cannot be that Little Nell was not present. When we read about (actual) historical events, the events also are at a remove. Nonetheless, when one reads accounts of the Danes wearing the Star of David en masse when the occupying Nazis commanded all Jews to wear it, one may well be moved to tears. When Jews were made victims, the Danes made themselves Jews. (Notice that the emotion here is neither sadness nor joy. One is sometimes touched when confronted by the noble.)

Does it matter whether an event described, in addition to being at some remove, never happened? (One may be stirred to tears by the Marseillaise scene in the film *Casablanca*.) In crying at fictions the tears are certainly real; the question is whether the associated sympathy or grief or whatever is real, whether the tears express emotion. Diderot raised the issue long ago: "Have you ever thought on the difference between the tears raised by a tragedy of real life and those raised by a touching narrative?" (20). Unfortunately, he goes on to give a misleading response to the question. He thinks that tears in real life are not mediated by thought and that real tears "come of a sudden, the others by degrees." But one should not confuse conscious thought and deliberation with all of thought. And even if one omits reference to less than fully explicit thoughts, the tears in real life are typically in response to situations perceived (that is, believed or thought) to have a certain character (e.g., involving loss). The mediation involved in thinking of a situation as of a certain kind need not involve calculation, and it is just such mediation that leads to tears. But we should note that mediation must also be understood in terms of socially recognized categories. While the physiological mechanism that produces tears when a person laughs violently may be the same that produces tears when a person wails in grief, in the latter case we regard the tears as an expression of the grief but in the former (when a person laughs to tears) we do not say the tears express amusement. In that case we regard the physiological mechanism as merely a mechanism. Being moved to tears is not a physical notion. If music makes one cry because it is too loud, that is, by its physical impact, that is not enough to make it "sad music." Tears must be mediated by thoughts of a certain (socially recognized) kind to count as emotional tears. That the thoughts may not be "true" (that they may be responses to fiction), and that one may not be moved to further action, does not necessarily change the character of the emotion.

And it should be clear that the thoughts need not be fully explicit. In the course of arguing for the importance of unmediated physiological responses to perceptions (what he calls reflex "effects due to the connate adaptation of the nervous system" [24]), James gives an example that seems to me to go against his own claims:

> The writer well remembers his astonishment, when a boy of seven or eight, at fainting when he saw a horse bled. The blood was in a bucket, with a stick in it, and, if memory does not deceive him, he stirred it round and saw it drip from the stick with no feeling save that of childish curiosity. Suddenly the world grew black before his eyes, his ears began to buzz, and he knew no more. He had never heard of the sight of blood producing faintness or sickness, and he had so little repugnance to it, and so little apprehension of any other sort of danger from it, that even at that tender age, as he well remembers, he could not help wondering how the mere physical presence of a pailful of crimson fluid could occasion in him such formidable bodily effects. (26)

It is difficult to believe that a boy of seven or eight could fail to have had innumerable experiences associating blood with injury and pain. He need not explicitly recall those associations in order for them to contribute to the effects of a perception (which, again, is itself a kind of thinking shaped by experience and social categories).

Psychological processes of identification, association, displacement, and so on may seem special adaptations on our part to the peculiar relation we have to fiction, but the same mechanisms are no less active in our interactions with the "real" world. The poet James Merrill reminds us, "Reality is fiction in disguise." In *On Love,* Stendhal describes how romantic love is characterized by "crystallization": we clothe the object of our love in virtues, just as a twig placed in certain caves becomes encrusted with salt crystals. In addition to such idealization (or "fictionalization"), Freud explains how all love is characterized by transference, how "the finding of an object is in fact the refinding of it" (1905d, 7: 222). Such psychological processes pervade our emotional life. Thus the person afraid of the shark while watching *Jaws* is no less afraid than the person who avoids beaches out of fear of sharks after watching it. Emotion may always be at a certain "distance," mediated by thought and perception, but that does not make the inner life of a person responding to fiction (any more than the inner life of a person responding to political news from afar) make-believe. The emotion of a person who while reading *The Adventures of Tom Sawyer* is concerned for Tom and Becky or who is sympathetically distraught with King Lear is no less real than that of a person worried about an absent loved one or confronting his own ungrateful children. The distinction between fiction and reality matters in all sorts of ways, but it does not undermine the psychological status of our emotional responses, turning the fear of, say, Dracula, into a pretend fear. If the fictional status of an object of emotion undermined the "reality" of the emotion itself, every irrational emotion (especially when it involved a bifocal awareness of its own irrationality) might also have to be demoted to a kind of play-acting, when it may be as truly felt as emotion more appropriately based. The education of the passions by books, plays, and movies runs the danger of sentimentality and may seem child's play, but it is the work of giving meaning to our world.

Psychoanalysis of Tears

If a thought can provoke tears, so can a displaced or even an unconscious thought. Freud gives a dramatic example of the emergence of an unconscious fantasy into tearful consciousness:

> After I had drawn the attention of one of my patients to her phantasies, she told me that on one occasion she had suddenly found herself in tears in the street and that, rapidly considering what it was she was actually crying about, she had got hold of a phantasy to the following effect. In her imagination she had formed a tender attachment to a pianist who was well known in the town (though she was not personally acquainted with him), she had had a child by him (she was in fact childless); and he had then deserted her and her child and left them in poverty. It was at this point in her romance that she had burst into tears. (1908a, 9: 160)

Pathological tears, or tears in the absence of context, point up the need for context in order for tears to be intelligible as expression of emotion. The psychoanalytic quest for unconscious fantasies in such cases is an effort to find the needed explanatory thoughts.

The psychoanalytic context may itself give special point to tears. It will be recalled that the girl in Sartre's example was crying in order to avoid confessing certain problems to her doctor (the famous contemporary of

Freud, Janet). What Sartre speaks of in terms of magical acts, psycho-analysts naturally speak of in terms of defense mechanisms. For example, as one puts it, "Weeping very often primarily represents an attempt to deal with aggressive energy by dissipating it in harmless secretory behavior" (Lofgren 1966, 380). This notion fits nicely with the observation that tears are the only human excretion uniformly and unequivocally regarded as a clean substance.[19] By contrast, saliva, urine, and feces are multiply con-nected with dirt and aggression both within psychoanalytic theory and in the popular imagination and ordinary (if vulgar) speech (Lofgren, 379). (Think what it means to "spit" on someone.) Moreover, "tears do make the other person difficult to focus on, or even difficult to see. It is hard to hurt someone you cannot see. At the same time, the tearful person, partially blinded, becomes a pathetic target and one not likely to be attacked" (Wood & Wood 1984, 126). Thus tears are especially suitable for dissipating ag-gression harmlessly, rather than threatening the object. This interpreta-tion also fits nicely with the fact that crying is typically felt as a relief; in-deed, it may sometimes help to explain that fact. Finally, it fits Hampshire's account of emotional expressions in terms of truncated actions, for weep-ing can be seen as the residual form of what was originally a tantrum. It should be clear that tears can be used defensively, whether to gain time and control or to dissipate aggression. And they can also be used manipula-tively. Children do it all the time.

Most interesting, however, in the midst of multiplying functions, is the reductive psychoanalytic claim that "there are no tears of joy, only tears of sorrow." The claim appears in an article by Sandor Feldman about "Crying at the Happy Ending" (1956, 485). The argument is based on the analysis of individual cases where a happy event is found to be merely the occasion of other thoughts that in turn provoke the tears. Feldman notes a person may indeed be happy and full of joy, but "the question is whether he cried be-cause he was happy or for some other reason which was stirred up at the oc-casion of the happy ending" (478). In case after case, he plausibly suggests that thoughts of loss or sorrow, conscious or unconscious, are brought up at the happy ending. In some cases, such as those involving relief at rescue, there may be delay of affect. In other cases, one may be reminded of a lost happy past or other concerns may be raised. Consider the parent at a wed-ding who becomes sad over the uncertain future of their beloved child or the individual who, watching a happy ending, is made to think of their own inadequate present (in the light of the other's happiness, one cries for oneself).

In any given case this may be plausible. Is it always? Note first that the active thoughts need not be unconscious. In fact, Darwin refers to associ-ated thoughts of grief at reunions (214–15). There need be nothing myste-rious or hidden about the emergence of delayed affect in such cases. All the relevant thoughts may be fully conscious. But suppose a person denies the presence of sad thoughts. There are tears, but the occasion is apparently one of unalloyed happiness. On Feldman's generalization, "There are no tears of joy, only tears of sorrow" (485), there must be operative unconscious thoughts of a sad character to explain the apparently happy tears. How is one to evaluate such a claim (especially in its causal aspect)? Short of a full psychoanalysis of every case, we must consider anew the relation of emotion and expression.

Suppose we accept the generalization as plausible (as I in fact think it is): that is, the actual or symbolic union of the typical happy ending gets associated with the pain and loss of (its opposite) separation, and it is the associated thoughts that produce the tears. Let us suppose that all tears (in particular tears at happy endings) are tears of sorrow. The result is dramatic. All my earlier references to tears of joy versus tears of sadness must be withdrawn. Does this also undermine the arguments that rested on those references? The result need not be devastating. Not if other cases of a single expression being tied to different types of emotion can be found. The coincidence of opposites (or at least the crowding of contraries) is in fact pervasive. One can run from fear, but one can also run from joy. Similarly, one can (it would seem) smile in amusement or in grief. Or if such smiles are dismissed as conventional or hysterical or otherwise don't seem enough, the grimace of disgust and of fear may be close, or, as with the Fore, the face of surprise and of fear. Freud writes of "The Antithetical Meaning of Primal Words" (1910e). He attributes the double and opposed meanings carried by many words in the oldest languages to the operation of the same factors that in the dreamwork allow an element to represent its contrary. He quotes the philologist Karl Abel: "Man was not in fact able to acquire his oldest and simplest concepts except as contraries to their contraries, and only learnt by degrees to separate the two sides of an antithesis and think of one without conscious comparison with the other" (1910e, 11: 158). The ambivalence in the language of emotional expression is not much different. While this may rescue some of my earlier arguments, the larger question of whether the relation of emotion to expression is necessary (tautological) or contingent remains. For the psychoanalytic hypothesis that reinterprets tears at happy endings as tears of sorrow, as well as other reductive psychoanalytic moves, seems to assume a one-to-one correlation of emotion and expression of the sort I have just (again) denied.

If we assume that all tears are tears of sorrow, that they can never really express happiness, are we going back to Ekman-like assumptions about all true facial expressions having a single universal meaning; are we perhaps even going back to a Jamesean identification of emotion with (felt) expression? Does psychoanalytic interpretation depend on such reductive assumptions? If so, to what extent can they be sustained? Hume denied them completely: "If nature had so pleas'd, love might have had the same effect as hatred, and hatred as love. I see no contradiction in supposing a desire of producing misery annex'd to love, and of happiness to hatred" (1888 [1739], 368). But Hume was surely wrong about love and hate being only contingently tied to appropriate actions. An apparent love would be rejected as love if we discovered that at the center of the passion was a wish for harm to the putative beloved. We would say the feeling was ambivalent or redescribe the situation in terms of the subject's beliefs (according to which the "harm" might not seem harm). Where a supposed lover acts in a harmful way, we presume something else is going on. And this is quite independent of psychoanalytic arguments. Psychoanalysis may extend the inferences (say to unconscious emotions), but the basic presumptions are similar. Certain aspects of couvade, for example, are best understood in terms of unconscious hostility. When certain Turks beat a confined woman with sticks, they explain the action in terms of the need to ward off demons, but since we do not believe in demons (and may doubt that they really do), we must regard the demons as the locus of a projected hostility that is the true motive of the beating. In psychoanalysis, one often infers to unconscious beliefs and desires when confronted with unintelligible behavior (such as apparently meaningless symptomatic activity—or the unaccountable tears that were understood in terms of unconscious fantasy at the start of this part of our discussion). When an agent has his own account, so the behavior is apparently intelligible, the beliefs or rationalizations of the agent, especially when shared by a wider group, complicate the situation (Neu 1981, chap. 14 here). But the inference to hostility from hitting in the case of couvade does not depend on a simple one-to-one correlation of emotion and expression. Hitting is only one way of expressing hostility, and not all hitting is motivated by hostility. But when it is not, one needs an acceptable alternative explanation. For dispositions to certain sorts of behavior in certain sorts of contexts (actual or notional) do constitute part of the identity of an emotion. The connection of emotion and expression is more than contingent, but only loosely necessary. The connection is defeasible when there is an explanation for why the ordinary presumptions fail. The ordinary presumptions are rooted in the conditions of language and communication. Biology and history conspire to forge the links. Our theories and images of emotional expression feed back into and reinforce our "natural" expressions of emotion.

What is the relation of sadness and crying? The ordinary view is that we cry because we are sad. James's suggestion was that we are sad because we cry. Sartre suggests that we cry to avoid (by magic means) being sad. According to Emile Durkheim (1965 [1915]), while we might in fact be sad, in mourning situations at least we cry because we are forced to, because societal expectations require it. Some psychoanalysts, such as Lofgren, point to internal psychological rather than external social functions, citing, for example, the role of crying in dissipating aggression. On all these accounts, crying may function to bring relief.

For Darwin the tears in crying are just an "incidental result" (175); associative and other processes produce tears as the result of a mechanism present for other reasons. Of course, according to the account by Darwin cited earlier (174, 206, 216–17), tears on happy occasions may be traced, via associative habits, to the physiological mechanism that leads to tears in connection with excessive laughter. On that account, tears of joy are no less basic than tears of sorrow, for the originating physiological mechanism (involving spasmodic breathing and protective squeezing of the orbicular muscles) is the same. Thus there would be at least one type of case in which the psychoanalytic claim that all tears are tears of sorrow would be false. Perhaps each type of case, and the relevant triggering thoughts, must be traced before we can be sure of the true range of the psychoanalytic claim. (Taken associatively, the extension may be limited to tears at happy endings.) Or perhaps we must reconcile ourselves to the complex and even conflicting meanings of our vocabulary for emotional expression, for that vocabulary (whatever its biological base) emerges from a complex and conflicting history. The antithetical meaning of primal expressions may be as basic and inevitable as the antithetical meaning of primal words.

Antithetical meaning is in fact open to two different interpretations. One is a simple associationist reading, on which the presence of an object or an experience brings up the thought of its contrary: so high makes us think of low, day of night, joy of sorrow. But I think Freud's point is more radical, for he is referring to a time at which the contraries are so far undifferentiated, before the concepts have been sorted out, and so the experience is itself undifferentiated. Indeed, the separate concepts are not yet available for associative or any other purposes. High/low is a dimension of experience, and joy/sorrow is a dimension of experience; and confronted with either extreme along the dimension we are confronted with both. They are in a sense equivalent. On this reading, all tears may be tears of sorrow, but not because there are no tears of joy or because on happy occasions there are associated sad thoughts, but because they come, ultimately, to the same thing. That we cry is a sign that we are moved, but that is an undifferentiated state, which we come (in time) to sort out in terms of associated situations and thoughts.

"Tears, Idle Tears"

There is little reason to believe that animals other than human beings weep, that is, shed tears in sorrow or grief.[20] But then there is equally little reason to believe that animals other than human beings blush, that is, redden in shame or embarrassment.[21] Should one fact be more surprising or puzzling than the other?

While it is difficult to think of another animal that *could* blush (the machinery needed for visible blushing would include capillaries near the surface of a face that is neither dark nor covered with fur), many animals have eyes that can water. Moreover, the skin reddening (say from cold) is not a blush; to constitute a blush, the physiological reddening would have to have a specific type of mental cause, such as the thoughts involved in shame. And it may well be that animals cannot have the specific thoughts requisite to shame. But with crying, emotional tears require only sadness (or sad thoughts), of which animals are surely capable. Thus while blushing is an emotional expression animals lack, we can easily explain that lack in terms of the relevant machinery and emotions (shame, embarrassment, etc.). But in the case of tears, other animals would seem to have both the machinery and the emotions. Why is there no emotional weeping in them?

First, the situation may be a bit more complex. It may be that only certain primates in fact have the machinery for crying. Collins argues that other animals have alternative mechanisms (e.g., "the nictitating membrane in air-breathing vertebrates below primates") to perform the physiological functions of crying in protecting the eyes (1932, 9–11). Whatever the availability of the machinery, if we distinguish the two main types of dangerous situation requiring protection (pressure on eyes when screaming/howling and irritating particles), and if only one of the two types of situation (direct irritation of the eye) arises and so stimulates the lacrimal glands in animals other than human beings, then we may have a basis for explaining their lack of emotional tears. For it is the other series of connections (screaming—spasmodic breathing—pressure in eyes—protective squeezing of orbicular muscles) that leads to emotional tears in human infants. There is a physiological chain that first produces tears in association with screams of physical pain or distress. Other occasions of suffering produce an inclination to cry out and so (via the same physiological links) tears. Hence tears come to serve as an expression of grief and other forms of psychological suffering. Other animals do not have the physiological mechanism linking pain—screaming—pressure in eyes—stimulation of lacrimal glands by squeezed orbiculars, and so do not associatively cry in emotional pain. But why shouldn't the other mechanism (direct irritation of the eye stimulating the lacrimal glands) be enough for associative generalization from physical pain? Because physical pain naturally provokes screaming (which produces tears), but it does not produce physical irritation of the eyes (which we are presuming is the only mechanism for producing tears in other animals). Animals don't cry in emotional pain or grief because (or for the same reason) they don't weep in physical pain either.

Darwin points out, "Children, when wanting food or suffering in any way, cry out loudly, like the young of most other animals, partly as a call to their parents for aid, and partly from any great exertion serving as a relief" (174). And he traces for us the physiological connections (via gorging of the blood vessels of the eye and contracting eye muscles) that lead to the secretion of tears in human infants, so that eventually "suffering readily causes the secretion of tears, without necessarily being accompanied by any other action." Painful, or even just sudden, emotional states may lead to discharge in the form of tears—but that we cry (rather than shed hairs) may just be "an incidental result, as purposeless as the secretion of tears from a blow outside the eye" (175). The protective watering of the eyes, whether from external irritation, hunger, sadness, grief, or other internal disruption, of course then becomes overlaid with many other meanings. It is associated with much in our lives. We are often stimulated to emotional tears by our emotional thoughts, and tears have more than reflex meaning for humans because we think. We cry when we feel moved, or touched, or vulnerable, and the associated thoughts are what give the tears their particular emotional characters.

Thoughts enter at two points at least: in interpreting the situation and in interpreting our (physiological) response. While James said we are sad because we cry, we have seen that in some contexts (and cultures), we may equally well be said to be angry or ashamed or something else because we cry. Physiology alone is not enough to settle the matter. When (as in certain aesthetic cases and in many sexual ones) perception leads (apparently directly) to a physical reaction, we think of the experience as by its nature psychosomatic. Part of the interest of tears (like the interest of sexuality) is that the two elements (of mind and body) seem fused from the start. While behavior may at some level be mediated by thought, it is not mediated by conscious thinking. The reaction is by its nature mixed. It is not just physiological, but it is also not a deliberate, calculated response, or perhaps even a well-defined and differentiated one. So we must remember there are at least two kinds of intellectual thing. Spinoza distinguishes between active and passive thought in terms of the explanation of the thought's occurrence. Imaginative thought tends to be passive: it mirrors physiology, and it is dominated by memory and association. It is only explicit thought with a normative and argumentative structure that is on the side of active emotion. If we are to be free and have control over our emotional lives, we must, according to Spinoza, seek to replace passive thought with active (rational and directed) thought. (See Neu 1977.) But the desire to displace imagination and passive emotion risks the elimination of aesthetic and sexual response—for in these areas memory, and association, and imagination are essential. By contrast, for Blake the difference between active and passive does not have these implications. For him, imagination involves energy and activity.

Crying at the Beginning

Newborns enter the world crying. More precisely, they enter screaming or gasping for air—tears come later. I have already noted that infants do not normally shed actual tears until several weeks after birth. Darwin argues that this could not be entirely due to lack of development in the lacrimal glands—for the glands readily secrete tears in response to direct physical irritation of the eye right from the beginning (152–53). It is only weeping from emotional causes that seems subject to delay. Could it be because infants do not yet think (at the appropriate level)? In a way yes, in a way no. First the no: even if they do not know how sad it all is from the moment of birth, it would be surprising if they could learn the lesson in only a few weeks, and surprising also that other animals with functional lacrimal glands never learn the lesson (they certainly, despite the lack of language, have some thoughts—why not the sorts of thoughts that provoke tears?). The problem turns, I think, on how we (the grown-ups) come to recognize the emotion behind the tears. When a baby first cries, we take it as a sign of distress, and we search for the cause in order to alleviate the suffering. This set of interactive responses doubtless has survival advantages for the species. Depending on the diagnosis, adults feed crying babies, change their diapers, and seek to remove other painful stimuli. While I suspect that babies sometimes cry just for the hell of it (to exercise their lungs, for pleasure), caretakers come to distinguish the different significances of crying, and crying gives babies a way of communicating their needs before they are capable of the more sophisticated communication enabled by language.[22] The addition of tears to verbal cries does not add much (though Montagu [1959] emphasizes the evolutionary advantages of the moistening and germicidal action of tears in relation to the nasal mucosa of the infant). The picture after a few weeks is of a diffuse response to pain or discomfort, though we may begin to allow the pain to be psychological (say, at separation from the mother) as well as physical. The tears only come to express particular emotions as we, the surrounding grown-ups, see in the tears responses to differentiated situations. Sometimes there is upset at the loss of a valued object, sometimes there is frustration at not getting what is wanted. As we come to ascribe the appropriate differentiating thoughts to the infant, these become tears of grief and tears of rage. How could it be otherwise? It is not as though infants enter life with a set of differentiated emotions built in, like little marbles of feeling, with the problems of finding the appropriate labels for the already well-defined feelings and of communicating to others which feeling they are currently experiencing. If that were the situation, the problems might be insoluble. We might never be sure that the words we attach to these isolated inner feelings match up with those used by others; our language for speaking of our inner lives might never make real communication possible. But the truth is that we enter a world with an already established language for speaking of the inner life, a social world into which we are initiated by others who take note of our behavior and responses. At the beginning, our inner life is an undifferentiated turmoil. But as others come to pick out certain of our behaviors, such as crying, as salient, they attach labels to them ("Baby is sad"), and we gradually come to connect what is going on within us in certain situations with these words. We come to divide up our inner life in accordance with the categories provided in the language we are born into, our mother tongue. Of course things develop and become more complex as time goes on, but now we can see another kind of truth in James's approach, a developmental truth. It is not quite the case that we are sad because we cry, but we do come to learn the meaning of sadness in a context where the expression of the emotion provides the first link to the vocabulary for describing the emotion. As Hampshire has put it, "In our classifications we move, as it were, inwards from expressive behavior to inner feeling" (1972c, 155). And, as he explains, things develop: "It is characteristic of the more refined concepts, which we use to distinguish between one sentiment and another, that the subject's own avowals are a necessary part of the conditions of their application. A person gradually acquires the power to apply these distinctions, both to himself and to others, in conjunction with his power to dissociate his inclinations from their immediate natural expression" (156)—the ability to control certain inclinations and to identify them, the ability to describe certain feelings and to have them develop together. Things start simply. A baby cries. The screams of distress, and the accompanying irregular breathing, are naturally attended by squeezed orbicular muscles about the eyes, leading to tears. What begins as an incidental and meaningless physiological response takes on many meanings. We come, through multiplying thought and experience, to be multiply moved to tears.

3

JEALOUS THOUGHTS

If someone imagines that a thing he loves is united
with another by as close, or by a closer, bond of Friendship than that with which he himself, alone, possessed
the thing, he will be affected with Hate toward the
thing he loves, and will envy the other . . . This
Hatred toward a thing we love, combined with Envy, is
called Jealousy, which is therefore nothing but a vacillation of mind born of Love and Hatred together,
accompanied by the idea of another who is envied.

Spinoza 1985 [1677], part 3, prop. 35

The slave revolt in morality begins when *ressentiment*
itself becomes creative and gives birth to values: the
ressentiment of natures that are denied the true reaction, that of deeds, and compensate themselves with an
imaginary revenge. While every noble morality develops from a triumphant affirmation of itself, slave morality from the outset says No to what is "outside," what
is "different," what is "not itself"; and *this* No is its
creative deed. This inversion of the value-positing
eye—this *need* to direct one's view outward instead of
back to oneself—is of the essence of *ressentiment*: in
order to exist, slave morality always first needs a hostile external world; it needs physiologically speaking,
external stimuli in order to act at all—its action is fundamentally reaction . . . While the noble man lives
in trust and openness with himself . . . the man of
ressentiment is neither upright nor naïve nor honest
and straightforward with himself. His soul *squints*.

Nietzsche 1967 [1887], first essay, sec. 10

Normal jealousy . . . is compounded of grief, the
pain caused by the thought of losing the loved object,
and of the narcissistic wound, in so far as this is distinguishable from the other wound; further, of feelings of
enmity against the successful rival, and of a greater or
lesser amount of self-criticism which tries to hold the
subject's own ego accountable for his loss.

Freud 1922b, *SE* 18: 223

Psychological problems are sometimes in some ways logical problems. Our lives do not simply fall apart, they collapse in structured ways, and the fault lines are marked by our concepts. Our ways of understanding and describing our psychological states often reveal (and sometimes limit) the potentials in those states themselves, the potentials both for development and for disorder. That this should be so may be explained through considering the roles of our concepts and beliefs in constituting our emotions and other mental states (Neu 1977). In this context, it is especially instructive to consider jealousy: partly because of its internal complexity, partly because of the richness of its conceptual surroundings, and partly because of its independent interest. That it has such rich surroundings, that we make such a wealth of fine discriminations in the area of jealousy (envy, resentment, indignation, Schadenfreude, begrudging, malice, spite, ill will, hatred, ingratitude, revenge, hostility, possessiveness, mistrust, suspicion, and so on indefinitely), is itself a sign of its interest and importance.

By tracing some of the tensions, some of the directions and complexities, built into jealousy, we may see some of the ways in which the forms and limits of our conceptions in this particular area shape our lives. Going beyond that, looking to a psychogenetic account of the origin and place of jealousy, I would like to raise some questions about how far and in what ways understanding our concepts may enable us to shape (and reshape?) them and so, perhaps, alter our lives. What are the limits here? What else would have to be different and what else would we have to give up if the possibility of jealousy were to be eliminated?

In what follows, I shall want to distinguish between jealousy and envy in relation to the hopes for emotional transformation connected with two types of ideals: communitarian and socialist. (The personal and the political are sometimes mistakenly assimilated. The ideal of the loving community is not the same as the ideal of the just community, though one might wish for, and work for, both.) I shall argue that despite the hopes of social reformers, the possibility of jealousy cannot be eliminated. It is wrong to think that jealousy is always necessarily misdirected, that it cannot have appropriate objects—on the contrary, it can. The presence and persistence of jealousy have more to do with the development of self-identity than with the possession of others; and while the underlying fears may make us prone to pathological forms of jealousy, it is also the case that jealousy is tied to certain forms of love—so the elimination of the possibility of jealousy might involve the loss of much else. On the other hand, the same difficulties do not, it seems to me, stand in the way of the hopes of social reformers in relation to envy. Which is not to suggest that envy can be readily dislodged from its place in human life, nor is it to say that the harmful consequences of jealousy cannot be ameliorated. In subsequent sections I will take up, successively, the questions of the eliminability of jealousy, of the relation of jealousy to envy and of malicious envy to admiring envy, and of the relation of jealousy to claims of right and to certain underlying fears. I shall conclude by juxtaposing the two faces of jealousy: the face turned to love and the face turned to lack of love.

Stalking the Green-Ey'd Monster

It was one of the hopes of the sixties (as of many other periods) that by restructuring social relations it might be possible to eliminate jealousy and other painful, "bourgeois" passions. This was the hope that inspired many in the commune movement. It has been largely, I think, a failed hope. Jealousy, envy, and possessiveness reasserted themselves despite the best efforts to keep them down. If this judgment is correct, the question becomes: "Why?" Was the failure a matter of changeable circumstance, or is the possibility of jealousy ineliminable?

It might be said that at the center of the typical commune problems was the fact that the makers of the new world were children of the old, and that they carried their pasts with them into the new institutions. And even their children, brought up under new arrangements, had to face the problem of "socialism in one country"—they had to relate to a wider world the inhabitants of which were not a party to the new arrangements. But these problems, while real and difficult, are merely contingent—one can imagine their being overcome.[1]

I think there are reasons for believing jealousy ineliminable (the possibility remains permanent), no matter what the social arrangements. And these are worth considering in some detail.

First, certain significant differences are ineliminable, and they are just the sort of differences necessary (and perhaps sufficient) for jealousy to get a foothold. Most basic perhaps is the difference between adults and children. It will always be the case that children, in the course of their prolonged dependency, will have needs and make demands which the supporting adults (whether or not they are the biological parents) will, because of needs and attachments of their own, be unable to meet. They cannot be constantly available in all the ways that children demand. The presence of siblings accentuates, but does not essentially change the situation. When loved persons are not available to us and they are (thought or felt to be) available to others, their absence will tend to be experienced as "loss to a rival." (Parents can also come, in this way, to feel jealous of their children; i.e., to experience *them* as rivals.) Jealousy forms one side of the Oedipal triangle because there is a natural (which is to say, biological) hierarchy. So far as the consequent inequalities, dependencies, and mismatches are universal and ineliminable, there must be room for jealousy.[2] (There certainly may be other differences—such as the differences between the sexes, e.g., in reproductive powers—with similar significance, but they may connect more with envy than jealousy, and I wish to come to and treat envy separately.)

Second, the development of children suggests that competitive possessiveness may be an ineliminable phase with permanent consequences. Consider the typical reaction of a two-year-old when it sees another child play with a toy it has just thrown aside. The primitive possessive behavior that emerges is apparently a cross-cultural universal.[3] I do not pretend to fully understand why this phenomenon should emerge just when it does or why it should be universal. Presumably it has something to do with a developing (biological?) need for control.

This primitive possessiveness is certainly an element in mature jealousy, but it needs to be understood that the character of possessiveness is itself problematic. It is too often said that what is wrong with jealousy is that it involves treating people as though they were things. What is more likely to be true in the psychogenesis of possessiveness is precisely the reverse, that is: we come to treat things as though they were people. The psychogenesis of possessiveness, and so jealousy, may perhaps be better understood if I introduce Winnicott's idea of the transitional object. In the beginning, when the difference between inside and outside is still unclear, there are no independent objects in the world of the infant and the notion of a possession has no place. ("The mother, at the beginning, by an almost 100 per cent adaptation affords the infant the opportunity for the *illusion* that her breast is part of the infant" [Winnicott 1958, 238].) Gradually, as the child comes to differentiate itself from its mother, it seizes on some object (typically a teddy bear or blanket) which has for it some of the properties of an independent object but at the same time forms an essential part of its identity: it may be given a name (as though it were a thing apart), but if it is changed (e.g., cleaned) or lost, its loss is felt as a loss of self. This transitional object is the child's first possession. The loss of the mother, contrasting with the time when she could be regarded as part of the self, contributes to the development of the child's attitude toward independent objects in such a way that the loss of an object can come to be felt as a loss of self. Identification with objects (so that they become "inside" while remaining "outside"), a process primarily begun and continued with people, gives possessions a special character and gives jealousy, insofar as it involves a fear of loss, a special place and force.

A third set of conditions that help give jealousy a place has to do with the character of love and intimacy. It may be that precisely what we most value about certain relationships also makes them essentially nonreplicable and nonshareable, and hence leaves a place for jealousy. For example, suppose one has a relationship characterized by "absolute openness," by a sharing of everything. Because one finds it so satisfying, one might wish to replicate it, to establish it with a second person. But imagine what would happen in the attempt. The second relationship would inevitably involve one in betraying the intimacies of the first. Thus it is the very thing that is most valuable about the first relationship that makes it impossible to replicate it. In trying to eliminate the possibility of jealousy here, one would be losing much else. Exclusivity is essential to the nature of the relationship.

There are at least two sorts of responses that might be made to this claim: First, that the relationship is replicable but that one must have the figure of a circle rather than a triangle (with unequal sides) in mind. That is, one could have absolute openness with someone and extend it to a second person, provided that person also has a relationship of absolute openness with the original partner. The notion is that no two people should be any closer than any other two. All share absolute openness. This returns us to the ideal of the commune. And there come the basic problems that currents of human feeling vary, that people are different, that not all are equally attractive to all (though the sources of attraction may have unconscious roots and we may not care to defend the sources of all our preferences—the preferences are nonetheless real), and finally that love has material conditions and limits. (I will consider this last point more closely in a later section.) We may defend the ideal of human equality and the notion that all have certain rights and entitlements, but can everyone be equally entitled to our love? Is our love something that can be dispensed on the basis of principle? And even if it could, would that be a good thing? It cannot be assumed that the ideals for the personal and the political are interchangeable. The principles of impartiality in distribution and of equal concern and respect that must govern institutional arrangements may be inappropriate if mechanically transferred to the governance of personal relationships. In any case, so long as we are involved (even if in different ways) with a number of people, there will always be the problem of *their* interactions and attitudes toward each other—which will always be complicated by our own ever-shifting needs and desires (and our equally shifting attitudes toward those needs and desires). Any apparent equilibrium (circular or triangular) is expectably unstable. A second response might claim that what is valuable in a relationship of absolute openness that compels it to be exclusive only seems valuable from the perspective of a bourgeois society. But the value may really depend on the value of *choice* in human relationships.[4] And is that value really limited to bourgeois societies? Is it wrong to value different people differently and for different reasons, and to desire different relationships with each of them (including exclusive relations with some of them)? Must we really desire (if we cannot in fact achieve) absolute openness with everyone? (Everyone in our society? in our city? in our commune? in our family? There may be natural limits in even this last, narrowest, category.) And where the value of choice is not at stake, security doubtless is. (That security may not be achieved does not mean that it is not sought.)

There is a third sort of response that becomes appropriate once one accepts the claim that certain valuable relationships have exclusivity built into them. One might wonder whether it is possible to preserve what is good in these special intimacies without having to bear the costs of jealousy. My belief is that one may be able to limit the consequences of jealousy and the suffering it involves, but that one cannot eliminate the jealousy itself. Think here of two special contexts. One is that of a person who has a relationship of (something like) absolute openness with someone, and then becomes the patient of a psychoanalyst. Psychoanalysis too calls for absolute openness. But here the first relationship has not been straightforwardly replicated. The intimacy is confined to a special sphere, and in particular the rules prohibit a full sexual relationship. (This connects with two further complications: what happens to the analytic relationship if there *is* the possibility of physical intimacy? Among much else, the analysis of one's life then threatens to turn into one's life; the isolation of the relationship is broken down. Second, what if one tries to establish a second relationship of absolute openness simultaneous with a first one, but limiting its sphere so that what belongs to the first relationship does not get brought up in the second. This involves, I think, a too narrow notion of "what belongs to the first relationship" and a too optimistic view of the possibilities of circumscribing the influence and connections of what may be the central set of experiences in one's life.) Returning to the analyst-patient relationship, we should note first that it is very special (e.g., the openness is one-sided and of limited, if not fixed, duration): social expectations give it a special place, and it would be as wrong to confuse the intimacy of a patient with his or her analyst with the intimacy between lovers, as it would be to confuse the intimacy between lovers with the intimacy between parents and children—they are all, of course, connected, but to confuse them is perhaps to put oneself in the position of a patient; one's problem begins to appear clinical. Second, and most important in connection with our topic, the lover of a patient may always raise the questions: "What is missing?" "What is the analyst providing that I am not?" "Are there things that my lover can say to her analyst that she cannot say to me?" "Do we really share everything?" and so on. To imagine the elimination of jealousy is to imagine the elimination of the possibility of these questions, for these questions *are* jealousy. To have these doubts and worries is to be jealous. (Jealousy is not a sensation or headache, it is in its essence a set of thoughts and questions, doubts and fears.) And these questions cannot be eliminated. They are real questions. What we must do is first recognize their appropriateness and then see that they are not given undue weight. (Which is especially a danger when a relationship is colored by narcissistic fantasies of omnipotence.) To raise a question is not the same as to give a negative answer. And even where the possibility of a gap and a loss amounts to a real gap and loss, we must not confuse something with everything: that there is something between an analyst and his or her patient need not exclude the lover from everything, need not be the end of that special intimacy, which is outside the analysis.

A second context where one might want to test the exclusivity of absolute intimacy might be same-sex (or at any rate, nonsexual) friendships that remain different and apart from the intimacy of lovers who are otherwise absolutely open and share everything. Again there is the possibility of questions: "What is it that she can share with her friend but not with me?" "What is it that the friend offers that I cannot provide?" Again the questions are, I think, real and cannot be eliminated. But this need not destroy the relationship. The recognition of the questions in their appropriate place with their appropriate force may in fact help allow a friendship which is not shared to strengthen a relationship that depends on everything being shared. This paradoxical strengthening would come about because a need that might otherwise go unmet gets satisfied outside the relationship it might otherwise disrupt. We may demand too much of ourselves and others if we demand that they or we not be jealous, where this means that we do not raise or contemplate the doubts and questions of jealousy.

Green Eyes and Evil Eyes

Othello is jealous, Iago is envious.[5] Jealousy is typically over what one possesses and fears to lose, while envy may be over something one has never possessed and may never hope to possess. Going with this, the focus of envy is typically the other person, rather than the particular thing or quality one is envious over (a thing that may not in itself even be desirable to the envier, whatever its perceived value to the present possessor). In jealousy there is always a rival, believed or imagined, but the focus of concern is the valued object. For jealousy, but not envy, the other must be seen as a genuine rival for the object: their gain is one's loss (the evil eye, on the other hand, can be directed at anyone who prospers; it needn't be at the envier's expense). Similarly, Schadenfreude (joy at another's suffering), the inverse of envy (pain at another's success), may be impartial in that the other's loss need not involve a material advantage to the person who takes pleasure at it. This (apparent) aloofness of envy may make it more intractable.

There are alternative ways of mapping out the terrain covered by jealousy and envy, but certain features of each may be illuminatingly brought together in the following way. Jealousy is typically over people, while envy extends to things and qualities. If we restrict jealousy to relations with people, the place of the desire to be desired and for affection comes into sharper focus. At the center of jealousy is fear, specifically fear of loss.

What is special about the fear of loss that constitutes jealousy is connected with what is special about people: while one could lose possession of a thing, one could not lose its affection—it has no affection to give or to be taken away. Things do not respond to our feelings. People do. And when they do, we may fear for their loss, not just as things (as objects of desire and love), but as feeling agents (as sources of desire and love). At the center of jealousy is insecurity, fear of loss, specifically fear of alienation of affections. At the center of jealousy is the desire to be desired or for affection, the need to be loved.

Envy extends to things and qualities. Because of this, we can see that its real focus is the rival (though, again, the rivalry need not be real—the quality one is envious of may even be nontransferable). In a way, the thing or quality drops out (as I have mentioned, in some cases the object need not be valued by the envier—he need not believe the thing or office or whatever would give him pleasure if he had it—he need only believe it valuable to the person who possesses it, either because he values it himself or because it increases his status or value in the eyes of others). Once the central relation is seen to be between the envier and the person envied (even if the envy is *over* a thing or quality), the alternatives of malicious and admiring envy become clear.[6] In the case of malicious envy, one wants to lower the other (to one's own level or below); in the case of admiring envy, one wishes to raise oneself (to become like the other). (More on this later.) I shall want to suggest that these two types of envy may have different instinctual sources and developmental paths; and that, as a result, malicious envy, unlike admiring envy and unlike jealousy, may not have appropriate objects, that is, the explanation for its occurrence may always involve pathology.

How are we to describe the emotional state of the third party in situations where there are two lovers, one of whom is jealous over the other and fears the encroachments of the third party, while the third party has not made any advances but certainly desires to supplant the jealous lover? (I leave open the feelings of the middle party.) Are we to say he is envious or that he is jealous? Ordinary usage would, I think, allow us to go either way. I think it better to say he is envious (in an "admiring" way—he wishes to have what the other now possesses), though here it is clear that the thing (person) does *not* drop out (and this may be distinctive of "admiring" envy).[7] If we were to say he is "jealous," we would lose the connection with belief in an established relationship that is necessary to "fear of loss." Jealousy is over what one possesses (or has possessed) and fears to lose.

Because of the differences between envy and jealousy, one would expect them to respond differently to different stratagems of elimination. Insofar as jealousy is over a *particular*, overcoming scarcity and inequality would leave it untouched, in this way at least: at the center of jealousy is fear of loss, and so long as sharing is felt as loss and exclusivity of relationship is demanded, one is liable to jealousy. One may of course be less likely to feel jealous if there is no scarcity of goods, so that others have alternatives to trying to seize your (particular) good. But the point of the commune movement (in relation to jealousy) will be better understood if it is seen less as an effort to overcome scarcity than as an effort to change attitudes toward sharing: so possession need not be exclusive possession.

Envy has to do with making people secure in their possessions (if at all) in another way. At the center of envy is invidious comparison, the perception of another as better off. It can be over things or even nondetachable (and so nontransferable) qualities: someone can envy another's good looks or intelligence, even though there is no way in which if they were taken away they could be given to the envier. And even where "sharing" is possible, it may not help. Indeed, the magnanimity of the wealthy can be met with ingratitude or accentuated envy: the magnanimity merely magnifying the perceived difference in position. And, again, overcoming scarcity is not sufficient. Everyone having enough is not enough; it doesn't obviate the possibility of relative deprivation, the resentment of the well-off toward the better-off. But, if everyone has the same (perhaps even if too little), invidious comparison of course becomes impossible. The important element is equality. So achieving equality of distribution (or redistribution) should overcome envy, should leave it no place. But this depends on what the sources of envy are, on the relation of objective equality to perceived equality, on whether equality is achieved through overcoming scarcity or by leveling, on what differences are possible objects of envy (are all of them open to equalization? are no goods unique and unopen to redistribution?), and whether the difference between "justified" and "unjustified" inequality also makes a difference to the possibility of envy.

Let us pick up a few of these threads and see where they lead. That magnanimity may be met by ingratitude does not mean magnanimity is futile. It does not follow, as some would have it, that because magnanimous foreign aid might accentuate envy one should not give such aid: people may be ungrateful, but the point of giving aid is not to win their gratitude, but to help solve their problems (at least if aid is given out of magnanimity). If people raise ungrateful children, would it follow that there had been no reason for raising them (were they brought up precisely to be sources of gratitude)?

That envy may be one reason for demanding equality does not mean that demands for equality are unjustified. For one thing, "envy" may be justified. (Where it is, it amounts to "resentment," which is a moral emotion in the sense that a moral principle must be cited in its explanation [Rawls 1971, 479–85, 533].) For another thing, there are other reasons, most importantly reasons of justice, for demanding (certain forms of) equality. But from another perspective the real issue is whether envy must form an inevitable obstacle to attempts to achieve justice and/or equality.

One point in the conceptual situation is I think clear: people may feel envy over some difference (some inequality) even if the difference is both justified and ineradicable. Given this, the most pressing questions become why one would feel envy (what are its sources), and whether this allows any remedy. And if it does not allow any remedy, what place should be given to envy in one's personal and political calculations?

Helmut Schoeck (1970), in a substantial recent study of envy, maintains that envy is to be expected always and everywhere. He points to the important influence of fear of envy as an instrument of social control, helping to make civilized life possible. The fear helps lead to modesty and the avoidance of ostentation, and produces concern for the opinion of others when one is tempted to deviate from social norms in pursuit of pleasure or material gain. He also suggests, very interestingly, that Americans are not afraid enough of envy. (This is evidenced in many advertisements that praise a product in virtue of the fact that it is liable to produce envy in friends and neighbors.) But (and this is Schoeck's main theme) it is also possible to fear envy too much. The ethnographic data reveal countless societies where every failure is viewed as due to the operation of the evil eye, and every success as magically achieved by holding others back. If a society is too afraid of envy it can have a terribly inhibiting effect. Superstition can hold back innovation and "progress."

If fear of envy can hold back progress, so (thinks Schoeck) can the desire for equality. Indeed, Schoeck (following a long tradition) tends to treat socialism and the desire for equality as always motivated by envy. He fails sufficiently to distinguish "envy" from resentment and indignation based on a sense of justice (or rather, he fails to give the sense of justice sufficient scope). And he moves too swiftly from the (alleged) ineliminability of envy to antiegalitarianism and antisocialism (or the dismissal of them as utopian). Socialism, unlike envy, calls for the redistribution of goods, not their destruction. Parodies of socialism often achieve their effects by using destruction, leveling, wherever redistribution is not possible. (There are serious questions about which things must and can be equalized and how. But the parodies tend to beg these questions by assuming everything must, in some crude manner, be equalized.)[8] In considering whether it is possible to overcome envy, one must distinguish the effects of overcoming inequality and overcoming scarcity. Schoeck tends to assume that equality can be achieved only through leveling (dragging down the prominent and better off), and that overcoming scarcity depends on maintaining inequality (that growth depends on inequality). Hence he thinks efforts to overcome envy are futile. The best we can do, on this view, is to go for growth. Growth in itself does not, of course, overcome envy (distribution of goods matters more than their quantity). Nonetheless, if one could overcome scarcity, it might be possible (contrary to Schoeck) to achieve equality without leveling. Admittedly, this may not be possible in every sphere (most interestingly, there are the problems of "positional goods" [Hirsch 1976]), but the evidence is not all in on the claim that inequality is necessary for growth. (Do we really need monopolies, bigness, everywhere? Is it always more productive and efficient?) Whatever the conditions for overcoming scarcity (do they include inequality?), and whatever its consequences (do they allow for overcoming inequality?), Schoeck counsels that we must in any case accept envy because it is in any case ineliminable.

He offers two sorts of argument. The first is that envy (fear of envy) is a condition of civilized life. But I fail to see why the socially valuable functions of "envy" ("fear of envy") could not be served by the more moral emotions (e.g., resentment and indignation) alone. Criticism of deviance should be limited to those cases where it can be justified on principle. What Schoeck (following Raiga) calls "legitimate indignation-envy" should be enough for the purposes of social control. The argument this leaves for thinking envy ineliminable is that envy is a given feature of human nature, in effect, an instinct.

But is this an argument at all, and if it is, what sort of argument is it? What follows if, as Schoeck insists, envy is an instinct, a basic (and therefore ineliminable) feature of human nature? Even if one were to overcome inequality, it is claimed, the envious person (all of us, in different degrees) would perceive reality in distorted fashion: he would see inequality where there is none and so find new grounds for envy. Certainly very small, seemingly insignificant, differences can be the object of envy. (Freud speaks of the "narcissism of minor differences" [1918a, SE 11: 199; 1921c, SE 18: 101–3; 1930a, SE 21: 114–15].) Can any (all?) differences be an object of envy? And even where a category may be susceptible of envy, if differences are eliminated, will people (all? many? some?) still distortedly perceive inequalities and so experience envy?

Presumably, anything may be an object of envy if anything can matter. Some things matter for everybody. Hence sexuality and the erotic provide a central arena for envy (as well as jealousy). What other things matter depends mainly on one's society or group. And perhaps anything can achieve sufficient (symbolic) importance to sustain envy. But this does not make it inevitable (1) that the things that matter cannot be distributed equally; or (2) that only leveling can produce equality; or (3) that even if equality is achieved in a sphere, some will perceive differences; or (4) that all valuable differences will inevitably produce envy rather than themselves being valued.

Much depends on whether envy must be viewed as a basic motive or instinct that will inevitably find an object, whatever the social arrangements (whatever society values and no matter how it is distributed). Schoeck gives us no good reason to believe it is, though he repeatedly makes the claim. There is evidence to suggest that "fear of envy" occurs in every society, but there is some distance from this to the claim that envy itself occurs (and must inevitably continue to occur) in every individual.[9] What is really needed is a psychogenetic account of envy. The best we have so far, that I am aware of, is the work of Melanie Klein (1975 [1957]; see also Joffe 1969) on destructive impulses and "spoiling" and some suggestions in Max

Scheler (1972) about a tie to impotence and a delusion of causal connection. Scheler writes:

> "Envy," as the term is understood in everyday usage, is due to a feeling of impotence which we experience when another person owns a good we covet. But this tension between desire and nonfulfillment does not lead to envy until it flares up into hatred against the owner, until the latter is falsely considered to be the *cause* of our privation. Our factual inability to acquire a good is wrongly interpreted as a positive action *against* our desire—a delusion which diminishes the original tension. Both the experience of impotence and the causal delusion are essential preconditions of true envy. (52)

So envy may begin to make more sense if we see that it is tied by an unconscious causal belief to felt impotence (so the other's possession of a good is, after all, seen as at our expense). What happens if we make that belief conscious? It is one of the lessons of Marx that the belief turns out often, surprisingly often, to be true. When that is the case, envy at inequality comes closer to being indignation at injustice.

To sort out the proportions of justified to unjustified "envy" in a given situation, one would need a theory of justice. John Rawls discusses envy in the context of his theory of justice (530–41). If someone would be made envious as a result of some advantage being given to someone else, even though the advantage is thoroughly just and justified (according to Rawls's principles of justice: even the worst off would be better off for the advantage being bestowed and none would be worse off), the envy should carry no moral weight against the arrangement. Rawls recognizes, however, that even where envy presents no moral problem, it may present a psychological, social, and political one. How big a problem, and how often, depends again on envy's sources (would it be a wild aberration in a just society, or rather something only to be expected no matter how we arrange our society?), and one feels again the need for a psychogenetic account of envy. What I want to emphasize here is that Schoeck's discussion of envy does not provide such an account, and moreover is dissociated from any explicit theory of justice, indeed, it is tied to a skepticism about the possibility of distinguishing illegitimate from legitimate inequalities, and so legitimate resentment from illegitimate envy.[10] While the latter must be morally discounted, it is a mistake to conflate legitimate resentment with illegitimate envy and then to assume that egalitarianism and socialism must be associated with motives of envy rather than principles of justice. A conservative antipathy to egalitarianism and socialism cannot be properly founded on a (proper) contempt for motives of envy. Even if one must ignore envy to achieve "progress," one must be careful not to ignore legitimate grievances and resentment in the process.

It should also be noted that the desire that others not have something thought valuable (by them) may be less an attack on the possessors (either malicious or based on a sense of justice) than on the thought that it is valuable. There is more to the moral psychology of negative desires than just envy and resentment. (The "desire that another not have" may nonetheless play a role in the analysis of envy comparable to the role of the "desire to be desired" in the analysis of jealousy.) A Savonarola may claim to be neither envious nor resentful, but merely to want others not to have or do certain things because it is *bad* for them to have or do them. (This is the standard claim of paternalists—and parents.) To properly judge such denials of envy, one would need, in addition to a theory of justice, a theory of the good.[11]

What is left of instinctual envy when we distinguish between justifiable and unjustifiable inequalities and between envy and resentment? Erik Erikson has claimed that people worry about *minimizing* envy when they should worry about *optimizing* it.[12] He argues that a certain amount of envy is developmentally necessary as part of the formation of an ego ideal. I would argue that one has to be careful here to distinguish between *admiring* envy (which may be necessary for an ego ideal, and so beneficial) and *malicious* envy (which the world could do just as well without). When someone *says* "I envy you," they can usually be taken to be saying: "I wish I were like you" or "I wish I had what you have" (admiring envy). But they would usually not be taken to be saying: "I wish you did not have what you do" (malicious envy), that is usually an unspoken thought. While both these types of thought may constitute envy, they are different, as different as the desire to be like and the desire to destroy (or the desire to have and the desire that the other not have). There is a common element in admiring and malicious envy: a desire to overcome inequality, but the desire comes from different directions, admiring envy involving a desire to raise (the self), malicious envy involving a desire to level (the other). Do these disparate desires really have a common instinctual source? Is it really inconceivable that we might overcome the sources of malicious envy without doing damage to the necessary foundations of an ego ideal?

It is of course a further question whether there is in fact any way to get at the roots of malicious envy. We need to know more about the sources and character of the Kleinian desire to destroy and spoil. Without pursuing that further here, we can ask whether there may not be a subtle, hidden, connection between the envy involved in forming an ego ideal and the malicious envy we should (otherwise) be able to do without. (So the desire to raise oneself might commit one to lowering the other.) The connection I have in mind is via the "delusional" (unconscious/magical/and, as I have said, perhaps sometimes, true) causal belief discussed by Scheler and the notion of self-esteem. Envy and jealousy come closer together if one always adds the assumption that life is seen as a zero-sum game, so rivalry is always experienced as real; the other's having something (*now* in the case of envy, *in the future* in the case of jealousy) is then always seen as at your expense. On this view, the otherwise unmotivated or maliciously envious desire that another be deprived becomes a part of a genuine competition or rivalry, an intelligible desire to enhance one's own position. Robert Nozick (1974) argues that even where a situation is not overtly competitive (someone else's gain is not your loss), the conditions of self-esteem are such as to give envy a proper foothold, and to preclude achieving equality as a way out (239–46).[13] His central notion is that self-esteem is *comparative*. Along any given dimension, a person will judge himself in comparison with others. It does not matter that someone's doing better than you is not at your expense: even though your absolute position on a scale is unchanged, the scale is extended by their performance and your relative position on the scale looks worse, so you must think less well of yourself. Moreover, the dimensions themselves are comparative:

> People generally judge themselves by how they fall along the most important dimensions in which they *differ* from others. People do not gain self-esteem from their common human capacities by comparing themselves to animals who lack them. ("I'm pretty good; I have an opposable thumb and can speak some language.") . . . When everyone, or almost everyone, has some thing or attribute, it does not function as a basis for self-esteem. Self-esteem is based on *differentiating characteristics*; that's why it's *self*-esteem. (Nozick 1974, 243)

It remains unclear to me why self-esteem must depend on being *better* than others (on some dimensions if not all). Certainly we only take *pride* in special accomplishments, but why shouldn't normal self-esteem rest on normal capacities and achievements? Granted we do not take pride in universal powers (e.g., speaking), but one need not be *outstanding* in a field to gain self-esteem from achievement. A person may be a good cook while recognizing that many others are also good cooks. It is not essential to self-esteem that there be none better. (It may be essential that there be some who are worse or at least some who do not engage in the activity at all. This seems to be the truth in the comparative point, though the comparison class may include one's past self.) Even where a situation is not directly competitive, Nozick argues it remains comparative (one must use a scale to judge oneself and so another's achievement on the scale can produce an indirect loss) for purposes of self-esteem. But why should self-esteem be destroyed by someone being better? I must count myself as *one*, but why more than one? The place of envy cannot be secured by the need for self-esteem; the conditions of self-esteem are not so grandiose. If envy is not an "instinct" (whatever that entails), there is no argument for it.

Jealousy and Rights

Jealousy is not a merely bourgeois passion, it is not confined to societies with capitalistic or monogamous social arrangements. (That it is not confined to a particular class within such societies goes without saying.) Every society that prefers and sanctions certain social arrangements over others, which is to say every *society*, will have room for jealousy: it serves to reinforce and protect the preferred arrangements (in particular, the preferred distributions of sexual affection). As Kingsley Davis (1936) has put it:

> Where exclusive possession of an individual's entire love is customary, jealousy will demand that exclusiveness. Where love is divided it will be divided according to some scheme, and jealousy will reinforce the division . . . Whether as the obverse side of the desire to obtain sexual property by legitimate competition or as the anger at having rightful property trespassed upon, jealousy would seem to bolster the institutions where it is found. If these institutions are of an opposite character to monogamy, it bolsters them nonetheless . . . Jealousy does not respond inherently to any particular situation; it responds to all those situations, no matter how diverse, which signify a violation of accustomed sexual rights. (400, 403)

While social arrangements may vary, whatever the social arrangements, jealousy serves to reinforce them.

It might seem that this functional view of jealousy nonetheless leaves it bourgeois in another sense, for it seems to depend on a notion of possession and property in personal relations. And it could be argued that such a notion is illegitimate, that property rights have no place in the sphere of human relationships.

The argument might have it that property rights are applicable only to things and that therefore, insofar as jealousy involves treating people as though they were things (as though we could have property rights in them), it will always be an inappropriate emotion, an emotion we should strive (through correcting the understanding, etc.) to eliminate from our personal relationships. The argument might continue that jealousy must be futile, for the right that is asserted is a right to love (a right to be loved), and such a right (even if it were intelligible—supposing it did not involve the illegitimate assertion of property rights in people) would be unenforceable. Love is not a matter of will; it cannot be given on demand. We cannot decide to love someone because we think they have a right to be loved by us; we cannot make ourselves love someone because we owe it to them. Moreover (and this is one of the many ironies of the human condition), even if love could be given on demand, that would not satisfy the claims of jealousy, for the love that is desired is usually a freely given love—a response to a desire (backed by a need) rather than a demand (backed by a threat).[14] A love that was coerced (presuming something that was coerced could still be regarded as love at all) would be the wrong sort of love. The love that was given in response to the demands of jealousy therefore could never really satisfy those demands. Thus property rights are applicable only to things, while jealousy is typically over people, specifically because of their power (in contrast with things) to respond (and fail to respond) to our desires: the response that can be given to a claim of right will never really satisfy the desire that lies behind that claim.

These are, I think, powerful arguments. They reveal part of what is troubling about the place of jealousy in human life. But I think that they also distort the situation somewhat and that they go too far; they might make it seem as though jealousy were simply a matter of conceptual confusion, as though it should have *no* place in human relationships because the notion of property rights should have no place in human relationships. I would want to argue against these (I think) misleading claims from several directions.

We can start by asking whether the existence of jealousy must depend on belief in a right. I am inclined to think that jealousy may not depend on a notion of rights at all (even a notion distinguished from and broader than that of property rights). At the heart of jealousy is fear of loss (specifically, fear of alienation of affections), and to fear loss all that is required is the existence or the believed existence of a state of affairs or relationship, and a desire that it continue. To be jealous over someone, you must believe that they love you (or have loved you), but you need not believe that you have a *right* to that love; you need not think yourself wonderful and so deserving of love (indeed, the fear of loss is typically tied to fears about one's lovableness), nor need you believe that the other has an obligation built up over time. Having detached jealousy from rights in this way, however, one is left with the question of how to distinguish "jealousy" from mere "disappointment" (or "grief" or simple "unhappiness")—clearly the contrast cannot be based on the presence of a claim of right in one case and its absence in the other. It may be based, however, on the fact that disappointment is tied to resignation while jealousy is tied to hope. That is, disappointment may be more a response to loss and jealousy to *fear* of loss (where one is not yet resigned to the loss, even if the fear is based on its apparently already having taken place). Moreover, jealousy, unlike disappointment, is always a three-party emotion (involving rivalry, hatred of the rival, etc.), that is, the loss suffered or feared is always experienced as a loss *to* someone else. This last point suggests a further possible contrast: jealousy may always involve anger, either at the rival or at the beloved, while mere disappointment may not involve any rival or any form of anger or resentment toward anyone.[15] Spinoza builds "hatred" toward the beloved and (via envy) toward the rival into his definition of jealousy. If a man of *extremely* low self-esteem thinks the woman who is involved with him is about to leave him for another, but feels no animosity toward his rival, and (aside from his fear of loss) feels only gratitude toward the woman for having given him as much attention as she has (for he believes she is in any case too good for him), we may be inclined to say his state of mind is not jealousy. The absence of anger at the woman or rival might make the man's fear of loss seem more like mere disappointment or apprehension. But there is a complication: if anger is neccssary to jealousy, it might seem that belief in a right is also. For what is the anger about? Betrayal? An underlying claim of right would give sense to feelings of betrayal and abandonment as grounds of anger. But while something like anger may be essential, irrational anger or anger at loss or deprivation (more like instinctual aggression or a response to frustration than a response to betrayal or violation of rights) may be enough. In the case described, one suspects the anger has been redirected against the self. (Is the man's state indifferent to circumstances, or does it deepen into depression with the impending loss? One wonders how much of even the initial "low self-esteem" is really anger turned inward.) Freud, in describing the components of jealousy, speaks of the "narcissistic wound" and "self-criticism" as well as loss and enmity against the rival. And perhaps anger (even anger turned inward) is not essential. Perhaps the mere existence of a rival may be enough to make the man's fear of loss (i.e., fear of alienation of affections) amount to jealousy. There may even be other ways to mark the contrast between disappointment and jealousy (but note that the difference is not to be looked for in raw feelings or blind sensations, but in the constituent thoughts involved), and in the end I think jealousy can stand independent of claims of right. One need not think one has a right to someone else's love in order to fear its loss: all that is necessary is that one believe one has the love to begin with. What claims may legitimately be made on the basis of jealousy, on the basis of fear of loss, is a separate and further question. For jealousy to exist all one needs is vulnerability, and we all have that in sufficient abundance.

What claims can one person make on the feelings of another? People are not property (indeed, part of the reason we value them is that *unlike* things they can respond to our desires with desires of their own), but that does not mean that claims of right are out of place in human relationships. What has to be said is that it is not a question of *property* rights (in the sense of ownership that allows for transfer, disposal, etc.), but it may be a question of rights nonetheless: there is room for obligations and legitimate expectations, and perhaps even for enforceable and (sometimes) waivable claims, in human relationships and human feelings. Think for a moment of an established couple, a man and a woman who have been together for twenty years. Now suppose that one of the partners suffers a physical calamity, suppose, for example, that the woman loses a limb (or has a mastectomy). The calamity is a shared calamity. The man cannot simply walk off saying: "Oh well, too bad for you. When I loved you, you were different. Thus altered, I no longer find you attractive. I wish you lots of luck in finding someone who is not put off by your new deformity and incapacities." What is most interesting, though much else could be said, is to consider what this attitude would reveal about his prior attitude (which he describes as love: "When I loved you . . ."): it would give the lie to his love, it would reveal it to have been something else (or a different kind of love). Who or what had he putatively "loved"? If it was that particular woman, are we to allow that the (admittedly drastic) change in her condition is a change not just *in* her but *of* her, that she is a different person? To suppose one could lose one's identity that easily would be to suppose that she was a bundle of properties, that the object of his love was not that particular woman but a set of qualities that she happened to instantiate. One must distinguish between two types of love: love of a particular person and love of a set of qualities.[16] Qualities are fungible in a way that people are not. We are more than the sum of our present attributes. (Which need not mean we are some hidden mysterious substance, or some unreachable and empty center of consciousness.) One sort of love would allow and expect the beloved to change in all sorts of ways. And other, unexpected changes would leave that love unchanged. ("Love is not love which alters when it alteration finds" [Shakespeare, Sonnet 116].) The other sort of love, being attached to a specific set of qualities, can move readily from person to person depending only on who best instantiates those qualities at a particular point in time. The two contrasting types of object may also be associated with different aims. When one is looking for a set of qualities, it is usually one's own needs that make one look and that set the criteria for satisfaction. And so far as those needs do not look to history, the past and future of the loved object are not tied up with the character of the present love. These features may all be typical of erotic desire and attachment. The other sort of object is tied to a more romantic conception of love, where the aim of love is the good of the beloved, and the love is characterized more by consideration and concern than desire (or rather, the desires involved tend to be selfless).

In the happiest situations, of course, all these features may come together. Part of what is disturbing in the case we were considering is that they there fall apart. What looked like one sort of love comes to look like another sort: it appears another woman would have done just as well all along, because it now appears (given the calamity) that another would do better. So the attachment looks like it was more an attachment to a set of physical properties than to a person. People are embodied and their physical properties matter, but there is more to them than that (this is obvious when we think of *ourselves* and how we wish to be thought of when we are an object of love for someone else). A proper understanding of the case would require a closer consideration of what properties are essential to what, and of precisely what changes with what. But for our immediate purpose, the main thing to note is that a man who has lived with and (putatively) loved a woman for twenty years owes her something. Even if their love was originally grounded in physical attraction, involvement over twenty years builds up a commitment. Their past has weight. It creates obligations. She has rights (though it would certainly be misleading to think of them as "property" rights). There remains the question of what she has rights to. Certainly she has rights to care, consideration, and concern. And presumably all of these rights would be granted by any decent man. But if they were not granted willingly, could they be enforced? (Certainly the state could require that support be provided, but can it require that the support be provided out of "concern"?) At any rate, a man who failed to feel concern in these circumstances would be properly criticizable for that failure. What of a right to "love"? What exactly the woman has a right to expect, beyond care, consideration, and concern, will depend on how far we (and she) believe the will extends in love. One has, I think, to distinguish its different aspects. Action (or at least outward behavior) is generally readily under control. Desire, while perhaps not directly susceptible to the will, may have complex relations to belief and principle. And affection may be even more complex (being bound to both desires for one's own good and desires for the good of the other). Perhaps the notion of a "right" does get overstretched here, but that may be because it carries with it a whole legalistic apparatus. Something goes awry when we use principles (and a language) designed to govern relations between strangers to govern relations between friends or lovers; the relations those principles get used to enforce may be defeated by their application.[17] The law reflects the irony of the human condition, where the love that jealousy demands may never be truly satisfactory because the love that is desired is a freely given love, not a love given in response to a demand. (This condition is not, however, universal. For some, the motivation of a response, whether selfish, selfless, or merely self-protective, may be irrelevant.) But what we have seen is that, whatever the problems with enforcement and so whatever the awkwardnesses with the notion of a "right to love," the character of love may require certain attitudes toward change. To be true to one's love (for one's love to have been true) it cannot "alter when it alteration finds." The existence of a certain sort of relationship creates what may be thought of as rights.

There is room for claims of right in personal relations. Sorting out the limits and types of claims that are appropriate is a complex process, but at least we have delineated some of the main dimensions that must be considered. The rights and claims that may be appropriate depend on love's *sources* (are they in the individual's control, a matter of his choice or choices?), its *objects* (particular/set of characteristics), and its *aims* (own good/good of the other).[18] And a full anatomy of jealousy would depend on a full anatomy of love. Jealousy may arise in relation to both types of love object. One can be jealous over a person thought of as a particular, where one's love is characterized by concern and affection. So far as the person is a particular and special, one may be more liable to fear loss or sharing and so more liable to feel jealous. But so far as one's love is truly unselfish and aimed exclusively at the good of the beloved (whatever you may believe about your essential role in bringing about that good), you may be less liable to feel jealous (and while the beloved remains irreplaceable for you, you may not regard yourself as irreplaceable for him or her). One can also be jealous over a person thought of as a set of qualities, where one's love is characterized by desire (in particular for satisfaction of one's own needs). Here one has to balance the countervailing tendencies involved in thinking of a person as a set of qualities. So far as this makes people fungible, one may be less liable to fear loss and be jealous. So far as it makes people more like things, one may be more liable to regard them as property and so more jealous of your possession and rights—though with this your jealousy may be liable to become perverse.

We have already seen in our discussion of the psychogenesis of jealousy that it may begin with our first possession. But the notion of "possession" should not mislead us into thinking that what is at stake is property rights. What is at stake is the self, is an individual's identity. The infant goes through a transitional period in which it recognizes a teddy bear, or whatever, as an independent object, but it does not want the object to change. Any change in the object is experienced as an assault on the self. I think this sort of attitude toward this first possession, this transitional object, is an attitude that begins with people (in particular the mother at the point where she is not distinguished from the self), gets extended to other things, and then comes back again to people. It makes sharing difficult without a sensed loss of self. So I would reiterate my claim that in the development of jealousy what is happening is not that we treat people as though they were things, but that we treat things as though they were people (ultimately, as parts of ourselves). This sort of identification is misunderstood if it is assimilated to simple "ownership."

Pathology

It is possible to feel the wrong thing or the wrong amount (including too little, as in the case of Camus's *Stranger*, who fails to feel grief at the death of his mother). Othello's jealousy, if it is pathological at all, is pathological in its intensity (in what it leads him to do). His belief about his beloved is false, but that does not (in itself) make it pathological. Whether a false (or even true) belief is pathological depends, most importantly, on the explanation for its being held. Othello's belief is imposed on him by Iago's manipulation of the circumstances; it is at least based on evidence. (What makes Othello susceptible to such manipulation and evidence is a further and more difficult question.) King Leontes's belief in *The Winter's Tale* is pathological on its face: it is not based on evidence. Of course, once one is jealous, anything and everything can be turned into evidence (the exquisite self-confirming power of paranoia).

Othello's jealousy is ill founded, but unlike King Leontes's jealousy, it is not unfounded. There is a difference between having a grounded (though false) belief and having an ungrounded belief (which may, in the end, turn out true). To believe without grounds, to believe in the face of contrary evidence, is irrational. Ungrounded beliefs, unfounded doubts, are characteristic of one form of pathology in jealousy. Why one would delude oneself against one's better interests, why one would seem to want to believe what one should hope is false, requires explanation. Freud, of course, makes some helpful suggestions.[19]

Freud suggests projected jealousy will typically be a defense against acknowledgment of one's own temptations to unfaithfulness, including (in true delusional cases) repressed homosexual desires. Temptations to unfaithfulness are inevitable. Why should the forces and mechanisms that lead one to love one person automatically cease to operate once one has formed an initial attachment? Indeed, adult attachments always have the infantile prototype of attachment to the parents (especially to the mother's breast) to fall back on ("The finding of an object is in fact a refinding of it" [Freud 1905d, SE 7: 222]), and so an "initial attachment" is really always the continuation of a process begun long before. Once one recognizes that temptations to unfaithfulness are inevitable, it becomes easier to see that the most unfounded jealousy will always have a level of reality to latch on to. A person may come to neglect his own temptations and focus exclusively on his partner's, picking up every sign the unconscious of the other betrays and adding on projected temptations of his own. Why one should succumb to unfounded jealousy will require separate explanation in each case. Another general thought to bear in mind is a remark Freud makes concerning a patient's obsessive-compulsive doubts about a range of topics (including his would-be fiancé's feelings): "A man who doubts his own love may, or rather *must*, doubt every lesser thing" (1909d, SE 10: 241).

Another source of doubt can be found in a certain type of object-choice:

it seems very evident that another person's narcissism has a great attraction for those who have renounced part of their own narcissism and are in search of object-love. The charm of a child lies to a great extent in his narcissism, his self-contentment and inaccessibility, just as does the charm of certain animals which seem not to concern themselves about us, such as cats and the large beasts of prey . . . The great charm of narcissistic women has, however, its reverse side; a large part of the lover's dissatisfaction, of his doubts of the woman's love, of his complaints of her enigmatic nature, has its root in this incongruity between the types of object-choice. (Freud 1914c, SE 14: 89)

A person who chooses to love another who loves only himself or herself has set up a situation which by its nature accentuates the liability to jealousy.

Irrational, unfounded jealousy should perhaps be considered in relation to cases where a person *urges* his partner to have an affair with another (which in turn should perhaps be considered in relation to cases of "making someone jealous," which we will come to in the next section). Where a person urges his partner to have an affair (rather than imagining that the partner is having one and resenting that imagined fact), a number of different things may be going on. First, there is an obvious denial of jealousy.

Second, the value of the partner may be increased when desired by or desirable to others. (Consider a husband's display of his wife, his "treasure," at a party—when does fear of envy and loss set in?) Third, it may be a route to a surrogate homosexual affair. (It is worth remembering that identification is a complex process. It may make a loved object seem a part of us and so make the fear of loss more acute. It may also, in the form of projective identification, make it possible for us to act through the loved object. Moreover, it is a process that can take place with rivals as well as loved objects. Indeed, the normal process of overcoming Oedipal jealousy and rivalry, the incest taboo, is supposed to involve identification with the rival.) And fourth, it may make the person feel freer to have an affair himself.

Irrational and obsessive beliefs, while one form of pathological jealousy, are only one form. We have seen that jealousy is sometimes dismissed as the misplaced application and assertion of property rights. (People are not things; they cannot be owned. Affection is not subject to the will; it cannot be owed.) While I want to say that jealousy *can* be normal, that it need not always involve mistaking people for things, it must here be recognized that there are cases of jealousy that do involve the misplaced assertion of property rights. Consider the swaggering bully who goes into a jealous rage if someone so much as looks covetously at his woman, while he regards the woman herself as useless and treats her as trash. While such a man may fear loss, the loss he fears is not of affection. What he values in the relationship is his domination or appearance of domination. Any threat to that is a threat to his "manhood." The fear of loss involved may be enough to make this count as a case of jealousy, but I want to suggest that it is a perverted and derivative case, that is, a pathological case. The central case involves fear of loss where the thing specifically feared is alienation of affections.

That we should fear the loss of valued goods when they appear threatened may not require special explanation. It is only to be expected that if the affection we believe to be ours is given to another we will fear a more permanent alienation of affections. It does require explanation, however, why the giving of affection to another should so often appear to us as at our expense. That depends, I believe, on certain assumptions we shall turn to shortly. It also requires explanation why jealousy (understood as fear of loss, specifically alienation of affections) should be so prone to pathological forms and exaggerations in intensity. I think that at least part of the explanation may be found in the fact that the fear of loss is tied to a deeper underlying fear: fear of annihilation.

The loss of an object is often felt as loss of self. This should not surprise us given what I have said about the development of our relations to loved possessions and people. Those relations are at points better understood in terms of identification than ownership. We are prone to pathological forms of jealousy because we are prone to identification with valued things and people—we are inclined to regard them as parts of our selves. The loss of a valued object may provide objective danger (the character of the danger depending on what was valuable about the object). The loss of affection from a loved person, in addition to the obvious gap it opens in one's life, may endanger one's identity. Spelling out this danger would involve going more deeply into processes of identification and identity formation. But here we can note the simple fact that if others do not love us, we may disintegrate. Who we are depends (in straightforward ways) on how others respond to us; and who we think we are may depend (in deeper ways) on what we believe is within our control. The loss of an affection that we felt to be as reliably at our disposal as the movement of our limbs may make the whole world seem to go out of joint.

As a fuller understanding of jealousy would require a fuller understanding of love, of the need to be loved, and the need to be secure in love, so a fuller understanding of the possibilities for pathology would require a fuller understanding of processes of identification and identity formation (including the contrast between introjective and projective identification), of how we think about ourselves and our love objects, and of the underlying fear involved in jealousy. Throughout, I think it most helpful if we think of jealousy as essentially involving fear of loss; more specifically, fear of alienation of affections; and, more generally, fear of annihilation.

The Two-Faced Green-Ey'd Monster

Jealousy has two faces. One face is as a sign of love. If a person does not feel jealous, or is incapable of feeling jealous, we tend to suspect that they do not really care. There is even the phenomenon, a staple of situation comedies on television, of "making someone jealous," where the point is not so much to persuade oneself of someone else's feelings as to get *them* to recognize them. What typically happens is that a person, in love with a second, but unresponsive person, pretends to be in love with a third person (who does, in fact, for the sake of the pretense, respond). The upshot is supposed to be that the second person becomes jealous and, seeing their jealousy, realizes that they loved the first person all along. Now this assumes that jealousy is easier to recognize than love (in ourselves). It assumes also that jealousy is a sign of caring. It is this second point that matters here, and as far as it goes, I think the point is made. But we must recognize that life is more complicated than the situation comedies would have it.

For one thing, it is highly questionable whether jealousy is easier to recognize than love in our own case. Jealousy is in fact a typical example of an object of self-deception and repression. In Freud's classic Oedipal cases (e.g., "The Rat Man" and "Little Hans"), jealousy is perhaps the archetypical object of repression. In those cases the love is acceptable enough, it is the jealousy that cannot be acknowledged. For another thing, pretense has an awkward way of slipping over into reality. The more plausible the third person in the "making someone jealous" stratagem is as a candidate for love (and so the more plausible the pretense), the more lively the possibility of real love becomes, and the more ambiguous becomes the pretense. And there is a further complication: suppose that someone is in fact made jealous, does it in fact follow that they must have cared all along? I think there are other possibilities. The jealousy may not be the sign of a love that has existed all along, but rather be attached to a new love that has sprung up in response to the desire of the third person. That is, the fact that the first person is desired by the third person may be enough to make him or her desirable to the second person. The jealousy means that the jealous person covets what is also coveted by another, but it may not have been the case that the object was valued independently of the third party's attitude. (A good test for this is whether the love persists after the third party has left the scene—in situation comedies the thirty minutes are usually up at this point, and the question is not raised.) Another possibility is that the jealousy is not a sign of love at all, neither old love nor new love, but simply a sign of selfishness. That is, the response might be less to the desire of the third party (producing recognition of the desirableness of the first, or simply making the first desirable) than to the (apparent) loss of the affection of the first. The jealous person, the person made jealous, may simply desire to be desired, not caring about the first person (the one who has done the maneuvering) except as a source of approbation (a desiring, not a desired object). (The test mentioned in connection with new but fleeting love won't discriminate between that and this form of selfishness.) Here however we should consider whether taking jealousy as a sign of selfishness (specifically, concern at not being desired rather than concern at the loss of a desired object) precludes or even contrasts with taking it as a sign of love. The answer here would have to depend on the place we give the desire to be desired in our account of the nature of love. That it must have some place seems to me certain.[20]

A full taxonomy of jealousy would require, as I have suggested, a corresponding taxonomy of love. Rather than pursue that here, let me raise another question: can jealousy strengthen a relationship? Certainly that is the point of the "making someone jealous" stratagem. And in the situation comedies, where the jealousy is taken as evidence of a prior (real but unrecognized) passion, precisely that happens. The central characters are united and strengthened in their love. But this depends, please note, on the special conditions in which the "making someone jealous" stratagem makes sense. The first person is an unrequited lover, not a person who has been involved with a second person and then becomes involved (for real) with a third person. In those, more typical, situations where the person is torn between (or at least tied to) two others, the jealousy of the second person gives no promise of strengthening the love of the first and second persons. In the situation comedies, the first person wants to make the second person jealous (and has always been ready to drop the third person). In most real-life situations, the first person wants to avoid the second person becoming jealous (typically through keeping him or her ignorant) and is not prepared to give up the third person. In the sitcoms the ground for jealousy vanishes with him or her and only the original love remains, strengthened because it was never really a conflicted love. In contrast with the special situation of "making someone jealous" and also with the typical conflicted situation, we have seen at least one special case (namely same-sex or nonsexual friendships in the context of an otherwise exclusive relationship) where jealousy may be appropriate and may persist without weakening a relationship. In that case, while the jealousy may not itself strengthen the relationship, it arises in response to features of the situation which in turn strengthen the relationship.

So far we can be sure that one face of jealousy is as a sign of love (though the *strength* of jealousy is more likely to be correlated with a person's degree of insecurity than the depth of their love; the overlap is perhaps marked by the degree of dependence involved in the love, the degree of desire rather than affection or selfish desires rather than selfless ones). Behind jealousy lies love. This side of jealousy is sometimes neglected, but it is extremely important (especially in relation to the question of the eliminability of jealousy). It reflects the fact that "jealousy" includes a positive evaluation of, or attachment or commitment to, the person (or thing or property) one is jealous over or about. One can be jealous only over something that is highly valued. This is reflected in one of the special senses of the word; as the *Oxford English Dictionary* (OED) points out, *jealous* can mean: "zealous or solicitous for the preservation or well-being of something possessed or esteemed; vigilant or careful in guarding; suspiciously careful or watchful." Someone who is "jealous of his time" values his time ("husbands it") and seeks to keep it in his control. The desire to keep implies that one already has (a contrast with envy), which brings us to the fear of loss and the second face of jealousy. Narrowing our focus again to interpersonal relations and love: jealousy can be a sign of lack of love.

Jealousy, in addition to involving an obvious lack of trust, may betray a deeper lack of love or, rather, lack of trust in love. That is, behind whatever personal insecurities (fear of loss, fear of not being lovable, etc.) that may surface in jealousy may lie (what I will call) a fixed-quantity view of love: the amount of love in the world, the amount in any individual, is limited. If we discover or believe that someone we love also loves someone else, that must mean that they love us less. The love for another is given at our expense. Life, or at least love, is a zero-sum game. This is the presumption of the jealous person, and it is a presumption we must now examine. It is one of the fault lines where relations and efforts at social reconstruction break.

The fixed-quantity view may seem immediately implausible once stated. In fact, most people are ready to reject it in their own case. That is, they can readily imagine being involved with one person, then meeting and becoming involved with a second person, and not caring any the less for the first person. The difficult thing, however, is to believe others capable of the same feat. There is a natural double standard (here not between men and women, but between self and other). It may have many roots, but the result is in any case the attribution of a differential capacity for love; and whatever the sources, the position is of course untenable.[21] Why should we believe ourselves capable of what we believe others incapable of, or why shouldn't we believe others capable of what we believe ourselves capable of? Certainly the fixed-quantity view must appear suspect insofar as it is a theory that seems plausible only in relation to others. But this does not settle matters. It could as well be true for all as false for all. What cannot be the case is that it be true for others and false for us (where the identity of "others" and "us" shifts with whoever is speaking).

If the fixed-quantity view is untenable, then *all* jealousy may seem pathological, even where the particular beliefs involved are true, for the background belief in a zero-sum aspect to love would seem a delusion. Can scarcity and exclusivity in the sphere of love be dismissed with the notion of quantity? I think exclusivity would have a place whatever we may think about the applicability of quantitative notions to love (a point we have seen in the discussion of eliminability), and in any event I do not think the notion of quantity can be so readily dismissed. I think there is something important and true captured in the fixed-quantity view of love, the view we are more ready to apply to others than ourselves. To bring it out, we should shift the emphasis from "zero-sums" to the notion of "limits." To make the shift, let us run down the path again: in one form at least, the fixed-quantity view is patently untenable, that is, if we hold that *we* can love two people without loving the first any less than before the growth of feeling toward the second, but deny that *others* can. Why should our capacity for love be any greater than that of others? But that is what must seem true if we hold, in our jealousy, that the love someone bears toward another must mean less love toward us, while we do not believe that in relation to ourselves. But before we, in our search for consistency, reject a fixed-quantity view of love for others as we reject it for ourselves—do we really reject such a view in our own case? Perhaps we believe we can love two people equally (with no loss of strength). But what of five? . . . of twenty? . . . of all mankind? What happens when one follows the Christian admonition and extends one's love to all? What can be the content of such a "love"? (See Freud 1921c, SE 18: 90–99, 134–35, 140–42; 1930a, SE 21, chap. 5.)

Clearly, there are limits. "Goodwill" may be inexhaustible, but there are features of love (at least the intimate, erotic love most associated with jealousy) that limit it (if not to one or two, at most to a relatively small number). There are material conditions of love. There may be things in the nature of love that allow of infinite extension, but there are also limiting parameters. One is time. Intimacy takes time, not just to grow, but to have the experiences the sharing of which is part of the body of love, of the lived experience. Shared experiences may be as mundane as going to the laundry together, but whatever their character, time is needed wherever love is to be built on intimacy. (Of course, it does not follow that because shared experience is a condition of intimacy, the more shared experience, the stronger the bond of love. Countless divorces go to the contrary.) Another limiting parameter is attention. One can devote only so much "loving care" at any given moment. (The Oedipal triangle doesn't emerge because parents do not love their children as much as their spouses, but because they must seem, to the child, to turn away when paying attention to the spouse or another, and may seem to the child to be turning away and abandoning for good.)

It is within such limits (whatever their precise character may be and wherever they may come from) that we must build our loves. And while living with our loves we may also have to live with jealousy. Once one appreciates the thoughts that underlie jealousy, their relative independence from claims of right and their attachment to basic fears, one can see that jealousy holds a place in human life as fixed as human vulnerability and the need for certain types of love. If we must live with jealousy, on what terms is it to be: must it persist, condemned but ineradicable, or distinguished from envy and detached from some of its noxious consequences, might we be better able to tolerate it for those aspects that serve to make it a sign of love?

Jealousy, where it is over particulars and has its special ties to love, seems secure of a place in human life. Some relations are essentially exclusive; the development of an independent identity seems to involve denying some people and things an independent identity (they become a part of us in a way that gets perceived by others as possessiveness); and in the course of development we find that we cannot always have what and who we want when and how we want them—people have desires of their own, and even where what we want is a thing, other people are liable to want it too—indeed it is part of our humanity that we are liable to desire and love what others are also liable to desire and love. Within the flexibility of attitudes to sharing, overcoming scarcity and overcoming inequality, we must draw the limits of jealousy as they reflect the limits of love.

4

JEALOUS AFTERTHOUGHTS

"Love seeketh not Itself to please,
Nor for itself hath any care,
But for another gives its ease,
And builds a Heaven in Hell's despair."

So sung a little Clod of Clay
Trodden with the cattle's feet,
But a Pebble of the brook
Warbled out these metres meet:

"Love seeketh only Self to please,
To bind another to Its delight,
Joys in another's loss of ease,
And builds a Hell in Heaven's despite."
William Blake, *Songs of Experience*,
"The Clod and the Pebble"

Some twenty years ago, I published an essay entitled "Jealous Thoughts" (1980a [chap. 3 here]) in which I argued (among other things) that the possibility of jealousy is not eliminable without the sacrifice of much else, including erotic attachment. While I don't believe the world has much changed in this respect, and so my basic view has also not changed much, I do have some further thoughts about jealousy—in particular in relation to issues of identity and of ambivalence. It is those that I would like to discuss here.

First, one needs to understand that jealousy is a complex, internally structured emotion, and that structure can best be understood through its component thoughts. That is, jealousy is not a simple unanalyzable sensation with a distinctive feel and little else that uniquely characterizes it, as David Hume, among others, thought all emotions to be. Jealousy is not best understood on the model of a headache, even a headache with characteristic causes and effects. It is crucially constituted by certain thoughts. Further, the constituent thoughts and beliefs provide a way into understanding the psychological and social conditions and implications of the emotion. I believe those thoughts centrally involve fear of loss, more specifically, fear of alienation of affections (loss to a rival), more generally and more deeply, fear of annihilation. Such fears are typically tied to hatred, hatred of one's rival (emphasized by Freud) and hatred of the betraying beloved (emphasized by Spinoza). Let us turn now to some aspects of fear of loss in relation to identity, approaching them via questions of irrationality, attention, and dependence.

Irrationality, Attention, and Dependence

In my original essay, I emphasized attention as one important dimension of intimacy, an aspect of love that makes for limits. Even if one wanted to love everyone, the natural limits of time and attention entail that the kind of love one can actually achieve is limited. Those forms of love that involve intimacy and erotic attachment, in particular, cannot be spread widely without thinning in the process. And this is part of what gives jealousy its ineliminable place in the human condition. While love is not exactly a zero-sum game, so that love given elsewhere is always at one's expense, people are not wrong to feel that time and attention given elsewhere have implications for the time and attention available for them. This in turn has some implications for the rationality of jealousy, as well as for the role of dependence and insecurity in jealousy. First, rationality.

Jeffrey Reiman, in an article concerned with the value of privacy protected by law, criticizes a certain view of intimacy on the ground that on that view "jealousy—the most possessive of emotions—is rendered rational" (1976, 33). The view he criticizes, the Rachels-Fried view, treats personal information and privileged access as the "moral capital" used to establish friendship and love relationships. "On this view, intimacy is both signaled and constituted by the sharing of information and allowing of observation not shared with or allowed to the rest of the world" (31–32). Reiman finds the view distasteful "because it suggests a market conception of personal intimacy" (32), and, as noted, because it renders jealousy rational. But I believe jealousy can be, at least in this regard, rational. While Reiman objects to "scarcity" views of human intimacy, his main complaint is about understanding intimacy in terms of "information" rather than in terms of, what he calls, a "context of caring." Yet he seems willing to acknowledge limits (namely, time and energy [35]) on caring. If he is, then jealousy still makes sense, even on his view emphasizing caring rather than information in intimacy. It is unavoidable that caring will be selectively and unequally distributed, and there may be value in that selectivity and its by-product "scarcity." Both caring and attention have limits (indeed, limits on attention are among the limits on caring) and they make an economic, zero-sum, view of love relations not wholly irrational.

Which is not to deny the existence of some, indeed much, irrational jealousy. Jealous thoughts, as Freud emphasized, are often unfounded or projected. And the thoughts and feelings may be especially intense because of backward-looking fears having to do with the infantile origins of identification and dependence (about which more in a moment) and also because of forward-looking fears of loss that can become exaggerated. Because time is often needed to recreate our most valued relations, if they can be recreated with another at all, the fears may sometimes be well-founded and it is difficult to gauge what the appropriate level of intensity might be. How jealous does it make sense to be in a particular case? There is no general answer to that question. The point here is to acknowledge that jealousy can be irrational, both ill founded and excessively intense, but also to insist that it can be rational, that some perceived dangers are real and sometimes love given to another is indeed, in some sense, at one's expense. But let us now look once more at some of the infantile sources of what can become pathological possessiveness, and in particular at the role of attention.

Amélie Rorty (1980), in an essay written partly in response to my original one, put focused attention at the center of what one fears to lose when one is jealous. I regard that attention as indeed crucial, and a very significant part of the "affection" one fears to lose when one is concerned about possible "alienation of affections"—what I take to be the heart of jealousy. Loss of attention is part of what one is visualizing when one becomes obsessed with images of the beloved paying attention to another, as people often do when they become obsessed with jealousy. Jealous thoughts involve fearful and angry questions, and they also quite characteristically involve images of abandonment and betrayal that are vivid forms of the fear of alienation of affections, including shift of attention, that constitute the emotion. Once more, jealousy centrally involves fear of loss, more specifically, fear of alienation of affections, more generally and more deeply, fear of annihilation. How exactly it involves fear of annihilation is worth further consideration.

Rorty pointed out in her discussion that the focused attention of others is an important part of how one forms one's own self-image. She writes, "The paradigm for such attention, that sets the model and expectations for later extensions, is direct gazing. That is how, as infants, we first experience attention and that is how we first experience the possibility of its loss, when the attention that was directed to us is turned away. At that level, anyone's gain, must be our loss" (469). Later, and in a variety of ways, who one thinks one is depends on who others think one is, on who they allow one to think one is, and the interest they attach to various aspects of ourselves.

Thus, for example, it is difficult to regard oneself as witty or attractive if no one else does.

The developmental importance of focused attention is perhaps best captured in psychoanalytic terms by Winnicott's notion that "the precursor of the mirror is the mother's face" (1974a, 130). The infant looks to his mother's face and, if he is lucky and she is not distracted or absorbed in herself, he sees himself reflected back. It is through the recognition, acknowledgment, and response to his states, especially his spontaneous gestures, that he learns what he feels and develops a sense of a continuous real self. He sees himself reflected back in her expression.

So we are dependent in a variety of ways on others, not just for affection, which is a nice thing to have and perhaps even a psychologically necessary thing to have, but for our very identities. I think this dependence is in fact very rich and complex. In my original essay I tried to suggest how Winnicott's notion of a transitional object helps us to better understand the psychological nature of possessions and our relation to them, how they can become important parts of who one is, so possessiveness may have less to do with concerns over ownership than concerns over identity.

Let me pause for a moment over the notion of a transitional object, repeating what I said. In the beginning, when the difference between inside and outside is still unclear, there are no independent objects in the world of the infant and the notion of a possession has no place. (As Winnicott puts it, "The mother, at the beginning, by an almost 100 per cent adaptation affords the infant the opportunity for the *illusion* that her breast is part of the infant" [1958, 238].) Gradually, as the child comes to differentiate itself from its mother, it seizes on some object (typically a teddy bear or blanket) which has for it some of the properties of an independent object but at the same time forms an essential part of its identity: the object may be given a name (as though it were a thing apart), but if it is changed (e.g., cleaned) or lost, its loss is felt as a loss of self. This transitional object is the child's first possession. The loss of the mother, contrasting with the time when she could be regarded as part of the self, contributes to the development of the child's attitude toward independent objects in such a way that the loss of an object can come to be felt as a loss of self. Identification with objects (so that they become "inside" while remaining "outside"), a process primarily begun and continued with people, gives possessions a special character and gives jealousy, insofar as it involves a fear of loss, a special place and force.

Winnicott has another observation which I think sheds significant light on the development of independence and the role that others must play in our lives (both in early stages and later). He speaks of "being alone, as an infant and small child, in the presence of mother" as the crucial step in the development of the capacity to be alone (1965, 30). This poetic notion of being alone in the presence of another seems to me to capture an important way in which we are held by others, held together by others, without their actually having to do anything or even to pay direct, focused attention. It is the root psychological value in the common notion of someone "being there" for us. In its infantile, its developmentally important, form it requires actual physical presence. But ultimately it is psychological availability, the assurance that the other will be there when needed, and the related assurance that others hold us in a certain regard, that is crucial. And in love that assurance, that security, is often achieved through identification, through internalization. Jealousy marks the breakdown of that assurance.

I wish to move to a discussion of identification through a consideration of idealization. Winnicott's developmental point about the capacity to be alone may help prepare us for the recognition, the perhaps surprising recognition, that identification is not a purely internal process; it may depend on the responses, on the responsiveness of others.

Reciprocity and the Desire to Be Desired

A central feature of many forms of love, especially romantic love, is idealization of the beloved. Plato's discussion of the nature of the ultimate object of love in his *Symposium* sheds useful light on this feature of love. In Diotima's account of ascending stairs, the lover develops from attachment to particular beautiful bodies to recognition of the beauty in many different bodies, and then in beautiful souls, moving eventually to an appreciation of "the great sea of beauty" to be found in social institutions, in knowledge, and ultimately in the abstract idea of beauty that gives a single common sense to the beauty found in all these diverse mundane objects. Plato's notion of the transcendent Form of Beauty, whatever its other philosophical advantages and its metaphysical difficulties, I think helps us understand the idealization involved in much love. What Plato would argue is that there is an ultimate object behind the idealized beloved, the real object of love. What is going on is that one loves the ideal as instantiated in the particular beloved, and comes perhaps to overestimate the individual who does the instantiating. The ideal itself can never be overestimated, it is perfect and unchanging. Plato would ultimately go on to insist that it is a mistake to remain attached to idealized individuals, and that the actual object of love and devotion should be the Form itself, an ideal object.

One of the problems with this move, from an idealized object to an ideal object, is that people drop out of the picture altogether as objects of love. A second problem, the one I wish to focus on here, is that even if one comes to love the Forms, the Forms cannot love one back. They are not people, not centers of desire. Such love is necessarily not reciprocated—is necessarily unrequited. It is strange to think that the most ideal love is necessarily unrequited. Why? This "why?" is not rhetorical. I think it a real question.

Perhaps one answer can be found by considering other ideal loves: the love of a mother for her child, the love of God for all. One's love for one's mother, one's love for God are necessarily requited—a mother's love, God's love, are supposed to be unfailing. Mothers and God are supposed to love one no matter what one does. They love you no matter what. The security of such love is reassuring. But the security is bought at a price: because the love is unconditional, it is nondiscriminating, it is given equally to all (at least by a mother to all her children, and by God to all his, that is, to everyone). So it does not select one out as its distinctive, special object. And one wants to be special, to be loved for one's very special self. (This, by the way, may be one of the sources for the desire for exclusivity in love, and so of jealousy.) That is, what one wants is in fact conditional love; one wants to be loved, at the least, because one is oneself, because one is special. So unconditional love, despite its advantages in terms of reliability, disappoints the hope to be picked out as special, the hope that only conditional love can meet.

Notice that the unconditional love of God and mothers is also distinctively nonerotic. Such love is selfless. The lover wants nothing for himself or herself (except perhaps what is best for the beloved). The loving God and loving mothers are supposed to demand nothing for themselves in return—though a loving God might demand that one love everyone, love everyone with that nondiscriminating good will characteristic of his love. The importance of the erotic suggests another answer to the question of why a necessarily unrequited love is so unappealing. Central to erotic love is the desire to be desired.

The importance of the desire to be desired is sometimes underestimated. Sartre, in his marvelous description of "double reciprocal incarnation" in his section on "the caress" in Being and Nothingness (1956 [1943]), does not underestimate it. He sees the importance in sexuality of one's awareness of the other's awareness and desire for one. Such self-constituting awarenesses and criss-crossing desires are also very present in the account of identity formation through recognition by the other in Hegel's Phenomenology (1977 [1807]). And Freud manages to link the themes of idealization, the role of the other, and identification in his discussion of "being in love" in Group Psychology and the Analysis of the Ego (1921c). But now idealization is not, as it is in Plato, a matter of an ideal object somehow behind and instantiated in the immediate object of one's love. Idealization in Freud is a transformation of narcissism. We are approaching the interplay of projective and introjective identification. Freud writes:

In connection with this question of being in love we have always been struck by the phenomenon of sexual overvaluation—that fact that the loved object enjoys a certain amount of freedom from criticism, and that all its characteristics are valued more highly than those of people who are not loved, or than its own were at a time when it itself was not loved

. . . The tendency which falsified judgement in this respect is that of idealization. But now it is easier for us to find our bearings. We see that the object is being treated in the same way as our own ego, so that when we are in love a considerable amount of narcissistic libido overflows on to the object. It is even obvious, in many forms of love-choice, that the object serves as a substitute for some unattained ego ideal of our own . . . The whole situation can be completely summarized in a formula: The object has been put in the place of the ego ideal. (1921c, 112–13)

We started with idealization and Plato. Freud gives us a way to move from idealization to a consideration of identification.

Identification

The superego, in particular the ego ideal, is the result of identification, of internalization via incorporation. The primitive model of this is oral incorporation, swallowing. Anthropologists report that in some societies, natives try to incorporate the virtues of others by literally eating parts of them. Infants in all societies explore the world and seek to assimilate the world through their mouths. As adults, we may incorporate, may identify, through unconscious fantasies. However that, at a deep level, may be, we should understand that there are at least two different types of identification. One, incorporation, the one I have been speaking of, involves an effort to become like the other. Another, a second kind, involves making the other like oneself, and is sometimes called projective identification. In that kind of identification, aspects of oneself are seen as features of the other, and often denied as aspects of oneself. (On a primitive level, spitting out as opposed to swallowing.) Freud (1922b) writes of certain neurotic cases of jealousy that involve projecting one's own impulses toward unfaithfulness onto one's beloved—leading one to suspect them of being unfaithful rather than admitting one's own temptations. And Melanie Klein makes much of projective identification as a form of defense and an effort at control. The Kleinians worked heavily with psychotics, and the projection of characteristics *onto* another in that context tends to become projective identification *into* another, the aggressive placing of rejected parts of oneself into external objects, done under an overriding fantasy of the omnipotence of thought. This can be seen and understood most readily in the transference relation between patient and analyst, where projective identification can become interpersonal actualization, with the patient manipulatively inducing the analyst into experiencing disowned feelings, especially hostile and painful ones. In effect the analyst gets drawn into the patient's fantasy world, and feels it in his own countertransference. This is a form of identification in which both parties experience the effects of the process. (Once more, as with Winnicott's being alone in the presence of the other, we get a hint of how what might seem an internal process may in fact be interactive.) If the evacuation of parts of the self, of aggressive impulses and other rejected parts of the ego, in projective identification seems to depend on the disturbed ego boundaries of schizophrenia and a related fantasy of the omnipotence of thought, the process of projective identification can be seen in a more normal form in communicative efforts at empathy. There one is said to attempt to put oneself in someone else's shoes. Inserting oneself into someone else's position is not so far from putting oneself inside another, and that is not so far from the inner world of objects, of fantasy manipulation of self and other, in Melanie Klein. In the more disturbed forms, people can come to structure their interactions by projection: only that part of reality that verifies the projection is perceived by the subject, as in the jealousy based on projected temptations to unfaithfulness discussed by Freud.

But here I do not wish to linger in the depths of neurosis and psychosis; I want to consider how certain crucial psychological mechanisms of identity formation may help us understand what is going on when we are jealous. Recall that I have been concerned to distinguish ordinary possessiveness with its ties to ownership from that kind of possessiveness, if it is possessiveness, which involves identification and is tied perhaps to "belonging." Possessiveness, insofar as it involves treating people as though they were things that we can own and control, seems to me to involve psychological illusion and moral error. If all jealousy were based on that sort of possessiveness, it too would involve psychological illusion and moral error. But I have wanted to argue that jealousy can be normal, can be rational, and can be allowed an acceptable place in human life (assuming we can control some of its harmful effects). To do that, we need to be able to see what may appear as possessiveness as more rooted in concerns about identity than ownership, and once we do that the fear of annihilation that may underlie fear of loss becomes more intelligible.

Going back to Plato's *Symposium*, there is the telling image in the myth ascribed to Aristophanes of the original humans, double-male, double-female, and androgynous, split in two for offending the gods and ever after searching for their "matching half." The myth is of interest for many reasons, one being the explanation it offers for heterosexuality, lesbianism, and homosexuality. It is significant that all three types of object choice are regarded as equally in need of explanation and that Aristophanes offers the same (mythological) type of explanation for all of them. But here, the myth is particularly interesting because of the image of the search for one's missing half. It is an image that has resonated throughout literature (remember Shakespeare's "The Phoenix and the Turtle": "two distincts, division none") and continues to resonate in individual experience. Another person may be regarded as part of oneself. It is not at all unusual for individuals in a couple to think of themselves more as parts of a "we" than as separate "I"s. The psychological reality out of which that "we" is constructed may be made up of processes of both projective and introjective identification. What are the conditions for such identification?

Suppose one thinks one has found one's other half, but the other disagrees? Who decides? What if one's presumed "other half" rejects one? Unrequited love, after all, is not all that unusual. Is identification then as much an illusion as possession doubtless is? Does identification depend on the attitude of the beloved or is it a purely internal matter? Much love lives in an ambiguous space between accepting independent identities and a transcendent shared identity. (Remember Winnicott's transitional objects which occupy a similar space.) Psychical reality may in some ways matter more here than material reality: a person may become "a part of" you even while, of course, not physically "inside" you. Certainly one can have a fantasy all by oneself, but it may be difficult to sustain particular fantasies without the cooperation of another. The "fear of loss" central in jealousy suggests that the other's attitudes and responses do matter, that one cannot identify no matter what the other feels. (This is a serious form of intersubjectivity.) Remember also that love, especially erotic love, includes the desire to be desired. Recognition by the other, as in Hegel, and reciprocity, as in Sartre, may be crucial.

The question is whether identification is as much an illusion as possession (understood in terms of ownership) doubtless is. If identification were simply a matter of internal and individual processes it would be relatively easy to understand. But then it might be unacceptably imperialist, it might seem you could appropriate another, make them a part of your identity, through simple one-sided infatuation. If love includes identification, perhaps then identification is better understood as involving a reciprocal element (as in the Bob Dylan lyric "I'll let you be in my dream, if I can be in yours"). To distinguish identification from "possession" it would seem to somehow require a reciprocal process in which the other is not simply a thing, but rather can respond, and how they respond matters. As Marx wrote, "If you love unrequitedly, i.e., if your love as love does not call forth love in return, if through the vital expression of yourself as a loving person you fail to become a loved person, then your love is impotent, it is a misfortune" (1975 [1844], 379).

We can distinguish identification from possession quite simply in terms of the desire to be like as opposed to the desire to have. In the context of a discussion of the Oedipus complex, Freud says, "It is easy to state in a formula the distinction between an identification with the father and the choice of the father as an object. In the first case one's father is what one would like to be, and in the second he is what one would like to have. The distinction, that is, depends upon whether the tie attaches to the subject or to the object of the ego" (1921c, 106). But, taking identification as internalization, the distinction is not so clear. Freud continues in the passage quoted, "It is much more difficult to give a clear metapsychological representation of the distinction. We can only see that identification endeavours to mould a person's own ego after the fashion of the one that has been taken as a model." We should recall that in the mechanism of superego formation spelled out in *The Ego and the Id* (1923b), the superego is the result of internalization, backed by what might be called a desire to be like the internalized external authority figures. But recall also that the object of self-reproaches, the strictures of the superego, described in *Mourning and Melancholia* is also thought by Freud to be the result of internalization, out of what might be called a desire to have and retain the lost object that precipitates the depression: "the shadow of the object fell upon the ego" in a "substitution of identification for object-love" (1917e, 249). Freud summarizes the complex picture of identification in *Group Psychology*: "First, identification is the original form of emotional tie with an object; secondly, in a regressive way it becomes a substitute for a libidinal object-tie, as it were by means of introjection of the object into the ego; and thirdly, it may arise with any new perception of a common quality shared with some other person who is not an object of the sexual instinct" (1921c, 107–8). This last is the basic mechanism of emotional imitation and has ties to empathy. We are back in the dialectic of introjective and projective identification that love may not permit us to leave. And ambiguity here may have interesting connections with ambivalence. In particular, it may help us to better understand how we come to hate those we love, not just in the context of jealous rivalry, where the threats to identity may make the fears and hatreds of jealousy readily intelligible, but also in the context of love, even reciprocated love, where it might appear hatred must find its roots in different fears.

I pursue the dialectic of dependence and mixed feelings further in "Odi et Amo: On Hating the Ones We Love" (1996 [chap. 5 here]), but here it may be useful to turn once more to Winnicott in order to learn from him a bit about how even hatred can play a constructive role in identity formation and the ability to love. For love to be possible, independent objects must exist and be recognized to exist. Winnicott's insight is that independent existence is confirmed for us by an object's surviving our destructive assaults (1974b). The point may be summarized by saying, "the object only becomes real by being hated; the infant can only find the world around him substantial through his ultimately unsuccessful attempts to destroy it" (Phillips 1988, 17). Resistance is one sign of reality. (This was a feature of Freud's earliest formulation of the nature of reality-testing in his *Project for a Scientific Psychology* [1950a (1887–1902)]: the fact that an object disappears when an infant turns his head is one sign that the object is real rather than a hallucination.) We are reassured of the reality of our beloveds, and of their love, by the persistence of them and their love despite the tests we put them to. How can one be sure of an untested love? While the exigencies of life may provide ample trials, is any test more sure than the challenge of our own hostility?

That one's own reality, one's own distinctive identity, may equally depend on surviving opposition and conflict with those we love is a point familiar to every adolescent.

Possessiveness and the Need to Know

Let me take up one further set of issues. In my original essay, I distinguished jealousy from envy and admiring envy from malicious envy, and also sought to argue that the things that give jealousy an ineliminable place in human life don't seem to create a comparable place for malicious envy. Further, that a proper understanding of self-esteem does not require envy and that envy is not the only source of a desire for equality. I do not wish to rehearse those distinctions and arguments here. But I do want to say a bit about the suggestion that jealousy should really be understood in terms of "insecurity" or that in any case its place is more narrow than I have suggested.

People sometimes seek to explain jealousy in terms of underlying insecurities, and then claim such insecurities, and so jealousy, are unjustified. On this I can be brief. If jealousy is defined in terms of "fear," as I do, it is not clear that it is distinguishable from (let alone explainable by) insecurity. Should "insecurity" itself be defined in terms of "fear of loss" (in which case it is hard to separate it from jealousy) or in terms of something else, say a sense of unworthiness? If something else, is it always a mistake to be insecure in that sense? (This *is* a rhetorical question.)

Some say the Bushmen or other tribes without a sense of "possession" never experience jealousy. That seems to me anthropological fantasy: do the Bushmen never have a feeling of needing a particular person, and fearing for their loss to a rival? If they do, that is enough for jealousy on my account. If someone claims they don't, my suspicion is they have not observed the Bushmen enough (or that the Bushmen are very discreet or private about their secret longings and fears). Many in our society deny jealousy, though it nonetheless often tends to manifest itself in their behavior. This is not to slight the fact that some people are less jealous than others or to claim that people must always be jealous whenever loss is likely or possible. It is simply to say that removing notions of "possession" from human relations is not enough to remove the possibility of jealousy, for, as I've suggested, the "possessiveness" involved may have more to do with identity than with ownership, and with fundamental vulnerabilities that come with forms of desire and dependence essential to love.

Still, it might be suggested there is another way to narrow the place of jealousy, a way comparable to the way I myself have sought to narrow the place of envy.[1] Some believe people cloak their envy in demands for equality, while the underlying desire is that no one have what one cannot have. By contrast, I believe the demand for equality need not be a kind of reaction-formation to defend against or hide envy. The desire for equality may involve a desire that all be raised up, rather than a demand that the advantaged be cut down. (One thinks here of Lenin's defense of his taste for first class travel on trains: "After the revolution, everyone will travel first class.") It may stem from principled moral considerations, as John Rawls would have it, rather than infantile malicious envy, as Freud would seem to have it (Forrester, 1996). Be that as it might, the suggestion is that the questions of jealousy, e.g. asking why one cannot provide one's beloved what some special friend or their psychoanalyst seems to provide, may be motivated by an undemanding, a giving love rather than, as I would have it, a fear of loss—just as there may be motives of justice instead of motives of envy behind attacks on inequality. The suggestion is that one needs an analysis of love comparable to that of justice, and that once one has it one may be able to narrow the place of jealousy just as I have sought to narrow the place of envy.

First, however, one should understand that I have never sought to equate jealousy with simple questions or bare thoughts. Of course one could raise questions, say about what one's lover shares with their friend or analyst that they cannot share with one, without any affect let alone jealousy in particular. But granting that bare thoughts are not enough for emotion, what more is needed? Let me sketch a brief answer. I would think any of at least three different types of thing might sometimes be enough. (And I think this for emotions in general, including fear, what I regard as the main component emotion in jealousy):

1. Affect or physiological tumult. But this is not essential. After all, there are intellectual, or what Hume called "calm," passions.
2. Motivational force (though here it should be acknowledged that the connection to action of what might appear jealous questions or thoughts could be via love rather than fear of loss),
3. Character of the thoughts themselves. Indeed, jealous thoughts are quite typically obsessive and quite often imagistic (one imagines the beloved giving focused attention to the rival).

But let us suppose the jealous thoughts I was talking about in my original essay were suitably obsessive, provided the motives for many actions, and even caused physiological tumult. It might be objected that one of the cases I discussed tainted the later argument. The case was one of "absolute openness," a case that might be supposed to eliminate the need for jealous questioning but that I argued might still not preclude jealousy. It might now be objected that the desire to know everything, one of the desires behind absolute openness, is itself jealously motivated. If the desire for exclusivity is a consequence of problems with "absolute openness" with multiple partners, perhaps exclusivity can gain no halo from that source. The desire to know all might be regarded as itself a form of the desire for possession and control.

A story might help illustrate the point. A well-connected American friend of mine had a very fancy wedding in France a number of years ago. Her American groom sat next to the Baroness de Rothschild at the reception. The baroness asked him if he had made any special requests of his bride. He responded, yes, he had told her she could do whatever she wanted so long as she always told him. The baroness was slightly shocked and replied, "My dear, when I married the baron, I told him he could do whatever he wanted on the condition that he *never* told me." This may point to a contrast between the old world and the new; it certainly points to two different points of view toward knowledge of the beloved. It is not obvious to me which is the more trusting, the more loving.

Suppose your beloved calls to tell you they are delayed and they won't make a planned dinner. Does it matter whether the delay is because of a broken fan belt or because the beloved is having an affair? I would have thought yes. The two causes have different implications in terms of voluntariness and in terms of priorities, and thus in terms of implications for the future. But then I may just be a child of the new world, and the significant differences that seem to matter to me may simply manifest desires for possession and control.

The argument against my view might suggest that there are two deluded ideals. One that insists on absolute openness, and is based on jealousy. And another that insists "ignorance is bliss" and that "what you don't know won't hurt you." The suggestion might be that there is a better ideal: lovers should share and know all that is "relevant." I suspect that there may be all sorts of problems in circumscribing what is "relevant" when it comes to what may be the central relation in one's life and what might threaten it. But be that as it might, the future remains a problem: of course it is a mistake to experience all types of "sharing" as a loss, but "sharing" may sometimes in fact involve a risk of loss. When is sharing itself a "loss," and when does it have the potential for loss? That is partly a matter of temperament and certainly varies with circumstances. But I have wanted all along to distinguish between jealous thoughts—the doubts, questions, and fears that may trouble one—and the actions (including verbal ones) those thoughts might motivate. Not all questions need to be voiced, not all fears need be or can be allayed. One may have to accept certain risks for the sake of love. Some say "the greatest love is to risk all." How much we are psychologically able to risk may depend on how reliably present the other is, internally if not externally. Independence may grow out of dependence, just as Winnicott suggests the capacity to be alone grows out of the experience of being alone in the presence of another. So while the vulnerability of identity may be part of what makes jealousy so painful and so difficult to eliminate, the mechanisms of internalization that help shape and solidify identity (mechanisms that may be importantly interactive and reciprocal) may also be what give us the ability to love and the strength to take risks.

5

ODI ET AMO: ON HATING
THE ONES WE LOVE

Catullus, in the midst of his unhappy affair with the woman he called Lesbia, wrote a two-line poem, beginning in Latin "Odi et amo": "I hate and love. Why I do so, perhaps you ask. / I know not, but I feel it, and I am in torment."[1] He is not alone in his experience, his pain, or his confusion. How can it be, and why should it be that, to vary Oscar Wilde's formulation, each man (and woman) hates the thing he (or she) loves?

Cycles

Hatred is supposed to be the opposite of love, and doubtless (in some sense) it is. But what does that mean? One thing it surely does not mean is that the two emotions are incompatible, if that is supposed to entail that they cannot be experienced toward the same object or at the same time. What is it then for one emotion to be the "opposite" of another? Putting that question aside for the moment, how is it that hatred, in particular, is so tied to its putative opposite, love, that it seems natural for them to occur together, if not simultaneously, then in constant alternation, in cycles?

Certainly relationships can go wrong, and do so for all sorts of reasons. There are possessive lovers, there are abusive lovers. Such relationships may be painful to *both* parties, and lead each to resent the other. We hate people for the evil they do us, but more interestingly if less justifiably, we also hate people for the evil we do them. If we become possessive and abusive, in addition to hating our victims for the real or imagined harms that led to our possessiveness and abusiveness toward them in the first place, we naturally hate those who harm those we love (in this case, ourselves), and we naturally reciprocate the hatreds of those who hate us (even those hatreds of which we are the cause). Spinoza works out some of these points in his logic of identification, what he calls "imitation of the affects" (1985 [1677], part 3, prop. 27).[2] And prior love produces greater hatred when one passion displaces the other (1985 [1677], part 3, props. 38 and 44). This can be seen in heightened form in connection with paranoia, which on Freud's account also involves a reversal from activity to passivity ("I love him" to "he hates me") that leaves the persecutor still an object of love (1911c, *SE* 12: part 3; 1922b, *SE* 18). The same is true from the other direction, when love displaces hate, as in the move from passivity to activity in defensive identification with the aggressor (A. Freud 1966 [1936], chap. 9). Such relationships and cycles may reveal pathology in love, though one must wonder whether there is a dynamic *within* love that tends to lead to such pathology. This is an important point, to which we will return.

But it is not difficult to understand how someone might love someone else *despite* their oppressive faults, especially if the faults are seen as aspects or outgrowths of love, albeit pathological ones. If someone loves another *because* they are abusive, the pathology is more complex, but the mixed feelings are not by themselves puzzling. Loving and hating different aspects of a person, or for different reasons, produces mixed feelings; but mixed feelings are by themselves puzzling only if one has some special theory suggesting they should cancel each other out, as in a chemical reaction in which acid and base neutralize each other. Some theories of mind, for example Hume's (Neu 1977, 32–34), do just that, making ambivalence inconceivable. Far from casting suspicion on the phenomenon, however, this should make such theories immediately implausible. A theory which sees no difference between the presence of two "contrary" passions and no passion at all is seriously defective. Ambivalence is a real and commonplace part of the fluctuation of our feelings, the fluid many-aspected character of our emotional lives. As Montaigne writes, "Whoever supposes, to see me look sometimes coldly, sometimes lovingly, on my wife, that either look is feigned, is a fool" (1958 [1588], 173). While Montaigne emphasizes the fleeting character of our emotions, and even Hume would allow the rapid fluctuation or alternation of conflicting feelings, there can be deep and simultaneous conflicts.[3] The pathological cases prove it. Freud makes the point a central feature of his picture of the human mind: "The logical laws of thought do not apply in the id, and this is true above all of the law of contradiction. Contrary impulses exist side by side, without canceling each other out or diminishing each other" (1933a, *SE* 22: 73).

But let us seek to go beyond pathology. Plato writes in the *Phaedrus:*

> Suppose we were being listened to by a man of generous and humane character, who loved or had once loved another such as himself; suppose he heard us saying that for some trifling cause lovers conceive bitter hatred and a spirit of malice and injury towards their loved ones; wouldn't he be sure to think that we had been brought up among the scum of the

people and had never seen a case of noble love? Wouldn't he utterly refuse to accept our vilification of Love? (243C, trans. Hackforth)

Trifling (and not so trifling) causes abound. Others hate us for the imagined harms we do them and, perhaps more intriguing though more perverse, they hate us for the real harms they do us. And of course we hate them in return. There is no problem about understanding hatred of those we love because they seek to control or abuse us. Does it make sense for us to hate them because they love us or because we love them?

Dependence and Mixed Feelings

The dialectic that Hegel elaborates in his famous description of the relation of master and slave, a dialectic of the development of self-consciousness and individual identity, is also the dialectic of our interactions (loving and otherwise) with others. At least that is the story Sartre tells in *Being and Nothingness* (1956 [1943], part 3, chap. 3). It is a story of the inherent futility of love. Aiming at the full possession of a free being, our desire must fail as possession insofar as the other is free, and it must fail in terms of freedom insofar as the other is possessed. Thus Sartre speaks of "the impossible ideal of desire" (394), "the lover's perpetual dissatisfaction" (377) and "the lover's perpetual insecurity" (377). Love falls into masochism and sadism. In Sartre's account, these have little to do with pleasure and pain, and much to do with freedom and control. Love is embedded in conflict, a war for recognition, in which Sartre concludes "it is indifferent whether we hate the Other's transcendence through what we empirically call his vices or his virtues . . . The occasion which arouses hate is simply an act by the Other which puts me in the state of *being subject* to his freedom" (411).

While Sartre's somewhat overheated metaphysics of sado-masochism is oddly detached from action and real interaction, and while it imagines a peculiar transcendent freedom too much always at issue, it nonetheless fruitfully explores in other terms the intricacies of identification, of introjection and projection; and the prosaic but important truth emerges and remains that the lover wants to be loved. Whatever may be the case for putative selfless loves on the one hand, or pure physical cravings on the other hand, it is true for erotic love that the lover wants to be loved.[4] And this has consequences.

Love brings with it dependence and vulnerability. And these are fertile grounds for hatred. The more dependent an individual is on another, whether for freely given love or for other things, the more opportunities there will be for disappointment. But possibility does not amount to actuality. Why should hatred be inevitable? No reason so far has been given unless dependence is in itself hateful. Is it? While men are often ready to assume that it is, that may be a gendered assumption. It may be that men in our society reject dependence as hateful while women accept it as a desirable aspect of relationships, and that their differing assumptions have to do with current and local conditions of psychological development. It has been argued that

> for boys and men, separation and individuation are critically tied to gender identity since separation from the mother is essential for the development of masculinity. For girls and women, issues of femininity or feminine identity do not depend on the achievement of separation from the mother or on the progress of individuation. Since masculinity is defined through separation while femininity is defined through attachment, male gender identity is threatened by intimacy while female gender identity is threatened by separation.[5]

Is the attitude toward dependence, whatever the facts of our particular society, in general socially formed and therefore variable? Why should dependence, especially interdependence, be experienced as a danger?

Dependence and vulnerability are problems of identity, of the self who is not self-sufficient, of who we are in relation to others. They are problems at the boundary (Brown 1966, chap. 8). The lover wants to be loved. If you want something, you risk not getting it. You also risk getting it. If your love is returned, you are open to reciprocal demands. And "you" are at risk. "You" may become "we." This might seem an unalloyed good; so much so that people are tempted to imagine it happens more often than it does, leading to illusions of commonality (of what Sartre, following Heidegger, calls the *Mitsein*). Merging has long been regarded as a valuable, not a hateful feature of love. But we should be aware that such merging involves the overcoming of individual separation and so the end of the beloved (as well as of oneself) as a separate individual, and so a kind of death. And that is what hatred also aims at accomplishing—even if by other means. This may be but one of many points at which love and hatred come together in their consequences, if not their nature. ("I love you so much that I could eat you up.") John Donne concludes in "The Prohibition":

> Lest thou thy love and hate and me undo,
> To let me live, Oh love and hate me too.

The intricacies are many, but it is in any case clear that dependence brings with it risks and dangers of various sorts. Risk and danger are the characteristic objects of fear, and it is to be remembered that fear is (arguably) the most common source of hate.

The desire to merge has infantile roots. Freud connects what he calls the "oceanic feeling" (1930a) with the earliest undifferentiated period of development, and Plato speaks in mythopoeic terms (through Aristophanes in the *Symposium*) of finding one's other half and becoming one as a return to our ancient state. We may bring other things back from our earlier condition. If dependence is not inherently hateful, infantile dependence, at least in adults, certainly is. And our later loves have infantile sources. Freud emphasizes how it is in the bosom of the family that we learn to love, how the finding of an object is always a refinding (1905d, *SE* 7: 222). Freud sometimes takes the history of displacement of objects as grounds for something like a Sartrean pessimism about love:

> It is my belief that, however strange it may sound, we must reckon with the possibility that something in the nature of the sexual instinct itself is unfavourable to the realization of complete satisfaction . . . the final object of the sexual instinct is never any longer the original object but only a surrogate for it. Psycho-analysis has shown us that when the original object of a wishful impulse has been lost as a result of repression, it is frequently represented by an endless series of substitutive objects none of which, however, brings full satisfaction. This may explain the inconstancy in object-choice, the "craving for stimulation" which is so often a feature of the love of adults. (1912d, *SE* 11: 188–89)

Of course, that there are infantile sources of love need not leave us stuck with infantile dependence as the central feature of mature love relations. Nonetheless, the desire for unconditional support (which may, when we were infants, have been met), and the desire to merge (which, when we were infants, may have been felt as an actual experience), continue to some degree, and their own history is one of conflict: conflict with the desires of others and with other of our own desires (including those for independence and individuation). Even the desire for unconditional love is itself internally conflicted. While some think God provides the unconditional love formerly bestowed by our mothers, God loves all indiscriminately. The lover in interpersonal contexts wants to be loved for himself in particular, and that means the love desired is conditional on him being him (whatever that involves), it must not be indiscriminate. So one wants the love to be unconditional and one wants it to be conditional. And the history of the development of our desires takes place in the midst of the family, in the midst of rivalry.[6] The ego itself is formed out of identifications, both introjections and projections. "The distinction between self and not-self is made by the childish decision to claim all that the ego likes as 'mine,' and to repudiate all that the ego dislikes as 'not-mine.'"[7] In love we are again in the midst of identifications, rivalries, and conflicts (some old, some new). For Sartre, this is a metaphysical point, for Freud, a psychological one.

Where does the fact that love has a history leave us? In ambivalence, I think. In Freud's early theorizing, he treats sadism (one of the poles of the failure of love according to Sartre—a denial of the other's freedom, as merging is a denial of the other's otherness) as a component sexual instinct, related to nonsexual instincts for mastery. In his later theorizing, he attributes it to a blend of life and death instincts.[8] Freud's later thought postulates an inclination to aggression, a "primary mutual hostility of human beings," and he suggests that aggressiveness "forms the basis of every relation of affection and love among people (with the single exception, perhaps, of the mother's relation to her male child)" (1930a, *SE* 21: 113). This provides no special explanation for hating those we love, for so far as hatred is instinctual it would equally explain hatred felt toward anyone. And hate is no more a simple instinct than love is. Both are attitudes felt by whole persons toward whole persons. But they connect with the instinctual reversals of activity and passivity that Freud explores in his consideration of sadism and masochism. Love and hate have instinctual roots, the convergence of which contributes to ambivalence. Freud saw this clearly even in his early theorizing, before the postulation of an independent death instinct, and he noted: "If a love-relation with a given object is broken off, hate not infrequently emerges in its place, so that we get the impression of a transformation of love into hate" (1915c, *SE* 14: 139).

Despite its changes, Freud's instinct theory remains determinedly dualistic throughout; the conflict is essential.[9] While love often enough appears to turn into hate, they are perhaps more often simultaneously present— the lapsing of love merely making the presence of the hate apparent. The hate that is in fact present all along may be unconscious or it may be a neglected (though perhaps not quite repressed) aspect of the love.

Ambivalence

It is one of the lessons of Freud that we should be suspicious of loves that appear too pure. When a love claims to be wholly unconflicted, the modern mind suspects denial or other forms of evasion (even in Freud's own favored case of "the mother's relation to her male child"). For all our loves have a history in the development of our patterns of loving, and that history has always involved conflict—with others and within ourselves.

While in fact normal (if universality is evidence of "normality"), ambivalence is especially pronounced in neurotics of the obsessional sort and Freud presents a graphic picture of ambivalence in an incident involving that classic obsessional-neurotic, the Rat Man, and his lady-love (who had, it should be remembered, previously rejected his marriage proposals) at a summer resort: "On the day of her departure he knocked his foot against a stone lying in the road, and was *obliged* to put it out of the way by the side of the road, because the idea struck him that her carriage would be driving along the same road in a few hours' time and might come to grief against this stone. But a few minutes later it occurred to him that this was absurd, and he was *obliged* to go back and replace the stone in its original position in the middle of the road" (1909d, *SE* 10: 190). (One wonders even about the Rat Man's first thought, the thought of possible harm to his lady-love. Despite its protective cloak, one wonders: where did *it* come from?) The Rat Man's ambivalence (and not just his) is also manifested in doubts of various sorts, and Freud tellingly points to their significance: "A man who doubts his own love may, or rather *must*, doubt every lesser thing" (1909d, *SE* 10: 241).[10] When love is interfered with and inhibited by hatred (especially unacknowledged hatred), doubts often emerge—jealous doubts among them.

Unconscious conflict can manifest itself also in the self-reproaches of mourning and the self-tormenting of depression and even in social practices and rituals such as taboos.[11] While Freud writes most often of repressed, unconscious hatreds, it should be noted infantile sources may fuel ambivalences of which we are only too well aware. A wholly unconflicted erotic love is, after Freud, unbelievable: "The evidence of psycho-analysis shows that almost every intimate emotional relation between two people which lasts for some time—marriage, friendship, the relations between parents and children—contains a sediment of feelings of aversion and hostility, which only escapes perception as a result of repression" (1921c, *SE* 18: 101).

Think again of what comes with love and the dynamics that follow. Love (on most accounts) naturally includes a desire to be with the beloved. Does wanting to be with the beloved lead (naturally? necessarily?) to wanting the intimacy to be exclusive, exacerbating fear of loss, and leading ultimately to efforts at control? Does the overestimation and idealization involved (naturally? necessarily?) in love, lead to disappointment when (inevitably) confronted with the reality of the beloved? If it does, expecting more of those we love, we may come to hate more deeply when they disappoint. Possessiveness and idealization may not be the only sources of hatred in love. Some of the traps may be built on apparent strengths of love, the comforts of security and identification. All the usual psychological mechanisms (displacement, projection, etc.) are available. So we may hate the people we love and who love us because it seems safe: assured of their love, we trust we will not lose them so we displace onto them the animosity we feel toward others that it seems too dangerous to express directly. Or we see ourselves mirrored in our loved ones, and project our own hated characteristics or self-hatreds onto them. Other twists and turns vary with the features one regards as essential to love—and the vast literature of love shows these to be indefinitely various.

All of this may seem to bring us back to pathology; but have we ever left it, can one ever leave it? In connection with sexual perversion, Freud writes, "In the sphere of sexual life we are brought up against peculiar and, indeed, insoluble difficulties as soon as we try to draw a sharp line to distinguish mere variations within the range of what is physiological from pathological symptoms" (1905d, *SE* 7: 160–61; Neu 1987b [chap. 9 here]). A similar point may be true for love. In his "Observations on Transference-Love," Freud spells out the ways in which transference-love, the patient's love for the analyst, is abnormal, emphasizing its role as resistance to the aims of therapy, its repetition of earlier patterns of reaction, and its disregard for reality. He immediately adds: "We should not forget, however, that these departures from the norm constitute precisely what is essential about being in love" (1915a, SE 12: 169). In the transference relationship between patient and analyst, the patient's feelings of love are more a response to circumstances than to the nature of the analyst, but we are all familiar in ordinary life with the phenomenon of "love on the rebound," where circumstances also seem to matter more than the nature of individual love objects. Perhaps all love is transference-love. After all, "the finding of an object is in fact a refinding of it" (1905d, SE 7: 222). Even the rationalist Plato, in the *Phaedrus*, recognizes and ultimately embraces the divine madness of love.

Emotional Opposition

What makes love the "opposite" of hate? Spinoza defines love as "a Joy [sometimes translated Pleasure], accompanied by the idea of an external cause," and hate as "a Sadness [sometimes translated Pain], accompanied by the idea of an external cause" (1985 [1677], pt. 3, Definitions of the Affects 6 and 7). Perhaps the place for us to start is with the apparently natural opposition of joy and sadness, pleasure and pain. Certainly typically, and on some accounts necessarily, one attracts and the other repels. Is the opposition of love and hate derivative?

Unfortunately, it is simply not the case that love is always pleasant and hatred always painful. Despite Spinoza's definitions of love and hate, which ground them in beliefs about the sources of pleasure and pain, we must all know from our experience that whatever the sources of feelings of love and hate, their manifestations and effects are not uniformly and distinctively pleasant or painful. While we might like to think love pleasant, we all know unrequited love is painful. Worse, we also know that even requited love can (perhaps must) bring pain in its train. For with the attachment of love comes the anxiety of loss and the pain of loss (whether actual or merely feared). Love makes us vulnerable in ways that enhance the possibilities of pain. Worse still, erotic love may in its very nature depend on absence and obstacle, lack and rivalry. It is not for nothing that eros is known as "bittersweet."[12] And looking from the other side, it is not unheard of for individuals to revel in hatred, to enjoy the passion and intrigue directed at enemies. It may even be the case that it is the intertwining pleasures and pains of love and hate that create a kind of equivalence between them, so that love and hate become the same, or rather, love-hate constitute a kind of passionate involvement that remains of a piece despite its cycles. So that the real opposition is not between love and hate, but between the intense passionate involvement they signify and indifference, a distancing emotional neutrality.[13] Detached, we neither love nor hate.

The possible equivalence of love and hate is worth pausing on. Such equivalence of apparent opposites is, according to Freud in "The Antithetical Meaning of Primal Words," characteristic of many of our most basic concepts (1910e; Neu 1987a [chap. 2 here]). It emerges in the double and opposed meanings carried by many words in the oldest languages, as well as in the factors in the dreamwork that allow an element in a dream to represent its contrary. At one level, this can be understood as a simple matter of association of contraries: so high makes us think of low, day of night, joy of sorrow. At a deeper level, however, the equivalence can be traced to a time at which the contraries are so far undifferentiated, before the concepts have been sorted out, and so the experience is itself undifferentiated. Indeed, the separate concepts are not yet available for associative or any other purposes. High/low is a dimension of experience, and joy/sorrow and love/hate are dimensions of experience; and confronted with either extreme along the dimension we are confronted with both. They are thus, in a sense, "the same." This provides yet another way of thinking about the persisting presence and influence of love's history referred to earlier. Freud traces aspects of that history in the following passage:

> Preliminary stages of love emerge as provisional sexual aims while the sexual instincts are passing through their complicated development. As the first of these aims we recognize the phase of incorporating or devouring—a type of love which is consistent with abolishing the object's separate existence and which may therefore be described as ambivalent. At the higher stage of the pregenital sadistic-anal organization, the striving for the object appears in the form of an urge for mastery, to which injury or annihilation of the object is a matter of indifference. Love in this form and at this preliminary stage is hardly to be distinguished from hate in its attitude towards the object. Not until the genital organization is established does love become the opposite of hate. (1915c, SE 14: 138–39)

Ambivalence and the equivalence of love and hate should also be seen in the context of more general issues and complexities concerning conflict, in particular the fact that denial can function as affirmation. This is the central point in Freud's essay on "Negation" (1925h, SE 19: 235–39). While the particular point has everything to do with the functioning of repression and the important psychological mechanism of splitting (which is especially significant in relation to ambivalence),[14] the thing to remember here is that emotional ambivalence itself is really but one of many manifestations of psychological conflict. The naturalness of ambivalent love and hate may thus connect not just with the problems of the self at its boundaries, and with the history and nature of love, but also with the inherent dividedness of the self itself and the nature of inner conflict.

Returning to our immediate theme, while love and hate may on some accounts be the models of emotional opposition, the underlying standard has not yet emerged. Their opposition certainly does not entail uniform concomitant pleasure or pain. So let us ask once more: what do we mean when we call one emotion the "opposite" of another? If emotions were simple sensations, though like flavors they might be grouped, it would become difficult to see what gave them a direction, a vector, as well as an intensity or strength. At any rate, there is nothing in the nature of sensations that makes the simultaneous having of a diverse variety of them difficult to imagine or problematical. But emotions are not simply sensations. Since emotions are essentially constituted by certain relevant thoughts (Neu 1977), perhaps we can give emotional opposition a sense in terms of the relation of the constituent beliefs and other thoughts.

Pride is often said to be the opposite of humility. But opposition, insofar as it suggests incompatibility, does not seem to capture their relation. Certainly one can be proud of one thing and humble about another, but even focusing on a single feature or aspect of oneself, one may be proud yet also humble about it (proud of one's cooking, yet humbly recognizing that there are many whose cooking is better). Shame seems a stronger candidate for the opposite of pride, at least so far as incompatibility is the issue. Again, of course, one can be proud of one thing yet ashamed of another, or proud of a given object in one respect yet ashamed in another. But to be both proud and ashamed of the same thing in the same way simultaneously does seem problematical. The underlying beliefs seem to conflict. Pride is characterized by the belief that something related to oneself is valuable or reflects well on oneself, while shame is characterized by the belief that something related to oneself is bad or inferior and discredits or lessens one. The conflict of beliefs readily amounts to contradiction.

Is the emotional opposition of love and hate grounded in their constitutive beliefs? Is our ambivalence best understood as a tendency to have different, indeed incompatible, beliefs—rather as with self-deception? But it is not obvious that love, in particular, is characterized by an essential belief. There may be certain ideals of love that require certain specific beliefs about the object, but love in general is not thought to require reasons (indeed, the citation of particular reasons can quickly come to seem like the bringing in of ulterior motives, motives that cast doubt on the description of the psychological state as love). Even supposing that particular beliefs essential to love and hate could be specified, does that make their opposition amount to conflict of beliefs, that is, to contradiction and incompatibility? Certainly we can both love and hate the same person. That is a common, if not the normal, condition. Insofar as that is because people are mixed bags, so we love them in one respect and hate them in others, the situation seems wholly unproblematical. (It becomes problematical when one engages in splitting, so that one denies one's feelings are in fact mixed feelings directed toward a single object or person.) One may love someone who is generous (loving them insofar as they are generous), and yet hate them insofar as they are abusive or possessive. Even focusing on a particular characteristic of the beloved, we can make sense of mixed feelings by bringing in external relations or divided interests in ourselves (e.g., we may both hate and love persons for their beauty, because while their beauty is attractive to us it may also be attractive to others and so become the grounds of painful jealousy). The more interesting question, however, is the one we started with, the question of whether we can hate a person for the very reason that we love them, indeed, hate them because we love them?

We have seen in our earlier discussion that the answer seems to be yes. If, for example, love brings dependence and dependence is hateful, a kind of bondage, or even just fearful, creating risk and danger, then love may well bring hate naturally in its train. This was an argument pursued by Hegel and by Sartre. What sense does it leave to the opposition of love and hate? Unlike the opposition of pride and shame, it cannot be a matter of a conflict between the relevant beliefs—at least not if such conflict amounts to contradiction. For even were the beliefs specifiable, the conflict would not amount to contradiction. One cannot simultaneously and with full awareness maintain contradictory beliefs. But one can (as Catullus assures us) maintain love and hate toward a single object at the same time. Perhaps the opposition is not in the beliefs, but in the constituent desires. When Hume analyzes love and hate along with the other emotions as peculiar and distinctive sensations ("impressions of reflection") he explicitly denies that their characteristic desires are essential: "If nature had so pleas'd, love might have had the same effect as hatred, and hatred as love. I see no contradiction in supposing a desire of producing misery annex'd to love, and of happiness to hatred" (1888 [1739], 2: 368). But in fact an apparent love would be rejected as love if we discovered that at the center of the passion was a wish for harm to the putative beloved. We would say the feeling was ambivalent or redescribe the situation in terms of the subject's beliefs (e.g., that the "harm" was not harm in his eyes). While particular beliefs may not be essential to love and hate, particular types of desires may well be. And if that is so, it is in terms of their relation that we can understand what we mean when we describe the love and hate as opposites. And it is important to see that opposition understood in terms of desire is rather different from opposition in terms of belief. While incompatible beliefs may be contradictory, so that they cannot be simultaneously and self-consciously maintained, incompatible desires need not "contradict" each other and can be simultaneously and self-consciously maintained (Williams 1973b). That is, incompatibility of desires typically amounts to the fact that they cannot be mutually satisfied. But that is rather different from the situation in which two beliefs cannot both be true. I may have many desires that cannot be simultaneously satisfied (I may wish both to eat and to sleep, or to buy both of two objects when I only have money enough for one), that is the typical position for most people most of the time. It does not follow that one of the conflicting desires, like one of two conflicting beliefs, must yield. It can persist, be maintained, even if it cannot be satisfied. This difference in the nature of conflicting beliefs and desires has important consequences in psychoanalysis. Freud indicated to his patients early on that "much will be gained if we succeed in transforming your hysterical misery into common unhappiness" (1895d, SE 2: 305). When a desire is unacknowledged, its unconscious functioning can produce neurotic symptoms. Making the unconscious desires conscious does not guarantee their satisfaction: there may in fact be good reason not to act on them or circumstances may not allow it or, as in the normal condition, they may conflict with other desires. But at least once made conscious one should be freed from the additional suffering produced by the emergence of unconscious desires in symptomatic form. Once desires are conscious, one is in a position to deal with them as one does with any conflicting desires, weighing alternatives and seeking opportunities for appropriate satisfaction, though one remains subject to the ordinary unhappiness that conflicting desires may bring. Thus, while there is hope, overcoming emotional ambivalence is not so simple as pointing out an intellectual conflict of beliefs and insisting that (as reason demands) one be abandoned.

While love and hate are doubtless opposites, there is no reason to think their opposition or emotional opposition in general has a single sense, any more than that psychological conflict in general has a single explanation. Pride and shame, which (unlike love and hate) require contrasting beliefs, also (like love and hate) are typically tied to contrasting desires and inclinations to action. Pride flaunts. Shame seeks to hide. The role of evaluations in all this is not straightforward, for evaluations can involve complex mixtures of desire and belief. Can one desire only the good? Socrates thought so, as perhaps did Mill (for rather different reasons). Yet we can understand Milton's Satan when he declares, "Evil be thou my good" (*Paradise Lost*, bk. 4, l.108).

Loving: Counting the Ways

While considering what we mean by saying two emotions are "opposite," by direction in emotions, I have too often been oversimplifying by speaking as though love and hate are not internally complex, and as though we all agree in ascribing a single clear meaning to each. While we use a single word in English, we nonetheless distinguish different types of love in terms of their objects and aims (e.g., family love, erotic love, love in friendship), and other languages employ different words for some of these.[15] And, as noted, the literature of love reveals no end to the different conceptions of the concept.[16] There have, however, been significant efforts at unification. Plato unified some of the forms of love in terms of a broad notion of desire (*eros*) and a narrow notion of egotistic motives. While Freud distinguished a separate affectionate current in love relations, he attributed great importance to what he called the sensual current (*libido*), and found it widely present—in particular in infantile development, family relations, and the sublimated forms of higher cultural activity (from science to art to making and hoarding money). But whatever the persuasiveness of the efforts at unification, erotic desire is itself internally divided. This is especially clear if one follows Plato in thinking of desire in terms of lack. So far as the desirability of the love object derives from its lack, so far as it reveals the insufficiency and limits of the self, and so far as the history of displacement leading to the current object in turn leads to dissatisfaction, the tension and pain of erotic desire are part of its nature.

I have said it is simply not the case that love is uniformly pleasant and hate uniformly painful. I think that is true. But perhaps it is not *simply* true. Emotions are not simple sensations. Really, when we are ascribing an emotion to ourselves, we are giving an interpretation of complexes of sensation, desire, behavior, thought, and much else. To ascribe love or hate is not to describe a sensation, it is to summarize many inner and outer perceptions, their context, and our individual and social understandings. As a consequence, the "directions" or relations of emotions as apparently simple as love and hate are also complex.[17] As a further consequence, trying to draw sharp lines between these and other emotions on the basis of linguistic usage is not likely to get us very far in understanding their relationship. For example: We tend to spend more time with those we love, providing more occasions for possible irritation, and so anger. Anger can be distinguished from hatred (it tends to be more focused on particular wrongs or slights, rather than on the whole person; the desires involved are more typically for retribution or revenge than for destruction, and anger generally does not require or generate the sort of intimacy hatred seems to—though these differences, like differences of intensity, may be matters of degree); nonetheless, occasions for anger can aggregate into sources of hatred. But we should not put too much weight on this point. First, because any distinctions we make between anger and hatred can be no more firm than the best psychological theory available to us. Linguistic habits do not alone suffice; after all, as often as not, "hate" is used as equivalent to "dislike," as in "I hate eggplant." And, secondly, because it overcivilizes our attitudes. As Freud says, "When . . . hostility is directed against people who are otherwise loved we describe it as ambivalence of feeling; and we explain the fact, in what is probably far too rational a manner, by means of the numerous occasions for conflicts of interest which arise precisely in such intimate relations" (1921c, *SE* 18. 102).

Love and hate are not social equals. We readily accept that we love, we do not so readily accept that we hate. Thus hate is more often suppressed and repressed. Love has all the time in the world. Hate, we think, must give way. When in love, we desire to keep on desiring. We do not want our state to change. We have no standard way to think our way from love to hate. Religion makes it its business to think a way from hate to love, to offer a path through atonement, forgiveness, and mercy.[18] But, as we have seen, love and hate come already mixed in the nature of erotic desire. Erotic love is not selfless, it desires its own satisfaction. It disturbs equanimity, lifting and troubling the spirit at the same time. Eros, in our imagination and experience, is "bittersweet." And this may have its value; as Blake insisted: "Without contraries is no progression. Attraction and repulsion, reason and energy, love and hate, are necessary to human existence" ("The Marriage of Heaven and Hell," 2: 7–9).

To retrace some of our steps briefly: That we should hate people we love because they abuse or betray us presents no mystery. After all, people are mixed bags and so there is no problem about loving them in some respects while hating them in others. The interesting question is why we should hate people precisely because we love them (presuming even that they love us back, that it is not unrequited love). Part of the answer, I think, is that love brings with it dependence, and so vulnerability and risk; we naturally come to resent those we love *because* we love them, because it makes us dependent. The next, deeper, question is why or whether dependence should be thought of as hateful (rather than merely risky). So far as our identities are at stake in love, death enters the picture and helps make extreme fear (which so often functions as a source of hate) intelligible. The naturalness of ambivalent love and hate may thus connect with problems of self-identity. Added to this the dividedness of the self itself (including instinctual dualism and other forms of mixed desire) and the inherent dividedness of love and other primal emotions (which may have its origins in the history of loving but persists in later development and gets complicated as other features are added by experience and varying ideals of love) make emotional ambivalence a natural manifestation of inner conflict.

What might have seemed a puzzle in our emotional lives, that we also hate those we love, is no accident; indeed—frightening thought—it may be inevitable. When it comes to love, as Freud teaches, the normal is pathological. The logic of emotional identification explored by Spinoza, the dialectic of the rivalrous desires to be free and to be loved explored by Sartre, as well as the history and dynamics of our conflictual life at our boundaries explored by Freud, lead to the ambivalence of love and hate. But then the other side of Freud's insight, that the normal is pathological, is that the pathological is normal. This should be some comfort.

6

BORING FROM WITHIN

Endogenous versus Reactive Boredom

Life, friends, is boring. We must not say so.
After all, the sky flashes, the great sea yearns,
we ourselves flash and yearn,
and moreover my mother told me as a boy
(repeatingly) 'Ever to confess you're bored
means you have no

Inner Resources.' I conclude now I have no
inner resources, because I am heavy bored.
Peoples bore me,
literature bores me, especially great literature . . .
(John Berryman 1969, "Dream Song 14")

Was Berryman's mother right? Is all boredom from within? The question is in fact ambiguous. Whether or not there should always be an internal cure for boredom, there is a separate question of whether the source of boredom is itself always internal (and yet a further question of whether self-generated emotions should be regarded as pathological by virtue of their source). Mrs. Berryman may have been more concerned with cure than source. Causal treatments, treatments that get at the root of a problem, must depend on the nature of the problem, in particular its source, but symptomatic treatments come from wherever they come from and work whenever they work. The two questions are, however, surely related, for the effectiveness of inner resources in overcoming a problem may depend on just what it is that needs to be overcome. Does the world or the person, life or attitude, need to change in order to overcome boredom? Is all boredom from within?

First, what is boredom? Saul Bellow, in his novel *Humboldt's Gift* (1975), has a character begin a series of reflections on boredom pleased at having in the past stayed away from problems of definition: "I didn't want to get mixed up with theological questions about *accidie* and *tedium vitae.*" But it isn't long before we find the same character saying: "Suppose then that you began with the proposition that boredom was a kind of pain caused by unused powers, the pain of wasted possibilities or talents, and was accompanied by expectations of the optimum utilization of capacities." That is not at all bad as a start. In fact, the notion of "a kind of pain caused by unused powers" is quite close to psychoanalytic definitions of boredom as a state of instinctual tension in which the instinctual aims and objects are repressed (Fenichel 1953 [1934] and Greenson 1953). Such an approach can be illuminating.

Greenson (1953) is especially helpful on the feeling of emptiness characteristic of much boredom. One experiences

> a combination of instinctual tension and a vague feeling of emptiness. The instinctual tension is without direction due to the inhibition of thoughts and fantasies. Tension and emptiness is felt as a kind of hunger—stimulus hunger. Since the individual does not know for what he is hungry, he now turns to the external world, with the hope that it will provide the missing aim and/or object. (19–20).

With the aim and object of desire repressed, only a feeling of emptiness remains; as Greenson penetratingly puts it, "we are dealing here with the substitution of a sensation for a fantasy" (16). Because of repression of aims and objects, there is in boredom a tension with no means of resolution. The feeling of emptiness combined with unresolved tension creates a feeling of hunger, or a need to satisfy an oral fixation. This is why boredom is commonly dealt with by eating, drinking, or smoking. Greenson describes a woman patient suffering from extreme boredom, unable to find or even imagine objects worth having: "Even in masturbation the patient would get bored because she had 'nothing to think about'" (11). While an absence of fantasies is a useful way of thinking about boredom, it is no use to think one can overcome boredom simply by conjuring up fantasies and desires. The frantic pursuit of excitement is generally unsatisfying. Greenson speaks of having the "wrong" fantasies (19). What this means is that satisfaction requires that desires be attached to their "true" objects. To make sense of this notion one must have, I think, a theory of human needs. (This is not a criticism. Psychoanalysis seeks to provide such a theory.) But imagination faces another obstacle, for it can play a double role in relation to boredom. On the one hand, it is one of those inner resources that may free one from or at least alleviate boredom, offering if not the "true" objects of desire at least alternatives to distract one's attention from present unappealing objects. On the other hand, imagination can also sometimes serve as a source of boredom when it brings one to see what one is doing at the moment or in one's life as a whole as but one of a number of alternatives, and an alternative less desirable or interesting than the others. One way of thinking of women's liberation (of the consciousness-raising kind) is as offering the enlightenment of boredom: getting women to see activities that they might have accepted as inevitable as really just imposed social roles that are in fact far less interesting than the alternative roles that have been made socially unavailable. The politically touchy issue is whether those who would bring enlightenment about the range of possibilities also mean to insist that women *should* feel bored or otherwise unfulfilled if they go on to choose as a matter of preference the activities and roles that had previously been simply imposed upon them. This too requires a theory of real human needs.

Returning to the main theme, the notion of repressed objects is additionally useful because it suggests a ready way to distinguish boredom from apathy or depression: if boredom can be thought of as centrally involving desire without an object, then depression can be understood as centrally involving an absence of desire. In boredom, one wants to do something, but doesn't know what. In depression, one feels will-less.

Still, the psychoanalytic understanding of boredom in terms of instinctual tension and repressed objects, despite its many advantages, is insufficiently specific, for all neuroses involve such repression, and it is so far left unclear why every neurotic is not bored. Without searching for further refinement, however, the contrast with depression mentioned a moment ago brings to mind a similarity between boredom and depression that in turn suggests another kind of limitation of the original definition. Depression is standardly distinguished into two types, depending on its believed sources. There is *endogenous depression* ("sadness without cause" [Jackson 1986, 315–17]), which arises somehow from within and comes to color the external world, and there is *reactive depression*, which begins as a response to particular events in the external world, such as the loss of a loved one. Similarly, there is boredom from within, which tends to color the whole of life, and there is reactive boredom, which seems to arise as a response to more particular objects.

The psychoanalytic approach tends to ignore reactive boredom. Consider Greenson's account. Defining *boredom* as "instinctual tension . . . without direction due to the inhibition of thoughts and fantasies" (19), and believing this state of affairs "characteristic for all boredom" (20), Greenson goes on to treat any attempt to place the source of boredom in the external world as a defensive maneuver, as denial. "Another aspect of the denial can be seen in the readiness of bored persons to describe situations and people as boring rather than to acknowledge that the bored feeling is within. 'It bores me,' is more ego syntonic than 'I am bored.' When one is bored even the most exciting events can be felt as boring" (17). This fits well with Berryman's mother's diagnosis.

Denial doubtless occurs. And the more widespread the individual's claim that external things are boring, the more plausible the suggestion that the failure is internal. But surely sometimes things *are* boring and being bored is an appropriate reaction. The philosopher Bernard Williams puts this strongly: "Just as being bored can be a sign of not noticing, understanding or appreciating enough, so equally not being bored can be a sign of not noticing, or not reflecting, enough" (1973d, 95). Williams's remark comes in the course of an argument that certain forms of repetition carried on long enough are necessarily boring. That argument may be in a variety of ways problematical, but surely a person watching Andy Warhol's movie *Sleep* who fails to be bored simply isn't paying attention. (For those unfamiliar with it, that 1963 movie consists of eight interminable hours of a fixed shot of a man sleeping. *Empire*, a 1965 Warhol film, offers a similarly endless shot of the Empire State Building.) Some things, one wants to say, are objectively boring.

"It Bores Me"

How is one to determine in a particular case whether an individual's boredom is reactive or endogenous? Obviously, whether boredom is regarded as reactive or endogenous depends on whether a feature of the object or of the person is thought to explain the state. But doesn't a reaction of boredom *always* depend on the particular person? Was John Berryman's mother perhaps right? Is all boredom from within, a sign of lack of inner resources? For it might be true that whatever the external circumstances, an appropriate shifting of attention or marshaling of internal interests should save one from boredom. But the fact that one might in certain circumstances *need* to be saved itself suggests that boredom can have an external source (even if an internal cure should always be available). What sort of features of an object are liable to cause boredom, and can they be regarded as "objective" rather than dependent on the individual's attitude (so once again blurring the line between reactive and endogenous boredom)?

Sometimes too little happens in too much time.[1] (The German word for boredom is *Langeweile*, literally "long while"—as frequently observed, time passes slowly when it is not filled with gripping events.) That is the problem with the proverbial "watching the grass grow" or the Warhol movies mentioned. The mind is given too little material to work on or to react to. Of course, diverting attention is one way to avoid boredom when the would-be object of attention is, as one might put it, "objectively boring," but the problem in the object is not thereby diminished. We are in the presence of Bellow's "pain caused by unused powers," and the problem here has an external source.

Certainly repetition can be boring. Kierkegaard wrote a rather boring book with that title (*Repetition*, 1843), and his lighthearted discussion of "The Rotation Method" in *Either/Or* (1843), which asserts that "boredom is the root of all evil" (indeed, of everything, for "The gods were bored, and so they created man" [282]), finds the cure in change (of a special sort: limited and so inventive and intense—one must not forget that empty stimulation and novelty can be boring too; that was the problem of Greenson's patient with the tiresome affairs and the "wrong" fantasies). But repetition itself need not be bad. Nietzsche reminds us of the possibility of a hopeful, even accepting and joyous response to that metaphysical extreme of repetition, eternal recurrence (1974 [1882], *The Gay Science* §341). Still, it must be admitted, Nietzsche's point has to do with the moral weight of the idea of recurrence, not the *experience* of repetition (indeed, each recurrence, being just the same as the others, bears no marks of being a recurrence).[2] Children often find repetition desirable. They often want stories endlessly repeated in exactly the same way. (Just as dogs seem willing to go on fetching sticks long after the game has lost interest for the person playing it with them.) This is a point not overlooked by Freud in his consideration of the repetition compulsion in *Beyond the Pleasure Principle*, where he notes that adults by contrast crave novelty (1920g, 18: 35). But Freud's main concern is the repetition compulsion in relation to the death instinct, the repetition of painful experiences. It is not so puzzling that children should want to have their pleasurable experiences repeated (though that "they are inexorable in their insistence that the repetition shall be an identical one" may suggest that even such repetition can be seen as a defense against anxiety, an effort at mastery, an assertion of a kind of control); it is more difficult to understand why we keep putting our tongues into the cavities in our teeth to test whether they still hurt, when we know they will. But leaving compulsions aside, even adults can find repetition desirable in the appropriate circumstances. What circumstances? What makes for meaningful repetition rather than monotonous dullness?

We have all heard boring lectures (perhaps even given some), and even if we have not seen Warhol's *Sleep*, we have all seen boring movies or read boring books. But monotony is not by itself sufficient to explain the boredom, or monotony should always lead to boredom. But it doesn't. Repetitious prayers are meaningful for many. Chanting and meditation can produce ecstasy. (Perhaps even less patterned forms of "too little happening in too much time" can be experienced as freeing the mind from distractions and so as an aid to inner peace.) And endurance athletes seem able to engage in marathon runs or long-distance swims without getting bored. Or should we rather say that they tolerate the boredom for the sake of some further end? (When some athletes say, however, that they value a daily dose of "boredom," they may actually mean something else—perhaps what they value is "tranquillity" or "absence of stimulation." It may be that "boredom" as such is necessarily painful and undesirable. But then there may be more varieties of masochism than found in the usual catalogues.) And monotony may in any case not be "objective," it may itself lie in the eye of the beholder. Certainly variety can be experienced as monotonous, "always the same," at least by those (like the Italian poet Leopardi) so disposed.

Whether repetition, even monotonous repetition, produces boredom may be relative to one's interests. A person sufficiently interested in the content of an otherwise boring lecture may be able to focus on the content rather than its pace or the monotone in which it is delivered. Or a shift of attention may do the trick, as in Kierkegaard's example of the philosophical bore with fascinating habits of perspiration while talking:

> There was a man whose chatter certain circumstances made it necessary for me to listen to. At every opportunity he was ready with a little philosophical lecture, a very tiresome harangue. Almost in despair, I suddenly discovered that he perspired copiously when talking. I saw the pearls of sweat gather on his brow, unite to form a stream, glide down his nose, and hang at the extreme point of his nose in a drop-shaped body. From the moment of making this discovery, all was changed. I even took pleasure in inciting him to begin his philosophical instruction, merely to observe the perspiration on his brow and at the end of his nose. (1959 [1843], 295)

But then, can one shift interests at will? Can one choose or create "arbitrary" interests? This is not quite the same as shifting attention at will. (We are getting closer to the nature of the inner resources Mrs. Berryman wished to call upon—resources of attention, self-motivation, imagination, and perhaps tranquillity.)

Even supposing one could shift interests at will (certainly one can at least cultivate them over time), how much could one change and still be the "same" person? This is a concern of Bernard Williams in his discussion of the Makropulos case, which centers on the story of a woman in a Capek play who had lived 300 years (at the constant age of 42) and ultimately decides to end her own otherwise eternal life because immortality leaves her bored, indifferent, and cold: "In the end it is the same, singing and silence" (1973d, 82). Williams wishes to argue that immortal life would necessarily be boring, basically because (in terms of the immediate case) "everything that could happen and make sense to one particular human being of 42 had already happened to her" (90). He assumes a relatively fixed character, and the assumption has a certain point. That one will be able to see more baseball games is not a reason for a person who hates baseball to live longer, and it is not entirely clear from what point of view an assurance that one would come to like baseball ought to be judged. Nonetheless, repetition is not necessarily always objectionable. People seem to enjoy having sex over and over again, even in the same way with the same person. And character can (and does) develop without the changes destroying an identity of concern. But without pressing issues of variation of character and stability of identity, are there objective goods that can motivate a desire to go on living (because they become the object of what Williams calls "unconditional" or "categorical" desires, that is, desires one has that are not dependent on the question of whether one will be alive)? To be objective, must they be universal? Are some things objectively good, objectively desirable in a way that makes life (interestingly, joyfully, or merely dutifully) worth living? And again, are some things objectively bad in a way that makes them intolerably boring, killing any interest in them if not in life?

Certainly it is a fact that different people react differently to the same external objects. But must a reaction to an object be universal in order to say the object causes it? After all, not everyone exposed to the tubercle bacillus falls ill. One's immune system doubtless plays a role in determining the result. Nonetheless, we can safely say the tubercle bacillus "causes" tuberculosis. And objects have colors even if some don't see them—which is not to deny that what colors one sees depends on one's individual apparatus for perception. Finally, and most relevantly, we can make sense of reactive depression though it also depends on internal (one could call them "subjective") factors, such as love for a person who has died or perhaps initial low self-esteem. We always pick out "the" cause from a multiplicity of causal factors, our explanatory or other concerns providing the grounds for picking out one from among the many necessary conditions as crucial. That something is boring may be a feature of it, a feature that explains, and is revealed by, its producing boredom in us.[3] Boredom provides one of our categories for evaluating experience—as does, perhaps more familiarly in philosophical discussions, "goodness." Insistence on a contrast between "objective" and "subjective" features may not ultimately be helpful in understanding the difference between reactive and endogenous boredom. (And we may in the end have to say something similar about the contrast between "particular" and "general" objects, the difference between being bored by something in particular and, like the grown-up John Berryman, finding life boring.)

The Good, the Bad, the Boring

The history of the philosophical understanding of the word "good" is instructive. "Good" is perhaps our most general and indeterminate term of evaluation, for things, experiences, actions, and even persons taken as a whole. Plato and many others have treated it as an almost perceptible quality of the objects evaluated. Plato understood that quality (in accordance with his general theory of meaning and value) in terms of an objective standard to be found in a supersensible Idea or Form of Goodness in which particular things in the observable world could be seen to "participate" (in different degrees). Leaving behind supersensible worlds, G. E. Moore (1903) early in this century treated "goodness" as a directly recognizable but simple and so indefinable property, like yellow. Another philosophical tradition has treated the application of the word "good" as an expression of individual and highly variable emotional responses. Spinoza argued that to call something good was to record the fact that one found it pleasant, and that to call something bad was to say one found it unpleasant or painful: "insofar as we perceive that a thing affects us with Joy or Sadness, we call it good or evil" (1985 [1677], *Ethics* 4 P8). Also in this line, in this century, A. J. Ayer (1936) and other so-called "emotivists" insisted that to call something good is little more than to say "I like it," a way of expressing one's (ethical) feelings and perhaps arousing similar feelings in others. In neither of these sorts of objectivist or subjectivist accounts of goodness are there definitive criteria of goodness, though there may be empirical concomitants of the characteristic, and proof or argument about value (about ends) becomes mysterious. Here as elsewhere the simply contrasting categories of objective and subjective may obscure more than illuminate.

Perhaps the most plausible understanding of the meaning of "good," at least as it functions in moral argument and deliberation, can be found by going back to Aristotle. As Stuart Hampshire has summarized it, "when we praise, and reflectively criticize, things of various kinds, the more or less vague criteria of our judgment are ultimately derived from the normal, or standard, interests that things of this kind have for us" (1972b, 82). The relevant criteria depend on the particular kind of thing evaluated and the interests such things are designed, or meant, or taken to serve. So one may or may not be interested in clocks, but to call a clock good is to say it serves the function of a clock (i.e., it tells time) well. Normal human interests help provide the relevant criteria. Of course, we can also reflectively evaluate human interests and try to set some order or priority among them—and the criteria for this are neither fixable *a priori* nor even necessarily consistent with each other (all good things may not be compatible). This does not reduce such evaluations to reiterations of present interests, purposes, and pleasures, nor does it leave them to rest in intuitive insight into the value of things. We can and do argue intelligently about how to live and what matters.

Boredom also has a history.[4] The first citations of *boredom* and *boring* in the *Oxford English Dictionary* are surprisingly late, from the mid-nineteenth century; and *bore*, in the relevant sense, does not appear till the mid-eighteenth century, and then it is first defined as "the malady of *ennui*, supposed to be specifically 'French,' as 'the spleen' was supposed to be English; a fit of ennui or sulks; a dull time." In fact, one could argue boredom was invented by the French in the nineteenth century, at least in that special form of weariness known even in English as "ennui." (Perhaps Rousseau having almost single-handedly invented sincerity in the eighteenth century, it was only to be expected. Baudelaire, Stendhal, Flaubert, et al. were Rousseau's children.) Certainly weariness, melancholy, spleen, dullness, apathy, listlessness, tedium, and the like have always had a place in human life, but the specific forms of detachment and sadness, the nature and understanding of that which holds or rivets attention and that which deadens passion and desire, are culturally shaped and expressed (different languages even provide distinctive vocabularies, including *taedium vitae*, *Weltschmerz*, and *mal du siècle* to describe the related, but different, conditions). *Acedia*, the special form of psychic exhaustion, sloth, and spiritual dejection suffered by medieval monks, had its character and place because of a constellation of beliefs and a set of associated social structures (Wenzel 1960). The aristocratic *ennui* of the French authors who have made their desolate and alienated mood a part of modern consciousness depends on a rather different set of circumstances and attitudes. Their "laments and loud yawns" (Peyre 1974, 29) may have emerged partly in response to the disappointments of the revolutions of 1848 in Europe and partly in response to the ever increasing embourgeoisement of society, but whatever the explanation, their despair and gloom is now often ours. Their writing has given us a way of conceiving and so experiencing disappointing lives in a disappointing world. Some would equate the Romantic and post-Romantic concept of *ennui* with the *acedia* of the early Christian ascetics, and certainly there are similarities (Kuhn 1976, 42, 53, 55), but the modern sensibility remains in some ways distinctive. Not the least of the differences between the religious torpor of the heart and modern estrangement is to be found in the sufferer's self-understanding. While both cases may seem to an observer to be independent of external circumstances, and in that sense endogenous, the religious sufferer thinks of himself as in a state of sin: his dejection, his loss of interest and joy, his sluggishness are thought of as personal faults. The sophisticated sufferer from *ennui* tends to think of his anguish, of the fog that descends between desire and life, as the fault of the world, especially of the established order. If the world is felt to have lost meaning, the inner emptiness is experienced as a response to a failure in the world. It does not come up to expectations. Whether the resultant state should be regarded as reactive or endogenous may thus depend on what one thinks we have a right to expect.

And so may whether the state should be regarded as pathological. Suppose one lived in a drab, gray society, say of the kind that typified Stalinist Eastern Europe not so long ago. Might not endemic boredom be the natural reaction? Societal change seems a more appropriate (and effective) remedy than individual therapy. Nonetheless, falling into desiring nothing, expecting nothing, can be a self-defeating reaction in the end indistinguishable from a self-generated despair. Of course modern boredom does not take the form only of "ennui." The mechanization of production came tied to a mechanization of life, and so made problematic the point of repetitious human activity. Why do anything more than once? But the industrial worker, Charlie Chaplin's man-as-cog in the film *Modern Times*, does not suffer from "ennui"—*that* requires sophistication and world-weariness.[5]

And one should not make the mistake of thinking that even a less pervasive reactive boredom must always be a relatively benign and passing state.
It can lead to or mask impotent rage (it may look like patient waiting), and
that rage can burst out in explosive aggression or implode in suicidal despair. That the boredom is in a sense imposed by external circumstances
and their constraints does not make the state any less devastating and destructive.

Williams writes of EM that she had been at life too long, that "her trouble was it seems, boredom" (1973d, 90). Would it be more accurate to say of
EM that she was depressed rather than (reactively) bored? She seems to
have run out of desires (at least the sort of categorical desires that make life
worth living), and lack of desires seems closer to depression than boredom.
In reactive boredom there is typically something else one would rather be
doing. Her reaction was to the whole world.

Still, the problem remains that it may be a mistake to think the standard
of health can be simply assumed. The appropriateness of an attachment to
life as opposed to an overwhelming feeling of nothingness or of the vanity
of ordinary pursuits may be more a matter for metaphysical disputation
than clinical resolution. (The doctors, of course, must not think this.)

Pathology and the Inner

Even psychoanalysts occasionally acknowledge that boredom can be "normal" or, as Fenichel (1953 [1934]) also puts it, "innocent":

> It arises when we must not do what we want to do, or must do what we
> do not want to do . . . In pathological boredom [something expected]
> fails to occur because the subject represses his instinctual action out of
> anxiety; in normal boredom it fails to occur because the nature of the
> real situation does not permit of the expected de-tension . . . One
> should not forget that we have *the right to expect* some "aid to discharge"
> from the external world. If this is not forthcoming, we are, so to speak,
> justifiably bored. (301)

The familiar boredom of young children (the plaintive "I'm bored, what
should I do now?") is also not pathological even though it arguably comes
from within. It is more like a pervasive mood than a response to anything
in particular. (More mature *ennui* is also typically a mood rather than a reactive and transient emotion. Neither is simply a sensation. They have and
give meaning to experience.) The child is waiting for desire to crystallize,
and asks help from outside. "Experiencing a frustrating pause in his usually mobile attention and absorption, the bored child quickly becomes preoccupied by his lack of preoccupation" (Phillips 1993, 69). Adam Phillips
usefully suggests that for a child such frustration need not mark merely an
incapacity, but an opportunity, an occasion for it to take its time to discover

its real interests, part of a needed "period of hesitation" in order to become more self-assured. As he puts it, "the capacity to be bored can be a developmental achievement for the child" (69).

When we grow up, we are supposed of course to know (more or less) what we want, but the world can frustrate us in our desires, and we may react to that frustration in a variety of ways, including boredom. How much we are entitled to expect of the world is of course disputable. If we expect too much, we may be condemned to *ennui*. (And if we expect too little, joy does not necessarily follow.) If we fail to become clear about what we want, like Greenson's patient, the restless feeding of our stimulus hunger will not overcome our boredom. If everything is boring, either because of excessive expectations or uncertain desires, our state might seem clearly pathological. Certainly it is painful (and so, on Spinoza's account, bad). What kind of pain? Bellow (1975) has suggested an answer: "a kind of pain caused by unused powers." *Pleasure is a form of attention; boredom is a failure of attention.* Whether the failure is caused by a feature of the object or situation or alternatively by some internal problem or attitude is what makes for the distinction between reactive and endogenous boredom. But what makes an attitude wrong or pathological, when is the problem the individual's and when is it the world's? What it means for the face of the world to smile on us cannot be determined by statistical inquiry; the metaphysics of individual happiness and meaningfulness is more complex than that. So, once again the quest for an understanding of boredom makes one feel the need for a larger theory of human nature, an understanding of the cycles of desire and fulfillment, of pleasure and attention.

Freud in "Mourning and Melancholia" remarks that, "although mourning involves grave departures from the normal attitude to life, it never occurs to us to regard it as a pathological condition and to refer it to medical treatment . . . It is really only because we know so well how to explain it that this attitude does not seem to us pathological" (1917e, 14: 243–44). Where the object of someone else's boredom seems to us too without interest, whether because of monotony or other features, we accept the reaction as normal. Where the object of the boredom is everything, we must wonder about the source of the attitude. But however painful the situation, it is not clear that we can choose to have or not have such attitudes nor is it clear how one is to judge their correctness. Freud observes, "In mourning it is the world that has become poor and empty; in melancholia it is the ego itself" (1917e, 14: 246). Adam Phillips remarks: "And in boredom, we might add, it is both" (1993, 72). To find the world full of interest, there must be an interested, a desiring and alive, self. What is worth wanting? This is not simply a medical question.

For Spinoza the primary affects, out of which all others are constituted, are pleasure, pain, and desire (all to be understood in his special senses). For the unfortunate Leopardi, pleasure, pain, and boredom are the basic passions. Black despair, *noia,* is pervasive: "All the intervals of human life between pleasures and displeasures are occupied by ennui" (Leopardi quoted in Kuhn 1976, 280).

To retrace some steps: It might seem that in order to make a distinction between reactive and endogenous boredom, one needs a notion of the objectively boring, and that to be objective a characteristic must be uniform if not universal in its effects. But if we understand by "reactive" something like "adequately explained by features of the object," then there is no need for a reaction to be universal in order for it to be recognized as a *reaction*. Indeed, either a very uncultivated or a very sophisticated person might be bored by something almost everyone else would find interesting, and we might all nonetheless recognize the emotion as a response to features of the object—while of course also recognizing that the response also depends on special features of the bored person. The uncultivated and the sophisticated are both bored, one because he notices and understands too little, the other because he notices and understands too much. Still the response would be adequately explained by features of the object, *given* the nature of the person (whose interests, we are supposing, are at least statistically not "normal"). Things would become different if they found *everything* boring, so features of particular objects were irrelevant. That would begin to seem like an extreme form of endogenous boredom, boredom from within. But can't one have a reaction to everything? Things seem, say, "always the same." Must the individual's nature at least allow for a spectrum of responses before we are prepared to say any particular response is adequately to be explained by features of the object, and so any boredom that appears is reactive? I don't see that there is any clear line to be drawn. An individual living in a lively and multicolored society might nonetheless find their life and their world drab and it is not obvious at what point we must say they are wrong, their perception distorted, and their boredom pathological. They are not getting what they want. What should they want?

What is interesting depends on what one desires. But then are desires simply given or are they criticizable and changeable? Certainly desires are modifiable and manipulable—much advertising is based on this fact. It aims to create and to shape desires. Desire can also be made to go away. People fight even addictions—there are a variety of conditioning and other techniques. The question is whether we can modify our own desires, not by self-alienated manipulation, but by reasoning about what is desirable and by the intelligent appreciation of experience. Education depends on that hope, as do self-education and self-development. Asking what is desirable (objectively?) and how we might come to desire it may be the best way to think about Berryman's claim that "Life, friends, is boring," the best way to confront Baudelaire's "monstre délicat" (1982 [1861], 184).

Freud concludes a discussion of "endogenous" versus "exogenous" factors in the causation of neurosis with the observation that "Psychoanalysis has warned us that we must give up the unfruitful contrast between external and internal factors, between experience and constitution, and has taught us that we shall invariably find the cause of the onset of neurotic illness in a particular psychical situation which can be brought about in a variety of ways" (1912c, 12: 238). He makes a similar point about innate disposition and accidental influences (infantile impressions) in shaping love and the erotic life (1912b, 12: 99n). The contrast of endogenous and exogenous may be equally false in the etiology of emotions in general. An understanding of pathology in the emotions cannot simply rely on internal causation as a criterion if it turns out that inner and outer factors are always in play. A different kind of theory is needed if the failure of attention in boredom, the "pain caused by unused powers," is not simply an issue of incapacity (whether attributed to lacking inner resources or an uninviting world, bad attitude or enforced inactivity) but a question of what is worthy of and what repays attention, a question of the "right" fantasies. Nonetheless, in cases of reactive boredom one typically does know what one would rather be doing. (Objects of desire are not pathologically repressed.) And perhaps that is enough to mark the crucial difference in ordinary life.

7

PRIDE AND IDENTITY

How is it that pride has gone from being one of the traditional seven deadly sins to becoming, in recent decades, the banner under which social movements have declared their objectives (Black Pride, Gay Pride, and so on)? How are we to understand the shift from a theology of sin to a politics of self-assertion (and an accompanying psychology of self-esteem)? Is it simply that times have changed? That, God having died, attitudes have changed—so that what once was thought to precede a fall now seems a condition of rising? Or is it perhaps that the nature of pride is to be understood differently in the two contexts? There may be an inherent ambiguity in pride: associating it on the one hand with arrogance, conceit, egotism, and vanity, and on the other hand with self-respect, self-esteem, self-confidence, dignity. (On certain readings, these may *all* be seen as different kinds or degrees of self-love.) Thus at different times, different aspects of the nature of the emotion come to be given prominence. Or is the difference in the objects? One place to start is with the recognition that the object, and the subject, of the traditional sin was the individual. The social movements that argue for pride are concerned with groups. How do individual and group identity come together in pride?

"We're Number One!"

"We're number one! We're number one!" It is the ecstatic chant of fans around the world when their sports team wins. The shout has gone up quite often in San Francisco in recent years from fans of the 49ers football team. But who exactly is the "we" that is claiming exalted status? It is most often not the players themselves. Their claim to victory and so status would seem straightforward enough. But what have the fans done to deserve credit? They have often watched the game (but is that necessary?) and cheered their heroes on to victory. Perhaps the cheers of encouragement do help (there is said to be a "home team advantage"). But if the watching is done through television, as it most often is, the cheers can hardly reach and so encourage the players. So the causal contribution of the ecstatic fans to victory may be minimal. But even where it is great, some would doubt that cheering itself is enough. The "49er Faithful" is a group of long-term fans who resent the Johnny-come-latelies who jump on the winning bandwagon to claim the 49ers as their own. After all, the Faithful had done their cheering and buying of merchandise during the many fallow years before a string of victories made the team so immensely popular. So is length of commitment a condition of group membership, and so credit for (subgroup) achievement? Is the motive of commitment relevant? Does it matter whether a fan decides to attach his or her good wishes to only winning teams or sticks (more or less consistently) to the home or nearest local team? Is identification with a winning team simply a matter of individual choice at all?

Surely some aspects of our identity are fixed independently of what we think or would like to think. Thus we can be embarrassed *by* something our parents say, where we might just be embarrassed *for* a stranger (such as an actor who forgets his lines on stage when we are in the audience). Thus also we can be ashamed of something our country does, even if we are part of a vocal minority that actively opposes the policy. (This was the situation of many Americans during the Vietnam War. [See Walsh 1970.]) For certain purposes, who we are is fixed by who others think we are. Their criteria are the relevant ones—though our endorsing and incorporating their perspective may also be crucial. (If we reject their perspective, we perhaps ought to be free of the consequent emotions.) If those around us take family membership to be determined by blood, and citizenship to be determined by place of birth or other factors not directly chosen or readily disavowable, then insofar as family membership or citizenship provides grounds for pride or shame, those emotions too can become independent of our actions and preferences.

Equally surely, some aspects of our identity depend on choices we make and allegiances we adopt. Sports fans are notably self-selecting—but as I have noted, there may be complications even there. The complications are especially obvious where the organization is more formal: joining an organization may be voluntary, but acceptance may be uncertain, and so membership may itself become a special source of pride. This is true for colleges, clubs, gangs, fraternities, and many other groups, including military organizations ("The Few, The Proud, The Marines"). Even where a voluntary choice is essential to group membership, and so to pride based on group membership, the reactions and other conditions placed on our choice by others may be equally essential.

But the complications of choice in relation to group membership and so individual identity are only a part of the picture. That they *are* a part of the picture, we should be clear, is due to the internal structure of pride. David Hume treats pride (like all passions) as a "simple and uniform impression" (*Treatise* 2: 277) that cannot be defined or analyzed into parts. Nonetheless, he manages to bring out some of what should be regarded as the conceptual conditions of pride (he himself mistakenly regarded them as simply causal conditions and consequences). His general scheme treats pride as a pleasure of self-approval, such "that all agreeable objects, related to ourselves, by an association of ideas and of impressions, produce pride, and disagreeable ones, humility" (*Treatise* 2: 290ff.; see Neu 1977, part 1). He includes *closeness to self* among the modifications or "limitations" to that scheme. According to Hume, the agreeable object must be *closely* related to ourselves (otherwise only "joy" and not pride is produced) and only to ourselves or at most to ourselves and a few others (hence the comparative and competitive nature of pride). Again, while Hume mistook these conceptual constraints for merely causal ones, a proper pride (here meaning a conceptually coherent pride, not necessarily a morally justified one) must indeed depend on a suitably valuable object being suitably related to one. For Hume, value was simply a matter of approval and disapproval, ultimately traceable to reactions of pleasure and pain. We shall see that the contemporary politics of pride must depend on a different notion of value and of what is valuable. And while individual identity was notoriously a special problem within Hume's narrowly empiricist philosophy of mind, tracing chains of credit back to a self must be problematic on any philosophy, at least so far as credit is taken to depend on group membership. Relation to self is a conceptual condition of pride, and closeness to self is, inevitably, open to complication and challenge.

Pride the Sin

Christian *pride* has some connections with classical *hubris* (and even Jewish *chutzpah*), but the Christian notion is wider than just insolence or defiance against the gods. Nonetheless, such defiance was what gave the sin its medieval preeminence. Pride was given first place (one might say, "pride of place") back in the seventh century in Gregory the Great's now-conventional list of seven deadly sins (Bloomfield 1952, 72–74). The arrogance of pride was for him the root of all evil, "the beginning of all sin" (Lyman 1978, 136). There is biblical ground for giving pride such primacy (Ecclesiaticus 10:15 in the Vulgate), though 1 Timothy 6:10 gives avarice the prize. (St. Thomas made one of his usual efforts to reconcile the texts [Bloomfield, 88]). Pride isolates and alienates from both God and society; it is a form of self-satisfied and self-sufficient withdrawal (Fairlie 1978, 42). For a medieval world committed to discipline, hierarchy, and corporate order, this made it particularly heinous. As Bloomfield puts it, pride "is the sin of rebellion against God, the sin of exaggerated individualism" (75).

The negative view of pride that has carried over to our more individualistic times picks up on the arrogance and error associated with the earlier notion, though a modifier is sometimes added to spell out the problem: *false* pride is explicitly seen as based on false beliefs, just as *overweening* pride is by definition excessive. Must pride by its very nature fall into error and excess?

Pride is, in part, a sin of judgment, an intellectual deviation, involving bias in favor of one's self. The bias is of course motivated, so the defect is not purely intellectual. Spinoza's definition captures this aspect of pride quite precisely: "Pride is thinking more highly of oneself than is just, out of love of oneself" (*Ethics* 3, Definitions of the Affects 28). The source of pride in self-love makes clear its link to self-esteem (understood in a sense that allows for excess), as Spinoza puts it: "Pride is an effect or property of Self-love. Therefore, it can also be defined as Love of oneself, or Self-esteem, insofar as it so affects a man that he thinks more highly of himself than is just." Oddly to the modern mind, Spinoza argues, "There is no opposite of this affect. For no one, out of hate, thinks less highly of himself than is just." But today's many self-help psychologies that insist on self-love and self-esteem as a precondition for a happy and effective life assume that failures of self-love are pervasive. Spinoza's argument actually depends on a rather special point: that if you think you cannot do something, you *therefore* cannot do it, certainly you will not try, and (however self-defeating) you therefore cannot be underestimating your abilities, for your estimate and your abilities are conceptually (in this negative direction) linked. Spinoza goes on to acknowledge a number of ways in which a person can think less highly of himself than is just and describes the relevant affect as "despondency" ("as Pride is born of Self-esteem, so Despondency is born of Humility," which is a form of sadness [Definition 29, Exp.]). Whatever the relation of pride and humility (is humility a virtue or simply an opposing error of judgment?) and of pride and shame (there are grounds for regarding them as true emotional, if not moral, opposites), we should not too quickly follow Spinoza in building error into our definition of pride. As a matter of modern usage, while pride may sometimes indeed be *false* and *overweening*, that we speak of *wounded* pride in connection with various forms of humiliation shows pride can also be a matter of dignity and self-respect. Similarly, Adam Smith remarks in his *The Theory of Moral Sentiments* (1969 [1759]): "We frequently say of a man that he is too proud, or that he has too much noble pride, ever to suffer himself to do a mean thing" (416). Spinoza himself tells us that "Self-esteem [sometimes the Latin is translated as "self-satisfaction," sometimes "self-approval," and is understood by many as what they mean by "pride"] is a Joy born of the fact that a man considers himself and his own power of acting" (Definition 25). He opposes such self-esteem to humility and tells us it "is really the highest thing we can hope for," so far as it arises from reason (*Ethics* 4, P52 Schol.). But that is not the point I wish to pursue here. I think we can now begin to see how an error of judgment can start looking like a sin in a God-centered world—at least when the error involves taking undeserved credit.

Spinoza picks up on Gregory the Great's vision of pride as bias in one's own favor, a tyranny of bad judgment: "it comes about that all the good things of others become displeasing to him, and the things he has done himself, even when they are mistaken, alone please him . . . he favours himself in his thought; and when he thinks he surpasses others in all things, he walks with himself along the broad spaces of his thought and silently utters his own praises" (*Moralia*, 24: 48, quoted in Payne 1960, 72–73). One might go further and think whatever praises are in fact due are due elsewhere, that when credit is traced to its ultimate source, pride in oneself is always misplaced.

Responsibility

One might think that responsibility should be a condition of pride—that, for example, pride should be for virtue and achievements rather than natural endowment and gifts. Responsibility in turn might be seen as conditioned on causal role or individual choice. (The relevant conditions depend on the various purposes one might have in allocating responsibility; and for certain purposes, e.g., legal ones, getting the conditions precisely right might be extremely important [Hart 1968].) But despite the many possible senses of "responsibility," responsibility is *not* a condition of pride. While there are conceptual constraints of other sorts on pride, there is no *conceptual* error in claiming to be proud where one cannot claim responsibility (whether one is proud of the 49ers, one's cultural heritage, one's parents, or one's height). If responsibility were a condition of pride, a politics of pride in group identity, where the characteristic defining group identity (whether skin color or sexual preference, ethnic or national origin) was not itself something deliberately chosen, would make no sense. The point of claiming such pride is different (and we shall return to it shortly), but it is worth lingering a moment longer on the temptation to condition pride on responsibility.

It might seem that, so far as group membership is dependent on factors outside of one's control, group membership cannot provide appropriate grounds for pride or, for that matter, for shame. One no more chooses one's family (or, more precisely, one's biological parents) than one chooses to be unattractive or unintelligent. Shame would seem as misplaced in the one case as in the others. But then, one typically does not become attractive or intelligent by one's choice and efforts; such advantages are typically gifts rather than achievements. So is pride appropriate in relation to such advantages? Certainly many are in fact proud of their looks or their intelligence. While such pride is not conceptually misplaced (responsibility is not, as a matter of language, a condition of pride), insofar as proper pride is thought to depend on achievements rather than gifts, it is perhaps morally misplaced. This may be part of the intuition of those who think of God as the author of our gifts, and so of individual pride in gifts as misappropriation of credit (if not sin). Leaving God aside, supposing one thinks proper pride must be limited to achievements rather than gifts (just as proper shame must be limited to faults rather than natural disadvantages or handicaps), the problem becomes most pointed when one asks whether perhaps *everything* is not a gift. After all, traced far enough, even apparent achievements depend on conditions outside one's control.

The notion of "moral" appropriateness here connects with Kant's emphasis on the distinction between moral characteristics and natural characteristics. One's moral identity, for Kant, depends on factors outside the natural order. Appeal to the noumenal realm may take one beyond what empirically makes sense, but Kant's point connects with the ordinary intuition that there are some aspects of our character for which we are responsible (whether we try to work hard or are simply lazy, what we try to do with our intelligence, etc.) and there are others that are not subject to our will, but are simply (say biologically) given, and so not appropriate grounds for moral judgment. But then, will there not always be some empirical explanation for why some are lazy, why some try to do good with their intelligence, and so on? If one traces the causal chains far enough, won't we always come to factors outside the sphere of the individual will? One comes to doubt the line that depends on appeal to the individual (nonempirical) will. Kant's desire to isolate the sphere of the moral, marking it off as a sphere of freedom and autonomy, where moral worth is a matter of virtue rather than natural endowment or talents viewed as gifts, may lead to a contracting self, a self with ultimately no content at all (Nagel 1979c). Certainly that is the result if everything ultimately is a gift. One writer, Arnold Isenberg (1980 [1949]), sees the difficulty but tries to differentiate shame and pride, regarding pride as widely appropriate and shame as widely inappropriate, because he thinks shame does no good—it just adds misery to misery, and the reflexive misery is avoidable. But the pleasantness of an experience does not itself make that experience well grounded, and even misery can sometimes do some good (the spurrings of painful conscience may redirect just as bitter medicine may cure). Whatever the savings in individual misery, a society of the shameless is not highly to be desired.

While responsibility is not a condition of pride, something like "closeness to self" is. Seen as "close enough to ourselves," however that notion is unpacked, we can be proud or, equally, ashamed of our family or our country: they are a part of who one is and, even if one has not chosen them, one cannot wholly dissociate from them. That shame arguably should not extend to certain things outside our control—some things that are not our fault, such as physical limitations, handicaps, or deformities—is more a matter of what we regard as our "essential" self and what counts as valuable than of responsibility or control or the will (though some, like Kant, would shrink the essential self to a transcendent will). What should be regarded as essential and what as valuable are obviously contestable. That the chain of credit, "closeness to self" in Hume's phrase, is open to question in cases of group pride, such as that of the 49ers fans, opens the way to the insight that the chain of credit is in fact *always* open to question, even in cases of individual pride. The world in which individual pride was inevitably a sin took certain views of essential identity and of value as obvious. The politics of group pride seeks to question such views.

Value

The political value of pride in identity politics partly derives from the internal place of values within pride. (When O. J. Simpson allowed as how he was "not proud" of his wife abuse, he was using "pride" to mark his choice of values, in this case to show his acceptance of community values.) On all accounts, the source of pride must be seen as an achievement or an advantage; pride involves positive valuation. Like "closeness to self," that is a conceptual condition.

The point of pride as a member of a group, the pride of belonging, depends on some distinctive virtue of the group, on its perceived value. Claiming group membership is a way of claiming the associated value for oneself. This reflects the conceptual dependence of pride on positive valuation. (On Hume's excessively mechanical account, lacking the belief in value, one would lack the double association needed to produce pride. Rather, I would say, lacking the needed belief, whatever was produced would not be considered pride [Foot 1978 (1958–59)].) That is, group pride, the pride of membership or belonging, like the pride of ownership, depends on value—the subject, like the owned object, is seen as valuable. The twist in recent identity politics is in the seeing of value.

Identity politics involves transvaluation, a reversal of received values. A previously despised property comes to be seen as valuable: "Black is Beautiful." Earlier majority values or norms are rejected as mistaken, biased, blind. A previous source of shame becomes a source of pride. The point is *not* that one should not be ashamed of one's skin color (for example) because one cannot help it, did not choose it, and so is not responsible. Rather, the point is that one should not be ashamed of one's skin color because there is nothing wrong with it in the first place.

One response is to see this as the politics of "sour grapes"—what "everyone knows" is valuable is rejected in self-defense against the shame of exclusion, of failure by the received standards. But if all that can be said in favor of a received standard is that "everyone knows" it is correct, that in itself provides grounds for suspicion. First there is the general bias in one's own favor that Spinoza warns of in connection with pride. The favored majority, the so-called "everyone," must beware of such self-reinforcing bias. Then there are more particular psychological tendencies to distortion, some especially prominent in recent local rivalries and nationalistic struggles. Issues of national identity are especially pressing in the many parts of the world where linguistic, religious, historical, and other divisions have taken on importance, sometimes leading to civil war. Such accentuation of small differences in the midst of overwhelming commonalities may be an inherent feature of human psychology, described by Freud under the heading of "the narcissism of minor differences." (The relation of such narcissism to identity formation and to aggression we will return to.) What differences are taken to matter and the value that is attached to the privileged position may very much depend on an individual's own situational circumstances and the accidents of history. Adjusting one's preferences to suit one's possibilities, making a virtue out of necessity (Elster 1983, 110), is as much a temptation for majorities as for minorities. Values are not to be reduced to uncriticized preferences. Better arguments, more grounded in human nature and human needs, must be provided if an accusation of "sour grapes" is to stick. And universal claims to dignity and justice weigh against it.

How is one to argue that one condition is better than another, that it ought to be preferred (even if it cannot be chosen, it is given or a "gift")? One should note first of all that such an argument does not by itself give grounds for preferential treatment. Indeed, preferential treatment, if any, might be better directed toward the socially disfavored condition. For example, it is plausible to suppose that it is almost always better to be intelligent than unintelligent (though during Red Guard purges of the intelligentsia and other such social upheavals, intelligence may come to have certain obvious disadvantages). But for educational purposes, it is arguable that a society that values equality should devote special resources to help the intellectually less gifted. What counts as a "special need" or, in the older terminology, a "handicap"? To say someone is "handicapped" is to say they are at a disadvantage. But disability is always relative to some purpose, and the value or disvalue of a disability must depend on the value, including the social usefulness, of the relevant power. Say one's powers of visual discrimination are limited, e.g., one is color-blind. Or suppose one lacks a power of discrimination that only a few in fact possess (tea or wine tasters or perfume sniffers, persons of fine palate and olfactory discrimination): the few can regularly note differences that those less empowered cannot, but are *most* of us thus handicapped? Is handicap necessarily a minority condition, so the norm is statistical? Is handicap necessarily a limitation of a socially important power, so lacking extraordinary powers is no handicap? Or is the value of a norm sometimes independent of the width of distribution and even of general social attitudes?

Thinking about deafness for a moment may help bring out the issues. The play (and movie) *Children of a Lesser God* makes an eloquent case for the beauty and power of signing as used by the deaf. Using sign language, one can even make points one cannot make or not make so forcefully in, say, spoken English (the play illustrates this when "veal" on a menu is explained by poignantly combining the signs for "cow" and "baby"). While sign language is obviously different from oral speech, it nonetheless constitutes a fully structured language that can facilitate thought and interaction; and the insistence that deaf people leave it aside and learn to speak, an insistence that prevailed in institutions for the education of the deaf for a long period starting in the late nineteenth century, can be seen as a benighted prejudice (Sacks 1990). It is nonetheless arguable that whatever the power and beauty of sign language as a language, whatever its intellectual and social usefulness, not hearing remains in any case a loss—and not just because the majority hear. In a majority deaf society, there might be a common language used by all (as in the Martha's Vineyard community discussed by Sacks [32–35]), and more accommodations might be made, but still most would be missing something, whether the warning noises of an approaching vehicle or the singing of birds. There are losses in not hearing, exclusions from aspects of life. In certain social conditions the losses might be less felt, but that does not make them any the less losses. (Though one must wonder whether if *no one* had the ability, it could still appear a loss. It would surely be odd for any human to experience the inability to fly as a "loss," as a handicap. But is that simply because it is odd for humans to compare themselves to birds rather than other humans?) None of this, again, is an argument against "Deaf Pride" as a political movement. That one might rather not be deaf is no reason to fail to respect the deaf, or to discriminate against them, or to fail to make accommodations. (Sacks writes: "The deaf do not regard themselves as handicapped, but as a linguistic and cultural minority" [138 n.147; 151].) Some disadvantages may be only socially imposed, and then the language of "handicap" or "special needs" may be inappropriate, but both socially imposed and natural disadvantages may often be ameliorated. In any case, the value claimed in all the movements that call for pride may ultimately be a matter of equal human dignity and respect and so may not turn on the difference between the chosen and the given or the socially useful and socially disfavored.

Another response is to think that rather than transvaluing an identity category, one ought to question the divisions and classifications themselves. Sometimes this is a matter of pointing out the predominance of gray. Sexual preferences and sexual activities allow for all degrees of exclusivity and combination. The exclusive heterosexual, in deed and fantasy, may be as rare as the exclusive homosexual. And even who counts as "black" is, despite what might appear a simple visual criterion, by no means always obvious. Lawrence Wright, in a *New Yorker* article entitled "One Drop of Blood," brings out how troubled the category is, in an interbreeding society, even for purposes of census taking (especially when tied to the distribution of social benefits). This is before issues of cultural and self-identification are introduced to complicate matters—whether a black child adopted and brought up by white parents in a white neighborhood is somehow thereby denied the blackness conferred by "black culture." An interracial society leads to multiracial individuals. But there are other problems with the socially constructed categories of invidious discrimination than being sure who fits in them. The problem is not just the existence of degrees of gray; some would reject the categories even in the supposedly clear cases.

Foucault and some of his followers urge that a truly radical politics should emphasize resistance rather than liberation. Liberation, it is charged, involves accepting the categories of the powers that be, even when liberation insists on transvaluation (that is, asserting the positive value of the denigrated, marginalized category). Resistance questions and rejects those categories. Thus David Halperin (1995) writes:

> The most radical reversal of homophobic discourses consists not in asserting, with the Gay Liberation Front of 1968, that "gay is good" (on the analogy with "black is beautiful") but in assuming and empowering a marginal positionality—not in rehabilitating an already demarcated, if devalued, identity but in taking advantage of the purely oppositional location homosexuality has been made to occupy. (61)

The rejection of categories in this sort of "queer" politics, a politics of positionality (of opposition, contrast, resistance) rather than identity, obscures (deliberately) the identity of the group being defended. That is, it objects to identity politics by attacking the terms of identity:

> To shift the position of 'the homosexual' from that of object to subject is therefore to make available to lesbians and gay men a new kind of sexual identity, one characterized by its lack of a clear definitional content. The homosexual subject can now claim an identity without an essence. (61)

But the lack of a clear essence makes the alternative politics of positionality rather unclear. In Halperin's version, "queer" politics (vs. "gay" politics) includes all sexually marginalized individuals: "anyone who is or who feels marginalized because of her or his sexual practices: it could include some married couples without children, for example, or even (who knows?) some married couples *with* children." All that unites the group is its felt marginalization in relation to social norms—a definition that seems rather too broad for an organized group politics. (Put differently, the "subject position" emphasized is perhaps too subjective, however true it may be that we are *all* gay, all women, all black, for we are all marginalized, denigrated, despised, under some heading or other some of the time.) Halperin acknowledges (64) that the vast range of sexual outlaws (including sadomasochists, fetishists, pederasts) can have diverse and divergent interests.

There is another paradox here in a politics of positionality: aside from the fact that we are all somehow, in some aspect, outside the accepted norms, the supposed de-essentialized subject position requires that one feel marginalized in terms of a norm that is the norm of society or of "the others." Therefore, those norms and their understanding—objectification— reenters the picture: one's self-identity for oppositional purposes must depend on categories and norms provided from outside (at least if it is to count as "resistance" to those categories and norms), just as identity politics depends on those categories and norms before it undertakes its work of transvaluing them. Self-identification through desire may remain the best defense: "De-gaying gayness can only fortify homophobic oppression; it accomplishes in its own way the principal aim of homophobia: the elimination of gays. The consequence of self-erasure is . . . self-erasure. Even a provisional acceptance of the very categories elaborated by dominant identitarian regimes might more effectively undermine those forces than a simple disappearing act" (Bersani 1995, 5).

The appealing inclusiveness of "queer" rather than "lesbian and gay" politics becomes especially problematical when one considers the history of the extension and enforcement of rights as it has developed in the United States through legal protections for particular classifications of persons. How flexible can such legal categories be and where do they (must they) come from? Gays and lesbians have sought antidiscrimination laws and social recognition of our intimate associations. But no one that I know of has seriously proposed civil rights legislation ensuring nondiscrimination in employment and housing for sadomasochists (of course both homosexual and heterosexual). Why does that seem such an unpromising political agenda? (The notion of ensuring pedophiles the right to marry the boys they love raises further, special difficulties.) Must potential employers inquire about their employees' private sexual preferences in order to avoid unknowingly discriminating against them? (Is unknowing discrimination discrimination?) I will return to problems of "visibility" in a moment. Morris Kaplan (1997), in a recent book on *Sexual Justice,* sensibly notes, "Adding 'lesbian' and 'gay' to 'heterosexual' in the repertoire of acceptable identities in our society would be a real but limited accomplishment in the struggle for full equality" (144). Anything short of equal treatment for all is rightly condemned as "limited," but civil rights for blacks were similarly "limited." The practices of discrimination, however, make some "limited" advances more pressing than others. (Are sadomasochists regularly discriminated against in employment and housing? Who would know?)

Whose oppression matters most? Here visibility plays a role, but it is multi-faced. The possibility of invisibility can provide protection, protection that the law may deny. But the fact that one can hide one's sexual preferences, keep them private, is small consolation to those who regard those preferences as an important part of who they are, a part they do not wish to be obliged to conceal (especially given that there are advantages in being identifiable to those others who happen to share one's preferences). And of course, another side of the possibility of concealment, of passing, is the possibility of mistaken identification, of misidentification. Suppose someone was mistakenly identified as a member of a currently protected category (say of religion or race, say an Episcopalian was mistaken for a Catholic, or a very tan individual for an African American) by a potential employer or landlord and improperly discriminated against on the basis of that mistaken identification? Surely there is an intention to improperly discriminate. Would the victim have standing to sue under the statutes (given that he or she was not in fact a member of the protected category)? But then, in a world where sexual orientation was given specific protection, could anyone self-declare and then obtain legal redress? Transvestites are widely and mistakenly believed to all be homosexuals. Would a heterosexual transvestite mistakenly discriminated against as a homosexual have standing to sue under civil rights laws that protected gays but not transvestites? Again one feels the push toward the universal. Who decides who is in what category? It is worth noting that there is at the moment a movement afoot among some Orthodox Jewish rabbis to denounce certain branches of Judaism, Conservative and Reform, as not-Jewish. Again, who decides? Is it the discriminators? The issue of attempted discrimination raises the question of whether the wrong is the mistake or the treating of *anyone* as though they were a second-class citizen, mistaken identification or correct notwithstanding. The question is whether antidiscrimination legislation can ultimately be understood as protecting individuals in certain categories, or all citizens. The rationale for such legislation turns on equal treatment for all, but the protections have had to be hard won in political contests, one despised category at a time.

Kaplan, like Halperin, may wish to protect all marginalized sexual outlaws, but in practice his argument has a narrower focus when he goes beyond those who would ask for no more than mere decriminalization of gay and lesbian sexual activity. Kaplan seeks specifically to add gays and lesbians to other protected categories (racial, religious, and ethnic groups, women, the physically and mentally handicapped, workers aged forty and older) for the purposes of protection against discrimination in employment, education, and housing. He argues: "The underlying rationale of the anti-discrimination provisions of civil rights legislation is the recognition that formal legal equality is inadequate to provide for equal citizenship under conditions of popular hostility and pervasive social inequality. It is precisely the intensity and extent of the prejudice against homosexuality that justifies the claims of lesbian and gay citizens to protection against discrimination" (43). And here he must have in mind extended histories of mistreatment, which have of course depended on identification by others, the mistreaters. Kaplan insists that "the definition of protected classes does not construct personal or political identities but rather forbids employers, landlords, and other decision makers from using such categories as race, religion, or sex to *impose* an invidious identity on a person rather than treating her in terms of her individual character and qualities" (45). He is certainly right about the point of such legislation. But if it is to be effectively enforced, it must specify the protected categories in a way that enables people to identify themselves under them for purposes of protection. And that risks the sort of rigidity and fixity that Kaplan wishes to avoid. I do not see how the law, for its purposes, which are indeed important, can avoid it. Moreover, the characteristics that are most significant, and so the ones most likely to be taken to be defining, are the very ones that decision makers (the discriminators and mistreaters) might be feared to improperly use—so perhaps it is the socially constructed categories, whatever the truth may be about essential characteristics, that become the most relevant ones. (As Hannah Arendt insisted: "If one is attacked as a Jew one must defend oneself as a Jew" [Kaplan 160].) Again, it is a history of popular hostility that makes something more than formal legal equality necessary.

Kaplan and Halperin are right to see the complexity, variety, and malleability of sexual desire. What follows for politics? Kaplan writes, "A politics based on fixed identities may foreclose the openness to contestation and negotiation required by justice" (112). That is surely a risk, but perhaps progress only gets made one step at a time. So far as Kaplan argues for antidiscrimination law, the groups to be protected must be defined in ways that make their members identifiable. A politics of legal reform must require the very "fixed identities" Kaplan seems to wish to deny. Of course they need not be fixed forever, or even for a lifetime, but they must be fixed for purposes of adjudication once one emerges from behind Rawls's veil of ignorance into a world where some are identified (by others, if not themselves) as gay or lesbian and discriminated against on that basis.

It is difficult to see *what* one does differently when resisting a category rather than liberating or expressing an aspect of self seen under that category. And *who* one does it with is politically problematic. Is "queer" politics supposed to unite all who are non-mainstream sexually? The "we" here might include all sorts of folks who fit very uncomfortably with each other. Not that all gay folks are comfortable together. Our political views (like our sexual activities) cover as wide a spectrum as those of heterosexual folks. It is very difficult to see heterosexuals as a group with homogenized interests. The only reason it is easier for those who march under the banner of gay pride to be so seen is that they do have one important interest in common: sexual liberation and nondiscrimination on the basis of orientation; but they may not feel that way about all aspects of sexual expression ("sexual orientation" is doubtless the way the relevant category would be described for purposes of legislation, but what exactly would it cover?). Similarly, there is a good deal of political and social diversity among blacks, though all might agree that skin color is no proper ground for shame or discrimination. Political and social coalition among *all* racial and ethnic minorities has had a hard history, even if all might agree that skin color, place of origin, and cultural background are no proper grounds for shame or discrimination. It also might become unclear who the opposed "majority" is.

Of course there are problems with traditional identity politics, some stemming from the admitted grayness of categories. The problems of inclusion may be more serious than those raised by the 49er Faithful. What and who is *in* the category? Even a category such as race, which might appear straightforwardly biological, can be problematical; as noted, skin color may provide no sure index of anything and we may all in the end be multiracial. And again, gay behavior, desires, inclinations, and attitudes can all vary in more ways than marked even by Kinsey's categories (exclusive, occasional, etc.), and that before account is taken of the unconscious. Who are "we"? And if we think of the gay-identified as excluding the repressed or closeted homosexual, we may be focusing too much on the voluntaristic aspects of identification (like 49ers fans), where identification is self-identification. But where the political problem may arise from the identification, and stigmatization, by others, perhaps a politically relevant notion of identification must be broader (even if it risks objectification of individuals and reification of the categories of the others—after all, the struggle is with or against those very others). Even when one is not asked, and does not tell, one may be discriminated against, one's life restricted.

So far as the politics of marginal positionalities is aimed at denying privileged valuations of *either* side of dichotomies, the message may ultimately be the same as "Black Is Beautiful" or "Gay is Good" or "Deaf Power." For the point, typically, is not to say black is better than white, or gay is better than straight, or deaf is better than hearing, but simply to deny the denigration of the minority position. The point is to demand political equality, equal concern and respect.

The Narcissism of Minor Differences

Freud observes that groups of individuals characteristically direct their greatest hostility toward those who, from a wider perspective, are in fact most similar to them. What is the source of this "narcissism of minor differences"? Is it an interesting but accidental sociological fact? Or is it somehow rooted in features of human psychology and the conditions for identity-formation; does it bespeak a natural polarity in thought?

Freud introduces the concept in his discussion of "The Taboo of Virginity" (1918a). There the topic is male hostility to and fear of women, and is complicated by the castration complex, but Freud is already prepared to take a point about individual separation and isolation ("that it is precisely the minor differences in people who are otherwise alike that form the basis of feelings of strangeness and hostility between them" [199]) and see in it "the hostility which in every human relation we see fighting successfully against feelings of fellowship and overpowering the commandment that all men should love one another" (199). When he turns to *Group Psychology* a few years later, he returns to the idea, there tying it to wider ambivalences as well as to narcissism (1921c, 101). He develops the idea most fully in *Civilization and Its Discontents* where he discusses it in terms of aggression, which in this form serves "cohesion between the members of the community" against outsiders (1930a, chap. 5, esp. 114). It is this final link, to what Freud regards as instinctual aggression, that may help clarify what may also be understood as a conceptual condition of identity formation. It makes conflict our normal state—and if pride is a sin, this (rather than intellectual error, even motivated intellectual error) may be its origin.

There is an old logical principle that holds "all determination is negation" (*Omnis determinatio est negatio*), and both individuals and communities often define themselves by opposition, by contrast, that is, in terms of what they reject. Stuart Hampshire (1996) elaborates the point in relation to incompatible conceptions of the good:

> Most influential conceptions of the good have defined themselves as rejections of their rivals: for instance, some of the ideals of monasticism were a rejection of the splendors and hierarchies of the Church, and this rejection was the original sense and purpose of the monastic ideal. Some forms of fundamentalism, both Christian and others, define themselves as a principled rejection of secular, liberal, and permissive moralities. Fundamentalism is the negation of any deviance in moral opinion, and of the very notion of opinion in ethics. (13)

People are who they are at least partly (and sometimes self-consciously) in terms of what they are not. The logical point is developed in Hegel and in F. H. Bradley. It is taken even further along a metaphysical dimension by Spinoza. As Hampshire puts Spinoza's vision: "Men and women are naturally driven to resist any external force that tends to repress their typical activities or to limit their freedom . . . It is a natural necessity for each distinct entity to try to preserve its distinctiveness for as long as it can, and for this reason conflicts are at all times to be expected in the history of individuals, of social groups, and of nations, as their paths intersect" (15).

In psychoanalytical terms, the individual ego (and more specifically, the ego-ideal) is formed out of identifications and introjections, the other side of which is the rejection—typically a violent spitting out—of those characteristics one does not wish to incorporate. "At the very beginning, it seems, the external world, objects, and what is hated are identical. If later on an object turns out to be a source of pleasure, it is loved, but it is also incorporated into the ego" (Freud 1915c, 136). As Norman O. Brown (1966) puts it, "The distinction between self and not-self is made by the childish decision to claim all that the ego likes as 'mine,' and to repudiate all that the ego dislikes as 'not-mine'" (142). The move from individual to group identity is explored in Freud's *Group Psychology and the Analysis of the Ego* (1921c), where his central concern is with groups, such as churches and armies, characterized by identification with a leader. The important role of unconscious mechanisms of identification via incorporation must complicate the too-simple voluntaristic picture of identity formation we started by considering in relation to the 49ers and other self-selecting groups of sports fans. As the existence of unconscious mechanisms should make clear, socially imposed identities are not the only alternative to consciously chosen identities. With unconscious mechanisms, ambivalence and aggression come to the fore. Others reject us, we reject others, and we project out "bad" and undesired aspects of ourselves while at the same time introjecting the desirable aspects of others.

Belonging to a group is tied to rejection of outsiders. Freud writes, "a religion, even if it calls itself the religion of love, must be hard and unloving to those who do not belong to it. Fundamentally indeed every religion is in this same way a religion of love for all those whom it embraces; while cruelty and intolerance towards those who do not belong to it are natural to every religion" (1921c, 98). One might think that toleration and the embracing of diversity should provide a ready alternative, but history suggests vast impediments to such an alternative, and psychoanalysis sees aggression in the very mechanisms that serve to create a distinctive self or group. Freud's skepticism about demands to "love thy neighbour" and even "thine enemies" is tied to his belief in fundamental instincts of aggression (1930a, chap. 5). The sources of division and ambivalence run deep, perhaps deeper even than any putative aggressive instincts. All determination is negation. An embraced identity entails a rejected identity. Even the very languages that help define the identity of certain individuals and communities (not all Frenchmen need live in France) isolate and separate at the very time they unite (the story of Quebec is but one of many, very many, examples [see Ignatieff (1993) for more]). The ambiguity that some see in pride (arrogance vs. self-respect) may have behind it a deeper ambiguity in self-love and in identity itself (rejection and isolation vs. affirmation and community).

The ambiguities and ambivalences inevitably play themselves out in identity politics as well. Identity politics is by its nature divisive: it separates and distinguishes—though of course the distinctive categories are typically provided by those who would discriminate against the minority, and the transvaluation of values is most often a form of (legitimate) self-defense. In narcissism, one rejects. In self-defense, one has been rejected. It is not enough to dismiss the imposed identities as false. New positive identities must be internalized and must be recognized. A universal identity and equality based on universal rights may be the ultimate aim, but the political question is how to get there from here. (And even a universal identity may have a price—one's distinctive ethnic, or religious, or sexual, or other identity may languish unacknowledged.)

When minorities engage in identity politics, asking for themselves what society should accord to all—dignity and respect and the equal protection of the laws—can they speak for all? When we gays and lesbians ask for antidiscrimination laws and social recognition of our intimate associations, who are "we"? Kaplan tells us that Eve Kosofsky Sedgwick "marks a vacillation, within both homophobic and emancipatory discourses, between 'minoritizing' views of homosexuality that define a distinct group with a common identity and 'universalizing' views that link homosexuality to tendencies shared by all human beings" (160). That tension is pervasive. Again I ask, who are "we"? Perhaps like the non-Jewish Danish king who put on a Star of David when the Nazis decreed all Jews must wear the star, the better to single them out for persecution, we should all be Jews in a world of anti-Semitism. But how do we get to a world where we are all in this together, where no one is oppressed?

Who are "we" for purposes of political organization and activism, for purposes of demanding nondiscrimination, and so on? In a sense, of course, we is everyone, every citizen entitled to equal concern and respect, and equal treatment under the law. But for purposes of the law, without denying or weakening the claims of anyone else, the adherents of gay pride can insist that experiencing same-sex desire or engaging in certain sexual practices with members of the same sex is no ground for invidious treatment, for discrimination in housing, education, or job opportunities. Perhaps one wants to say the same for other sexual minorities (and other nonsexual minorities as well). But so long as discrimination law singles out special categories for protection, one must be precise. There is not much to be gained by denying the reality of the very categories under which one is asking protection. If equal treatment for all is not enough to protect gays and lesbians, and we need to ask for specific protection, why should we be surprised if other sexual minorities need to do the same? Marginalized groups might wish to band together, but "queer" identity by itself may not do what is required.

Self-Respect and Self-Esteem

The absence of sinful pride is called humility or modesty, but these apparent virtues hide their own faults and failings. Humility can give way to servility and obsequiousness—an exaggerated enhancement of the other's and a slavish devaluation of one's own worth. Modesty can lead to extremes of self-effacement, denials of one's existence and value that threaten social withdrawal or personal extinction. Poised somewhere between sinful vanity and self-destructive submissiveness is a golden mean of self-esteem appropriate to the human condition. Straying too far from it in either direction leads to active evil or passive victimization. (Lyman 135)

Aristotle's "proud" man is supposed to be a mean between the foolishly vain and the unduly humble (*Nicomachean Ethics*, 1123b–25a). (I am here following those translators who take *megalopsychia*—literally "greatness of soul"—to mean "pride." Others translate it as "magnanimity" and others still as "high-mindedness." It is the virtue "concerned with honour on the grand scale" and seems to essentially involve an ideal of pride and confident self-respect.) While the proud man's self-evaluation is supposed to be accurate (he "thinks himself worthy of great things, being worthy of them . . . he claims what is in accordance with his merits" [1123b]), and so his pride is a virtue ("Pride, then, seems to be a sort of crown of the excellences" [1124a]), Aristotle's portrait of aristocratic disdain and self-sufficiency makes him sound as though he suffers from what the later Christians regarded as the sin of pride. Aristotle's ideal great-spirited man has a lofty detachment from particular goods. He cares most for honor, yet little even for that: "at honours that are great and conferred by good men he will be moderately pleased . . . for there can be no honour that is worthy of perfect excellence" (1124a); and tends to have detachment and disdain for the world in general ("honour from casual people and on trifling grounds he will utterly despise" [1124a] and "the proud man despises justly" [1124b] and "he is free of speech because he is contemptuous" [1124b]). He strives, all-in-all, for "a character that suffices to itself" (1125a).

Aristotle's proud man "is the sort of man to confer benefits, but he is ashamed of receiving them; for the one is the mark of a superior, the other of an inferior" (1124b). Even today, individuals who are described as "fiercely proud" are typically being singled out as especially independent. Some find it humiliating to be indebted, especially deeply indebted. Even a gift can humiliate. This can be understood broadly in terms of a general need to repay or reciprocate in human life: a whole theory of punishment flourishes under the heading of "retribution." Insults must be repaid, so must gifts—all are debts and create a burden. There are standards of reciprocity in human relations that can be felt as burdensome. (Some of the complexities here are nicely delineated by William Miller 1993.) Of course, not accepting help (like, more obviously, not helping) can be a kind of aggression. The pride connected with independence and freedom from indebtedness can also be understood in terms of dependence (a central concern of Hegel) and power (a central concern of Nietzsche—who of course looked beyond virtue and sin). (See Neu 1996, chap. 5 here, on the unease of dependence.)

Some would distinguish between pride the sin and pride the emotion in terms of the former being a general character trait, though a person with the self-satisfied character trait might be especially liable to experience the corresponding emotion on a variety of occasions (as in Ryle's dispositional analysis of character traits such as vanity [1949, 85ff.]). As a matter of motivation, pride is expansive and goes with a tendency to display and show off (while shame is of course tied to a desire to hide, to disappear and become invisible). It is arguable that, even as a character trait, pride may not be a sin, or at least no longer a sin. Lyman suggests narcissism and pride are now a psychic necessity because of the need for individual strength in "the modern lonely age":

> The pattern of parental overestimation and excessive indulgence helps establish the psychic institution that must replace the now defunct social institutions of human conservation. Emancipation of the individual requires him to abandon his dependence on social security in favor of a hardly developed psychic self-sufficiency. The personal character appropriate to this liberating social structure is one in which pride must hold an important place. Less a sin than a necessity in the modern lonely age, pride is absolved from much of its guilt as the individual is freed from most of his constraints. (157)

The *sinful* character trait then might be equated to a kind of arrogance, as Solomon Schimmel puts it "exaggerating our worth and power, and feeling superior to others" (1992, 29). We are back to Spinoza's understanding of pride as bias in favor of oneself and excessive self-esteem. On the other hand, Gabriele Taylor distinguishes the sin and the passion in terms of the sin involving a character trait where one's worth is taken for granted, and so one's high expectations may make particular occasions of pride the passion become relatively rare (1980, 394ff; 1985, 36ff). This may, like Aristotle, take the error out of the attitude. So, as sin, does the character trait necessarily involve error or not? Is a person with the character trait more or less likely to experience particular occasions of pride the emotion? Such occasions are based on particular reasons (one is "proud of this" or "because of that"). The generalized character trait of pride may need no reasons. But then "taking one's worth for granted" may be a matter of having a due regard for one's rights, may amount to self-respect. Self-respect also needs no reasons—in which case pride the character trait does *not* obviously amount to a sin, need not amount to presumptuous arrogance or anything more than self-assurance, or indeed, simple dignity.

There may be a contrast between self-esteem and self-respect that is helpful here. The pleasure that Hume discerns in pride is ultimately a form of self-approval (Davidson 1980 [1976]; Neu 1977). But self-approval is ambiguous in a way that may help explain the dual attitudes, sin to be avoided and virtue to be sought, toward pride itself (whether regarded as a character trait or a passion). We can understand the ambiguity in terms of certain contrasts between self-esteem and self-respect. Self-respect, having to do with one's rights and dignity as a person, may be noncomparative. Self-esteem, having to do with one's merits and self-valuation, may depend on the standards of value in one's society and how one compares with other members of that society. Put crudely, of self-respect one cannot have too much, of self-esteem one obviously can. Put more precisely, the idea of too much self-respect is at best problematic, while that of too much self-esteem, like those of either too little self-respect or too little self-esteem, poses no difficulty. (See David Sachs [1981]. Cf. Rousseau's contrast of *amour de soi*, which is supposed to be natural, noncomparative, and tied to self-preservation, and *amour propre*, which is supposed to be social, comparative, and other-directed; see *Discourse on the Origin of Inequality* [1950 (1755)] and *Emile*, [1969 (1762)], Book 4.) Thus a person might have low self-esteem and yet have self-respect. As Sachs puts it, "it could be categorically true of a person both that he takes no pride in anything whatever, and yet that he has his pride" (350).

So far as pride is a matter of self-respect, one must have a certain amount. This point is developed by Thomas Hill (1991 [1973]), who interprets certain forms of objectionable servility as resulting from misunderstanding one's moral rights or placing a comparatively low value on them, a lack of a certain type of self-respect, a respect that is owed one as a person, independently of special merits. That is, self-respect is a matter of appreciating one's equal moral rights as a person and (also perhaps) of living by one's own personal standards—not an issue of merits. Respect for one's merits, or esteem, is to be distinguished from respect for one's rights. Such a distinction helps clarify Edith Sitwell's attitude toward pride. While insisting it should not be confused with silly vanity or foolish obstinacy, Edith Sitwell declared: "Pride has always been one of my favourite virtues" (1962, 15). She recognizes that pride "may be a form of love" (17), and she refers to "ugly humility" (19) and notes that "A proper pride is a necessity to an artist" (21). She sees it as a form of self-defense needed by the original against inevitable attacks by the envious and untalented. Such self-confidence needs to be understood in relation to self-respect (something essential to all) and self-esteem (which can be greater than justified, but also has a "proper" level). Everyone needs self-respect and is, moreover, entitled to it. It is a condition of moral identity.

One of the errors of certain recently popular self-help psychologies is to suppose that increasing self-esteem is simply a matter of changing one's attitude rather than the more strenuous activity of changing one's life. So far as esteem depends on merit, a pride that simply depends on deciding one is "ok" whatever one does becomes like the sinful individual pride of old: one falls into unjustifiable self-satisfaction. Group credit too, or "bragging rights," does little to advance claims based on merit unless responsibility (as well as "nearness") can somehow be claimed. So far as group pride gives self-respect and asks for respect from others based on one's common humanity and equal moral rights, there is no sin, no error. But one should be careful of too simply tying the contrast between pride as sin and as virtue to the contrast of self-esteem and self-respect, for while self-esteem can be excessive (people can think too well of themselves), there is surely a "correct" or justified level of self-esteem, which might be quite high in some cases (even if not quite so high as in the case of Aristotle's great-souled man).

We have seen that nearness to self is necessary to distinguish pride from mere happiness or joy; that is, pride is self-enhancing. Taking credit for a valuable object expands our identity, enhances our self-esteem. So one can see how pride can be competitive, concerned as it is with ego-identity and its enhancement, and it is thus subject to envy and liable to fall into sinful arrogance. Arrogance may be the heart of (certain understandings of) pride the sin. It is the antithesis of the concern for equality in self-respect. It is the excessive self-esteem emphasized by Spinoza, a bias in favor of oneself that may seem more a general character trait than a particular emotion. If self-esteem is understood as based on perceived merits, then it is perhaps more like pride the emotion which is also based on particular reasons. Enough such pride amounts to conceit, the character trait of thinking too well of oneself (even if one has particular reasons). But self-respect needs no reasons and so is more like a generalized pride that is more like a char- acter trait—but, again, it is then *not* obviously a sin, need not amount to presumptuous arrogance or anything more than self-assurance or dignity.

The cardinal (or chief) sins were in the beginning not necessarily mortal (or deadly) ones. Their importance attached to those temptations with spe- cial significance from a monastic point of view—which was the point of view of Evagrius of Pontus and John Cassian, the fathers of the seven car- dinal sins in the fourth and fifth centuries. There is the familiar phenome- non of pride in one's humility. Cassian points out that "Pride is the most savage of all evil beasts, and the most dreadful, because it lies in wait for those who are perfect" (quoted in Payne 1960, 68). The early lists some- times had eight sins—sometimes, for example, distinguishing *vana gloria* (vainglory) from *superbia* (pride). The lists later came to serve penitential purposes with priests using them as a helpful aid in the examination of conscience for confession, and the distinction previously made between cardinal and deadly sins dropped away. As St. Thomas pointed out, a sin is called capital "simply because other sins frequently arise from it" (*De Malo* 9.2–5, quoted in Bloomfield 1952, 88).

Pride's special importance among even the deadly sins Aquinas attrib- uted to its general character which made it arguably the source of all sins insofar as it involves a turning away from God (1995 [1269], 314ff.). The specific sins each in their own way involve rebellion against the law of God, but such rebellion is the essence of pride as a general sin. In its more spe- cific form, vainglory, it involves an inordinate desire for honor and renown, a special admiration of one's own excellences. And it was of course vanity rather than pride that became the focus of (the relatively godless) later French moralists. Vanity is especially concerned with public reputation. Pride is the sin of not knowing one's place and sticking to it. It is of course Faust's ambitious sin. Challenging God—going above your place.

Greek *hubris* (thinking oneself superior to the gods), like Christian pride (thinking oneself independent of God, self-sufficient), involves placing one- self above one's station. This is one of the features of pride that makes it pe- culiarly appropriate as the banner for political movements that seek to change the station of those in them—i.e., that seek a transvaluation of values. Both identity politics and a politics of marginal positionalities, whatever their views on whether God has died, deny that the social valuations and positions that denigrate certain groups and privilege others are ordained by God. Times have changed. The death of God would leave the concept of sin with little conceptual foothold. But even in a world where God is still believed to preside, an attack on social hierarchy need not be regarded as sin, for it is not an attack on God: social hierarchy is not a matter of natural law, is not God-given. These political movements are challenging positions in the political world rather than a God-given order. And, as we have seen, on an individual level, the self-approval that is characteristic of pride may be ambiguous, and the different significances may be understood in terms of a contrast between self-esteem (which can be excessive and unjustified) and self-respect (which does not depend on invidious comparison and may be essential to human dignity). A politics of self-respect, where the self has a social identity, may not be so ungodly after all.

8

PLATO'S HOMOEROTIC
SYMPOSIUM

Plato's *Symposium*, the greatest book ever written about the nature of love, centers on homoerotic desire. Does that make a difference? What it says is certainly shaped by the assumptions of the society in which it was written and by the interests of the man who wrote it. Not only are the exemplars of love discussed most often homosexual, they are exemplars of a very special socially sanctioned form of pederasty, characteristic of Plato's time and class. Does that affect what can be learned from it by individuals in other times and other societies, with other assumptions, customs, and interests?

Homoerotic Love—Pausanias

Several of the speakers at this feast of speeches in praise of love make explicitly clear that, in their view, the ideal love relationship is between a male and another male. Some of them suggest that the reason for this is to be found in the social benefits of the practice. Thus Phaedrus argues that an army of lovers would be undefeatable, since a lover would be ashamed to show lack of courage before his beloved (178D–79D). That this should be regarded as important in a world of many divided city-states in frequent armed conflict with each other is hardly surprising. And if in modern wars soldiers are supposed to be inspired by concern for loved ones back home, surely there is something to be said for the power of concern for loved comrades by one's side. But this is no less an argument in favor of women in the military (and a liberal attitude toward "fraternization" in the ranks) than in favor of particular gender alignments in love relations. Other speakers point to social advantages beyond the narrowly military. Aristophanes maintains that youths who pursue other males "are the best of boys and lads, because they are the most manly," citing in proof that "these are the only kind of boys who grow up to be politicians" engaged in public life (191E–92A). But the endorsement here may be ironic, and more important, the benefits to public life might be equally achievable by other practices, given a different social context. Plato himself (through Socrates/Diotima) speaks of the beauty of a beloved boy as the catalyst for the creation of wisdom and virtue, poetry and laws (208E–9E, 211B). But if, as Plato insists, there is a single Form of Beauty instantiated in all beautiful things (however otherwise diverse), the gender of the bearer of inspirational beauty should be irrelevant to its power. (Thomas Mann's Aschenbach has his Tadzio, Dante has his Beatrice.) In our time, Freud too has suggested that homosexual erotic energy might contribute to socially spirited and productive activity; though unlike the Greeks, Freud seems usually to think it is the sublimated forms of that energy that are most effective.[1] Plato's own view of sexual sublimation is complex and will need closer scrutiny.

Pausanias gives a fuller picture of the ideal love relationship in classical Athens. It is unsublimated, but it is crucially asymmetrical. Although the lovers are of the same gender, they are of different ages. The ideal love relationship is between an older man and an adolescent youth (described as "beardless" by Phaedrus [180A] and as "showing the first traces of a beard" by Pausanias [181D]). The needs that are fulfilled by the relationship are also thought to be different. While the youth (the beloved, *eromenos*) offers his beauty and sensual satisfaction, the older man (the lover, *erastes*) is supposed to provide moral instruction, spiritual and intellectual guidance. The relationship is importantly educational.

Pausanias spells out the assumptions of the Athens of his time in connection with a contrast he draws between two types of love, Heavenly and Common. The lower form of love is aimed purely at physical pleasure and may be directed at very young boys or even women. (Women are generally denigrated throughout the theoretical discussions of the *Symposium*, though a few—such as Alcestis and Diotima—are accorded respectful treatment.)[2] Because Common love is inspired by physical attractions, which inevitably fade, it is unreliable and of short duration. Heavenly love differs in aim, object, and duration. Although it may include physical intimacy (the lover desires "favors"), it centrally aims at spiritual communion and the development of the beloved. Its objects are older youths, of high spirit and high intelligence. And the love is stable and of lasting duration. Indeed, the key test for differentiating Heavenly from Common love involves time and the overcoming of obstacles, provided through a whole etiquette of courtship and interaction. The youth is expected to be at first coy and to avoid giving in too soon or for base motives (as would be suspected were he to give in to a rich or famous person who could not offer a suitable mentor relationship in pursuit of virtue and excellence). The ideal structure involves a bargain, but (on Pausanias's account) a long-term and high-minded one. One should be aware that some of Pausanias's statements may be self-serving; he is, as Aristophanes indicates (193C, cf. *Protagoras* 315D–E), the long-term lover of Agathon, the honored tragic poet and host of the feast. Diotima's later praise of pederasty ("loving boys correctly" [211B]), however, must be regarded as disinterested.

The sexual asymmetry in the relationship deserves a note of emphasis. In Pausanias's picture, the youth is not supposed to be particularly physically attracted to the older man, and in any case sexual gratification is not his aim. Aristophanes, by contrast, seems to allow that the youth may enjoy the physical aspects of the relationship ("While they are boys . . . they love men and enjoy lying with men and being embraced by men" [191E]). The conventional attitude was that the youth was expected not to enjoy the physical intimacy as such, indeed the range of physical interaction (at least in conventional depictions, as on vases) was rather limited. The assuming of what to the ancient Greeks as to many modern "macho" cultures would appear a passive and so womanly sexual role was problematic and was supposed to be a passing phase (the youth eventually becoming *erastes* to another youth and husband to a wife)—the gratifications involved were supposed to be nonsexual. A strong statement of the view is attributed to Socrates in Xenophon's *Symposium* (8.21): "the boy does not share in the man's pleasure in intercourse, as a woman does; cold sober, he looks upon the other drunk with sexual desire." [3] Of course depictions of cultural expectations should not be mistaken for accounts of actual practice and experience.

In a remarkable passage, in the course of praising the Athenian arrangements, Pausanias directly links sexual repression with political repression. While the idea is a now familiar one, from the work of Marcuse and many others, Plato's Pausanias is the first (so far as I am aware) to make the link. He explains:

> The Persian empire is absolute; that is why it condemns love as well as philosophy and sport. It is no good for rulers if the people they rule cherish ambitions for themselves, or form strong bonds of friendship with one another. That these are precisely the effects of philosophy, sport, and especially of Love is a lesson the tyrants of Athens learned directly from their own experience: didn't their reign come to a dismal end because of the bonds uniting Harmodius and Aristogiton in love and affection?

> So you can see that plain condemnation of Love reveals lust for power in the rulers and cowardice in the ruled. (182B–82D, trans. Nehamas and Woodruff)

Matching Halves—Aristophanes

At the start of his *Three Essays on the Theory of Sexuality*, the greatest book ever written about the nature of sex, Freud speaks of "the poetic fable which tells how the original human beings were cut up into two halves— man and woman—and how these are always striving to unite again in love." If this refers to Aristophanes' speech in the *Symposium*, Freud's account is seriously misleading.[4] After specifying the two halves as "man and woman," Freud goes on to say, "It comes as a great surprise therefore to learn that there are men whose sexual object is a man and not a woman, and women whose sexual object is a woman and not a man." But, of course, this is no surprise on Aristophanes's theory. His story of the division of the original human beings into two halves, and their subsequent quest to reunite in love, allows for all three alternatives. Aristophanes starts with *three* original sexes: double-male, double-female, and "androgynous." Thus the myth offers an explanation (the *same* explanation) of homosexuality and lesbianism as well as heterosexuality.

The Greeks in general tended to think of sexuality as involving a single desire aimed at the beautiful, whether the beauty is embodied in a male or female, and they thought of attraction to a person of the same or the opposite sex as equally natural.[5] This accords with Freud's own preferred view:

> psycho-analysis considers that a choice of an object independently of its sex—freedom to range equally over male and female objects—as it is found in childhood, in primitive states of society and early periods of history, is the original basis from which, as a result of restriction in one direction or the other, both the normal and the inverted types develop. Thus from the point of view of psycho-analysis the exclusive sexual interest felt by men for women is also a problem that needs elucidating and is not a self-evident fact based upon an attraction that is ultimately of a chemical nature. (1905d, *SE* 7: 145–46n)

For psychoanalysis, as for Aristophanes in the *Symposium*, heterosexuality and homosexuality are equally in need of explanation, and the same type of explanation is offered for both. No special explanatory factors or pathology is involved in either object choice.

Aristophanes's myth shares another important feature with Freud's views: for both, love involves "a need to restore an earlier state of things" (Freud 1920g, *SE* 18: 57).[6] So far as later objects are imperfect substitutes for the original object (one's "matching half" [191D]), one's striving for wholeness may have to remain incomplete and restless (cf. Freud 1912d, *SE* 11: 188–89).

The obsessiveness of love may have an even deeper source. Although Aristophanes's picture of restoration of oneness, a blissful merging, as the aim of love resonates through later literature and meshes with much individual experience, a close reading of Aristophanes's myth makes it questionable whether lovers, even on his account, ultimately aim at oneness alone. Anne Carson suggests

> Aristophanes' judgment ("no lover could want anything else") is belied by the anthropology of his own myth. Was it the case that the round be-

ings of his fantasy remained perfectly content rolling about the world in prelapsarian oneness? No. They got big ideas and started rolling toward Olympus to make an attempt on the gods (190b–c). They began reaching for something else. So much for oneness. (1986, 68)

Incompleteness (and also triangles) may form an inevitable aspect of the bittersweetness of eros. Restless striving may be part of its nature. When Plato moves us from Aristophanes's myth to Diotima's transcendental erotics, it becomes explicitly clear that the aim of erotic desire is not the *possession* of the beautiful, but "reproduction and birth in beauty" (206E). (The aim never was simple intercourse, even on Aristophanes's account: "No one would think it is the intimacy of sex—that mere sex is the reason each lover takes so great and deep a joy in being with the other" [192C–D].) Beauty is the object (both on the conventional Greek and the etherealized Platonic accounts), but creativity is the aim of love. Desire is endless, not only because its object (as in Aristophanes's myth) is a forever lost and unrecoverable earlier state, not only because its object (as in Socrates/Diotima's vision) is a transcendental Form, but because what is wanted is creativity inspired by beauty, an activity (not passive ownership).[7]

The aestheticizing of the object of sexual desire may seem puzzling. But it was not for the Greeks in general, who assumed the beautiful is desirable, nor for Plato in particular, who enshrined the Form of Beauty as the ultimate object of desire. Yet so far as "the beautiful" picks out an objective type (especially a visual type), it is not clear that desire in fact always aims at beauty as its object. (Socrates himself was notably ugly; only a shift in gaze from the outer to the inner man enabled Alcibiades to see him as "beautiful" [215B, 217A].) The objects of desire (in particular sexual desire) are subject to all sorts of psychological conditions, "beauty" being only one possibility. It might be a particular scar or a turn of speech that appeals, despite a person's ugliness. Of course if one defines beauty in terms of desirability to the individual, it will follow that whatever one desires, one will believe to be beautiful (cf. Sappho).[8] Freud suggests such a subjectivizing standard when he writes: "There is to my mind no doubt that the concept of 'beautiful' has its roots in sexual excitation and that its original meaning was 'sexually stimulating'" (1905d, *SE* 7: 156 n.2, cf. 209). This is a familiar philosophical move in relation to "good" (defining goodness in terms of desirability). But Plato's Form of Beauty is not subjective, his metaphysics insists on objective standards. So understood, desire need not always in fact aim at beauty. Moreover, there are subjective notions of beauty that do not tie beauty directly to desire. Thus desire need not always aim at beauty—whether one takes beauty itself as subjective or objective. Nonetheless, the special place Plato gives to Beauty (and Goodness) in his account of love may help us better understand the place of idealization in our experience of love.

Longer is Better, Forever is Best—
Socrates and Diotima

Diotima's vision of "rising stairs," which take the lover on an ascent from particular beautiful bodies, to beautiful souls, activities, and laws, and ultimately to knowledge and the very Form of Beauty (210A–11C), contains both unexamined bias and fruitful insight. The progressive abstraction in the objects of love, which may have connections with the special educational functions of homosexual love in Plato's time, moves the lover away from that passionate attachment to a particular person that is perhaps most characteristic of modern views of erotic love. The loss in such detachment is very real (and we will come back to it in relation to Alcibiades). On the other hand, the move toward an ideal object as one ascends Diotima's ladder may reveal some of the importance of the idealization of the object perhaps most characteristic of modern views of romantic love (discussed, for example, by Stendhal in terms of "crystallization"). An ideal abstract object and idealization of a particular object are not the same, but metaphysics and romantic fantasy may here share a common aspiration.

The aim of love according to Plato is creativity, the achievement of immortality through "reproduction and birth in beauty." Given the homoerotic context, it is perhaps not surprising that the principle of procreation is male (though it is presented in the female voice of Diotima, as reported by Socrates): it is the men who are "pregnant," both in body and in soul, and spiritual and intellectual children are to be preferred to the fleshly variety (208E–9E). The beauty of the beloved is the catalyst for the creativity. There is in Plato's account, in addition to a bias for the male, a bias for the abstract and for the eternal. Creativity might in the ordinary Greek practice be expressed through the education and cultivation of the beloved. And this may involve overvaluation, an idealization of the object of love. Plato makes no direct mention of such overvaluation in the *Symposium* (romantic idealization of a particular individual would seem short-sighted delusion in the face of the Forms), but he recognizes it quite clearly in the *Phaedrus* as involving a projection of desired characteristics (252D 53C).[9] Diotima insists that love depends on the ideal, and Alcibiades idealizes Socrates (although it is a question whether rightly or as a delusion). Idealization of the object of love is later crucial to the nature of love according to Stendhal, Proust, Freud, and countless others. Freud suggests that such overvaluation of the beloved is the result of transferred narcissism,[10] and the importance Plato attaches to an egoistic desire for immortality (even in the case of Alcestis's sacrifice of her life—apparently—for her husband's sake [208C–E]) accords with such a source. (Plato would of course deny that the "idealization" involved when the Forms, rather than particular individuals, are the objects of love constitutes *over*valuation.) If the source seems low, the aspiration remains high. Idealization points to a value beyond the immediate object. Plato makes an important contribution in distinguishing the two. The problem emerges when one considers whether the value of the manifest image of the transcendent is itself enhanced or diminished in virtue of its intermediary role. In the *Symposium*, the message is that those who see aright will recognize that the immediate object of love really stands in for or represents an ultimate value. The unfortunate implication is that, once this is understood, the particular individual can drop out of the picture. Thus, Socrates rejects Aristophanes's notion that we love the missing part of ourselves in the other, and insists that we love only the good in the object (205E). The particular beautiful object is used to move to the vision of the Form, which in itself is not visible to the senses, having neither face nor hands nor "anything else that belongs to the body" (211A). On this account, what gets left out is love of the individual as a whole (with and even despite his faults), love of the individual as (perishably) embodied, and love for the sake of the beloved (as opposed to for the good of the lover). (See Vlastos 1973.)

The Platonic ascent sublimates particular attachments in favor of what results in a kind of social creativity (yielding poetry and laws), but it is motivated in his account by an egoistic desire for immortality. In this we see his bias for the eternal.

That more stable, long-lasting relationships are better is an assumption built into Pausanias's test for Heavenly love. Surely if longer is better, forever is best. But people change and ultimately perish. The highest objects of love for Plato are unperishing. Individuals aim at immortality for themselves, and in their objects seek the immortal. People inevitably drop out of the picture altogether. Even when love of particular people has a place—at the bottom of Diotima's ladder—it is aimed only at the good in them, and loving them is only a way to the Forms. Plato (and many since) makes a profound assumption that in love, and in everything else, the everlasting is better, the unchanging is better. Is it? Plato speaks of the absolute Form of Beauty as "not polluted by human flesh or colors or any other great nonsense of mortality" (211E). But is an artificial rose that lasts indefinitely "better" than a living rose, with its ephemeral, passing beauty? And, in case one thinks an artificial rose is a thing different in kind from a rose, would a rose that lasted forever, that never wilted or withered, inevitably be better? Is it unthinkable that part of the beauty and appeal of a rose lies precisely in its natural cycle from bud to bloom through death? Would the shape of a human life necessarily be more satisfying if it had no end? If finite life is meaningless or absurd, might not unending life be infinitely meaningless or infinitely absurd (see Nagel 1979a)? And it has been argued that eternal life, far from being desirable, would inevitably be boring (see Williams 1973d).

Freud, here as elsewhere, offers valuable insight. Writing in the midst of World War I, he argued against the "view that the transience of what is beautiful involves any loss in its worth. On the contrary, an increase! Transience value is scarcity value in time . . . The beauty of the human form and face vanish for ever in the course of our own lives, but their evanescence only lends them a fresh charm. A flower that blossoms only for a single night does not seem to us on that account less lovely" ("On Transience," 1916a, *SE* 14: 305–6).[11]

Ideas of immortality and the desire for a reliable (ultimately unchanging) object seem tied to narcissistic desires for self-sufficiency that may be incompatible with love as a relationship. The aspirations in Plato's vision, like Spinoza's "intellectual love of God," may lead to a life in which individual relationships and individual persons as objects of love drop out. The philosopher contemplating the Forms is a model of self-sufficiency, like "Socrates, who was impervious to drink, to cold, to the naked body of Alcibiades" (Nussbaum 1986b, 203; see also 1986a, 183–84, 199).

Why Say No to Alcibiades?

When Alcibiades joins the company, we learn from him that years before Socrates had rejected his advances. At the time, Alcibiades had been commonly viewed as the most promising, beautiful, and desirable youth in Athens, and Socrates (as presented in Plato's portrait) was the wisest and the best man. So the relation, if consummated, would have exemplified what Pausanias had described as the ideal: a relation for mutual benefit between an older man and a younger boy, the man enjoying the youth's sensual beauty and the youth receiving valuable instruction. What is unusual in Alcibiades's story in terms of Athenian ideals is the reversal of conventional courtship roles, with the younger man pursuing the older. But surely this was not enough to make Socrates turn away, especially since it is clear that Alcibiades was as desirable to him as to everyone else.[12] Why then did Socrates's view of love require him to reject Alcibiades?

When Socrates rejects Alcibiades, he speaks contemptuously (ironically?) of being asked to give "gold in exchange for bronze" (219A). But is Socrates in fact being offered an unfair bargain? Granting the evaluation of his and Alcibiades's assets in terms of gold and bronze, what would Socrates be giving up? For unlike gold, which once given is gone, wisdom can be given to another and yet retained, that is, shared without loss or sacrifice. (If Socrates's point is that he lacks the wisdom Alcibiades means to be bargaining for, that in itself is no reason not to indulge in sexual relations—so long as fraud and deceit are avoided.) Perhaps the problem is not supposed to be the unfairness (what Socrates would have to give up), but the insufficiency of the inducement. On Diotima's account, the enlightened lover would have no desire for what Alcibiades was offering. That is, on one reading, once one has achieved later and higher stages on the ascending ladder of love, one would have abandoned the earlier and lower ("When he grasps this, he must become a lover of all beautiful bodies, and he must think that this wild gaping after just one body is a small thing and despise it" [210B]).

But why should that be so? Why should there not be room for both interests, even if one is thought of as higher and the other as lower (because of a bias for the eternal)? Aristotle, and many others before and since, have insisted that human beings are of mixed nature. While partaking in the nature of both gods and animals, we are not simply either. We may achieve insight into the eternal Forms, but we are also embodied creatures with mortal needs. No one can live a life devoted exclusively to doing mathematics or contemplating the Forms—even if such moments constitute the high point of particular days. Even Socrates himself, with his great powers of concentration and in his extreme self-composure, is better considered not as a person beyond temptation, but as a person of extraordinary temperance and self-control and of extraordinary calm and contentment within his self-control (Vlastos 1991, 37–41).

Perhaps Socrates means to be teaching Alcibiades a lesson. What then is it? Alcibiades's own desires seem already to fit the hierarchy in Diotima's ladder. Alcibiades's feelings for the outwardly unattractive Socrates reveal that he has already moved beyond the first step, love of mere bodily beauty. In approaching Socrates he says: "Nothing is more important to me than becoming the best man I can be, and no one can help me more than you to reach that aim" (218D). He comes seeking intellectual instruction, improvement of his soul (not gross physical pleasure) from Socrates. He is clearly not acting out of simple lust or for the sake of money or some other low aim.[13] So when Socrates denies himself sensual pleasure, he is *not* showing Alcibiades that he should seek higher things than sensual pleasure. Alcibiades already knows that and in offering himself to Socrates is trying to further the pursuit of those very higher things at which Diotima and Socrates would have him aim. It would of course be another sort of error if Alcibiades thought he could acquire what wisdom Socrates had by sleeping next to him, by some form of osmosis. That is an error Socrates attacked at the start of the *Symposium* with the analogy of the string and water (175D–E). But Alcibiades does not think physical contact is all that is needed. He wants to be close to Socrates so he can discuss philosophy with him and learn. But then again, Socrates would freely discuss philosophy with anyone, he did not require payment like a sophist or an exchange of sexual favors like the predatory wolves that lovers of boys, on some views, turn out to be.[14]

As noted, Alcibiades's design seems to fit Pausanias's ideal (in which a youth exchanges beauty and sensuousness for a mature man's wisdom and instruction). Perhaps then the ideal described by Pausanias was not in fact pervasive in the Athens of his time (despite much corroborating evidence [Dover 1964]), or even if it was, perhaps Socrates wished to reject that ideal: either regarding it as incompatible with the contemplation of higher things or simply regarding it as unseemly for a dignified older man to be in hot pursuit of pretty boys, however much he might enjoy the distraction from his more demanding intellectual pursuits.

There is in fact a speech to that effect in the *Phaedrus*, where Plato has

Socrates criticize "May-December" romances in terms of divergent interests, compulsive behavior, and "unseasonable fulsome compliments" (*Phaedrus* 240C–E, trans. Hackforth; cf. Xenophon, *Memorabilia* i 2.29f). But that speech is later repudiated, at least in part, in favor of the divine madness of love. Still, despite the approval of passionate attachment in Socrates's more considered speech (his speech of recantation), there abides an antipathy to physical gratification of love—and it should be noted that it extends to intercourse of any kind, whether homosexual (*Phaedrus* 256A–B) or heterosexual (*Phaedrus* 250E).[15] That repugnance, quite apart from issues of age difference, may account for Socrates's rejection of Alcibiades's embraces as he sleeps through the night beside him.

If Socrates meant to be giving Alcibiades a lesson in abstinence, then Diotima's ideal differs from Pausanias's in more than just its vision of the Form. Pausanias would allow the beloved to grant "favors" and perform "any service for a lover who can make him wise and virtuous" (184D). The question becomes why Diotima's ideal calls for abstinence, either through the despising and abandoning of earlier objects or, more peculiarly, through precise sexual limitations. The abstinence (as spelled out most clearly in the *Phaedrus*) is required only beyond a certain point, marked by intercourse.[16] Why?

To start on the path to contemplation of true Beauty, there must be self-denial and self-control, and specifically there must be physical abstinence. Socrates's dissociation from his own body as he ascends the ladder is evidenced in many of his distinctive characteristics, from imperviousness to alcohol and cold to imperviousness (beyond a certain point) to the charms of Alcibiades. But Socrates did not feel obliged to abstain from alcohol. Why should sexual relations seem more threatening? Perhaps because he was more susceptible to their appeal. Certainly sexual arousal had greater power to disturb his equanimity (see *Charmides* 155C–E). Still, more may be at stake than Socrates's (or any would-be philosopher's) self-sufficient impregnability and imperturbability. Plato, at various points in his development, subscribes to beliefs that might make him (and Socrates in his account) shy away from intercourse with a beloved. In the *Phaedrus*, despite initial lust for "a monstrous and forbidden act," the lover exercises restraint because of "modesty" and "awe and reverence" for the Form of Beauty reflected in the beloved (254A–B), and ultimately because of "reverence and awe" for the beloved himself (254E). Later, despite mutuality of desire, caresses stop short of intercourse because of "reverence and heedfulness" and the desire for "self-mastery and inward peace" (256A–B). Yet it is difficult to see how this is based on anything other than the sort of suspicion of the body and antipathy to intercourse that pervade Plato's works (as well as, of course, later Christianity).[17]

The specific problem of intercourse for Plato (recall that passionate physical interaction, up to but not including intercourse, is permitted in the *Phaedrus*) may be based on the specially intense pleasure of orgasm.

Regarding the soul as the prisoner of the body, and believing that intense pleasure nails the soul to the body, making it impossible to detach and free oneself and distorting one's sense of reality (*Phaedo* 82D–83D), Plato understandably has a metaphysical horror of such experience (Vlastos 1991, 39). But it is a false metaphysics that seeks to separate the mind from the body, and it is a false respect that seeks to separate out disembodied virtues of the beloved. In addition, in the *Laws* and elsewhere, Plato explicitly regards homosexual intercourse (though not homosexual desire in general) as "unnatural" (cf. *Phaedrus* 250E, *Republic* 403B–C, *Laws* 636, 836B–41E). That view is of course, where intelligible, untenable: animals do engage in such intercourse; and, whatever is true of other animals, one must remember that humans and their diverse desires are also part of the natural order.[18]

Whatever Plato may have believed, false respect and false natural lines (and behind them, the need for control and the need to avoid passivity) cannot be taken by us as proper grounds for guiding behavior. If physical limits placed on passionate attachment are not to be based on false beliefs or on a simple and unjustified rejection of sexuality in general, other matters must come into consideration. In addition to issues of the "exploitation" of youth (after Freud it is not possible to deny the presence of sexual desires in even the very young, but neither is it possible to assume they take the same form as adult sexual desires),[19] there may be implicit in Plato's views a doctrine of sublimation, in which energy with a certain object and aim gets deliberately turned to higher objects and aims, strengthening the passionate pursuit of knowledge and virtue (cf. *Republic* 485D). This sexual energizing of the quest for the transcendental ideal would in some ways anticipate the explicit doctrine of sublimation in Freud, which goes beyond Plato's both in scope and in operations. Freud adds the complications of infantile pregenital sexuality while Plato restricts only certain consummating activities of adult sexuality, and not the correlative desires, and not homosexual activity in general. Freud further introduces unconscious mechanisms while Plato is concerned with self-conscious self-control.[20]

It might be suggested that Socrates also objected to the double standard built into the Athenian ideal of his time. Pausanias's model includes a double standard which, while focused on age rather than gender, is not wholly unlike the more familiar Victorian variety. Older men are encouraged to pursue younger boys, but the boys are encouraged to play hard to get. This is, according to Pausanias, to test the seriousness of the man's intentions; but it may also reflect a natural variation, in a society where women were segregated, of the same conventions that governed a later society where women were allowed more freedom of movement (Dover 1978, 81–91). Finally, it may reflect in the conventional terms of the time the seductiveness of unattainability, the essential tension of erotic desire that connects attractiveness with lack and obstacle.[21] Whatever the significance of the double standard ("we do everything we can to make it as easy as possible for lovers to press their suits and as difficult as possible for young men to comply" [184A]), if Socrates did object to it there is no evidence that he did in the *Symposium*. Alcibiades in fact switches traditional roles in relation to Socrates ("as if I were his lover and he my young prey" [217C]), and there is nothing in the *Symposium* to suggest that Socrates (or Diotima in her quoted speech) rejects the hierarchy of age and status, not to speak of the sexual asymmetry, between lovers generally accepted in Greek society.[22] Plato's emphasis on creativity rather than on possessiveness in love, the sublimation of physical desire, and the move to an ideal object are all truly distinctive, but they do not come tied to any notion of equality or reciprocity in love. Indeed, not only is the model of love in the *Symposium* generally between unequals, but as one ascends Diotima's ladder other people drop out as the object of love, their place taken by the Forms—and Forms *cannot* reciprocate love. The question then becomes whether one can make the ascent alone, without the company of (human) lovers (whether equal or unequal). Socrates himself has a guide or teacher, namely Diotima, on the way to the highest vision of love; and a beautiful inspiration seems important at least in the earliest stages (according to the account in the *Symposium*) and perhaps throughout the quest (according to the account in the *Phaedrus*). The question nonetheless remains whether one can make sense of an erotic love in which ultimately the lover does not himself desire to be loved.

I have noted that one cannot explain Socrates's rejection of Alcibiades by a lack of homosexual desire in general or attraction to Alcibiades in particular. And Socrates's view of love, like the conventional one of his time, included neither horror at homosexuality nor modern notions of equality between lovers. By the time Plato wrote the *Symposium*, however, he and his audience would have been aware that Alcibiades had come to a bad end (he was murdered in 404 BC, after betraying Athens and contributing to its defeat in the Peloponnesian War; the likely composition date for the *Symposium* is between 385 and 378 BC [Dover 1965]). But if we suppose Socrates at the time of the attempted seduction had a premonition of Alcibiades's bad end, he would have been rejecting Alcibiades for his (later) bad character. Although this might accord with the notion of loving only the good in the beloved (which Socrates insists on in opposition to Aristophanes's notion of love of one's other half), he makes no mention of it. Moreover, it does not accord with love of whole persons (with or despite their faults). Not that all faults must be accepted, but if people are all mixed in character, the result for Socrates would be that individuals (even with minor flaws) disappear as objects of love (for moral as well as metaphysical reasons). Some in Athens doubtless blamed Socrates for the corruption of Alcibiades and other of his followers (cf. the *Apology*), and some might read the *Symposium* as a response to the charge, showing preexisting flaws in the pupil who preferred political glory to philosophical pursuits—but then it could also be read as revealing Socrates's failure as a teacher. For he failed to give Alcibiades whatever was needed to change him (whether or not he should be blamed for his "corruption"); unlike his teacher Diotima, it could be said he frustrated his students with his insistent disavowal of knowledge. And the failure here may be thought of as a failure of love (Vlastos 1958, 16–17; Gagarin 1977, 22–37; Nussbaum 1986a).

Conclusion

Does the fact that Plato's *Symposium* focuses on homosexual love affect what it has to teach us about erotic desire? The perhaps obvious answer is: in some ways yes, in some ways no. The advantages of homosexual relations as perceived by Plato's symposiasts, like the perceived disadvantages of homosexual relations in some modern societies, are largely social artifacts, the variable and changeable effects of local customs and attitudes. Attraction to members of one's own or of the opposite sex is, as Aristophanes's myth suggests and as Freud's theory confirms, explainable in terms of a single underlying set of factors; neither preference is to be regarded as more natural than the other. And as the classical Greek practices reveal, neither preference need be exclusive or fixed for life. Plato's preference emerges in Diotima's image of male pregnancy. The gender of the immediate object of love certainly affects the possibilities of procreation, and dubious presumptions about the superiority of the male and the spiritual as opposed to the female and the bodily come into play, but the distinguishing of an ultimate object beyond the immediate one as well as the nature of that ultimate object and of the aims of erotic desire (whether or not one accepts Plato's particular account) remain unaffected. Plato's emphasis on creativity in love may indeed have been influenced by the educational functions of the homoerotic practices of his time. Even the refusal of the sort of physical consummation that Pausanias's ideal would have allowed may be seen as aimed at strengthening the passionate pursuit of knowledge and virtue, thus according with the educational aims while revising the practices. But the case for (what through modern eyes must be seen as) intentional sublimation rests neither on Plato's personal preferences nor the customs of his time. The Forms as the ultimate objects of love and the restrictions on sexual activity are based on Plato's metaphysics, a metaphysics that makes the Forms the supreme reality and that sees the human body as an ephemeral prison for the soul. Plato's call for sublimation can be no more persuasive than that metaphysics. Nonetheless, Plato's expansion of the scope of eros (205A–D), like Freud's later expansion of the scope of sexuality, offers explanatory insight. Plato's metaphysical flight up Diotima's rising stairs takes us away from the conventional objects of love (of our own and also, it should be emphasized, his own time), but takes us closer to understanding both the obsessiveness (due to the unobtainability of the ultimate object and aim) and the overvaluation (due to the ultimate value represented by the immediate object) characteristic of erotic love. And other insights, such as those concerning the role of creativity as opposed to possessiveness in love and the one voiced by Pausanias concerning the relations of sexuality and politics, are independent of social convention and individual preference; indeed, they help us understand such conventions and preferences.

9

FREUD AND PERVERSION

The first of Freud's *Three Essays on the Theory of Sexuality* (1905d) is entitled "The Sexual Aberrations." Why should Freud begin a book the main point of which is to argue for the existence of infantile sexuality with a discussion of adult perversions? (After all, the existence of the adult aberrations was hardly news.) While many answers might be suggested with some plausibility (e.g., to ease the shock of the new claim; or, medical texts typically begin with pathology), I believe Freud's beginning can be usefully understood as part of an effective argumentative strategy to extend the notion of sexuality by showing how extensive it already was. Freud himself (in the preface to the fourth edition) describes the book as an attempt "at enlarging the concept of sexuality" (7: 134). The extension involved in the notion of perversion prepares the way for the extension involved in infantile sexuality.

The book begins on its very first page with a statement of the popular view of the sexual instinct:

> It is generally understood to be absent in childhood, to set in at the time of puberty in connection with the process of coming to maturity and to be revealed in the manifestations of an irresistible attraction exercised by one sex upon the other; while its aim is presumed to be sexual union, or at all events actions leading in that direction. (1905d, 7: 135)

But it quickly becomes obvious that this will not do as a definition of the sphere of the sexual. Sexuality is not confined to heterosexual genital intercourse between adults, for there are a number of perversions, and even popular opinion recognizes these as sexual in their nature. Popular opinion might wish to maintain a narrow conception of what is to count as *normal* sexuality, thus raising a problem about how one is to distinguish between normal and abnormal sexuality, but the more interesting and immediate problem is to make clear in virtue of what the perversions are recognized as sexual at all. And it is here that Freud makes an enormous conceptual advance. He distinguishes the object and the aim of the sexual instinct (decomposing what might have seemed an indissoluble unity), and he introduces the notion of erotogenic zones (thus extending sexuality beyond the genitals), and is thus able to show that the perversions involve variations along a number of dimensions (source, object, and aim) of a single underlying instinct. Heterosexual genital intercourse is one constellation of variations, and homosexuality is another. Homosexuality, or inversion, involves variation in object, but the sexual sources (erotogenic zones or bodily centers of arousal) and aims (acts, such as intercourse and looking, designed to achieve pleasure and satisfaction) may be the same. Thus what makes homosexuality recognizably sexual, despite its distance from what might he presented as the ordinary person's definition of sexuality, is the vast amount that it can be seen to have in common with "normal" sexuality once one comes to understand the sexual instinct as itself complex, as having components and dimensions.

Freud makes the complexity of the sexual instinct compelling by drawing on the researches of the tireless investigators of sexual deviation such as Richard Krafft-Ebing and Havelock Ellis. He makes the complexity intelligible by distinguishing the few dimensions (source, object, and aim) of the underlying instinct that are needed to lend order to the vast variety of phenomena, providing an illuminating new classificatory scheme. Once each of the perversions is understood as involving variation along one or more dimensions of a single underlying instinct, Freud is in a position to do two things. First, to call into question the primacy of one constellation of variations over another. And second, to show that other phenomena that might not appear on the surface sexual (e.g., childhood thumbsucking) share essential characteristics with obviously sexual activity (e.g., infantile sensual sucking involves pleasurable stimulation of the same erotogenic zone, the mouth, stimulated in adult sexual activities such as kissing), and can be understood as being earlier stages in the development of the same underlying instinct that expresses itself in such various forms in adult sexuality. Freud is in a position to discover infantile sexuality. To briefly retrace the steps to this point: Perversions are regarded as sexual because they can be understood as variations of an underlying instinct along three dimensions (somatic source, object, and aim). The instinct has components, is complex or "composite" (1905d, 7: 162). If adult perversions can be understood in terms of an underlying instinct with components that can be specified along several dimensions, then many of the activities of infancy can also be so understood, can be seen as earlier stages in the development of those components. But now I wish to focus on the newly problematic relation of normal and abnormal sexuality. Is one set of variations better or worse than another? The mere fact of difference, variation in content, is no longer enough once one cannot say one set of variations is somehow natural and others are not. Once one sees sexuality as involving a single underlying instinct, with room for variation along several dimensions, new criteria for pathology are needed. Moreover, insofar as variation is thought-dependent, rather than a matter of biological aberration, the question arises of whether there is such a thing as a pathology of sexual thought. Is there room for a morality of desire and fantasy alongside the ordinary morality governing action?

Homosexuality

Freud initially distinguishes inversion from perversion. Inversion involves displacement of the sexual object from members of the opposite sex to members of the same sex. Inversion includes male homosexuality and lesbianism. Insofar as it involves variation in object only, it may appear less shockingly "deviant" than other sexual aberrations. But insofar as the point of singling out inversion is to contrast it with aberrations involving displacement in aim rather than object, it might as well include a wider range of aberrations, aberrations where displacement is to someone or something other than members of the same sex. From that point of view, bestiality, necrophilia, and so forth are more like inversion than like the other aberrations—and Freud in fact treats them together as "deviations in respect of the sexual object" (1905d, 7: 136). If we include these less common and more troubling variations in object, inversion may no longer seem a less problematical form of sexual aberration. Moreover, the distinction between inversion and perversion tends to collapse in the course of Freud's discussion of fetishism (is the deviation in object? in aim?—1905d, 7: 153). And it should be remembered that homosexuality is itself (like heterosexuality) internally complex, encompassing many different activities and attitudes. I shall use "perversion" broadly, as Freud himself usually does, so that homosexuality counts as a perversion within Freud's classificatory scheme.

Is that a reproach? In the *Three Essays*, Freud states explicitly that it is inappropriate to use the word "perversion" as a "term of reproach" (1905d, 7: 160). But that is in the special context of exploring the implications of his expanded conception of sexuality. In the case of Dora, published in the same year as the *Three Essays*, he refers to a fantasy of fellatio as "excessively repulsive and perverted" (1905e, 7: 52). A reproach seems built into the reference. It could be argued that Freud is forced to use the vocabulary of the view he wishes to overthrow, and that it carries its unwelcome connotations with it. Indeed, he in the same place argues that "We must learn to speak without indignation of what we call the sexual perversions—instances in which the sexual function has extended its limits in respect either to the part of the body concerned or to the sexual object chosen" (1905e, 7: 50). Perhaps Freud's own feelings, about the term if not the specific acts referred to, are ambivalent. The important question is what the appropriate attitude is and whether Freud's theory offers any light. So, again, let us consider homosexuality. Supposing it is a perversion, is that a reproach? Is the fact that it counts as a perversion a reason for disapproving of it in others or avoiding it oneself?

One could take the high ground and claim that it is pointless to disapprove what is not in a person's control, and then argue that choice of sexual object or sexual orientation is not in a person's control. But this does not really take one very far. Perhaps one has no or only marginal control over whether one contracts diabetes, but this does not stop us from recognizing that diabetes is a bad thing (while it does compel us to treat diabetes patients as victims). Even if we had an etiological theory that assured us that homosexuality is not a matter of choice, and so perhaps not properly disapproved, that would not settle the question of whether it is a good or a bad thing (something we should avoid if we could). Moreover, even if sexual orientation is a given, outside the individual's control, what is given is a direction to desire. There remains the question of whether the individual should seek to control and suppress, or act on and express, the given desires.[1]

Freud does not in fact take the high ground. His own etiological views seem to leave open the extent of biological and other dispositional factors in leading to homosexuality. Whether homosexuality is innate or acquired is for him an open and a complex question (1905d, 7: 140). And, to whatever extent it is acquired, the conditions of its acquisition are also complex (1905d, 7: 144f.). The so-called "choice" of a sexual object is thus multiply obscure, and it is unclear to what extent the relevant causal conditions are within the individual's control (though one might also question whether and when control should be regarded as a condition of responsibility—see Williams [1981] and Nagel [1979c]). Freud nonetheless argues, on other grounds, that the "perversity" of homosexuality gives no reason to condemn it:

> The uncertainty in regard to the boundaries of what is to be called normal sexual life, when we take different races and different epochs into account, should in itself be enough to cool the zealot's ardour. We surely ought not to forget that the perversion which is the most repellent to us, the sensual love of a man for a man, was not only tolerated by a people so far our superiors in cultivation as were the Greeks, but was actually entrusted by them with important social functions. The sexual life of each one of us extends to a slight degree—now in this direction, now in that—beyond the narrow lines imposed as the standard of normality. The perversions are neither bestial nor degenerate in the emotional sense of the word. They are a development of germs all of which are contained in the undifferentiated sexual disposition of the child, and which, by being suppressed or by being diverted to higher, asexual aims—by being "sublimated"—are destined to provide the energy for a great number of our cultural achievements. (1905e, 7: 50)

This passage actually contains at least two different types of argument. One is an appeal to universality across individuals, another an appeal to diversity across cultures. There is no doubt that sexual standards are culturally relative: different societies approve and disapprove of different sexual activities. But one might still wonder whether some societies are perverse in a pejorative sense. There is no avoiding direct consideration of the question of the criteria for perversion. Do they allow for something more than culturally relative, or even individually relative (whatever pleases one), judgments of sexual value?

Criteria for Perversion

Once one accepts Freud's view of the complexity of the underlying sexual instinct, the old content criterion for perversion and pathology must be abandoned. As Freud writes, "In the sphere of sexual life we are brought up against peculiar and, indeed, insoluble difficulties as soon as we try to draw a sharp line to distinguish mere variations within the range of what is physiological from pathological symptoms" (1905d, 7: 160–61).

It might seem simple enough to provide a sociological or statistical specification of perversion, but there are difficulties. For what precisely would the statistics reflect? One's questionnaires or surveys might seek to discover what the majority regards as perverse, but that would leave one wanting to know what perversion is (after all, members of the majority might in fact be applying very various standards). One might try to avoid direct circularity by, without mentioning the concept perversion, trying to elicit information revealing of which sexual desires the majority disapproves. But circularity reemerges on this approach because there might be all sorts of different grounds for disapproval (aesthetic, moral, religious, political, biological, medical, to name a few), and what one wants is to single out those desires and practices which are disapproved of as (specifically) perverse. It appears one's questions and evidence would have already to be applying some standard of perversion in order to achieve that singling out. Parallel and further problems would apply to surveys of actual sexual practices. (Are perversions necessarily rare? If a practice became popular, would it therefore cease to be perverse? And if a practice were rare, e.g., celibacy or adultery, would that be sufficient to make it perverse?) Surely perversion is meant to mark only a certain kind of deviation from a norm. And there is another difficulty. For whatever method one uses, it will turn out that what counts as perversion will vary from society to society, will vary over time and place, in short, will be culturally relative. So insofar as one's concern is wider than the views of a particular society or group, insofar as it is a concern with general psychological theory, with the nature of human nature, no sociological approach will do. Moreover, insofar as one's concern is personal, or perhaps even therapeutic (unless one's standards of therapy are simply adaptation to local and contemporary prevailing norms), that is, if one is concerned to know how one ought to live one's life (including one's sexual life), a sociological approach will not do. For one's society may be wrongheaded, prejudiced, misguided, or in other ways mistaken. One has only one life to live. It might be necessary to resist one's society's demands or even to leave it. So one must look further.

Perhaps perversion can still be defined in terms of content if we are willing to start (again) with the popular view of normal sexuality as consisting of heterosexual genital intercourse between adults: then, any sexual desire or practice that goes beyond the body parts intended for sexual union, or that devotes too exclusive attention to a form of interaction normally passed through on the way to the final sexual aim, or that is directed at an object other than an adult member of the opposite sex, might be regarded as perverse.[2] One might insist on this stand independently of what the members of any particular society happen to think. But as we have seen, once one accepts Freud's analysis of the sexual in terms of a single, but complex, underlying instinct, while it becomes clear why the sexual perversions count as sexual, it becomes unclear why they are perverse. What privileges heterosexual genital intercourse between adults? Is there some further criterion that transcends individual societal views?

One might consider disgust. That is, we might try to pick out sexual activities to be condemned as perverse on the basis of a, presumably natural, reaction of disgust. Extensions of sexual activity beyond the genitals, alternative sources of sexual pleasure, would be perverse if disgust at them were sufficiently widespread. So fellatio and cunnilingus might count as perverse were disgust widely felt at oral-genital contact (as Freud reveals it was in his society at the time of the Dora case). But disgust is itself generally culturally variable and often purely conventional. As Freud points out, "a man who will kiss a pretty girl's lips passionately, may perhaps be disgusted at the idea of using her toothbrush, though there are no grounds for supposing that his own oral cavity, for which he feels no disgust, is any cleaner than the girl's" (1905d, 7: 151–52). Nonetheless, Freud seems to think that a content criterion can be preserved in certain extreme cases "as, for instance, in cases of licking excrement or of intercourse with dead bodies" (1905d, 7: 161). Perhaps some things, such as licking excrement, are thought to be objectively, universally disgusting. But perverse practices reveal that is not true, and Freud should know better.

Developmentally, children must learn to be disgusted at feces. This fact may not be obvious, but Freud was well aware of it. During the period of his earliest speculations about anal erotism, Freud wrote a fascinating letter to his friend Fliess:

I had been meaning to ask you, in connection with the eating of excrement [by] [illegible words] animals, when disgust first appears in small children and whether there exists a period in earliest infancy when these feelings are absent. Why do I not go into the nursery and experiment with Annerl? Because working for 12 1/2 hours, I have no time for it, and the womenfolk do not support my researches. The answer would be of theoretical interest. (1985 [1887–1904], 230, letter of February 8, 1897)

(This letter reminds us how little Freud's theories about infantile sexuality were based on the direct observation of children. Which, to my mind, far from undermining his achievement—given its substantial confirmation by subsequent observations—makes it all the more remarkable. Freud was not the first person to observe that children suck their thumbs, but it was only with his conceptual innovations that he and others could see this and other infantile activities as sexual.) The answer to his question about excrement was well known to Freud by the time he wrote the *Three Essays*. Children will play quite happily with their little turds, and as Freud writes, the contents of the bowels "are clearly treated as a part of the infant's own body and represent his first 'gift': by producing them he can express his active compliance with his environment and, by withholding them, his disobedience" (1905d, 7: 186). And Freud elsewhere develops the analogy between feces and other valued possessions, such as gold (1908b).[3] Disgust at the excremental is itself in need of explanation.

> Where the anus is concerned . . . it is disgust which stamps that sexual aim as a perversion. I hope, however, I shall not he accused of partisanship when I assert that people who try to account for this disgust by saying that the organ in question serves the function of excretion and comes in contact with excrement—a thing which is disgusting in itself—are not much more to the point than hysterical girls who account for their disgust at the male genital by saying that it serves to void urine. (1905d, 7: 152)

It is true that Freud singles out disgust as one of the triumvirate of "forces of repression" (disgust, shame, and morality—1905d, 7: 162, 178), and it may be that the forces of repression are ultimately instinctual and so present in every society, but that need not fix the content of the reaction. That is, it *may* be that everyone is necessarily (meaning biologically) bound to feel disgust at something, while still leaving room for variation in the objects of disgust. It should be no more surprising that the objects of disgust (as an instinct) are variable than that the objects of sexual desire (as an instinct) are variable. So if the objects of sexual desire have no fixed or determinate content, neither do the objects of sexual disgust. We must look elsewhere if we are to find usable criteria for perversion and pathology.

Before looking elsewhere, we should note that there is another problem in a content criterion for perversion, which stems not from the variations I have been emphasizing, but from the universality I have mentioned only in passing. Freud points out that we can find apparently perverse desires not only in (otherwise admirable) other societies, but also within ourselves. In the case of homosexuality, he points out that our desires are responsive to external circumstances. Many will turn to homosexual pleasures given the appropriate favorable or inhibiting circumstances (e.g., "exclusive relations with persons of their own sex, comradeship in war, detention in prison"—1905d, 7: 140). And even more strongly Freud concludes:

> Psycho-analytic research is most decidedly opposed to any attempt at separating off homosexuals from the rest of mankind as a group of a special character. By studying sexual excitations other than those that are manifestly displayed, it has found that all human beings are capable of making a homosexual object-choice and have in fact made one in their unconscious. (1905d, 7: 145n.)

There is a sense in which all human beings are bisexual. Moreover, the universality of perversions other than homosexuality is exhibited in the role they play in foreplay (1905d, 7: 210, 234). The prevalence of perversion (and the "negative" of perversion, neurosis) receives its theoretical underpinning in terms of the universality of polymorphously perverse infantile sexuality. But for now the point is to see that a simple content criterion for perversion will not do. Given the facts of variety in cultural practice and of uniformity in individual potential, it is difficult to see how any particular object-choice (to focus on one dimension) can be singled out as necessarily abnormal. The nature of the sexual instinct itself sets no limit, for as Freud concludes, "the sexual instinct and the sexual object are merely soldered together" (1905d, 7: 148).

An alternative criterion for perversion and pathology emerges in connection with Freud's discussion of fetishism. Freud characterizes fetishism in general in terms of those cases "in which the normal sexual object is replaced by another which bears some relation to it, but is entirely unsuited to serve the normal sexual aim" (1905d, 7: 153). (Note that the variation seems to affect both object and aim.) But he shows that it has a point of contact with the normal through the sort of overvaluation of the sexual object, and of its aspects and of things associated with it, that seems quite generally characteristic of love. He continues:

> The situation only becomes pathological when the longing for the fetish passes beyond the point of being merely a necessary condition attached to the sexual object and actually *takes the place* of the normal aim, and, further, when the fetish becomes detached from a particular individual and becomes the *sole* sexual object. These are, indeed, the general conditions under which mere variations of the sexual instinct pass over into pathological aberrations. (1905d, 7: 154)

Freud spells out the general conditions in terms of "exclusiveness and fixation":

In the majority of instances the pathological character in a perversion is found to lie not in the *content* of the new sexual aim but in its relation to the normal. If a perversion, instead of appearing merely *alongside* the normal sexual aim and object, and only when circumstances are unfavourable to *them* and favourable to *it*—if, instead of this, it ousts them completely and takes their place in *all* circumstances—if, in short, a perversion has the characteristics of exclusiveness and fixation—then we shall usually be justified in regarding it as a pathological symptom. (1905d, 7: 161)

But this really will not do as a general criterion either, for reasons provided by Freud himself in a note a few pages earlier:

psycho-analysis considers that a choice of an object independently of its sex—freedom to range equally over male and female objects—as it is found in childhood, in primitive states of society and early periods of history, is the original basis from which, as a result of restriction in one direction or the other, both the normal and the inverted types develop. Thus from the point of view of psycho-analysis the exclusive sexual interest felt by men for women is also a problem that needs elucidating and is not a self-evident fact based upon an attraction that is ultimately of a chemical nature. (1905d, 7: 146n.)

Once it is recognized that the instinct is merely soldered to its object, that there are wide possibilities of variation in the choice of object, then every choice of object becomes equally problematical, equally in need of explanation. Exclusiveness and fixation cannot be used to mark off homosexuality as perverse without marking off (excessively strong) commitments to heterosexuality as equally perverse. Thus, exclusiveness and fixation are no help if the point of a criterion for perversion is to distinguish the abnormal from the normal, and if heterosexual genital intercourse between adults is to be somehow privileged as the paradigm of the normal. We need some norm for sexuality if the notion of perversion is to take hold. From where can we get it? Is there any reason to suppose that it will take the form of the popular view of normal sexuality?

Development and Maturation

Freud in fact, as we have seen, operates with multiple criteria for perversion and pathology. We have also seen that his own views provide material for a critique of those criteria if one attempts to generalize them. But there emerges from within his theory yet another criterion, a criterion which is meant to be ultimately biological and so not culturally relative. As Freud puts it at the start of the third of his *Three Essays*: "Every pathological disorder of sexual life is rightly to be regarded as an inhibition in development" (1905d, 7: 208). Perverse sexuality is, ultimately, infantile sexuality. While consideration of the adult perversions prepares the way for the extension of our understanding of sexuality to infantile activities in the course of Freud's book, infantile sexuality prepares the way for both normal and perverse sexuality in the development of the individual.[4] It is through arrests in that development, or through regression to earlier points of fixation when faced by later frustration, that an adult comes to manifest perverse sexual activity. We can pick out sexual desires and activities which count as perverse if we have an ideal of normal development and maturation.

Freud's theory of psychosexual development, with its central oral-anal-genital stages, provides such an ideal. The dynamic is at least partly biological. At first, the infant has control of little other than its mouth, and in connection with its original need for taking nourishment it readily develops independent satisfaction in sensual sucking (1905d, 7: 182). That the anus in due course becomes the center of sexual pleasure and wider concerns ("holding back and letting go") is not surprising in the light of a variety of biological developments: As the infant gets older, the feces are better formed, there is more sphincter control (so the child begins to have a choice about when and where to hold back or let go), and with teething there is pressure for the mother to wean.[5] Next comes the genital phase, which gives way to latency and then culminates in puberty and the possibility of reproduction. But one should not totally biologize what is at least in part a social process. There may be a confusion between the ripening of an organic capacity with the valuation of one form of sexuality as its highest or only acceptable form. The subordination of sexuality to reproduction, and the importance attached to heterosexual genital activity, is after all, a social norm. Freud does not claim that there is a biological or evolutionary *preference* for reproduction; the individual preference, if any, is simply for end-pleasure. Even if the preference for end-pleasure or orgasm over fore-pleasure (1905d, 7: 210–12) is biologically determined, the conditions for such pleasure are not. Whether end-pleasure takes place under conditions that might lead to reproduction depends on a wide range of factors, and whether it *should* take place under such conditions is subject to both circumstance and argument. Even if one attaches supreme importance to the survival of the species, other things, including sexual pleasure (which may in turn depend on a certain degree of variety) may be necessary to the survival of the species. And for most of recent history, overpopulation and unwanted conception have been of greater concern than maximizing the reproductive effects of sexual activity. Under certain circumstances homosexuality might have social advantages.[6]

In terms of Freud's instinct theory (not to be confused with standard biological notions of hereditary behavior patterns in animals), every instinct involves an internal, continuously flowing source of energy or tension or pressure. Freud adds, however: "Although instincts are wholly determined by their origin in a somatic source, in mental life we know them only by their aims" (1915c, 14: 123). Given Freud's fundamental hypotheses concerning the mechanisms of psychic functioning, the aim is in every case ultimately discharge of the energy or tension. And given Freud's discharge theory of pleasure (or tension theory of unpleasure), the aim must ultimately be understood in terms of pleasure. Freud is well aware of the problems of a simple discharge theory of pleasure, especially in relation to sexuality (where, after all, the subjective experience of increasing tension is typically as pleasurable as the experience of discharge). (See Freud 1905d, 7: 209f., and Freud 1924c.) The point here, however, is that on Freud's view the essential aim of sexual activity (as instinctual activity) must be pleasure, achievable by a wide variety of particular acts (under a wider variety of thought-dependent conditions). Sexuality may serve many other purposes and have many other functions and aims from a range of different points of view. Among these are reproduction, multilevel interpersonal awareness, interpersonal communication, bodily contact, love, money.[7] Within Freud's theory, perversion is to be understood in terms of infantile, that is nongenital, forms of pleasure. This approach has its problems. For one thing, homosexuality, in some ways the paradigm of perversion for Freud, is not necessarily nongenital and so not obviously perverse by this criterion. Moreover, insofar as other perversions, such as fetishism, aim at genital stimulation and discharge, they too are not purely infantile. (Cf. Freud 1916–17, 16: 321.) In practice, of course, Freud collapses the individual's experienced concern for genital pleasure together with the biological function of reproduction, so that the development and maturation criterion for perversion reduces to the question of the suitability of a particular activity for reproduction.

One should not confuse the (or a) biological function of sexuality, namely reproduction, with sexuality as such. Freud is at pains to point out that sexuality has a history in the development of the individual that precedes the possibility of reproduction. The reproductive function emerges at puberty (1916–17, 16: 311). An ideal of maturation that gives a central role to that function makes all earlier sexuality of necessity perverse. The infant's multiple sources of sexual pleasure make it polymorphously perverse. And the connection works both ways. Sexual perversions can be regarded as in their nature infantile. As Freud puts it:

> if a child has a sexual life at all it is bound to be of a perverse kind; for, except for a few obscure hints, children are without what makes sexuality into the reproductive function. On the other hand, the abandonment of the reproductive function is the common feature of all perversions. We actually describe a sexual activity as perverse if it has given up the aim of reproduction and pursues the attainment of pleasure as an aim independent of it. So . . . the breach and turning-point in the development of sexual life lies in its becoming subordinate to the purposes of reproduction. Everything that happens before this turn of events and equally

everything that disregards it and that aims solely at obtaining pleasure is given the uncomplimentary name of "perverse" and as such is proscribed. (1916–17, 16: 316)

I believe Freud may well provide an accurate account of the link in our language between perversion and nonreproductive sex. On the other hand, I don't believe Freud's theory is committed to maintaining that link (the theoretically necessary aim is pleasure, not reproduction). Moreover, even if detachment from the possibility of reproduction is a necessary condition of regarding a practice as perverse, it cannot be sufficient: otherwise, sterile heterosexual couples or those who use contraceptives would have to be regarded as perverse. (More on these matters in a moment.)

In privileging heterosexual genital intercourse between adults, if only for the purpose of classifying the perversions, one is making a choice based on norms. Freud's discussion of reproduction reflected prevailing social norms, and so the fact that they were norms was perhaps concealed. The norms of the sexual liberationists, such as Herbert Marcuse and Norman O. Brown, are in some ways perhaps continuous with the standards built into Freud's model. Does polymorphous perversion include sadism? Should it? Contemporary debates over the appropriate ideals of sexuality cannot be decided by simple appeals to biology. "Regression" is doubtless an empirical concept, but it gets its sense against a background provided by social norms of development (not purely biological norms of development). In picking out the perversions we apply an external standard to sexuality. Which is not to say that we should not. It is to say only that we should be self-conscious about what we are doing and why. Calling perversions "infantile" may in fact describe them, but the immature is usually regarded as inferior. And if that judgment is to follow, one needs more grounds than those provided by biology. After all, if we live long enough, we eventually decay. Later does not necessarily mean better.

More on Homosexuality

Is homosexuality a perversion? On a content criterion, whether ultimately based on a reaction of disgust or something else, the answer will vary over time and place, and it is arguable that the reaction of disgust is at least as malleable as the desire to which it is a reaction. On a criterion of exclusiveness and fixation, it is no more or less a perversion than heterosexuality of equivalent exclusivity. On a criterion of development and maturation, or arrest and regression, the answer is less clear. Many say that homosexuality is a developmentally immature stage or phase. I do not believe, however, that Freud's theory (despite incidental remarks) commits him to such a view. In the *Three Essays*, Freud notes that homosexuality "may either persist throughout life, or it may go into temporary abeyance, or again it may constitute an episode on the way to a normal development." He goes on, "It may even make its first appearance late in life after a long period of normal sexual activity" (1905d, 7: 137). In this case, it is heterosexuality that is the earlier phase. In passing, in the lecture on anxiety in the *New Introductory Lectures on Psycho-Analysis*, Freud indicates that "in the life of homosexuals, who have failed to accomplish some part of normal sexual development, the vagina is once more represented by [the anus]" (1933a, 22: 101), thus presumably explaining why the vagina is avoided or (in the case of homosexuals who prefer sodomy) how the anus comes to take its place in sexual activity. But the main point (at 100–1) concerns the persistence of anal erotism in heterosexuals: in the course of "normal sexual development" there is an equation of anus and vagina (that is, heterosexual intercourse involves displaced anal erotism), so homosexuals who prefer sodomy may in some sense be more direct. The point to notice here is that anal erotism (in its various forms) may be equally important for homosexuals and heterosexuals.[8] Freud does say that infantile sex is characteristically auto-erotic (1905d, 7: 182), that is, involves no sexual object. In that respect, homosexuality is clearly not infantile. But then foot fetishism and bestiality also involve objects. Would one want to conclude that they are also not infantile, also not perverse? The presence of a whole person as object in the case of homosexuality doubtless makes a significant difference. (Inversion as such may, after all, be importantly different from perversion as such.)

Freud does occasionally seem to refer to homosexuality as an immature or arrested form of sexuality, for example in a letter in response to a mother who wrote him about her homosexual son (see also 1919e, 17: 182 and 1940a [1938], 23: 155–56). Freud wrote:

> Homosexuality is assuredly no advantage, but it is nothing to be ashamed of, no vice, no degradation; it cannot be classified as an illness; we consider it to be a variation of the sexual function, produced by a certain arrest of sexual development. Many highly respectable individuals of ancient and modern times have been homosexuals, several of the greatest men among them (Plato, Michelangelo, Leonardo da Vinci, etc.). It is a great injustice to persecute homosexuality as a crime—and a cruelty, too . . . What analysis can do for your son runs in a different line. If he is unhappy, neurotic, torn by conflicts, inhibited in his social life, analysis may bring him harmony, peace of mind, full efficiency, whether he remains homosexual or gets changed. (1960a, 419–20, April 4, 1935)

Without support from his theoretical writings, the "arrest of sexual development" must be presumed to refer to (the social norm of) reproduction. At a theoretical level, it is only in the case of lesbianism that there looks like there is a stage-specific point to be made about object-choice. That is, given the basic premises of psychoanalytic theory, it is not entirely clear why all women are not lesbians. (Or, more tendentiously, how anyone can love a man.) Up to the genital phase, their development parallels that of little boys, and the beginnings of object relations should tie both little boys and girls to their mothers as the main supporting figure. Girls, unlike boys, are supposed to switch the gender of their love objects in the course of going through their Oedipal phase. The incest taboo is supposed to lead boys to exclude their mothers, but not all women, as possible sexual objects. Under pressure of the castration complex, and through identification with their father, boys are supposed to search for "a girl just like the girl who married dear old dad." Girls, on the other hand, are supposed to switch from a female to a male love object. Why they do this is open to various accounts: Some accounts are in terms of penis envy (which needs more elaboration than can be provided here—in any case, biological accounts in terms of a switch in interest from clitoris to vagina will not work). Some accounts are in terms of rivalry with the same-gender parent (something girls have in common with boys—it is just that their same-gender parent happened previously to have been the primary object of dependence and so love). Some accounts are in terms of a desire to please the mother (involving getting a penis for her). Whatever the account one gives of female psychosexual development, there is little reason to regard male homosexuality as involving arrest at or regression to an earlier phase of development, and so as infantile and (on that criterion) perverse.[9]

Still, perhaps something further can be extracted from Freud's general theory of development. It might be argued that there is a sense in which the basic mechanism of homosexual object-choice is more primitive than the mechanism involved in heterosexual choice. Freud distinguishes two basic types of object-choice: anaclitic and narcissistic (1914c, 14: 87–88). On the anaclitic (or attachment) model, just as the sexual component instincts are at the outset attached to the satisfaction of the ego-instincts, the child's dependence on the parents provides the model for later relationships. On the narcissistic model, the individual chooses an object like himself. It might seem obvious that homosexual object-choice is narcissistic, and that narcissistic object-choice is more primitive than the other type. Neither point is correct. While the homosexual certainly has an object that is in at least one respect (gender or genitals) like himself, there are many other aspects of the individual, and in terms of those other aspects even heterosexual object-choice can be importantly narcissistic.[10] Moreover, the mechanisms of homosexual object-choice are various (e.g., Freud sometimes emphasizes the avoidance of rivalry with the father or brothers), and the similarity of the object to oneself may not be crucial in all cases—indeed, an anaclitic-type dependence on the object may be much more prominent.[11] That narcissism as a stage, in the sense of taking oneself as a sexual object, may be more primitive than object-choice, in the sense of taking someone else as a sexual object, does not make the narcissistic type of object-choice more primitive than the anaclitic type. In both cases, unlike primitive narcissism, someone else is the object, it is just that on one model similarity matters most, on the other dependence matters most. Even if narcissism is considered the first form of object-choice (after auto-erotism), dependence is present from the very beginning (and a whole school of psychoanalysis would argue object relations are present from the very beginning). Freud himself wrote:

> At a time at which the first beginnings of sexual satisfaction are still linked with the taking of nourishment, the sexual instinct has a sexual object outside the infant's own body in the shape of his mother's breast. It is only later that the instinct loses that object, just at the time, perhaps, when the child is able to form a total idea of the person to whom the organ that is giving him satisfaction belongs. As a rule the sexual instinct then becomes auto-erotic, and not until the period of latency has been passed through is the original relation restored. There are thus good reasons why a child sucking at his mother's breast has become the prototype of every relation of love. The finding of an object is in fact the refinding of it. (1905d, 7: 222)

Homosexuality is no *more* a return to earlier modes of relationship than any other attempt at love.[12]

The American Psychiatric Association (APA) has struggled with the question of the classification of homosexuality. The classification is not without practical implications, and it is not surprising that the debate has taken political turns.[13] Nosology is not simply a matter of etiological theories in any case. At the minimum, classification sometimes takes account of symptomatic patterns and treatment possibilities as well as etiology. The argument against classifying homosexuality as a disease could well include the notion that it *should not* be treated (whatever its origin) as well as the political claim that the disease classification contributes to inappropriate discrimination (e.g., in jobs—should homosexuality be grounds for dismissal? should schizophrenia?). In 1973 the Board of Trustees of the American Psychiatric Association voted to remove homosexuality (as such) from the list of disorders in the *Diagnostic and Statistical Manual of Mental Disorders* (DSM-III, 1980, 281–82). Nonetheless, something called "ego-dystonic homosexuality" was included. That is, if a homosexual does not desire his condition, or suffers distress at his condition, the condition is then regarded as a disorder. Clearly the criteria of mental disorder employed by the APA in this connection are not "neutral": distress and undesirability can be traced to social attitudes (what produces distress and is therefore undesired in Iowa may be very different from what produces distress and is undesired in San Francisco—so homosexuality might be a "disorder" in Iowa but not San Francisco).[14] In any case, it does not follow from the etiological and developmental theories of psychoanalysis that homosexuality must produce distress and so be undesired.

It must be acknowledged, however, that even if homosexuality involves no developmental arrest or inhibition, even if homosexuality is as "genital" and mature as heterosexuality, it is, as things currently are, detached from the possibility of reproduction and in *that* sense perverse. Any sexual activity that must be detached in its effect from reproduction can be, and has been, regarded as perverse. (Note that the relevant detachment is in effect, not in purpose. If the purpose of the persons engaged in the activity was what mattered, most heterosexual genital intercourse would have to be regarded as perverse.) Granting this sense to perversion, however, one should be careful what one concludes about people whose activities are in this sense perverse. For one thing, reproduction would in fact be excluded only if their activities were exclusively perverse. For another, whether it is socially beneficial to *bear* children (the care and upbringing of children is not excluded by perverse—that is, nonreproductive—activity) depends on circumstances (other features of the parents and social circumstances such as overpopulation). Moreover, new reproductive technologies may make the reproductive limitations of perverse activity of lesser concern, just as new contraceptive technologies have made the dangers of unwanted conception of lesser concern in "normal" sexual activity. Whatever the biological place of reproduction in human sexual life, it cannot settle the appropriate attitude to nonreproductive human sexual activity. Granting that it is the case that reproduction is one of the purposes of sex, it is equally certain that that purpose can be successfully achieved (and the survival of the species assured) without all engaging in only reproductive sex. And after all, normal sex, that is, heterosexual genital intercourse between adults, can be multiply defective. There can be failures of reciprocity and mutuality, or of interactive completeness (private sexual fantasies may make intercourse closer to masturbation in its experience, even if not in its possible effects). And even sex normal in the present sense, that is, of the kind that could in appropriate circumstances lead to reproduction, may fail in its actual effects (most intercourse does not lead to pregnancy, and intercourse between sterile partners or involving the use of contraceptives is most unlikely to). Does detachment from reproductive concerns in one's sexual activity make an individual defective? There is no reason to believe so. Freud frequently points out the great social contributions of homosexuals in history, sometimes even tying the contributions to the sexual orientation, deriving social energies from homosexual inclinations.[15] Not that Freud is blind to defects; he does not assume all homosexuals are mainstays of civilization: "Of course they are not . . . an 'elite' of mankind; there are at least as many inferior and useless individuals among them as there are among those of a different sexual kind" (1916–17, 16: 304–5). Whether homosexuals contribute to society may be relevant to the question of the appropriate attitude to take toward homosexuality, but the same can be said for heterosexuals and those of mixed inclinations; there is no reason to expect uniformity of contributions within such groupings. It remains unclear whether homosexuality should be regarded as a perversion: it depends on which criterion for perversion is adopted (e.g., content, with disgust the marker; exclusiveness and fixation; or development and maturation, with reproduction the marker), and given certain criteria, on which developmental and etiological theories are believed. But it does seem clear that even if homosexuality is regarded as a perversion, that in itself gives no ground for condemning it or thinking it worse than heterosexuality—no reason to disapprove it in others or avoid it in oneself.

Foot Fetishism

One could reasonably conclude that Freud offers no systematically sustainable concept of perversion as pathological, and nonetheless should still recognize that his consideration of the issues provides valuable insight into what we mean by perversion and, more important, what perversion means—its psychological significance. If anything is a perversion according to prevailing attitudes, foot fetishism is, and Freud's discussion of exclusiveness and fixation helps us understand why.[16] But other criteria for perversion (content, maturation, reproduction, completeness) would doubtless yield the same result—indeed, it might be a condition of adequacy for such criteria that they yield that result. Classification is not the problem. Understanding the source and point of this sort of unusual interest in feet is.

Usually, when confronted with a desire one does not share, one can sympathize with the unshared desire at least to the extent of having a sense of what is desirable about the object. Part of the mystery of fetishism is making sense of the extraordinary value and importance attached to the object. Bringing out the link of fetishism to more ordinary overvaluation of sexual objects (which can in turn be tied to narcissism—1914c, 14: 88–89, 91, 94, 100–1) goes some way toward making fetishism intelligible (1905d, 7: 153–54), but it still leaves us wanting to know why desires should take such peculiar directions. Partly this is a question about the mechanism of object-choice, but, more important, it is a question about the meaning of object-choice. What is it about a foot that makes it so attractive? Why are some particular feet more attractive than others? How can they come to satisfy (or be seen to satisfy) needs? Psychoanalysis offers answers. In the central cases, "the replacement of the object by a fetish is determined by a symbolic connection of thought, of which the person concerned is usually not conscious" (Freud 1905d, 7: 155). In the case of foot fetishism, in condensed form, psychoanalysis argues (among other things) that "the foot represents a woman's penis, the absence of which is deeply felt" (Freud 1905d, 7: 155n.). Thus condensed, the answer may seem wildly implausible. But in his paper on fetishism (1927e), Freud traces a chain of experience, fantasy, and association that suggests how a foot might come to provide reassurance about castration fears and so become the focus for sexual interests. Thus filled in, the story may still seem implausible. But notice that the question of plausibility enters at two levels: one is the plausibility of the beliefs ascribed to the fetishist (how could anyone believe anything as implausible as that a foot is the mother's missing penis?), and the second is the plausibility of the ascription of the (implausible) beliefs. The genius of the psychoanalytic account is not that it seeks to make bizarre or ad hoc beliefs plausible, but it takes beliefs that it gives us other reasons for ascribing to people and shows how in certain cases they persist and give direction to desire.

Some of the relevant beliefs (e.g., in the ubiquity of the male genital) are to be found in infantile sexual theories. Much of the evidence for such beliefs, as well as for symbolic equations, comes from the study of neurotics; which is as it should be, for, as Freud repeatedly points out, "neuroses are . . . the negative of perversions" (1905d, 7: 165). We should perhaps pause for a moment on this point. The sexual instinct, we have seen, is complex, has several dimensions (1905d, 7: 162). It is not the simple, "qualityless" energy of much of Freud's earliest theorizing (1905d, 7: 168, 217). It is thus possible to reidentify the "same" instinct in different contexts because variation in (for example) object may leave the source clearly the same. Instincts, unlike qualityless energy, meet one of the conceptual restrictions on "displacement": a change in object can be seen as "displacement" (rather than mere change) only against a background of continuity. One of the things that may have concealed the underlying continuity between infantile and adult sexuality is that the infant is "polymorphously perverse" (1905d, 7: 191)—and the tie to adult sexuality is clearest in relation to perverse sexuality (not heterosexual genital intercourse). Similarly, the role of sexuality in the neuroses was concealed partly because the sexuality involved is typically perverse: as Freud puts it, *"neuroses are, so to say, the negative of perversions"* (1905d, 7: 165)—so the sexual nature of neuroses tends to be hidden. What Freud means by the famous formula is spelled out a bit more fully in a note: "The contents of the clearly conscious fantasies of perverts (which in favorable circumstances can be transformed into manifest behavior), of the delusional fears of paranoiacs (which are projected in a hostile sense on to other people) and of the unconscious fantasies of hysterics (which psychoanalysis reveals behind their symptoms)—all of these coincide with one another even down to their details" (1905d, 7: 165 n.2). To make this claim persuasive, one must bring out the content of the unconscious fantasies of hysterics, but this is made simpler by the fact that, in the case of neurotics, "the symptoms constitute the sexual activity of the patient" (1905d, 7: 163), and "at least *one* of the meanings of a symptom is the representation of a sexual fantasy" (1905e, 7: 47). Thus Dora's hysterical cough could be analyzed in terms of an unconscious fantasy of fellatio (1905e, 7: 47–52). None of this is very surprising if one remembers that neurotic sexuality, like perverse sexuality, is infantile (1905d, 7: 172)—whatever shape the sexual instinct eventually takes, it inevitably has its roots in infantile sexuality.

Returning to foot fetishism, whatever one thinks of the psychoanalytic story, it is clear that some story is needed. The attachment is, without further explanation, too peculiar. It is hard for one who does not share the desire to see what is desirable. With suitable hidden significances, the desire at least becomes intelligible as desire. Such understanding is needed for true sympathy. By the standard of exclusiveness and fixation, fetishism is doubtless perverse. But that does not take one far, and I have argued that the criterion of exclusiveness and fixation is itself inadequate if applied quite generally. Certainly there is something peculiar about fetishism, and insofar as psychoanalysis can help us understand that peculiarity, it may help us achieve an appropriate attitude toward perversions in general. In the case of fetishism, while we might not share the beliefs, we can see how given certain beliefs, certain objects and activities might become desirable. Fetishism allows a kind of simultaneous denial and acceptance of uncomfortable facts. It does not follow that all desires become equally uncriticizable once understood. The beliefs may have wider implications and having the beliefs and desires may have wider effects. So some perversions may be objectionable. Our ordinary standards for judging human action and human interaction do not lapse in the face of perversions, but the mere fact of perversion is not an independent ground for moral criticism. Remember, all of our desires are equally in need of explanation, they all have a history (more or less hidden), we may just feel the need for an explanation less in the case of more familiar desires.

Again, foot fetishism demands some explanation. Those who wish to reject the psychoanalytic account of foot fetishism have the burden of supplying an alternative. I believe that a simple stimulus generalization account will not do. Psychoanalysis readily includes the standard associationist points, though sometimes adding less standard associative connections as well. For example, Freud notes:

> In a number of cases of foot-fetishism it has been possible to show that the scopophilic instinct, seeking to reach its object (originally the genitals) from underneath, was brought to a halt in its pathway by prohibition and repression. For that reason it became attached to a fetish in the form of a foot or shoe, the female genitals (in accordance with the expectations of childhood) being imagined as male ones. (1905d, 7: 155 n.2; cf. 1927e, 21: 155)

But Freud is also properly wary of attributing too much to early sexual impressions, as though they were the total determinant of the direction of sexuality:

> All the observations dealing with this point have recorded a first meeting with the fetish at which it already aroused sexual interest without there being anything in the accompanying circumstances to explain the fact . . . The true explanation is that behind the first recollection of the fetish's appearance there lies a submerged and forgotten phase of sexual

development. The fetish, like a 'screen-memory', represents this phase and is thus a remnant and precipitate of it. (1905d, 7: 154 n.2)[17]

The connections Freud emphasizes are typically meaningful, rather than mere casual associations. The more general problem with simple stimulus generalization is that it tends to explain both too little and too much. Why do other people exposed to the same stimuli not develop fetishistic attachments? (Psychoanalysis may also have trouble with this question. See Freud 1927e, 21: 154.) Why do fetishists often attach special conditions (such as smell) to their preferred objects? (Here psychoanalysis has some interesting suggestions. See 1909d, 10: 247; and 1905d, 7: 155 n.2.) If stimulus generalization stands alone as an explanatory mechanism, it can appear able to explain actual particular outcomes of an association only at the expense of appearing equally able to explain any other outcome of a given early impression. The factors pointed to by the conditioning theorists are simply too pervasive and nondiscriminating. Something that would explain everything explains nothing. (See Neu 1977, 126–27, and 1995b [chap. 12 here].)

The desires of the fetishist are typically highly thought-dependent. He sees the fetish object as of a certain kind, as having certain connections. (This "seeing as" is another aspect of the situation generally neglected by behaviorist approaches. See Taylor, 1964.) Psychoanalysis seeks to trace out these connections (some of them hidden from the individual himself) and their history. It seeks to understand their compulsive force and to enable the individual to specify more fully what it is that he desires in relation to the object. The thought of the object (including the thought of the reason for the desire or of the feature that makes the object desired desirable) specifies the desire. A proper understanding of the relevant thoughts may be a necessary condition of freedom, of the possibility of altering desire via reflective self-understanding. A too exclusive attention to the behavior involved in perverse sexuality may neglect the thought and so the desire behind the behavior. People may do observably the same thing for very different reasons: sometimes one person wants to, while another person might be paid to—the different meanings of the same behavior may be revealed in associated fantasies, conscious and unconscious, and other thoughts. Because of this, behaviorist specifications of perverse activity, like sociological accounts of perverse activity, may inevitably miss the point. If we are to understand perverse (and also "normal") sexual desires (and activities) we must look to the thoughts behind them.[18]

The Mental and the Physical

Plato draws a line between physical love and spiritual love, thinking the latter higher than the former. The line between the physical and the mental does not correspond to the line between the sexual and the spiritual. For whatever one thinks of spirituality and mentality, sexuality is not purely physical. Indeed, if it were, one might expect the objects and aims of sexual desire to be fixed by biology. But while human biology is relatively uniform, the objects and aims of sexual desire are as various as the human imagination. There are psychological conditions of sexual satisfaction. Sex is as much a matter of thought as of action. While the machinery of reproduction, the sexual organs themselves, the genitals, have determinate structures and modes of functioning, sexual desire takes wildly multifarious forms. Sexuality is as much a matter of thought or the mind as of the body. To think one can get away from sexuality via the denial of the body is to mistake the half for the whole.

While it would be an exaggeration to say sex is all in the mind, it would be less of a mistake than the common notion that sex is purely physical. Freud came closest to the truth in locating sexuality at the borderland or bridge between the mental and the physical. Writing of instincts in general, Freud explained his meaning:

> By an 'instinct' is provisionally to be understood the psychical representative of an endosomatic, continuously flowing source of stimulation, as contrasted with a 'stimulus', which is set up by *single* excitations coming from *without*. The concept of instinct is thus one of those lying on the frontier between the mental and the physical. (1905d, 7: 168)

Thus the sexual instinct is not to be equated with neutral energy (as in Freud's earlier theorizing, e.g., in his *Project for a Scientific Psychology*— 1950a [1895]). It has direction (aim and object) as well as a somatic source and impetus (or strength). The instinct involves both biologically given needs and thought-dependent desires. It is our thoughts that specify the objects of our desire (however mistaken we may be about whether they will satisfy our real needs). Via transformations and displacements of various sorts, our sexual instinct takes various directions. As Freud at one place puts it, "In psycho-analysis the concept of what is sexual . . . goes lower and also higher than its popular sense. This extension is justified genetically" (1910k, 11: 222; cf. the discussion of "The Mental Factor" at 1905d, 7: 161–62). The analysis of sexual desires starts with an instinctual need derived from a somatic source. But the psychical representatives of this instinctual need develop in the history of the individual, attracting him to a variety of objects and aims (modes of satisfaction). Given different vicissitudes, our original instinctual endowment develops into neurosis, perversion, or the range of normal sexual life and character. Our character is among those (perhaps "higher") attributes that Freud traces back to sexuality. In his essay on "Character and Anal Erotism" Freud says we can "lay down a formula for the way in which character in its final shape is formed out of the constituent instincts: the permanent character-traits are either unchanged prolongations of the original instincts, or sublimations of those instincts, or reaction-formations against them" (1908b, 9: 175). I cannot pursue the puzzles raised by these alleged transformations, and by the psychoanalytic explanation of the normal, here (I make a start in Neu 1981 [chap. 14 here], especially the final pages), but it should be clear that our sexual character in large measure determines our character, who we are: whether directly, as suggested in the formula, or indirectly, as the model for our behavior and attitudes in other spheres.[19]

There are lessons in multiplicity to be learned from Freud. At a minimum, I hope readers take the following from this essay on Freud's *Three Essays*:

1. Sexuality, far from being unified, is complex. The sexual instinct is made up of components that can be specified along several dimensions (source, object, aim). It is a composite that develops and changes, and can readily decompose. In particular, the instinct is "merely soldered" to its object.
2. The criteria for perversion are multiple, and no one of them is truly satisfactory if one is searching for a cross-cultural standard founded in a common human nature. Not that there are not ideals of sexuality (with corresponding criteria for perversion), but they too are multiple, and must be understood in connection with more general ideals for human interaction.
3. The purposes, functions, and goals of sexuality are multiple. It is not a pure bodily or biological function. There is a significant mental element that emerges perhaps most clearly in relation to the perversions, where the psychological conditions for sexual satisfaction are dramatically emphasized. Here we might find the beginnings of a defensible (Spinozist-Freudian) ideal in the sphere of the sexual: health and maturity involve coming to know what we really want and why we want it. Further, since what we want depends on what we think, if we wish to change what we want, we may have to change how we think.

Who we are is revealed in who or what and how we love. The structure of our desires emerges in the course of the transformation of the sexual instinct as we learn to live in a world full of internal and external pressures and constraints, as we learn to live with others and ourselves.

10

WHAT IS WRONG WITH INCEST?

A friend wanted to have an affair with her cousin. She asked me if I could think of any reason why she should not. I could not (on just that basis) think of any. But then, are there any grounds other than affection that are admissible in limiting the choice of sexual objects (especially in those cases where affection is presumably most natural)? Are all possible relations open? Are taboos silly? Is everything (in the sphere of sexuality) permissible? If we cannot think of good reasons for existing institutions or practices, does that mean that the institutions or practices are dismissible? What is a "good reason"? . . . I thought some more:

Defining Incest

What is "incest"? I shall take it to cover prohibited sexual relations where it is the identity of the persons involved rather than the nature of their acts that is essential, and where the relevant features of the parties are defined in terms of social roles or positions. Social roles or positions may or may not in turn be defined (within a particular society) in terms of biological relationships. This notion is broad enough to include prohibited sexual activities other than male-female genital intercourse (e.g., homosexual relations between fathers and sons), so long as the objection depends on the persons rather than the activity. The notion is narrow enough to exclude sexual prohibitions, say against homosexuality or particular perversions (e.g., shoe fetishism or bestiality), that do not include essential reference to particular parties (specified by social position) to whom the activities are prohibited. If an activity is prohibited to all in relation to all, the prohibition is not an "incest taboo." Thus, "incest" is meant to pick out a particular type of objection to sexual activities: objection based on *who* people are in relation to each other, on social position, that is, on nonsexual relationships.

What is wrong with incest? As I am using the term, incestuous relations are by nature objectionable, and the problem is what in their nature makes them so. Posed in this way, I doubt that the question admits of an informative general answer. The answer will vary from society to society, with the types of social relationships leading to prohibitions, and the basis for drawing distinctions among social positions and relationships. Some more general insight may perhaps be obtained if we narrow our conception of incest to objections to sexual relations on the basis of social closeness rather than distance. So rules of exogamy (where these cover sexual relations—whatever else may or may not be included in "marriage" relations) would be included, but rules of endogamy would not. (Of course there are restrictions on sexual relations within endogamous societies, the question is whether it is helpful to treat the restrictions on sexual relations with outsiders, the rules of endogamy, as themselves cases of "incest" prohibitions.) And the fact that a woman may be prohibited in a certain society from marrying a man of lesser wealth does not necessarily reveal much about that society's view of the interdependence of class and sexuality. Such a prohibition might serve a vast range of functions and be based on a wide variety of beliefs. The same would be true were the prohibition to make reference to the man being of equal or greater wealth or even being "too close" in wealth. This suggests a further narrowing of the conception of incestuous relationships so that specifications of social role having to do only with "family," and not (say) "class," would be relevant. But this sort of distinction is very difficult and would require elaborate discussion, and we would risk losing the generality I had hoped to obtain by not taking "incest" as simply sexual relations between blood relatives. So I will try to take some first steps toward the problem by discussing a particular conception of incest, ours, and a particular incestuous relationship, father-daughter, bearing in mind their connection with the broader concept we started with.

Problems with Father-Daughter Incest

What is wrong with father-daughter incest in the eyes of the West? Or rather, what reasons might there be for prohibiting father-daughter incest in our society if a prohibition did not already exist?

1. An easy, but inadequate, answer is that it leads to genetic disaster. That discovery (if the claim is true) may well have come long after the prohibitions it is meant to explain, and in relation to the present, modern contraceptive technology makes it irrelevant. And the truth is that under certain conditions, as animal breeders can tell us, inbreeding can actually help maintain desirable traits. In any case, since sexual relations need no longer carry with them the danger of procreation, one need neither calculate nor fear the genetic consequences of incest.

2. The next answer is far more significant: mother will not like it. This difficulty is real and serious. A person who has a right to consideration and affection is sure to be hurt. The Oedipal triangle exists (and conceived broadly enough may exist in every society),[1] and so the suffering comes inevitably (though allowing special exceptions) with the incest. This difficulty is structural and rather different from (say) the problem that daughters may not happen to find their fathers sexually attractive: lack of physical attraction may arise as an objection to any sexual partner, but the suffering of an important third party, while not peculiar to incestuous relationships, is inherent in them. Other affairs in other circumstances may, it is true, leave third parties unhappy (the usual case with adultery). But, outside of incestuous situations, there is nothing to guarantee that any third parties who might be involved will be significant to *both* participants in an affair. Mothers are bound to their daughters as well as to their husbands. Societal structure ensures that they are significant figures to both, and entitled to the concern of both. And the impact may be reciprocal: from harm to the mother's feelings there may follow danger to the daughter's developmental needs. That is, if the mother has even the fantasy that she is raising her daughter to be a sexual object for the father (and it is significant that humans can have such fantasies and that there is no reason to believe that other animals can), she may be less willing and able to provide the needed mothering. The taboo is a barrier to certain thoughts (including fantasies) as well as to action.

3. A third answer is one that attracted Freud's interest in *Civilization and Its Discontents* (1930a): it is difficult enough to break out of the family as it is, with the addition of sexual relations and dependence it becomes virtually impossible. Incest is (literally) antisocial. Dependence comes with the relations. Sexual urges (in the context of incest prohibitions) are among the leading forces for breaking out of the family and forming complex social structures and relationships—necessary conditions for civilization. It may also be true, as Freud suggests, that sex (even non-incestuous sex) is by its nature antisocial. The parties may become sufficient unto themselves. But where they are part of the same family, society is more likely to break up into little divided family enclaves, perhaps cooperating where they must but never forming a community.[2] If we add a further assumption about limited psychic energy, so that what is given over to sexuality is not available for social purposes, the difficulties for society are obvious. (We should note, of course, that this added assumption makes matters no worse in the case of incestuous sexual relations than for other kinds.) From the point of view of the individual, in addition to the loss of the advantages of larger society and civilization, if the family encroaches on sexual as well as all other needs, she becomes so much the more the prisoner of the family. And, of course, should the affair fail she may have to go on living in the midst of a ruined prison. (And even if she need not stay, the family may be ruined—though that involves a different sort of loss.)

4. This relation of dependence brings us to a fourth objectionable feature of incestuous relations, or at least the form we have been focusing on. And it is perhaps the feature that contributes most to making incest seem worse than merely odd or disagreeable. The power structure, the structure of dependency, is such that the propositioned daughter is put in an unfair position. (This way of putting it assumes that the father makes the initial overt move, even if in response to a seductively active daughter. But the point holds in any case.) Too much is at stake. The situation may be compared to that of the boss who insists on sexual relations with his secretary. She may fear for her job. Her refusal is not a simple refusal of sexual relations, for she remains involved and dependent in other ways. The situation is even more extreme in the case of the father who propositions his daughter. Even if there is no direct threat of breaking the many other ties, a refusal of sexual relations may be experienced (by both parties) as a rejection on more levels than that of the original approach. Society's disapproval takes the burden off the daughter (and father) by helping ensure that the question does not arise. Teacher-student affairs may also provide an analogy, perhaps a better one than bosses and secretaries, for here the age-gap, custodial obligations, and societal disapproval are clearer. Some taboos are irrational. Some, when understood, have a variety of virtues.

Taboos and Reasons

Now, where do these points take us? Some way, to be sure; but, unfortunately, not terribly far nor terribly deep. If we were a daughter wondering whether to have an affair with our father (or vice versa), we would now have some general reasons not to. These reasons are independent of whether or not a taboo against this form of incest happens to exist in our society. But precisely because the reasons are independent reasons for a prohibition, they do not explain why the prohibition should take the form of a taboo (I have only "rationalized" the taboo). Taboos allow no questioning. Reasons, precisely because they are reasons, leave room for questioning. The reasons I have brought forward depend on features (admittedly, broad structural features) of our society; and so, in a given case, may not apply. What if (looking to my second point) mother does not mind, or, what if she is dead? The inevitable suffering of a significant third party may no longer seem so inevitable. And who would be the aggrieved third party in brother-sister incest? To explain the taboo here one might have to consider that a father who cannot have his daughter may nonetheless be jealous of her and so place her off limits for his son as well. (Of course, he might wish to stop all rivals, but he can most readily enforce his jealousy against the rival who is in his home. In any case, there is a question about whether the jealousy is justifiable.) Clearly, not all of the four factors I have brought out underlie all incest taboos in all cultures, nor are they the only factors even in our own. And certainly more must be done to distinguish factors connected with incest from factors that may apply to more general sexual prohibitions. For example, what makes father-daughter incest more than just a special case of prohibitions on adult-child sexual relations? For one thing, incest taboos, as I have said, are a matter of closeness and adult-child (as opposed to parent-child) prohibitions are a matter of distance. For another thing, objections to father-daughter incest presumably hold even when the daughter has become an adult. But (thinking back) are the objections to incest really the same or as strong when the child has become an adult as when she (or he) is an adolescent or prepubescent? (In this connection, it might be useful to consider the different applications and consequences of laws against statutory rape and incest laws.) So far we have only a beginning or a fragment of an analysis; a hint at the character of some of the nonsexual objections to sexual relations involved in "incest" (understood in the broad sense we started with). It should be noted, however, that the points made already extend beyond a narrowly biological conception of incest: I rejected the objection to father-daughter incest that depended on genealogy and genetics, and the other points made would all (in our society) be as applicable to step-fathers as to fathers. (Lawyers speak of "consanguinity" and "affinity.")

Though the points I have so far brought forward may justify certain incest prohibitions, they neither justify nor explain incest taboos—even within our society and even restricting our view to father-daughter incest. They may provide reasons for obeying an incest prohibition for someone who does not accept the prohibition as a taboo. But there may be good reasons why the prohibition takes the form of a taboo—a form that puts the demand for reasons out of place, and that imposes strict liability and so puts the offering of excuses out of place as well. Moreover, every society, every way of life, has its taboos, and these taboos always include (so the anthropologists tell us) incest taboos. No society allows all forms of sexual activity among all of its members. Every society prohibits absolutely (that is, unconditionally) certain sexual relations between certain persons on the basis of their social closeness. Why should this be so?

Oedipus

Let us look at a famous case of parent-child incest. What is the tragedy of Oedipus? Why is Oedipus so upset? As far as is in his power he does no wrong, at every point he makes what (in his culture) would be the right choice, and yet, despite his best intentions and efforts, he kills his father and sleeps with his mother. In reality, he has no choice. When he comes to know of what he has done, he recognizes that his actions, though they fulfill his fate and are not his fault (he did not know what he was doing, indeed he did what he did precisely in order to avoid his predicted fate—and so, by the standards of post-Kantian morality and perhaps by those of Sophocles's own later play, *Oedipus at Colonus,* he is not responsible), nevertheless constitute a misfortune. As far as the four factors brought out in relation to father-daughter incest go, it is not even clear what the misfortune in his case is. Ignorance, and the other circumstances in his case, would seem to make his actions unobjectionable. But surely something is wrong. We may wish Oedipus had not blinded himself—the punishment may seem extreme—but what would we think if he had merely chuckled and said, "Oh well, too bad, I tried to avoid it but fate seems to have won through"? Part of the point of tragedy, like the point of taboo, is that it allows no excuse. It was *his* fate and *his* misfortune. Despite circumstances, certain losses cannot be canceled and certain hands cannot be made clean. Ancient morality leaves important room for the actual, for what in fact happens (detached from one's will and intentions), and it may still have a place in modern morality marked, perhaps, by taboo, by strict prohibitions.

What stands on the surface of ancient morality may perhaps be understood with the help of the depth vision of modern psychology. Though Oedipus knew not what he did at the time he did it, he nonetheless *meant* to do it. It was his unconscious wish. And that it was his unconscious wish, that it included a sexual desire, that that desire was the object of an incest taboo, that incest taboos (of one form or another) are universal, and that the particular form of incest taboos is patterned on features of a given society's social structure—none of these things are accidents. I mentioned earlier that the Oedipal triangle, it conceived broadly enough, may exist in every society. Let me sketch briefly what I mean and why it is a consequence of the conditions (biological and social) for human development that such a constellation of desires and emotions should exist, and be the object of prohibitions.

Born a helpless mammal into the world, if the human infant is to survive there must be a supporting figure (or figures)—typically, in our society and in most (here consider the facts of lactation and who is necessarily present at the birth as well as at conception), the mother. A dependency relation is formed, and this early attachment is a primary form of love. But with the supporting figure there always comes a rival. And it is not a mere accident that there is a rival, that there is another party that takes the child's "mother" as a love object. That there was at one point, at least, a third party is a biological necessity, a matter of the conditions for procreation (though technology may change this). That there continues to be a third party (or parties) after the child's birth—though it need not be the child's biological father—also has a biological basis. The mother is herself a mammal with needs and desires of her own, needs and desires that cannot be met by her infant, and that impel her to establish and maintain relations with other adult mammals. And these others come to be seen, by the child, as rivals for the love, affection, time, and concern of the mother. Hence the Oedipal triangle is complete, and the essential emotional constellation established on the basis of the biologically prolonged dependency of the mammalian child and the biological needs and relations of the supporting mammalian adults. Breaking out of the triangle of dependent love and concomitant jealousy involves a long and complex process of growth. The conflicts themselves become most acute at a particular stage in the child's growth and development, a stage determined by biological conditions and the conditions for socialization. The shape of a particular society will help determine who the loved supporting figures and who the hated rivals and socializing authority figures will be. In the end, according to psychoanalytic theory, a superego is formed as the result of identification and introjection of the figures who restrain one's Oedipal wishes: moral prohibitions arise out of fear of punishment by or fear of the loss of love of an authority figure on whom one is dependent. In telling his complex story (and the story is doubtless more complex for women), Freud employs (in *Totem and Taboo*) the myth of the brothers who band together and slay and eat (and so literally incorporate) the primal father. The incest taboo emerges because their (ambivalent) love for the father comes to the fore after his slaying. The sons then identify with his prohibitions (incorporated in their superegos). What is prohibited is what father would not have liked. The taboo emerges also because the liberated brothers might otherwise renew among themselves the conflict over the women that led to their revolt against their father in the first place—without the taboo they might all continue their strife for their father's role. (Note that these two points have important connections with the second and third points in my discussion of father-daughter incest, points about mother not liking it and breaking out of the family for social cooperation.) It may be a condition for the maintenance of each society that it be true to its origins. The superego and its requirements, the strict liability that it imposes on us all, may be conditions for the formation of mature object relations and societal order. That every society must feel those prohibitions (in one form or another) may follow (perhaps not simply, but nonetheless may follow) from the conditions for its existence as a society.[3]

Developing an Identity

More has to be done, I think, to show how taboos may connect with the conditions of a moral consciousness and how, in the light of their universality, they connect with the conditions for any society. Taboos, particularly incest taboos, may be essential to the development of character, to the development of the superego and to full object relations, to the shape of a way of life. Unless we were able to feel guilt at incest, perhaps we could not feel guilt at anything, or be fit for social relations. A person undisturbed by incest might be undisturbable by any social prohibition. In my too brief sketch, it can be seen that we get our superego from precisely those whose love we fear to lose. Granted that we do not want their disapproval, however, why should they disapprove incest in particular? I hope that discussion of the nature of incest, of the nature of incest prohibitions, and of the place of drives toward incest in the development of individuals and societies may help us to see how the pieces fit together.

I cannot carry that discussion much further here, but perhaps I can at least suggest that the (or a) key may be in the notions of identity and identification. Each generation must win its identity, partly through struggle with the older generation and partly through something like mourning for its loss. The "something like mourning" amounts to identification. But the identification makes sense only through difference, as a culmination of the effort to overcome infantile dependence and achieve autonomy. Incest destroys difference: categories collapse, people cease to have clear and distinct sexual and social places (consider the scene in the film *Chinatown* where the confusion bursts out in the anguished "sister/daughter, sister/daughter" confrontation); and with the destruction of difference people cease to have the possibility of shifting from one place to another as they develop. Perhaps that might make incest seem attractive to some. But I suspect that violation of incest taboos would not itself be an effective revolutionary act. While destroying difference and confusing roles and perhaps undermining authority, it would not overcome dependence—which, as I have said, I think is a biological and social necessity. Violation of incest taboos or their abolition would not, I think, allow the establishment of a stable, mature, independent identity.

If one turns to the clinical literature to confirm one's suspicions about the effects of incest on development, one encounters a number of problems. First, there is not much data. Second, the paucity is apparently systematic, i.e. in our society father-daughter incest is the form most commonly reported, but there is reason to believe sibling incest is the most common in occurrence. Mother-son incest is extremely rare in published accounts and homosexual incest is hardly ever even mentioned. Perhaps sibling incest is not usually reported precisely because its effects are not particularly deleterious, or perhaps precisely because it is so common. There are also questions about *who* would report it—is there a victim? an aggrieved third party?—and what exactly is the line between childish or adolescent sex play and incest? (If we understand sexuality in the broad way suggested by Freud in his *Three Essays on the Theory of Sexuality*, then incestuous desires and acts need not involve genital intercourse.) Third, the data are clinical (or even less helpful, criminal) and therefore of course reveal (if they reveal anything) severe psychological disruption. It is extremely difficult to get data on cases where consummated incest is not harmful. (Louis Malle's film, *Souffle au Coeur*, plays on the assumption, or wish, that such cases are possible.) Fourth and finally, it is difficult to distinguish, in those cases where there is harm, how much of it is attributable to the existence of the prohibition rather than the incest itself. That is, is the harm a product of the prohibition or an independent reason for having a prohibition? The prohibition itself may cause problems, or given the prohibition perhaps only people who are already otherwise disturbed engage in incest. All this makes it difficult to isolate its consequences.

Taboos and Reasons Again

But perhaps this sort of calculation of consequences is wrongheaded (or really only illuminates one special aspect of our question). For the prohibition is a taboo. It is unconditional. That is, in one sense of unconditional, it is not a means to an independently valued end, but a necessary part of a way of life and ideal of human relationship. And these notions of a "way of life" and an "ideal of relationship" may be more central than the conditions for development of the superego in understanding the role of fixed boundaries or prohibitions in morality. The simple calculation of psychological consequences may miss the importance of "identity," where the identity of the individual is intimately connected with the coherence of a way of life distinguished by the characteristic virtues and vices and patterns of relationship recognized within it. When one says taboos are absolute and unconditional but may not be irrational one should compare them with something like ideals of justice which are also not simply assimilable to utilitarian calculations. There are in fact a number of ideals in various spheres which make for absolute prohibitions. One must not betray friends, not simply because they might become angry, but because they would no longer be "friends," indeed, the betrayal might reveal that they never were. Certain sorts of loyalty may be necessary to certain sorts of friendship. And those sorts of friendship are valuable. One must beware too narrow notions of what counts as a reason here. Certain sorts of love demand certain sorts of trust. And certain sorts of trust may rule out certain sorts of reasons. To trust because one has weighed the evidence (where one is willing to waver if the evidence does) may be as bad as not trusting at all. One's love may then be of the wrong kind. A certain ideal of love lies behind unquestioning trust. And the value of that ideal, its place in a way of life, may count as a reason for valuing that sort of trust and excluding certain sorts of doubts. Unquestioning attitudes are needed for certain kinds or qualities of relationship. The role of faith in religion might provide another way to get a handle on this difficult set of issues. (We should remember that "taboo" is itself originally a religious notion.) I am inclined to think that these sorts of cases, and especially the restrictions placed on action by ideals of justice (which make certain actions "unthinkable" or "unconscionable"), provide the most useful parallels for understanding the restrictions that incest taboos place on sexual relations.

There may be prohibitions that are necessary (to morality, to society, to humanity) even though they may not be justifiable within a narrower conception (e.g., utilitarian) of morality and justification.[4] It is not an accident that every society has incest taboos, that every society prohibits some sexual relations on grounds independent of the intrinsic character of the activity involved (which is, in other circumstances, approved) but based rather on social relations. It may be that it is a condition of social relations that members of a society be able to feel the force of (if not obey) such prohibitions. The pattern of the prohibitions may vary from society to society and with the structure of social relations, but there could be no society without some such prohibitions and the possibility of respect for them. And the fact that the prohibitions are sexual may have to do with the conditions for psychosocial development of the individual, and so have a biological basis. (Restrictions on impulses to murder, on aggression, may similarly be universal, and necessary, and absolute, and also have a biological basis.) Prohibitions that are absolute within a particular society (even if they are different in different societies) even though they cannot be fully understood or justified (in a narrow sense) may be essential to morality (in a broader sense) and to society and so to humanity (insofar as man is a social animal). The key to understanding taboos, as opposed to other sorts of social prohibitions (legal, utilitarian, etc.), may lie in those very features of taboos that are most puzzling to modern moral consciousness: taboos are universal (every society has some, including, in particular, taboos on murder and incest), and absolute (are unconditional and allow no questioning), and impose strict liability (allow no excuse). These features may not be irrational. But while we must consider this possibility, we should also be aware of how paradoxical it is to reach this sort of conclusion, which calls a halt to questioning, after the sort of questioning or as the result of the sort of questioning we have just ourselves engaged in. The taboo is, of course, meant to extend to thought and not just action. Some things (incest, betrayal of a friend) are supposed to be unthinkable. Is there a line between "thinking" and "thinking about"?

In Summary

Incest taboos should be seen as involving nonsexual objections to sexual relations, that is, objections based on who people are in relation to each other, rather than their activities. What is at stake is brought out by considering certain objections to father-daughter incest and certain features of taboos. The objections that matter do not depend on social ties and distinctions having a biological basis, but there is nonetheless a biological element in incest taboos. To see it, one must look to the nature of the Oedipus complex, and to the conditions for the development of the individual and of society. There may be prohibitions that are necessary (to morality, to society, to humanity) even though they may not be justifiable within a narrower conception (e.g., utilitarian) of morality and justification. And so taboos that are universal (occur, in one form or another, in every society), and absolute (allow no questioning), and impose strict liability (allow no excuse) may not be irrational: they may mark the boundaries that shape a way of life.

11

FANTASY AND MEMORY

The Etiological Role of Thoughts according to Freud

"Hysterics suffer mainly from reminiscences" (1895d, 7). This early formulation, though it underwent drastic revision as Freud's psychoanalytic thought developed, contains two elements that remained central. It places one source of psychological disorder in *thoughts*, and it treats the hysteric as somehow the victim of his or her *past*. The hysteric is unfree, a prisoner of individual history. The maxim brings the past into play through thoughts, specifically thoughts about the past, that is, memories. That our past can influence our present behavior in devious ways is an important insight, that one of those ways is through thoughts proves an even more important insight. A cluster of questions arises around these points. Is it actually our past, or (better) our actual past, that influences our behavior in the areas Freud discusses? How is one to distinguish the causal efficacy of reality and fantasy? Is their efficacy "causal"? How and why is "memory" brought in as intermediary? How is one to distinguish memory of reality, memory of fantasy, and fantasy of memory? And do any of these distinctions matter to the individual's unfreedom and the possibilities of overcoming it? In this essay I will be taking only some first steps toward answering these questions.

Hypnosis, Cure, and the Role of Thoughts

What were the grounds at the beginning of psychoanalysis for believing that there *could* be an "analytical" therapy? Why should "analysis," "understanding," "interpretation," "insight" be of value in treatment? Part of the answer is to be found in the belief that certain disorders are psychological in origin. If thoughts lay behind problems, then unraveling thoughts might help solve those problems. The connections here are in fact very complex, and the character of the thoughts involved is so far left open, but we can start with this question: why should thoughts be assigned a role in the production of certain disorders; in particular, why should hysteria be regarded as ideogenic?

According to the theory presented in *Studies on Hysteria* (Freud & Breuer 1895d), undischarged affect leads to hysterical symptoms either because the associated experience occurred while the victim was in a susceptible, "hypnoid," state or because the experience was "incompatible" with the subject's self-image. Excess "affect" (psychical energy) must be discharged. According to the "principle of constancy": "The mental apparatus endeavors to keep the quantity of excitation present in it as low as possible or at least to keep it constant" (Freud 1920g, 18: 9; cf. 1940d, 1: 153–54). Affect is produced by experiencing events, and where the experience is so traumatic that the affect cannot be discharged as required by the principle of constancy, it can produce pathological results. I shall have to treat the question of what makes an experience "traumatic" (it is not simply strength or intensity), and in particular the notion of "incompatible ideas." At this point, however, the thing to emphasize is that it is the persisting memory of an actual event (from which affect arises) that is said to cause hysteria.

Charcot's use of hypnosis to *remove* hysterical symptoms was of therapeutic importance, but perhaps of greater theoretical importance was his discovery that it could be used to *induce* such symptoms in normal people. It could be argued that cures reveal nothing about the nature of hysteria, because hypnosis might simply introduce countervailing factors (and so alleviate symptoms) rather than remove exciting causes. (Just as the physical treatment of ulcers does not prove that ulcers are purely organic in origin.) The *production* of hysterical symptoms by hypnosis, on the other hand, provides convincing evidence that ideas (i.e., thoughts) can play a role in the production of mental disorder.

It has been charged that Charcot's demonstrations of hysteria were faked (Szasz 1961, 32–34). But these charges may apply only to the grand epileptoid hysterias of which he was the putative discoverer; and, whatever may have been the case with Charcot's demonstrations, it is clear that hysterical symptoms *can* be duplicated under hypnosis. There are, however, two further difficulties with this argument. First, what makes a symptom "hysterical"? What is the justification for describing hypnotically induced behavior as "hysterical symptoms"? Given Freud's theory, to call a symptom "hysterical" would be to imply that it is ideogenic. But the etiological implication and consequent circularity that might later be involved in such a description do not arise at this early stage. The same justification could be provided for describing the hypnotically induced behavior as hysterical as for the naturally occurring behavior (in both cases reference being made only to the character of the observable behavior and, perhaps, the lack of organic disorder). Still, it is important to note that as used now the characterization of behavior as "hysterical" (or even "neurotic") depends on the belief that a certain type of explanation—namely "psychological" rather than "physiological"—holds. Indeed, certain behavior will count as a "symptom" only in the context of certain beliefs about its cause or explanation. The "facts" are thus theory-laden. There is no neutrally describable set of behaviors which are, as such, hysterical. Freud did, however, at one time believe that there are specific (objective) hysterical symptoms (Freud 1888–89, 78ff.; cf. Andersson 1962, chap. 3). This brings us to the second difficulty with the move from hypnotically induced hysteria to the role of ideas. There was dispute whether the mechanism of hypnosis was itself somatic (Charcot) or psychical (Bernheim and the "suggestion" school), that is, whether it was the result of physiological changes or the effect of ideas. Because of his belief in an objective symptomatology of hysteria, Freud argued against direct suggestion, but noted: "This does not imply any denial that the mechanism of hysterical manifestations is a psychical one: but it is not the mechanism of suggestion on the part of the physician" (1888–89, 79). Freud went on to favor a form of "suggestion" account of hypnosis (1889a, 97–98, 101), and eventually to offer a sexual theory of hypnosis (1905d, 150n.; 1921c, 127–28). The essential thing from our point of view is that, whatever the mechanism, the *content* of ideas has to be assigned a role in the hypnotic process.

The ideas that Freud and Breuer focus on in their "Preliminary Communication" are persisting memories. The "persistence" is important, for otherwise there might be no reason not to attribute the symptoms directly to the traumatic event, without appealing to memory or thoughts at all. They insist that "the psychical trauma—or more precisely the memory of the trauma—acts like a foreign body which long after its entry must continue to be regarded as an agent that is still at work" rather than an *agent provocateur* that merely releases the symptom, which then goes its own way (1895d, 6). The evidence cited is the evidence of "cure" (i.e., removal of symptoms). In treating hysteria, Freud (following Breuer) had from the very first made use of hypnosis in "another manner"; apart from directly suggesting the disappearance of symptoms, he would use hypnosis in getting the patient to trace the origins of his symptoms (Freud, 1925d, 19):

> each individual hysterical symptom immediately and permanently disappeared when we had succeeded in bringing clearly to light the memory of the event by which it was provoked and in arousing its accompanying affect, and when the patient had described that event in the greatest possible detail and had put the affect into words. Recollection without affect almost invariably produces no result. (Freud & Breuer 1895d, 6)[1]

This is the classic pattern exhibited, for example, by the cure of Anna O.'s inability to drink by her recovery of the memory (with disgust) of her lady-companion allowing her dog to drink out of a glass (1895d, 34–35). We shall have to consider the importance of arousing accompanying affect, i.e., cathartic abreaction; but the evidence of cure may again be of dubious value in any case. They say (speaking of a putatively epileptic girl who, hypnotized, had one of her attacks and relived the chase by a savage dog that had preceded her first attack): "The success of the treatment confirmed the choice of diagnosis" (1895d, 14). But Breuer himself admits (in discussing Anna O.): "As regards the symptoms disappearing after being 'talked away,' I cannot use this as evidence; it may very well be explained by suggestion" (1895d, 43). In context, Breuer is referring to evidence for the *truth* of the patient's statements (not the doctor's diagnosis); but it is these statements that identify the "precipitating cause" and so the quotation (and the difficulty) is applicable to the diagnosis as well.

Failures to cure, on the other hand, need not be devastating to the claims. Among other things, the situation can be complicated by new associations with an original trauma preventing complete cure by the cathartic procedure (1895d, 74n.2). But even where there is cure, and no question of suggestion, other countervailing factors, or untruthfulness, the production of a memory and subsequent relief of symptom are not sufficient to show that the symptom had its source in memory. The most radical difficulty for this argument for etiology is that the memories produced may be only putative memories, or (at best) memories of putative events. This is the difficulty that led Freud to fruitful consideration of fantasy, instinct, and infantile sexuality. It is not a difficulty that calls for the rejection of the influence of ideas (fantasies are no less thoughts than memories) suggested by the efficacy of hypnosis (in eliminating *and* inducing symptoms) and by Breuer's cathartic method; but it does call for a reexamination of that influence.

Idea and Affect

The central explanatory notion in the Breuer-Freud theory of hysteria is that all types of hysteria (not just "traumatic" hysteria or attacks where it is clear that the subject is hallucinating the event that provoked the original attack) have symptoms that are *meaningful* in the context of a precipitating trauma. Ideas are essentially involved because behavior can be understood as a response to a situation (i.e., as "meaningful") only if the agent is aware (in some sense) of the situation. So far, however, this calls only for perception, not memory. But the event being responded to is in the past. The symptom makes sense as a reaction to an event. The symptom is pathological because one is responding to past reality rather than present reality. Hence, "hysterics suffer mainly from reminiscences" (1895d, 7) which are mistaken for present perceptions and responded to as such. This picture of Freud's early theory requires correction along several dimensions. Perhaps most important, the situation is complicated by the fact that in addition to the confusion of perception and memory, there is a contrast (and so a possible confusion) between the memory of an actual event and a fantasy.

It is not strictly correct to say that symptoms are meaningfully related to the precipitating trauma because memories are mistaken for present perceptions and responded to as such. This for two reasons. First, the argument (for the role of ideas) required that "meaning" be interpreted narrowly so that the symptom could be understood as a behavioral response to a situation as seen by the subject (e.g., as flight is to danger; 1895d, 91). Though the Freud-Breuer theory certainly claims that the symptom is "strictly related to the precipitating trauma" (1895d, 4), the relation need not be that of an intentional response in order to be intelligible. The symptomatic behavior might simply be *associated* with the original experience without being a rational reaction to it. For example:

> A girl, watching beside a sick-bed in a torment of anxiety, fell into a twilight state and had a terrifying hallucination, while her right arm, which was hanging over the back of her chair, went to sleep; from this there developed a paresis of the same arm accompanied by contracture and anesthesia. (1895d, 4)

Alternatively, the relation might be merely *symbolic* and the symptom a "mnemic symbol" (1895d, 90). "For instance, a neuralgia may follow upon mental pain or vomiting upon a feeling of moral disgust" (1895d, 5). But whether a matter of response, association, or symbolism, some sort of awareness of the original situation is required and so (a slightly modified version of) the earlier argument for the role of ideas, whether the trauma is perceived, remembered, or fantasied, still follows through. The possibility of fantasy, however, brings us to the second point needing elaboration. The originating cause of the symptom may not be a "precipitating trauma" if this is taken to involve an external event. There must be affect, but this may arise from instinct (i.e., an internal stimulus) rather than event (external stimulus). In either case, the vicissitudes and relations of affects and ideas must now be traced.

Freud's views on idea and affect undergo considerable development. The "affect" or "sum of excitation" attached to an idea, however, remains an underlying hypothesis: it is

> the concept that in mental functions something is to be distinguished—a quota of affect or sum of excitation—which possesses all the characteristics of a quantity (though we have no means of measuring it), which is capable of increase, diminution, displacement and discharge, and which is spread over the memory-traces of ideas somewhat as an electric charge is spread over the surface of a body. (Freud 1894a, 60)

Sometimes Freud uses a mechanical rather than a field-theory model in his discussions of psychical energy. The underlying hypothesis is meant to be neurological, or at any rate physical-chemical-biological, but the ambiguity suggested by the psychological-feeling connotations of "quota of affect" is also present in the theory.

The most important characteristic of the pathogenic *idea* (which, it must be remembered, is a thought rather than an isolated image) is that it is "incompatible," that is, it conflicts with the set pattern of the person's life, what he believes or wants to believe. An idea may also be "incompatible," and hence traumatic, because there is no adequate reaction "as in the case of the apparently irreparable loss of a loved person" or because social circumstances make a reaction impossible (1895d, 10).

The idea is rejected. At this stage (e.g., 1895d, 116) Freud treats this rejection as an *intentional* repression. The patient has motives for "forgetting" and these are what lead to the resistance to the recovery of the memory (1895d, 111).[2] There are, of course, problems with deliberate repression. All the problems of self-deception: of simultaneously knowing and not knowing. Intentional forgetting seems to require following a rule under conditions that do not allow you to knowingly follow it, in which case it becomes unclear in what sense you are (actively) *following* the rule rather than (merely) acting in accordance with it. (Cf. the child's playful injunction: "Don't think of elephants!") How can one deliberately forget? Must one also forget the forgetting? Perhaps Freud could simply allow that one forgets without effort the deliberate forgetting—because once the affect is detached from the idea, no energy is needed to keep it from consciousness. Whether or not he would say that, these complications may have helped Freud move (later) to the view of repression as itself an unconscious process.

On this view the unconscious becomes a collection of individually repressed ideas, which form

> a nucleus and center of crystallization for the formation of a psychical group divorced from the ego—a group around which everything which would imply an acceptance of the incompatible idea subsequently collects. The splitting of consciousness . . . is accordingly a deliberate and intentional one. (1895d, 123)

The repression is intentional, but the unconscious ideas are memories and not intentions: no hint yet of dynamic ideas (impulses or desires) or the unconscious as process rather than isolated bundle. This may seem satisfactory where there is an obvious external trauma, independent of one's desires. But how could Freud believe this to be true in general? How could he even describe those cases that seem precisely the denial of desires (e.g., Lucy)? Perhaps he would say that you can repress a desire, but the unconscious desire (e.g., Lucy's love?) does not act *as* a desire. The energy gets attached to an associated idea and *converted* into a symptom, not *executed* into a symptom (the desire is manifested, not expressed). But I suspect that the problem simply does not arise for Freud at this point because he does not think through all of his examples. It later does become a problem because the notions of infantile *pleasure* and desires force recognition that it is sometimes desires that become or are unconscious. But we shall return to these developments. Note also that the "second consciousness" or bundle of thoughts formed by repression is rather different from the trauma-producing "hypnoid states" that Freud came ultimately to reject (1896c, 194–95).

In the defense against the incompatible idea by repression, the affect is detached but remains to be dissipated. The idea is defused and safely hid. The form of disposal of affect varies, and with it the character of the disorder. "The hysterical method of defence . . . lies in the conversion of the excitation into a somatic innervation" (1895d, 122). The affect now forms a symptom; the content of that symptom depends on the idea that has been repressed. The physical symptom may be a response, an association, or a symbol of that idea. The idea is a memory. But now a third correction is in order. In a hysterical attack, the sufferer need not *mistake* the memory for a perception. First, the attack may in no sense be an *active* response to a perceived situation, even a mistakenly perceived one. And, secondly, even where it is such a response (e.g., Frau Emmy's "Keep still!—Don't say anything!—Don't touch me!" formula, 1895d, 56–57, 95), the sufferer may still be totally *unconscious* of the originating memory. Even where there is a memory with the force of a hallucination (e.g., Emmy, 49, and Anna, 34), it may be only a screen. But in all cases the symptom *itself* is, so to speak, a memory. Whatever its connection with the pathogenic incompatible idea, it is itself a *mnemic symbol* (see 1895d, 90n.1).[3] So, for example, Emmy's pains are "memories of pains . . . mnemic symbols of the times of agitation" (1895d, 90), and Miss Lucy's "consciousness [plagued by the smell of burnt pudding] now contains the physical reminiscence which has arisen through conversion . . . and suffers from the affect which is more or less clearly attached to precisely that reminiscence" (122–23). The mechanism explains the symptom without appealing to a confusion between memory and perception, a confusion which is in some cases (no doubt) also present.

This does not leave ideas as odd appendages to some sort of truly pathogenic affect. According to the theory, it is the ideas that determine which affects must seek abnormal discharges (the usual paths of association, forgetting, and abreaction being unavailable). The theory of the ideogenic nature of hysteria is also the most secure element of Freud's early account. I rejected the evidence of hypnotic cure as uncertain, but the danger of interference from suggestion, at least, can be minimized. Initially, hypnotic therapy consisted entirely of suggestion, instructions from the doctor to the patient for the relief of symptoms. But with the development of the cathartic "talking cure" (1895d, 30), the content of hypnotic sessions surprised the doctors and the results were unexpected (at least by Breuer in the first case, that of Anna O., 1895d, 7, 46). I have already mentioned the confirmation provided by the duplication of hysterical symptoms under hypnosis. That cures continued to be effected by the cathartic procedure after Freud had given up the use of hypnosis (e.g., Miss Lucy R.) increases their evidential value still further. The "pressure technique" and, even more, free association (where there is no command to trace memories to initial trauma) eliminate straightforward "suggestion," and though it may reenter in the form of "transference," fresh evidence is also provided as one can observe the role of ideas in witnessing the process of development of symptoms in the transference relation. Stuart Hampshire provides a clear statement of this sort of evidence (not depending on cure) for the importance of *persisting* memories in the neurotic:

> to say that he recognizes the unconscious memory as the *explanation* of his inclination and conduct is not to attribute to him the discovery of a correlation between two classes of events. When the repressed memory is revived, there is an instant recognition of the continuity and unbrokenness of the memory discernible in a consistent misreading of situations confronting him. When the memory is recognized as a memory, he recognizes also the consistent superimposition of the notional past upon the present . . . with his now fully conscious memory of the past situation as he conceived it, the inclination to behave and act in the same way returns to him with the same force, even though now, recognizing the past as past and unalterable, he restrains himself. (1972a, 173–74)

This sort of evidence, however, already takes a further step toward treating the discovery of memory as the discovery of a "reason" or "motive," the idea as object of impulse or part of the background of belief in which impulse operates, rather than a causal accompaniment of strangulated affect. Before we take that step, there is another type of evidence to consider. The role and influence of ideas in hysteria seem most definitely confirmed by that feature of hysterical symptoms which distinguishes them most clearly from organic symptoms: "hysteria behaves as though anatomy did not exist or as though it had no knowledge of it" (Freud 1893c, 169). The symptoms are clearly ideogenic, for not only is there no evident organic cause for the disorder but it is the *sufferer's ideas* of the working of his body and not the facts of anatomy that determine the pattern of his disorder.

Or it would *seem* that hysteria must be ideogenic. For does the anatomical ignorance of hysteria depend on the ignorance of the hysteric? One would expect that if it is the sufferer's ideas that shape his symptoms, then more sophisticated hysterics (e.g., anatomists and medical students) would have more sophisticated symptoms. The expectation is difficult to confirm and its implications are not as clear-cut as one might suppose. To begin, classical conversion hysterias are now a clinical rarity. When they do occur, it tends to be among the uneducated poor. Where, in a rare instance, a medical student may exhibit a transient conversion symptom, the report may be unsophisticated ("pain in my knee"), but we cannot be certain of the relation of the report to the symptom. That is, the level of reporting required or expected is important. Even with the unlearned, one can elicit medically quite accurate and specific symptoms (for, say, myasthenia gravis) by appropriate questioning. (Cf. the charge that the symptoms of Charcot's hysterical patients were due to suggestion and coaching; Szasz 1961.) It may be presumed that the medical student would elaborate or correct his report of symptoms in accordance with medical knowledge if he thought such detail expected. (Consistent ideology might even force him to be cured by application of the usual, chemical, procedures.) Even if symptoms in medical students were persistently unsophisticated and medically implausible, it would in any case not show that hysteria was not ideogenic. The operative ideas might be unconscious fantasies. Indeed, it may be part of the nature of hysteria that displacement and conversion occur at the unconscious level and so the ideas invoked are necessarily some sort of fantasy. The unconscious remains infantile and therefore unsophisticated even if the man no longer is. Evidence concerning the effects of the sexual enlightenment of children would tend to confirm this suggestion. Children may be informed of the sexual facts of life and yet somehow forget. In a sense, the information does not register and the sophisticated knowledge is unavailable or unused. An informed five-year-old can persist in the pumpkin seed theory (i.e., oral impregnation fantasy), at least in play: "The baby got in the doll because an elephant with long trunk squirted something in her mouth." Even medical students exhibit such regression to early "knowledge": will talk of the vagina as "a dirty, smelly hole," and make the same sexual and excremental confusions that so troubled Little Hans.[4]

The etiology goes through unconscious ideas, which are ideas nonetheless. This leaves a number of further questions. Among them, what is the character of the fantasies involved in unconscious knowledge? In what sense does one "know" when knowledge is unconscious, and in what sense does one "not know" when conscious knowledge is displaced by unconscious?

Finally, leaving this digression on the hysteria of anatomists, the existence of resistance to the recovery of memories and the interlocking and mutually supporting theories of repression and the unconscious provide evidence for the role of ideas at a more sophisticated level. *That* ideas are important in the genesis of hysteria is, I think, certain. How they are important and what sort of ideas they are is not yet entirely clear.

Affect and Abreaction (Discharge)

Reintegrating the "incompatible" ideas into consciousness is not enough for cure. Breuer and Freud emphasized the need for "arousing its accompanying affect." Freud observed many years later, in his theoretical essay on "The Unconscious," that "If we communicate to a patient some idea which he has at one time repressed but which we have discovered in him, our telling him makes at first no change in his mental condition" (1915e, 175). And elsewhere he says:

> If knowledge about the unconscious were as important for the patient as people inexperienced in psycho-analysis imagine, listening to lectures or reading books would be enough to cure him. Such measures, however, have as much influence on the symptoms of nervous illness as a distribution of menu-cards in a time of famine has upon hunger. (1910k, 225)

Insight is not enough. What more is needed? The early abreaction theory calls for affect. The difficulty brought on by the splitting off of the incompatible idea was that the affect originally attached to the idea could not be discharged in the usual ways (abreaction, association, etc.). The idea was weakened and removed from consciousness, but the affect remained, in the case of hysteria, to be "converted" into symptoms. So it is not enough for cure that the repressed idea be retrieved, the affect must be reattached and then discharged. Here there are theoretical difficulties.

It seems that Breuer and Freud found that, in most cases, the retrieval of the memory of the traumatic event was accompanied by an accentuation of the related symptom and then its disappearance (1895d, 37). But how is one to distinguish a new affective reaction from the abreaction of the original undischarged quantity? The relation of energy in the symptom to the original undischarged affect is also problematical. The problem arises especially acutely when affect is not converted immediately into symptoms, that is, there is a delay in the first occurrence of symptoms (1895d, 168ff.). Freud speaks in these cases of "recollected affect" (Rosalia case, 1895d, 173), but the patient is not aware of it in the interval and it is unclear in what form it is preserved. What is the criterion of identity and individuation for affective energy? What happens once a sum of excitation has been put to another use, that is, been converted? Why can it not be released or "used up" in its new form? The trauma in Freud's "Neuro-Psychoses of Defence" (1894a) remains a precipitating cause, but it is less clear whether it is still an agent at work or a "directly releasing cause." That is, how detached is affect once it is put to a new use? Does it lead an independent life once its new form has been determined by the associated idea? Can it have an independent death? If it can, is the "memory" then still essential to the existence of the neurosis (admitting its essentialness to the content), and need it be recovered in order to effect cure? If it cannot, why not? The start of an answer *may perhaps* be found in the notion of a "psychical mnemic symbol." For insofar as the symptom is itself a memory, the energy may be no more open to release in its new form than in its original one—it may just be more bearable. It becomes dischargeable through association, consolation, abreaction, and so on, only once it becomes conscious memory. It is therefore the role of psychoanalysis to bring affect and idea together again. It is of course important that the conditions that kept the affect from being discharged in the original situation not be duplicated in the analytic situation (hence the analyst must be accepting, etc.). Other constraints should also be considered, but I doubt that further light is to be found until one has examined closely Freud's instinct theory and the nature of the connection between idea and affect within that theory. (See also Freud's *Project for a Scientific Psychology*, 1950a [1887–1902].)

There are further theoretical difficulties connected with the identification and reidentification of the energy involved in symptoms and abreaction. But first I wish to explore another aspect of the notion of abreaction.

Abreaction and Expression

What sort of "discharge" of emotional energy is "abreaction"? Is the connection of energy involved in discharge behavior to the emotion such that the emotion is the "motive" of the behavior? Must it be a conscious "motive" or may it be unconscious (i.e., is abreaction necessarily conscious)? One way of approaching these questions is through another: Is "abreaction" a species of "manifestation" or of "expression" of emotion?

That difference rests, I want to claim, on the intentionality of the behavior. Expression *must* depend on the subject's thoughts. The problem is whether those thoughts may be unconscious or must be conscious. One can *manifest* an unconscious emotion (meaning that the thought involved is unconscious—whatever the status of the "affect") in all sorts of ways: Elisabeth's love of her sister's husband manifested itself in somatic hysterical symptoms (especially localized in pains in the left thigh), intrusive thoughts ("Now he is free again and I can be his wife" at her sister's deathbed, 1895d, 156), and significant behavior (e.g., overzealous defense of his appearance, 1895d, 158). The emotion could be said to be "expressed" in as many ways, where "expression" here equals "manifestation," but *she* is not *expressing* the emotion on these occasions. For that to be true, she would have to know that she loves him, and intentionally do the relevant actions because of that love. Behavior, if it can be intentional, must be intentional to count as "expression." (See Wollheim 1966.) To bring this out, imagine that "A hits B." Suppose that is all you know of their behavior. What emotion is A expressing? One might be inclined to say "anger" and perhaps "jealousy" and other emotions in that range (unpleasant and hostile). But why not, say, "gratitude"? Perhaps A is grateful to C, who hates B, and expresses that gratitude by hitting B. Perhaps A is grateful to B, but B has strange ways of deriving pleasure (or at least A believes B derives pleasure in those strange ways). The point is that any bit of behavior, neutrally described, can express (almost) *any* emotion. (It might also express no emotion. After all, A might punch B on a bet.) But to know what emotion is being expressed, if any, you must know the thought behind it, why the agent is doing it, you must know the intentional description of it as an action. (See MacIntyre 1971.)

"Catharsis" might seem a matter of the discharge of neutrally described energy, but as embodied in the "abreaction" theory, such an account cannot be adequate. Catharsis and abreaction as treated by Freud seem to be species of expression (despite many misleading statements), in the sense in which expression requires conscious intention. Because you do not discharge *that* particular energy, you do not abreact that particular emotion, unless your behavior is intentional action (where the relevant intention involves expressing *that* emotion). Otherwise running around the block or other activity (or conversion into a symptom) should always be sufficient "discharge" of any emotion. But it is a central claim of the abreaction theory that strangulated affect *cannot* be discharged in just any way, most particularly not by symptomatic actions. Incompatible ideas must be reintegrated back into consciousness, and reattached to their original affect, before the affect can be adequately discharged. General release of energy (e.g., from running) may bring relief by lowering the vitality of the entire system, and so lowering the level of suffering along with it, but it does not discharge the particular troublesome energy. To tell what emotion is being discharged or abreacted you must go through the patient's thoughts.

My question was whether those thoughts may be unconscious. The answer is that they must be conscious for the emotion to be expressed rather than merely manifested, and it seems that "abreaction" requires the thought to be conscious because it is a species or type of "expression." It might seem an empirical claim of the abreaction theory that the energy is not discharged unless discharged in connection with (the appropriate) conscious thought. I hope it is now clear that that is actually a conceptual point: we do not know what *the* energy is (what emotion is being expressed rather than merely manifested) except through the conscious thoughts. We identify the energy through the behavior, which in turn we identify through the intention. That abreaction is a species of expression is a consequence of how we tell what emotion is being discharged or abreacted.

We can't discharge the energy of strangulated affect, unconscious emotion, until the associated idea is made conscious because "discharge" really means "express." Symptoms can manifest unconscious feeling. But even if symptoms disappeared without the thought becoming conscious, the emotion would not have been "abreacted."

Affect and Abreaction Again

Further theoretical difficulties are raised by the need for an *adequate* reaction in order to discharge affect (1895d, 8). This *should* be a quantitative notion. If a reaction is inadequate in the first place, the affect remains attached to the idea in memory. They become detached in the repression of the idea, and adequate reaction (or discharge) is thereafter impossible. The notion of adequacy becomes more than neatly quantitative, because the detached affect seems to require an "appropriate" discharge. Appropriateness seems to be determined by the original associated idea, and so adequate reaction cannot be achieved until affect and idea are rejoined. No reaction, however great in magnitude, can achieve the adequate discharge of a detached and "strangulated" affect. Again, this is a consequence of identifying (discharged, abreacted or expressed) energy through behavior as conceived by the subject. Appropriateness is also actually one of the constraints (the other is "traumatic force") that Freud puts on etiological claims: the content of a trauma and the nature of the symptom must be appropriately connected, the former must be a "suitable" determinant of the latter before we can accord it a primary etiological role (Freud 1896c, 193–94).

A final difficulty. Associative discharge, an alternative to motor discharge, also tends to obscure the economic or quantitative picture. Conscious ideas, according to *Studies on Hysteria,* are subject to "rectification by other ideas" (1895d, 9). This is very much like the correction of beliefs:

> After an accident, for instance, the memory of the danger and the (mitigated) repetition of the fright becomes associated with the memory of what happened afterwards—rescue and the consciousness of present safety. Again, a person's memory of a humiliation is corrected by his putting the facts right, by considering his own worth, etc. (1895d, 9)

So long as an idea is conscious, accompanying affect can be made to disappear through a process of association. But the economics of this process is not entirely clear. Is the affect somehow spread over the associated ideas, or is there some sort of canceling affect (negative cathexis?) attached to the correcting ideas? How does the process differ from whatever occurs in the process of reasoning by which we correct non-affectively charged beliefs? And why does not a similar process bring relief in obsessional neurosis? According to Freud's early model, obsessional neurosis is produced by detached energy that gets displaced onto other ideas (rather than converted into physical symptoms as in hysteria). For example, the girl who suffered from obsessional self-reproaches for crimes she did not commit because of the displacement of her guilt from masturbation (1894a, 55). Why do the displacement and associations to innocence not bring relief? Here there is not quite the same difficulty we saw earlier in reidentifying the affect in its different connections. In hysteria we are dealing with a neutral energy that gets converted, here we are dealing with "affect" in the sense of an emotion (guilt) which gets displaced. So far as an emotion is identified through its object, however, to call a change in object "displacement" would raise the same difficulty. A thing can be perceived as "displaced" or "converted" only against a background of continuity—too much change (i.e., change in essential identifying respects) leaves it no longer the "same thing." In any case (leaving the analysis of "displacement" for elsewhere—see chap.

12 here), the question remains of why the affect cannot be successfully discharged in its displaced form. If there is an additional source of energy sustaining the symptom, what is it and why must *it* be re(?)joined to the original idea?

A way out of this tangle may perhaps be found if we return to examine the original idea and its connection with affect—which is what we shall do in the next two sections.

The Seduction Theory

Is the hysteric responding to past *reality*?[5] For some time (first reference in letter to Fliess of 8 October 1895; see Stewart 1967, 106–10) Freud believed he must be. Freud was prepared to believe that in some cases the "traumatic event" consisted of a sexual assault by the father on his innocent child. This "seduction theory" was developed as part of a broader theory of the sexual etiology and "choice" of neurosis. The broader theory was based on a schematic picture of sexuality in chemical and quantitative terms. Neuroses arise, in accordance with an "etiological formula," from problems in the unburdening of the model of internal excitation. Hysteria is produced by the passive seduction by an adult of a child before the age of eight. A variant "active" sexual experience leads to obsessional neurosis. These are two of the neuropsychoses of defense. They are distinguished from another group of "actual" neuroses by the fact that the victim is (in a sense) aware of the instigating forces (and defending himself against them) and that the sexual factor belongs "to an epoch of life which is long past" (Freud 1898a, 267). The actual neuroses, such as neurasthenia and anxiety neurosis, are supposed to be derived from "current deleterious sexual practices," such as masturbation and coitus interruptus (Stewart 1967, 43).[6] Here the symptoms are not symbolic or "meaningful," but rather toxicological consequences of inadequate discharge. Freud did not correct the errors in his toxicological theory of anxiety until 1926 (1926d, 94); the difficulties in his "seduction theory" became evident much sooner. It was a theory Freud tried to avoid, even admitting to having twice suppressed the identity of the seducer as the father (1895d, 134n.2, 170n.1; in the cases of both Rosalia and Katharina a "bad uncle" is substituted). But the theory had the virtue (as well as neatly fitting the physicochemical etiological formula) of avoiding infantile sexuality, that is, impulses attributed *to* the child, even while having to admit sexual experiences *as* an infant or child. This, of course, led to grave theoretical difficulties. For example, the earlier events were said to act through the mediation of memories. But why should the *memory* of an infantile trauma be more serious in its consequences than the actual experience of it at the time (prepuberty and, presumably, presexuality)? Freud made efforts to explain how memories from a presexual period could become traumatic (1896b, 166–67n.), but was forced eventually to abandon the whole attempt to preserve the innocence of childhood. In a letter to Fliess (21 September 1897) he announced that "I no longer believe in my *neurotica*" (1950a, *SE* 1: 259). The childhood seductions had always been implausible (especially in the numbers required), and became more implausible as his own father seemed implicated by the neuroses of his sisters (Jones 1953, 354). Freud's own self-analysis (which he had just begun) and developments in technique (free association leading to sexual thoughts) also must have played a role in his growing doubts. Limited therapeutic success should also be mentioned, but most significant from our point of view, "the certain discovery that there are no indications of reality in the unconscious, so that one cannot distinguish between the truth and fiction that is cathected with affect" (Freud 1950a, *SE* 1: 260) moved Freud to abandon the "seduction theory." The path was open to the discovery of infantile sexuality and the Oedipus complex, and the understanding of pathogenic ideas as representations of wish and impulse in childhood. The emphasis on fantasy is a step toward placing the etiology of neurosis in the persistence of unconscious (repressed) desires rather than buried reminiscences. In rejecting the "seduction theory," Freud raises a further question, connected with the larger issue of the objectivity of history, and that is whether it is necessary that the fantasy should occur in childhood: "It seems to have become once again arguable that it is only later experiences that give the impetus to phantasies, which then hark back to childhood" (1950a, *SE* 1: 260; cf. 1899a, 321–22, and discussion of sexualizing the past in Rat Man, 1909d, 206–7n.). So history might be fantasy of memory rather than memory of fantasy.

Action and Abreaction

What did Freud discover when he abandoned his "neurotica" for unconscious fantasies? First, that the memories of traumatic seductions reported by his hysterics were false, or rather, they could be, they need not be memories of actual events to produce their effects. Second, and more important, that they were the psychical representatives of instinct, that is, the (distorted) representations of the object of unconscious wish. Originally, "Hysterics suffer mainly from reminiscences." The task of analytical treatment was to recover these memories so as to allow release of the associated affect (discharge through abreaction). But it became clear that there must have been an element of pleasure in the original attack (the experience is not simply "neutral" or traumatically unpleasant) and so Freud came to reject the abreaction theory: "A hysterical attack is not a discharge but an *action;* and it retains the original characteristic of every action—of being a means to the reproduction of pleasure" (Letter 52, 1896, Freud 1950a, *SE* 1: 239). The failure of the hysterical defense is not due to the failure to discharge inappropriately bound energy derived from an external trauma. (If all there was was the external energy, it would remain a mystery why the symptoms could not successfully use up that energy.) It fails because it is a compromise between impulses derived from earlier impulses and forces of repression. Hence Freud's later formula: the neurotic "repeats instead of remembering" (1914g, 151). The task of analytical treatment becomes the working through of resistances in the transference relationship, to overcome frustration and repetitive "acting out" by recognizing present impulses and their relation to earlier impulses (repression and regression)—not simply *discharging* old (external) energies in connection with recovered memories.

The developments in Freud's thought that led to his abandoning his *neurotica* and to his emphasis on fantasy can be traced in his *Project for a Scientific Psychology* and his correspondence with Fliess (1950a [1887–1902]). In his *Project*, which he worked on just after the publication of *Studies on Hysteria* (1895d), Freud's mechanical model for the operation of the mind had suggested that the "primary process" of the brain leads to hallucinatory gratification. This provided the essential clue for the wish-fulfillment theory of dreams, and for the importance of fantasy. There is an initial or innate drive and preference for fantasy gratification. It is only the "exigencies of life" and the need for "specific actions" that lead to "secondary process" thinking.

Fantasy gratification, or hallucinatory wish-fulfillment, has certain analogies with genuine "satisfaction" (i.e., discharge of energy). First, there is some energy that is used up in over-cathecting an idea to hallucinatory force. Second, the desired object is perceived as present; but, of course, since it is not really present, there is inevitable frustration. The instinctual needs keep pressing for genuine satisfaction, which requires the presence of an appropriate external object and "specific action" (e.g., sucking on breast) leading to discharge. It is the exigencies of life and frustration that lead to the secondary process. But the *Project* model fails to give a mechanical explanation of neurotic defense, of repression. Why should memories be repressed (*SE* 1: 350)? Clinical experience seemed to show that repressed ideas were sexual and unpleasant—but why should sex be unpleasant? The theory had it that the original sexual event was very early, prepubertal, and memory of it was triggered by a post-pubertal event causing retroactive traumatizing of the event, leading to displacement and repression. The intercession of puberty might explain the new forcefulness of the revived memory, but is that the same as unpleasantness? The energy of sexual awakening might be added to the original cathexis of the memory—but why should this (mechanically) lead to repression? On the model, one would have thought that it would lead to hallucinatory strength rather than unconscious activity.

The revisions of the *Project* psychopathology began almost immediately. Among them was the idea that the original event was not neutral, but unpleasant. This left a problem of explaining the initial unpleasure. Freud first speculated that shame and morality were the repressing forces and that they were organic in origin (*SE* 1: 221–22). But he recognized that the geography of the body (the proximity of the sexual and excremental organs) was inadequate to provide an explanation. Why should there be disgust at the excremental (children are quite happy to play with feces—see Letter 58), and why would there not *always* be disgust at sex on this account (*SE* 1: 222)? A full theory of sexuality was needed, but still, if the original event was experienced as unpleasurable, it must have been repressed right away. So instead of a later conscious (intentional) repression, the theory seems to call for a primary repression (which the patient does not remember and which remains theoretical and is later connected with "fixation"). When the memory is reawakened, there is a second repression (*SE* 1: 222–23).

Freud's father died in October 1896. Shortly after, Freud was putting a new emphasis on the element of pleasure in the original attack (*SE* 1: 236, 238). He had already noted the peculiar pleasure in the way patients sometimes recounted the event (1895d, 137). The pleasure, being nongenital, seemed "perverse." The notion of sexual release being obtainable from many parts of the body in childhood led to the notion of "erotogenic zones," and to hysteria as the "negative" of perversion (the same impulses can lead to different results) (*SE* 1: 239, 243n.5). Most importantly, it led to the break with the abreaction (discharge) theory: "A hysterical attack is not a discharge but an *action*" (*SE* 1: 239).

The concept of "fantasy" enabled Freud to connect the two disparate ideas of hysteria as the residue of an earlier event working through memory and hysteria as action to yield pleasure in the present ("the missing piece," Letter 59, 1950a [1887–1902]). The fantasy was a way of harking back to the primal seduction scene, a fulfillment of the adult wish to return to that scene. So what is repressed is not memory, but impulse: "the psychical structures which, in hysteria, are affected by repression are not in reality memories—since no one indulges in mnemic activity without a motive—but *impulses* which arise from the primal scenes" (Letter 61, 2 May 1897, 1950a, *SE* 1: 247; cf. 1915e, 177). "Remembering is never a motive but only a way, a method. The first motive for the construction of symptoms is, chronologically, libido. Thus symptoms, like dreams, are *the fulfillment of a wish*" (Letter 64, 31 May 1897, 1950a, *SE* 1: 256; cf. 252). The motive for formation of symptoms is libido; symptoms are sexual activity aimed at producing pleasure. So hysterical symptoms are "meaningful" in yet another sense: in the sense in which actions with a purpose behind them have a "meaning" supplied by that purpose. A feeling revived from the original "seduction" scene produces or revives an impulse. At this point the original scene might still have been regarded as real. But if symptoms and fantasy in the present represent instinctual impulse, why could not earlier impulses have taken the form of fantasies? This approach dooms belief in the original seductive attack. That was acceptable as long as the experience was viewed as neutral.

But for an impulse to return to exist, it must have been pleasurable, so that the child must (insofar as pleasure is the satisfaction of impulse) have had sexual impulses to enjoy in the first place. If there was pleasure, given Freud's view of pleasure, there must have been discharge of energy, so the seduction scene must allow discharge of internal impulse and not merely the addition of unpleasurable tension from the outside. But if the child has its *own* impulses requiring discharge, there is no need to postulate or believe in an actual seduction. The child had its own desires to fulfill in fantasy and lead to symptoms in adulthood. The road to the full theory of infantile sexuality becomes clear, and it passes through the notion of "fantasy."[7]

In this new context, Dora's "cough" appears as an action (Freud, 1905e, 46–52). This symptom is connected with her unconscious love of Herr K. (the cough appearing during periods of his absence), but Freud also interprets it as a manifestation of unconscious fantasies of oral intercourse involving Frau K. and Dora's father and a return to infantile pleasures of sucking (51). The cough is a much distorted compromise satisfaction. Here, as elsewhere, we can see the contrast of abreaction and action (arising from inner conflict rather than external trauma). If the problem were one of abreaction (discharge) there is no reason why symptoms should not solve it, that is, why they should not be a successful form of discharge. Freud's early theory does not really explain why they fail (the energy assumptions, besides being difficult to support, are not sufficient). The underlying theory of pleasure, as a form of discharge, is itself open to challenge. But in any case, if the problem is one of action, one can understand how reinterpretation and insight would help guide one's actions so that they more successfully achieve their ends (of pleasure in the face of a given, but changeable, reality), rather than result in unsuccessful symptomatic compromises. What appeared as "abreactive" catharsis may in fact have been but a part of the more complex process in which unconscious impulse is made conscious and seen to be inappropriate to present reality and to have led to distortion in perception and response to that reality.[8]

The Power of Fantasy

With the rejection of the "seduction theory," Freud concluded that "as far as the neurosis was concerned, psychical reality was of more importance than material reality" (1925d, 34). Many traumatic events that Freud had taken for reality might have been fantasies; the ideas or memories nonetheless had pathogenic force equal to what reality would have had. There is an important complication once the "memories," whether veridical or fantasies, are seen to be not simply memories, but the embodiment of instinct and impulse. Once this is recognized the indifference in effectiveness of reality and fantasy may perhaps be explained if it is the underlying impulse or desire which is responsible for pathogenic force, so force may remain constant despite variations in the character of the associated ideas. And we may begin to understand why insight or recapturing memories is not enough for cure. But before we can discuss this complication, there is a prior question: is the indifference of which it would be a theoretical explanation a fact? In a recent article O. Sachs notes:

> Pragmatically almost, there seems to have developed an attitude that it made little difference whether a remembered traumatic event occurred or was fantasied; the latter, subjective, drive-dependent, experience came to be accorded the primary ætiological significance. (1967, 416)

He claims that it does make a difference: "There appears to be more masochism and guilt created from acts of reality than fantasy if these occur when superego formation is already well developed" (421). But Sachs offers no theoretical reason for believing this to be true. A case is discussed in which, it is claimed, failure to distinguish reality from fantasy leads to regression into earlier obsessional symptoms. It is important that the failure is the analyst's. Other cases are cited where the difference between fantasy and reality is indeed important. For example, a

> patient, having witnessed an unsuccessful suicidal attempt by his mother when he was 3 1/2, had been told that it had not actually happened, that he must have had a nightmare. The conflict between perception and parental denial, as well as the overwhelming affect involved, resulted in severe defects in distinguishing fantasy and reality and in consequent feelings of derealization. (421)

But here the difficulty is the patient's, and so the case seems irrelevant to the question of the role of fantasy and reality in etiology. For our question is: given that the patient takes a certain event as having really occurred, does it make any difference to the development of symptoms or possibility of cure if the event was merely fantasy? The main case Sachs discusses is similar to the above in that, as he says, "an important element was that of parental lying and denial about reality events which had been more or less correctly perceived and understood by the child" (421). This case might seem similarly irrelevant, because it speaks to the issue of: given that the patient takes a certain event as having been mere fantasy (as a result of psychoanalytic treatment), does it make any difference to the development of symptoms or possibility of cure if the event was actual? This is the reverse of our former question, but an answer to it is not irrelevant because both ask for differences in the etiological roles of fantasy and reality. Unfortunately, I think Sachs gives a misleading account of the force of his case. The case is of a young secretary, who in an earlier analysis had reported on a visit when she was six and a half to the doctor with her mother:

> she remained in the waiting room while mother was "next door." She had listened to the sounds, thinking something sexual was going on,

with feelings of strong resentment, jealousy—and excitement. At the time she told me of these happenings I had interpreted "the pattern" in terms of her experiences in her parents' bedroom, and her later sexual fantasies stimulated by her uncle's medical books. (420)

The patient accepted the interpretation of the event as part of the Oedipal fantasy pattern, but a few years later she is troubled by anxiety and an obsessive question of "should I tell" or "may I tell" a fiancé about certain love affairs and a lie about age. These new symptoms are now traced via dreams, identification, and so on, to "an important sexual accusation against her mother, about which she had been strongly admonished not to tell." The event is the one described, but Sachs's account is misleading because it is not the *reality* of that event as opposed to its supposed fantasy status that leads to the reemergence of symptoms. It is rather the admonition, the repressed admonition, that has force. It is the admonition that leads Sachs, as it had led the young girl, to accept the reality of the event:

> I brought this incident back to her and suggested that the truth of her suspicions about her mother's affair must have been confirmed for her by a strong admonition from her mother *not to tell* anyone of the visit. The repressed element, her mother's command not to tell, had been the confirmation of the truth of her suspicions as a child as it was now essential for the analytical understanding and confirmation. (420)

So the girl's confusion of fantasy and reality is important, as Sachs says:

> The distinction in reality between who was lying, who was guilty of sexual misbehaviour, she or mother, were vital to the resolution of her obsessional symptoms and of her anxiety. Guilt had first to be distinguished from "borrowed guilt," and for this distinction, the reality had first to be understood and delineated from the patterns with which it had become interwoven. (421)

Though the girl's confusion is important, the analyst's is not. What is significant is that taking the event as fantasy left his analysis incomplete, and the incompleteness of his analysis is what allowed him to treat the event as fantasy. The admonition is what makes the difference between taking the event as real and as fantasy, but that the event is real is not what makes the difference to the case. It was the event plus the admonition to deny the event that led to regression. Is there any reason to suppose that the effects would have been different if both event *and* admonition (like most castration threats) had been fantasy? Sachs gives none, and his argument seems more a case of incomplete initial analysis than of traumatic reality reasserting itself.

It is worth noting, however, that though the status of the event as fantasy or reality seems not to matter, it does matter (as I have said) whether the patient thinks the event real or fantasy (or is confused), and it does matter *in some ways* (as should now be obvious) what the analyst believes the status of the event to be. But this last point is actually very complex, and differences in interpretation are only one dimension along which his beliefs will affect his procedure. For example, in Freud's case of the eighteen-year-old Dora, the initial reason for treatment was that the girl's father, for his own reasons (an affair with Frau K.) wanted her convinced that an actual seduction attempt, or attack (by Herr K.), had been a fantasy. Though Freud does not fall in with this scheme, he does fail to take proper account of the intolerable nature of the girl's actual circumstances. He badgers her with interpretations, failing to see that Dora might perceive him as a seducing Herr K. or threatening father figure. (For example, he interprets a "jewel-case" in a dream as female genitals—she says, "I knew you would say that"—and he interprets that as resistance. Freud 1905e, 69.) He admits failing to interpret the transference, but the failure goes deeper than that. As Erikson suggests,

> The nature and severity of Dora's pathological reaction make her, of course, the classical hysteric of her day; but her motivation for falling ill, and her lack of motivation for getting well, today seem to call for developmental considerations which go beyond (although they include) the sexual conflicts then in the focus of Freud's studies . . . The question arises whether today we would consider the patient's active emphasis on the historical truth a mere matter of resistance to the inner truth; or whether we would discern in it also an adaptive pattern specific for her stage of life, challenged by her special conditions, and therefore subject to consideration in her treatment. (1964, 169–70)

This is just a hint at the rather different perspective object-relations theory might add. The main point is that Freud treated Dora's problem as too much an internal one, arising merely from failures to adjust to instinct. (He even goes so far at one point as to suggest that he would regard her as hysterical even if she did not exhibit symptoms simply because of her pure disgust at a sexual attack: "I should without question consider a person hysterical in whom an occasion for sexual excitement elicited feelings that were preponderantly or exclusively unpleasurable; and I should do so whether or not the person were capable of producing somatic symptoms" [1905e, 28].)

Why should there be no difference in the etiological consequences of fantasy and reality, between childhood experiences and childhood fantasies of such experiences or between those and later fantasies projected back into childhood? It should first be admitted that it is not quite true to say that there are no differences. The point of this admission is not to suggest that for any given account of the origin of a symptom in childhood experience an alternative account in terms of fantasies cannot be constructed. I wish to suggest that one always can. The point here is rather that experience counts. That is, what does actually happen in childhood does have important consequences. That these consequences could result from alternative causes does not mean that these causes are not different, and the difference need not be confined to the first link in the causal chain. What actually happens in childhood is especially important because even though events might be plausibly reconstructed with the substitution of fantasy for reality, it is only in very few cases (the "primal fantasies") that it is at all likely that the fantasies would actually have been constructed in the absence of the experiences.

The Force of Thoughts

Finally, why should fantasies produce the same effects as memories had been alleged to? I have not shown, and it has not been shown, that the effects are in general equal. Perhaps actual traumas do (sometimes, or even always) produce more severe neuroses. That is an empirical issue. But we can speculate on how it is that fantasies can produce neuroses with the same content as those produced by actual traumas, and why they should be equally severe, *if* they are. It might simply be a matter of the balancing of factors. The effects of *deprivation* in increasing the satisfactions of early fantasy and so chances of regression might just compensate for the *"facilitation"* by actual gratification of early impulses in leading to regression. But if thoughts are important, a more general explanation is possible.

Some events have effects bypassing our thoughts about them. If someone breaks his leg, it becomes more difficult for him to walk no matter what he thinks. But if it is the perception of an event that has effect, how a person sees the event becomes its privileged description. If the event is repressed, it is *his* view of what happened that is repressed, and there is no neutral description (however obtained) that is more important. It is the consciousness of the happening, rather than the actual happening, that has causal efficacy. Of course, a person may distort the event in his perception, and the greater the distortion the more inclined we are to say it is a "fantasy," though so long as there is some public event to which it maintains an intelligible relation, we are not forced to give it that description. (Conversely, fantasies are not necessarily "false," in that, like certain accurate masturbation fantasies, they can aim at and achieve the content of a veridical memory.) If the differences among thoughts (perceptions, fantasies, and memories) were themselves matters of degree of force or quantity of energy (in Humean fashion), we would expect differences in consequences based on type of thought and not just content of thought. Such an account is, however, arguably false. (For such arguments, see Neu 1977, appendix C: "On a Humean View of Fantasy.")

In the cases we have been considering, thoughts are important. But not because there is some event (perceived, remembered, or fantasied) which results in symptoms through our thoughts about it, but because there is an impulse (instinct, wish, desire) and that impulse essentially involves thoughts. In the absence of that impulse, actual events would not have the pathogenic significance they do have. An assault might indeed be neutral rather than traumatic without a background of desires and beliefs. The unconscious fantasies to which Freud traces hysterical symptoms are real insofar as they embody impulse. The fantasies are the mental aspect of the impulse, which is to say that the impulse essentially involves thoughts, for we know our desires through our fantasies and other manifestations to which we can attach thoughts: we identify our desires through the associated thoughts (conscious and unconscious). The explanation of that involvement is the explanation of unconscious fantasy, and the beginning of an understanding of the nature of neurosis. An explanation of unconscious fantasy and the development of fantasy from primary process mental functioning would help us see why insight is necessary. We always act against a background of beliefs and memories that function in reasons and motives, that give the objects of our desires. Current impulse, informed by unconscious memory or fantasy, becomes repetition, or an attempt (unconsciously) to alter the past. The source of the thought (whether fantasy or memory) does not matter, it can play the same role in guiding impulse and action. Fantasy and memory may have comparable effects because they are not simply "causes"; past experiences are not connected by general laws to present symptoms (or at least, that is not the Freudian claim). Rather unconscious fantasy and memory provide the (unrecognized) motives and reasons for present conduct, inclinations, and symptoms. So long as they are unconscious, they can operate with equal force—they can be equally inappropriate as perceptions of current reality and so as background for action. It is not the undischarged energy of earlier periods of childhood that persists, but the memories of earlier satisfactions and frustrations and the fantasies connected with them, and these become involved in giving direction to present energy. Accepting impulses, or changing attitudes toward them, may be an important therapeutic step. The discharge of externally derived (traumatic) energy would leave the equal influence of fantasy and memory a mystery, along with the mysteries of the identification, reidentification, and conditions for discharge of energy. With an appreciation of the relation of thought to impulse we can begin to understand the operation of insight as a force for change in analytic therapy—and why insight is not enough.[9]

12

"DOES THE PROFESSOR
TALK TO GOD?"

Learning from Little Hans

Freud never worked with children. Indeed when, early in his psychoanalytic theorizing, a question arose for him about the excremental interests of children, he wrote to his friend Fliess asking for information, adding: "Why do I not go into the nursery and experiment with Annerl? . . . I have no time for it, and the womenfolk do not support my researches" (1985 [1887–1904], 230, Letter of February 8, 1897). Freud at one point in his *Three Essays on the Theory of Sexuality* suggested that his lack of experience with children did not matter:

> None, however, but physicians who practise psycho-analysis can have any access whatever to this sphere of knowledge or any possibility of forming a judgement that is uninfluenced by their own dislike and prejudices. If mankind had been able to learn from a direct observation of children, these three essays could have remained unwritten. (1905d, 133, Preface to the Fourth Edition, 1920)

Surely he had a point: Freud was not the first to note that children suck their thumbs, but it was only his new conceptual understanding of the sexual instinct (as made up of components analyzable in terms of source, object, and aim) that enabled him to argue persuasively that such activity should be seen as an early manifestation of that instinct, as a form of infantile sexuality. (See Neu 1987b [chap. 9 here].) Elsewhere in the same work, however, he seems to treat the direct observation of children as necessary, though subject to misunderstanding. He admits, of course, that psychoanalysis too has its disadvantages, in particular that it "is made difficult by the fact that it can only reach its data, as well as its conclusions, after long detours" (1905d, 201).

However much psychoanalysis has to say about the sources of adult character, sexuality, and neurosis in childhood, it was not based (initially at least) on the direct observation of children and childhood development.

It was based on inferences from the analyses of adult patients. Freud's case study of Little Hans records the first actual child analysis. Little Hans was not analyzed (indeed, was not even born) until after the turn of the century; but Freud's account offers a unique window into the ways in which the observation of children may be relevant to the confirmation of psychoanalytic hypotheses themselves not originally inspired by such observation. (Which is not to say that direct observation never itself suggests new hypotheses—it has and it does.) Freud himself did not enter into the nursery; even in the case we will be considering only one direct meeting between Hans and "The Professor" is reported (41). The analysis of Little Hans was conducted through an intermediary, the boy's father. This makes for a rather significant additional "detour."

Little Hans's father, Max Graf (1875–1958), was a distinguished music critic and musicologist, an early follower of Freud, and a founding member of the Vienna Psychoanalytic Society (Freud 1974, 587n.; see also Graf 1942). Hans's mother had herself been a patient of Freud's (141–42). And we now know that Little Hans, Herbert Graf (1903–1973), despite his early difficulties, went on to a successful career as an opera stage director in New York and elsewhere (1974, 587n.; Holland 1985, 246–80). Freud himself noted Hans's "inherited musical gift" (138n.). While we will come to the complications introduced and questions raised by a parent performing a psychoanalysis on his own child, my immediate interest in the case has to do with what it has to offer in terms of a better understanding of psychoanalytic evidence and explanation. First, it provides direct information about the sexual theories of children. Second, it provides direct evidence for developmental and other psychoanalytic theories, particularly those of Freud's *Three Essays* (Oedipus complex, castration anxiety, ambivalence, among others). When I say that the evidence here is "direct," I mean the contrast to be with the sort of reconstruction and inference that is inevitable when one moves from the study of adult patients to theories of infantile development. The observation of children is itself of course theory-laden, that is, involves interpretation (and so could be said, in that sense, to be "indirect"). But the demand for neutral, uninterpreted data involves, I shall argue, a fundamental misunderstanding of the nature of evidence (in general, but especially in relation to psychoanalytic claims). And third, it provides a study of a class of neurosis—namely phobias—which is of independent interest and concern.

Chronology and the Phobia

To quickly review the main events of Hans's early childhood: He was born in April 1903 and his parents started sending their first reports, emphasizing his interest in widdlers, to Freud in 1906. The summer of 1906, when Hans was three and a quarter to three and a half, was the period of his first visit to Gmunden. His sister Hanna was born in October of that year, when Hans was three and a half. It was around this time that his mother made her castration threat. The first reported dream (that he was back at Gmunden with Mariedl [12]) took place when Hans was three and three quarters and shortly later, when Hans was four, the family moved to a new flat. The summer of 1907, when Hans was four and a quarter to four and a half, was the period of his second visit to Gmunden, which included the episode of the biting horse. At four and a half there is the first report of a distorted dream (about being made to widdle—distorting and repressing his earlier pleasure in exhibitionism [19–20, 61]). In January 1908, when Hans was four and three quarters, the episode of the falling horse occurred and his horse phobia began to unfold. By the time Hans was five, in May 1908, the analysis had come to an end.

Horses were common in 1908, of course, so a horse phobia in cosmopolitan Vienna at that time was not as strange as it might be today. But one should not attribute too much to the chance precipitating event of seeing a horse fall down (49). Those who think the "entire disorder" (Wolpe & Rachman 1963 [1960], 216) can be explained by this incident are mistaken. For one thing, Hans's apprehensiveness started *before* that "precipitating" incident (136). If one takes a comprehensive enough view of Hans's disorder, attributing exclusive causal force to seeing the horse falling would involve the nonsensical notion of the onset of the symptoms *preceding* their supposed cause. But more on this later.

Hans's problems began as an unfocused anxiety, and only emerged as a specific phobia gradually (24, 47, 124): including fear of horses biting (22, 24, 29, 50), horses falling down (46, 50), horses coming into the room (24, 115), focusing on specific types of horses (41, 47, 49), extending to other large animals (33) and heavy carts and vans (49, 51, 53, 124). What marks Hans's problem as a "phobia" is the strength of his fear (as measured both by the trouble taken to avoid "danger" and by the physiological upset involved) and the irrationality of the fear. It is these two criteria, in general, that make a fear a phobia, though they are not independent. It is not the strength of a reaction by itself that makes a fear a phobia. The normal reaction to an extreme danger may involve violent physiological upset and dramatic action, but it is only when the strength of the reaction is unwarranted, disproportional, or irrational that it comes to seem abnormal. Little Hans's fear of horses is irrational in at least two ways. In one of its aspects it is unintelligible. Why should Hans be afraid of a horse *falling down?* Given the object, what is the point of the fear? (That is, what is the danger to Hans?) In another aspect, while intelligible, the fear is unrealistic. While horses were more common in 1908, the probability of their *biting* was very low. One can know the object and the point of a fear, but still regard it as irrationally unrealistic. Today, it would not be foolish to be afraid that a dog might bite one, but it would amount to a phobia if one permitted that concern to keep one from ever going out of one's home or if it produced enormous anxiety whenever one managed to venture forth.

Freud's Explanation

Freud actually offered a number of explanations of Little Hans's phobia. Like all symptoms, it was overdetermined. (Cf. Freud's remarks on the multiple meanings of Dora's cough, 1905e [1901], 52–54, 82–83.) I will be focusing here on four strands of Freud's analysis.[1]

The Toxicological Theory of Anxiety

The first strand of Freud's interpretation postulates the repression of Hans's libidinal impulses toward his mother, and the transformation of those impulses into an anxiety that becomes attached to horses (26, 114–15, 119). This seems to me (and came to seem to Freud [1926d]) the least tenable aspect of his account. Let us consider its elements and their support.

It is clear that Hans experienced a heightened attachment to his mother as a consequence of the birth of his sister and the family's return from Gmunden, where Hans had had many other children to play with (26). As a result, Hans regressed to some of his old pleasures, to a need to be taken care of, and in other ways exhibited jealousy of the attention given to the new baby. The evidence for his attachment to his mother seems clear and overwhelming, but the evidence for repression of those feelings is not. (The issue is slightly complicated because Hans does repress his masturbation and his excremental exhibitionism with the onset of symptoms [108]—and I will return to these complications in a moment.) Hans's desire for his mother is, after all, open and remains open throughout the period under consideration. He wants to "coax" with his mother when he feels anxious (23–24). He has a prior anxiety dream of his mother going away (23, 118). And he wants on at least two occasions to seduce her into stroking his penis (19, 23, 25). He later talks of marrying her and becoming a Daddy (92), and has a masturbation fantasy of seeing his mother naked ("I put my finger to my widdler . . . I saw Mummy quite naked in her chemise, and she let me see her widdler" [32]). And of course he has a central and reiterated desire to sleep with his mother (23, 26, 39, 111). So it would appear that increased feeling for his mother and anxiety were simultaneously present, making it difficult to believe that the anxiety was the transformed product of repressed feelings.

Freud at this time accepted a special causal theory of the transformation of libido into anxiety that required repression of libido to get going. Certainly Hans was experiencing conflict, but since his need for his mother was clearly conscious, the case for repression of those feelings needs to be made out. Freud argues that Hans's longing for his mother is really "pathological anxiety" because it is not satisfied by the presence of the object longed for, and therefore must involve repressed longing (26n.). Hans must want more than he consciously admits to when he asks to "coax" and the like.

There is evidence for repression of some aspects of Hans's libido (108): he represses his masturbation (24, 27, 30–31) and he represses his (excremental) exhibitionism. This latter we see in his distorted widdling dream at four and a quarter (which, by the way, was before the incident of the falling horse [19–21]), and in his disgust at his mother's yellow drawers (57). One might argue that his anxiety was due to the repression of aggressive propensities—hostile ones against his father and sadistic ones against his mother—but Freud at this point, as opposed to Adler, denied a separate aggressive instinct, treating it instead as part of libido (138–41). The real problem is that the forces of repression (fear of castration in particular) already contain anxiety, and so it is a mistake to think that anxiety has to emerge *after* repression has taken place and as the result of some sort of chemical transformation. It was only Freud's special causal theory (that repressed libido is turned into anxiety) that led him (for a time) to think so.

The explanatory theory behind this strand of Freud's analysis was the *toxicological* theory of anxiety, a chemical theory of the transformation of substances (i.e., libido into anxiety). It was connected with Freud's theory of the *"actual"* neuroses, which are distinguished by the importance of current deleterious sexual practices (rather than symbolic transformations going back to past events) in their causation. Deficiencies in current sexual life (e.g., coitus interruptus), on this model, lead to the transformation of libido into anxiety. Similarly, masturbation would lead to neurasthenia (another "actual" neurosis). Freud later rejected his toxicological theory (at least for phobias [1926d, 110]). He rejected it partly for reasons of temporal order: it is more plausible to hold anxiety (particularly signal anxiety) leads to repression than that repression leads to anxiety. Hans's castration anxiety leads to repression, in terms of Freud's later structural theory: ego anxiety rather than id libido leads to repression. When one looks at the forces of repression—here fear of castration—anxiety is already present. As Freud puts it, "the anxiety felt in animal phobias is the ego's fear of castration" (1926d, 109; 101–10, 124–31). Moreover, the toxicological theory is at a different level from most of Freud's psychological hypotheses, and as a chemical theory seems untestable (no one has ever identified the relevant sexual and anxiety "substances").

Perhaps worst of all, the attachment of Hans's anxiety to horses would be accidental on this account. No meaning is given to horses as the object of fear. It would seem the anxiety could attach itself just as well to anything. The explanation in this strand is mechanical rather than purposive; it leaves out reference to beliefs and desires in the explanation of inhibitions and symptoms.

Fear of the Father

In the second strand of Freud's analysis, the horse *is* given meaning: fear of horses represents fear of the father. More particularly, fear of being bitten stands in for fear of being attacked by his father, while fear of a horse falling stands in for fear for his father. This latter fear is particularly justified in light of Hans's wish (unacknowledged, of course) for the death of his father (52). Hence the deeper fear behind the fear of being bitten is the fear that his father will punish him for his evil wishes (41–42, 126).[2] Castration anxiety is to be seen as the main force of repression, and the horse is a symbol, a displacement object or substitute for the father.

It also could be argued, however, that the fear of horses represents fear of the mother. After all, it was she who was the actual maker of a castration threat (7–8, 24). She also threatened, perhaps frequently, to abandon the naughty Hans (44–45), apparently often threatened to beat him with the carpetbeater (81), and he expressed concern she might let him drown in the bath (67). She was the one explicitly said to have a widdler as large as a horse's (10, 22, 27). And she was the object of the fantasy of beating horses (81, 129–30)—though the father interprets her role there as a defensive and evasive substitution for himself, since after all he was the one questioning Hans, and Freud sees it as "compounded of an obscure sadistic desire for his mother and of a clear impulse for revenge against his father" (83). She was also the object of the "sadistic" premonitions of copulation (as something violent and forbidden and done by the father too [41, 122–23, 135, 139]). These premonitions were the fantasies of "forcing his way into a forbidden space at Schönbrunn" and "of his smashing a railway-carriage window on the Stadtbahn" (122). (These are first described on 40–41; in each case the boy and his father are arrested by a policeman.) At one point Hans claims to remember his sister Hanna whipping horses at the time she was still inside her mother (75–76). Also, his mother was the crumpled giraffe in that significant fantasy (37–40), an animal Hans had been afraid of at Schönbrunn (33) and that Freud ties to the horses anxiety (122). In his later thought, Freud complicates his understanding of the Oedipal complex, exploring the ambivalence of the male child toward the mother as well as the father (e.g., 1923b). Still, in this case study, it is the interpretation in terms of the father that Freud develops.

The emotions in this strand of the interpretation are clearly present. There is love of the mother and a desire to get rid of the father. For the first, remember my discussion of the first strand of interpretation. For the desire to get rid of the father there is both indirect evidence and direct evidence. Indirect evidence includes the giraffe fantasy, in which the big giraffe is upset over the "possession" of the crumpled one by Little Hans, a fantasy that reproduces the morning ritual in which Hans climbs into bed with his mother and his father objects (37–39, 123; cf. giraffe drawing with widdler added by Hans [13]). And there is the most direct evidence of Hans's desire to have his mother alone in bed and to get rid of his father—he ultimately admits as much (82, 130; cf. 42). There is the association to the boy (Fritzl) who fell and bled: Hans acknowledges he thought of his father when the boy fell (82). And Freud (taking up an interpretation made by the father) suggests Hans also may have thought of his father when the horse fell (51–52). Then there was the experience of sleeping with his mother in the summer, during his father's absences (26, 45). The experience of closeness to his mother was conditional on those absences (111). And finally there are the various bits of "acting out" in which Hans butts or hits and then caresses his father (42n.1; Hans playing horse and biting father, 52; butting stomach like a goat, 88, 112, 125). These incidents are pictures of ambivalence.

Granting that the postulated emotions exist, the question remains of why they should be displaced. The answer could be put in terms of Freud's early notion of "incompatible" ideas, but is perhaps clearest in terms of "ambivalence." The reason for, the need for, displacement is given clearly in Hans's conduct: whatever his hostile feelings, Hans also loves and needs his father, and so fears the loss of his love. (Consider the incident where Hans claims he is coming into bed to be with his father rather than with his mother [43–44].) Ambivalence can be dealt with by both displacement and reaction-formation (1926d, 102–3—this is not to mention splitting and other defense mechanisms). (Hans's impulses toward both his father and his mother are at least partially thwarted [134–35]: his Oedipal hostility toward his father, and his over-fondness toward his mother [1926d, 107]). So Hans has a motive for displacement in his mixed feelings, and it is of course easier to avoid horses than his father (if he stays in the house, he may avoid horses, but his father is still liable to be at home [1926d, 124–31]).

Given the emotions, and given the need for displacement, why horses? Horses were particularly suitable displacement objects in relation to Hans's father. Hans's father actually had played horse for him (126–27). And in general animals and people are close in the minds of children (1926d, 103). (Interestingly, on the occasion of Hans's third birthday, long before his troubles, Freud himself—as a family friend—brought him a gift of a rocking horse [Graf 1942, 474].) Hans's nursemaid too had played horse for Hans (30). Horses, like Hans's parents (including his mother [10]), had big widdlers. The horses that Hans feared most had black things about their faces which corresponded with his father's moustache and glasses, making them resemble him more closely, a point first noted during the visit with Freud (41–42, cf. 49, 52, 53, 69, 123—see Wolpe & Rachman, 213, and Neu 1977, 127). Hans speaks of his father "trotting away" (45), which connects with his sometimes ambivalent fear of his father leaving him. There is also the scene of going away involving another father and a particular white horse (111). That Hans in fact identified horses and his father seems abundantly clear. The path to motivated displacement is made persuasively smooth.

Fear of His Mother Having
Another Child

Freud accounts for Hans's fear of horses falling down in terms of a fear of his mother having another child (connected with sibling rivalry [113–14]). This particular fear also was connected, of course, with the precipitating incident (49) at the start of Hans's phobia, and with Fritzl's falling down and bleeding when the children were playing at horses at Gmunden (58, 82, 126, 136). And we have seen that it also can be connected with Hans's hostile wishes against his father (e.g., 90, 111–12). "Thus the falling horse was not only his dying father but also his mother in childbirth" (128).

The emotions and beliefs involved in this strand of the interpretation are rather plainly present. Hans repeatedly shows that he hates his sister and does not welcome her competition in the household: he says that she has "no teeth" when she is praised, and during a fever after her birth says, "But I don't *want* a baby sister!" (11). He also indicates desires for his baby sister, variously, to fall in the bath and drown (67, 72, 128) and to fall off the balcony (68). He also makes it plain that, in terms of his parents' misinformation, he does not want more babies from the stork or in boxes on the way to Gmunden (68–72).

There is an equation in Hans's mind between his mother being heavily laden, as in pregnancy, and the body being laden with feces (91, 95). Moreover, as Freud puts it, "all furniture-vans and drays and buses were only stork-box carts, and were only of interest to Hans as being symbolic representations of pregnancy" (128; cf. 78, 81). The links between the explicit fears and the hidden meaning are multiple. One bridge that helps make the crossover easier is provided by the German word for delivery, "*niederkommen*," which also can be used to describe the horse falling down (95–96, 128). (Cf. the English description of a cow giving birth in terms of its "dropping" its calf.) Most interesting, for a variety of reasons, is the fact that Hans's neurosis takes a path to its concern with babies and childbirth that goes through an excremental complex (74–75, 105, 127).

Excremental themes emerge in Hans's story rather unexpectedly and in profusion. The falling horse had made a "row with its feet" (50; cf. 53, 79), and Hans associates the making of such a row with both resisting doing "lumf" (his word for feces) and the sound of lumf falling (54, 64, 66, 95). The concern about "making a row with the legs" also may be linked with the primal scene (135–36), one of the primal fantasies we will be considering later. It should be recalled that Hans slept in his parents' bedroom till the age of four (10, 17, 99; when his family moved to a new flat, 15), so there is perhaps more reason in his case than in most to think him likely to have in fact witnessed the primal scene. The making of a row also is connected by Hans with the "row" his sister makes with her screams (72). Then there are verbal links between Hans's name for his fantasy child, "Lodi," and a baby sausage (93–95, 131), like lumf in appearance, and a general equation of children with lumfs. There is the incident with his mother's yellow drawers, where Hans's professed disgust can be understood in terms of a repressed pleasure in watching his mother at her excretory functions (55f., 62–63—a symptom *for* the Professor, one he was glad to have his father write Freud about, 56). In this connection, Freud also follows the father in noting the verbal link for the young Hans between "lumpf" (which the English translators reduce to "lumf") and "strumpf" (the German word for stocking [54; cf. 59n.]).

The upshot is that it is very plausible to suppose that Hans believes the equations: baby = feces (68n., 95, 74, 131) and body with feces = body with baby (95–96) = heavily loaded cart and horse falling (55, 131). There is a link between Hans's perception of carts driving through the gateway across from his house and feces leaving the body (68, 96, 127); indeed, the first mention of the fear of horses falling down is made in connection with the observation of the carts at the gateway (46). Hans equates buses and the stork-box (78, 81), and he equates defecating and childbirth and horses falling (95—and one should not forget the blood Hans noted on the occasion of his mother giving birth, 10; or the bleeding Fritzl who hit a stone with his foot and fell while playing at horses, 58, 82). All of this corresponds with Hans's infantile theory of childbirth, a theory quite common among children, built partly on associations with the child's notion of feces as something that he makes of which he can be proud (indeed, it is a kind of "gift": think of the eagerness with which parents encourage their children to defecate at the right time and place "for them"), which passes out of his body. It corresponds also with what his parents tell him (his father tells Hans the baby is pressed out of the body like feces [87; cf. 89]). Hans after all knew that his baby sister was not brought by the stork, she was in his mother's body (e.g., during the trip to Gmunden [69f., 129]).

Note that Hans brings up the "lumf" theme on his own (in connection with the "row with his feet" [54; cf. 74]), so Freud quite legitimately can use it to answer the charge of "suggestion" (105) that we will turn to shortly.

It should be understood that Hans's linking of reproduction and excretion is not idiosyncratic or an isolated case. Other dramatic cures have been based on unraveling just such reproductive and excremental confusions. (See Erik Erikson's account of Little Peter [1963, 53–56]. In the light of Little Peter's problems, it might be worth reconsidering Little Hans's constipation [55–56, 65–66, 99, 112n.] and connecting it with his thoughts about his own "pregnancy" [85–86, 94–96, 133–34].) While it might seem surprising on some views that Hans's neurosis should take a path to its concern with babies and childbirth that goes through anal erotism, it is not surprising from a psychoanalytic point of view. The psychoanalyst need not "talk to God" to see such connections and foresee related developments (42, 105), he need only pay attention, as the theory requires, to infantile sexuality and infantile sexual theories.

Finally, Hans himself identified with horses, and so his horse phobia can also be understood in terms of fear of his own impulses. The phobic restrictions are connected with curbing his own impulses, both sexual and destructive. Little Hans recalls the incident where a father admonishes his child: "Don't put your finger to the white horse or it'll bite you" (29–30, 119, 137), and the concern here finds a ready verbal link to warnings against masturbation via the phrase *"Es beisst mich"* (it bites me) used to describe a genital itch (30n.1).

These fears of his own impulses are ultimately grounded in fears of castration. That such fear is present, there can be little doubt. There is the mother's explicit threat (7). His father also explicitly encourages him to stop masturbating ([29–31] partly provoked by Freud's concern with Hans's excessive interest in widdlers, including his own [28]). And the father tells Hans (again at Freud's behest [28]) that girls and women have no widdlers (31), which leads to a masturbation fantasy centering on his mother's widdler (31–32, 120). There is Hans's craving for reassurance that his widdler is fixed in and that it will get bigger (34), arguably a deferred response to his mother's earlier castration threat and the fear engendered by the new information about little girls (31, 35–36). And there are the recurring plumber fantasies (65, 98–99, 127–28, 131), all of which Freud connects with Hans's castration anxieties. There is also ample evidence that these anxieties lead to restraint by Hans of his own impulses. There are his efforts to repress masturbation (27, 31), his repressed exhibitionism (the distorted widdling dream at four and a half—before the horses [21]; and the disgust at the yellow drawers [57f.]). There is the fear of his father and the fear for his father, the combined hostility and affection (45).

The fear of his own impulses can be seen in his disgust at things that he previously had enjoyed (e.g., watching his mother at her functions—disgust at yellow drawers [57f.]), and in the ambivalent butting and caressing of his father (42). Hans makes his identification with horses plain when he announces "I'm a young horse" while playing at being a prancing horse (52, 58). As Freud puts it, emphasizing the aggressive impulses, "For Hans horses had always typified pleasure in movement . . . but since this pleasure in movement included the impulse to copulate, the neurosis imposed a restriction on it and exalted the horse into an emblem of terror" (139).

Phobias in general, Freud tells us, can be understood as flights from pleasure (59n.). Freud later encapsulates the point in a phrase, saying a phobia "is nothing else than an attempt at flight from the satisfaction of an instinct" (1920g, 42).

I believe these various strands of interpretation taken together form a coherent whole: Hans suffers from an Oedipus complex with aggressive components, aggravated by sibling rivalry and lies (unsatisfied curiosity), and resolved in the face of a castration complex by repression and fantasy.

So far as many of these features of Hans's situation are universal or near-universal, one might wonder why everyone is not (at least at some point in their lives) a phobic. In fact, we all do have fears. Whether those fears become accentuated to the point where they must be regarded as phobias may ultimately depend on issues of endowment and over-determination (how sometimes separately sufficient factors come together in a particular case). Psychoanalysis does not provide a basis for predicting when various factors will be strong enough to produce a phobia. The measure of their strength may be given only in the outcome (cf. 1920a, 167–68). And of course not all phobias are the result of Oedipal or instinctual conflict. Some are the result of simple conditioning or otherwise depend on unpredictable external factors. (See Watson's case of Little Albert [1924, 125f.].) At best, psychoanalysis gives a retrospective, or historical, explanation of why what happened happened and of what it means. The situation may be compared to the understanding of hysteria that psychoanalysis was left with once Freud had abandoned his seduction theory. Accounts in terms of external trauma could answer neatly the question why everyone was not an hysteric (or a phobic): those free of external trauma would be free of neurosis. Once one recognizes the importance of internal drives and subjective (indeed, unconscious) meanings, for which one can offer no "objective" measure, there may be a gain in understanding of some aspects of neurotic problems, but it must be acknowledged that we may lose ready answers to other questions. That the internal factors must be given heavy weight, nonetheless, is one of the enduring lessons still to be learned from Freud.

Suggestion

Of course there are alternatives even to Freud's multifaceted account. But the mere existence of alternatives does not make them preferable, does not discredit an explanation. Competing explanatory power and plausibility must be probed. Suggestion is one possibility Freud himself considers. And modern critics have pressed the charge further.

The complex web of evidence and argument sketched above might be dismissed as really all the product of "suggestion." (Wolpe and Rachman in their critique speak of "leading questions" and "indoctrination" [1963 (1960), 202, 205n., 206n., 207n.].) The problem is especially acute in the case of Little Hans, who in any case might be regarded as an impressionable young boy, because his analysis was carried out by his father. An analyst is usually a stranger. A father might be expected to exert a specially powerful influence on his young son. The charge here would be that Freud's interpretations ultimately rest on suggestion by the father; and the more general charge is that psychoanalytic interpretations always get what support they have as the result of suggestion by the analyst (102). It is a charge that must be confronted, and that, as mentioned, Freud in fact does confront.

Unfortunately, in his anxiety to respond to the charge of suggestion, Freud gives multiple and perhaps contradictory responses, becoming like the man described in the *Interpretation of Dreams* "who was charged by one of his neighbours with having given him back a borrowed kettle in a damaged condition. The defendant asserted first, that he had given it back undamaged; secondly, that the kettle had a hole in it when he borrowed it; and thirdly, that he had never borrowed a kettle from his neighbour at all" (1900, 120). Each response might be adequate on its own, but when they are offered together, each undermines the others.

In discussing Little Hans, Freud first claimed that the effects of suggestion can be distinguished from evidentially valuable avowals (103); he then admitted that suggestion raises problems but claimed that they do not matter: "For a psycho-analysis is not an impartial scientific investigation, but a therapeutic measure. Its essence is not to prove anything, but merely to alter something" (104). In the end, however, he came back to the view that "Therapeutic success . . . is not our primary aim; we endeavour rather to enable the patient to obtain a conscious grasp of his unconscious wishes" (120). I think this final stance is the one that must prevail if psychoanalysis is to be of "scientific" interest and not a magical mystery cure. If therapeutic efficacy were all that mattered, psychoanalysis would be left with no theory (except perhaps the empty notion of "suggestion") about why it worked. Psychoanalysis, like many other therapies, might work, but we would be left with no way to understand the scope of its working or why it worked when it worked. All treatment would be equally symptomatic, with no way to tell which treatments were also causal, that is, which worked by reversing the originating causes rather than by merely counteracting symptoms. In psychoanalysis, the theory of therapy and the etiological theories are interdependent. (See Neu 1977, part 3, and 1981 [chap. 14 here].) The content of interpretations certainly does matter. It is only on something like the psychoanalytic account that clearing up excremental and reproductive confusions in a child should make the difference it in fact makes in the case of Little Hans and other cases. One cannot cure a phobia with the sort of causal history Little Hans's had by simply reassuring the patient that the object is not dangerous (as certain deconditioning approaches such as Wolpe and Rachman's might suggest). And much else goes unexplained if one sets aside the truth of the theoretical claims and settles for the power of suggestion. The lumf theme, after all, was brought up by Hans, not suggested by his father, who was taken by surprise (54). It was also Hans who brought up the bath theme on his own in connection with his castration fears (65–67, 98), and overall Freud rightly emphasizes Hans's active role in the analysis (105, 126).

Even if the charge of suggestion were to stand, however, one would have to explore further the nature of "suggestion" and the question of why a patient would accept it. Otherwise "suggestion" could serve only as empty name-calling rather than as an alternative theory. (The charge of "suggestion," "indoctrination," and even "brainwashing," is broadcast widely by Grünbaum [1984] and other recent critics. The need for "infilling" and a theory of suggestion itself is pointed out by Fine and Forbes [1986] and Wollheim [1993].) The necessary exploration would require understanding the special authority of the father, and the general importance of transference, and so would, I believe, bring one back to psychoanalytic theory.

The Behaviorist Critique

While Freud considers one alternative to his account, in terms of "suggestion," there is a second type of critique, grounded in behaviorism, which is far more thoroughgoing. Most fully developed in an influential article by Wolpe and Rachman (1963 [1960]), it goes beyond the first in offering not only an alternative account of the apparent effectiveness of psychoanalytic therapy, but also an alternative explanation of the origin of Little Hans's problem. Indeed, it offers fundamental criticism of what Freud counts as "evidence" for his views, etiological as well as therapeutic. (Wolpe and Rachman's critique has been described as "a classic" by H. J. Eysenck [1965, 107] and strongly endorsed by Clark Glymour [1980, 264n.] and others.) On the contrary, however, I believe that Freud's account (claims based on the toxicological theory of anxiety aside) is powerful and persuasive, and that it is the behaviorist approach that fundamentally misunderstands and distorts the character of evidence and argument in cases such as Little Hans's.

To begin with, Wolpe and Rachman leave much out of account altogether. They make no mention, for example, of the lumf theme, which as Freud points out, Hans brings up spontaneously and so counts against the "suggestion" charge. While the theme is a significant part of the intricate web of evidence and argument for a psychoanalytic explanation, it is irrelevant to the problem on a behaviorist view. Wolpe and Rachman also leave out Little Hans's dreams (though they do mention the giraffe fantasy [1963 (1960), 203]). Excremental interests and dreams are dismissed because they provide only "indirect" evidence in relation to Hans's problem, his horse phobia. But of course the psychoanalytic account is in terms of unconscious desires and beliefs, and such psychological states can be attested only by indirect evidence. It is wrong-headed to expect direct avowal of unconscious states. Even for the person whose states they are, they are by their nature a matter of inference. We ascribe them, just as we ascribe conscious states to other people, because of the range of phenomena such ascriptions explain. Evidence for the unconscious must be, in this sense, "indirect." It is only a "science" that dismisses *a priori* the possibility of unconscious psychological states that can dismiss such evidence as inappropriate or inadequate. The crude demand for "confirmation by direct observation" (1963 [1960], 219) is as misplaced as a demand to be shown electrons.

One need not believe in the unconscious to see the problem here. Many thoughts that we ascribe (both to ourselves and to others) are less than fully explicit without being withheld from consciousness by dynamic forces of repression. Thus, I might explain to the police officer who stops me for jumping a light that "I thought the light had turned green." In such a case (assuming I am being as honest as I can), I am not claiming that I explicitly thought "the light has turned green and now I can go forward," any more than when I change gears I (as an experienced driver) have to think explicitly, "I am in neutral and must now shift into first." Such actions are intentional (I don't, usually at least, shift gears by accident), they are done knowingly, but they do not require conscious explicit spelling out of their guiding thoughts. Indeed, we only reach for the thought as an explanation for our behavior when things go somehow awry in our usually semi-automatic behavior (and when we can rule out alternative explanations, such as a mechanical failure in the car causing it to lurch forward before the light has changed). In sum, we use the concept of "thought" in both explanatory and phenomenological senses. Sometimes we ascribe a thought on the basis of being explictly aware of it. (That is the phenomenological sense.) Sometimes we ascribe it on the basis of its filling an explanatory need. (Wittgenstein is full of examples of thought in this second, explanatory, sense.) And all of this is part of the perfectly ordinary understanding and functioning of the concept of thought. It does not require any commitment to belief in the psychoanalytic concept of unconscious (dynamically unconscious rather than descriptively unconscious) thoughts. To rule out "indirect" evidence of thought would be to deny the explanatory use of the concept of thought and thinking, a use essential to self-understanding and our understanding of others.

Along similar lines, Wolpe and Rachman complain that interpretations are presented as "observed facts" (1963 [1960], 208, 219). But facts in this area (as perhaps in most) inevitably must be theory-laden, must depend on interpretation through the lens of a theory. (That "facts," in general, are theory-laden has been a point familiar in philosophy of science at least since Duhem [1954 (1905)].) Without an appropriate theory the facts are invisible, unintelligible. Recall how infantile thumbsucking can be perceived as a manifestation of infantile sexuality only through an appropriate theoretical understanding of the nature of sexuality. A theory, like that held by the man in the street or "popular opinion" (Freud 1905d, 135), that defines sexuality only in terms of heterosexual genital intercourse between adults never can recognize thumbsucking as a form of sexuality. But then, such a narrow theory has equal difficulty in explaining how adult sexual perversions (which precisely do not involve the supposedly definitive heterosexual genital intercourse) nonetheless can be recognizably *sexual* perversions. Such narrow theories are not refuted by brute "observed facts," but by the range of phenomena that they cannot adequately interpret and explain. The correct question to ask when presented with an interpretation is not whether it is "direct" (presumably meaning something like "independent of theory") or "indirect" ("theory-laden"), but whether the theory informing it and the web of interpretations that follow are plausible, whether they have explanatory force. So, for example, Wolpe and Rachman complain, "When Hans observes that Hanna's widdler is 'so lovely' the father states that this is a 'disingenuous' reply and that 'in reality her widdler seemed to him funny.' Distortions of this kind are common in the father's reports" (1963 [1960], 208). While not based on Hans's direct avowal (the only sort of evidence they seem to recognize for his psychological states or thoughts), the father's interpretation is in fact well-founded, based on informed observation (observation that takes in more than just Hans's direct affirmations). In context, Little Hans had been *laughing*, and that is the ground for regarding his statement as disingenuous—a very good ground given the ordinary understanding of laughter. Indeed, in context even the disingenuousness of the response becomes intelligible in terms of the doubtless defensive nature of the laughter. (The relevant passage reads: "Hans [aged four and a half] was again watching his little sister being given her bath, when he began laughing. On being asked why he was laughing, he replied: 'I'm laughing at Hanna's widdler.' 'Why?' 'Because her widdler's so lovely.' Of course his answer was a disingenuous one. In reality her widdler had seemed to him *funny*. Moreover, this is the first time he has recognized in this way the distinction between male and female genitals instead of denying it" [21; cf. 74].) Similarly, Wolpe and Rachman dismiss Hans's father's observation of Little Hans's hostility toward his sister because of "several clear statements by Hans of his affection for his sister" (1963 [1960], 208), thus simultaneously missing the vast range of evidence (both direct and indirect) for sibling rivalry discussed earlier and showing a lack of understanding of the nature and pervasiveness of ambivalence. They equally miss and dismiss the evidence for Hans's hostility to his father (1963 [1960], 213; see above and Neu 1977, 126–28). Again, what matters is the persuasiveness of a given interpretation, taking everything into account, not whether it is somehow privileged by direct testimony.

Wolpe and Rachman's general failure to understand the nature of evidence for unconscious psychological states is most dramatically evident when they deny that "Hans had an oedipus complex which implies a sexual desire for the mother" (1963 [1960], 212). Of course, they, like the "popular opinion" that Freud criticizes in his *Three Essays on the Theory of Sexuality*, equate such sexual desire with a "wish to copulate with her" (1963 [1960], 212). But that is precisely what infantile sexual desires cannot be expected to amount to—at least not simply or at first. Freud goes to some trouble to show that the sexual desires of children are based on their own (sometimes bizarre) sexual theories, which in turn are based on their own level of bodily functioning. (More on this shortly.) It would be remarkable if infantile sexual desires took the forms of "normal" adult sexuality (e.g., desire for genital union—few four-year-olds can conceive explicitly of such a union, let alone conceive of it as desirable). The sexual relations desired in Oedipal contexts must be understood more broadly. That they are nonetheless "sexual" Freud demonstrates at length in his *Three Essays* (1905d). Even so, there is evidence even for genital desires in the case of Little Hans. Wolpe and Rachman miss such "interpreted" evidence as the smashing window fantasy as a premonition of copulation (41) and the "borer" fantasy (65, 98, 128), they downplay Hans's efforts to get his mother to stroke his penis (19, 23, 25), and they completely ignore (as their narrow and untenable view of sexuality forces them to) nongenital sexuality, that is, polymorphously perverse infantile sexuality. For example, they ignore Little Hans's anal erotism in relation to his mother, his interest in watching his mother at her excretory functions (57, 63), his interest in his mother's widdler (7, 9–10)—including the masturbation fantasy with "Mummy quite naked in her chemise" showing her widdler (32; cf. his interest in the maid, 30)—and his interest in wiping "his" children's bottoms just as his mother did his (97). That he has imaginary children with his mother (97) and that he admits to wanting to marry his mother and being jealous of his father (89; cf. 82) also seem significant. Wolpe and Rachman are anxious to take Hans at his word. But one should remember that neither patient denials nor patient confirmations of interpretations should be taken as conclusive. Verbal reports may be taken as one kind of behavior, particularly useful as signs of belief, but they are only one kind of behavior and one kind of evidence—never conclusive by themselves.

In their alternative conditioning account, Wolpe and Rachman insist "that the incident to which Freud refers as merely the exciting cause of Hans's phobia was in fact the cause of the entire disorder" (1963 [1960], 216). To suppose that Hans's witnessing the fall of the horse that drew the bus could explain everything is to take a much too simple view of Hans's "entire disorder." It leaves too much out of account, and raises many questions to which it offers no hint of an answer. What makes the horse's falling down "traumatic"? There is no suggestion that an experience or event that gets singled out might be connected with Hans's own interests, desires, and development at the time it occurred. If they do not matter, why shouldn't such incidents be traumatic for everyone, and why shouldn't other incidents (e.g., a friend cutting his foot [58, 82, 126]) have been traumatic for Little Hans? Why, too, did the symptom "generalize" from horses "falling" to horses "biting"? Is this choice of one "generalization" and rejection of others to be explained by "'resemblance" or "similarity"?

The evidential situation in relation to the second strand of Freud's interpretation, the one in terms of displaced fear of the father, contrasts sharply with the behaviorist alternative that invokes "stimulus generalization" to account for the particular objects of Hans's fear. The conditions for claims of "stimulus generalization" are in fact far less rigorous than those for the application of the psychoanalytic concept of "displacement." (See Neu 1977, 126, 128.) Stimulus generalization rests on claims of similarity. The problem with this is that similarity is all pervasive. For any two items in the universe, it will always be the case that there are *some* respects in which they are similar (and, one should immediately add, some respects in which they are dissimilar). Similarity and dissimilarity are always relative to specific terms and contexts of comparison (they are "incomplete predicates"), and one can always find contexts that will yield the preferred results. Why does Little Hans's initial trauma of seeing a horse fall down (the initial conditioning on which the behaviorists focus) generalize to fear of horses biting? (Are these similar? More similar than fear of horses falling down and fear of horses *kicking?*) Why does Little Hans's fear of horses spread to include his mother's yellow drawers? Doubtless some similarity could be found. (Or disgust at yellow drawers might be distinguished from fear of yellow drawers. But what shows the two reactions to be independent or related?) But if stimulus generalization based on similarity can explain all possible objects, then it can explain no particular actual object. By explaining everything, it explains nothing. By contrast, the psychoanalytic account in terms of "displacement" rests on three distinct elements: First, there is actual (even if unconscious) fear of the father. Second, there is a motive for displacement. Without this, one might simply have two fears (fear of the father *and* fear of horses). And third, there is identification of the father with horses, which makes the transition or interplay possible. (Identification rests on perceived similarities or associations, not "objective" similarities or those perceived by the explainer only.) It is this conceptual and evidential complexity of claims of "displacement," which requires the bringing out of underlying continuities in the face of surface change, that makes the account of Hans's fear of horses biting him in terms of fear of his father so persuasive. One can be seen as a displaced form of the other. Of course, particular aspects of the displaced fear and other objects may call for additional assumptions and other explanations, as in the third strand of Freud's explanation discussed earlier.

But the most severe problem with the conditioning alternative was pointed out by Freud fifty years before Wolpe and Rachman put it forward: "Chronological considerations make it impossible for us to attach any great importance to the actual precipitating cause of the outbreak of Hans's illness, for he had shown signs of apprehensiveness long before he saw the bus-horse fall down in the street" (136; cf. 26, 49, 118). Hans's apprehensiveness is the central feature of his disorder, though it comes to take on many specific objects especially involving horses, and that central apprehensiveness crucially precedes the proposed precipitating incident. There may be some confusion about the matter because, when the incident of the bus horse falling is first mentioned, Hans claims both that he saw the horse fall "Once when I went out with Mummy in spite of my 'nonsense'" (49) (which suggests, as his father says, that Hans already had his "nonsense") and that "No. I only got it then. When the horse in the bus fell down, it gave me such a fright, really! That was when I got the nonsense" (50). The apparent contradiction is most simply resolved if we understand that "nonsense" in the second statement refers to the fear specifically of horses (which Hans describes as a compound fear that horses would "Fall down and bite" [50]), rather than the general anxiety that is really the larger problem, which began earlier and has to be explained, as Freud insists, by something other than the incident of the horse falling. As Freud puts it, "at the beginning of his illness there was as yet no phobia whatever present, whether of streets or of walking or even of horses" (25) and "there is good reason for keeping the two [Hans's anxiety and his phobia] separate" (24).

The over-simple and chronologically impossible interpretation persists (it is reaffirmed by Frank Sulloway in his recent generally dismissive review of Freud's case histories [1991, 252]). Awareness of the role of general anxiety in the case should save one from confusion. John Bowlby, who emphasizes issues of attachment in childhood phobias in general, and focuses particular attention on Hans's mother's threats to abandon him (44–45), details how "both the sequence of events leading up to the phobia and Hans's own statements make it clear that, *distinct from and preceding any fear of horses*, Hans was afraid that his mother might go away and leave him" (1975 [1973], 327). Despite differing emphases, Bowlby and Freud agree that Hans's "enormously intensified affection" for his mother is "the fundamental phenomenon in his condition" (24–25, 96, 114) and that his problems significantly precede the apparent "precipitating incident."

In general, efforts to test psychoanalytic hypotheses informed by the behaviorist ideals of Wolpe and Rachman tend to be systematically misleading, partly because the criteria used for the application of psychoanalytic concepts are too crude, but especially because the significance of an experience for the individual, its unconscious meaning, is (perhaps inevitably) left out. Consider, for example, Alvin Scodel's (1973 [1957]) often cited attempt to test (what he took to be) "the Freudian orality hypothesis" (Grünbaum's phrase 1979, 138–39) on the basis of breast-preferences. The test, using a population of 169 male undergraduates, reveals a correlation between preoccupation with dependency themes and preference for women with small breasts. Scodel concludes that this is the opposite of what psychoanalytic theory would lead one to expect. On the contrary, it seems to me that the terms of the test neglect the fact that we are dealing with the unconscious, a realm of meanings, and it is unclear what relevance the results have to *any* psychoanalytic hypothesis. Taking the attractiveness of large breasts as a sign of oral dependency needs (either reinforced, as Scodel would have it, or frustrated, as Scodel claims psychoanalysis would have it) seems to depend on an equation of breast size with femininity in general, and nurturance in particular, an equation as crude as taking penis size as a measure of masculinity. Doubtless patients, and even experimenters, do make such equations, but that they hold in a particular case requires evidence and argument. Why, in any case, is breast size a criterion for orality? One would have thought the size of the breast is less important than how the individual thinks of it and what he wishes to do with it. Those who suck their thumbs need not prefer large thumbs—indeed, it may be important to them to be able to envelop the whole object. Similarly for breasts. Or the desire may not even be to suck, but rather to stroke. Does that make a concern for large breasts more a manual or tactile than an oral interest? And, moving back from hand to mouth: as suckers of thumbs and other objects show, lack of interest in breasts (large or small) does not necessarily show absence of orality. (The poet W. H. Auden used sometimes to explain his homosexuality as due to "insufficient weaning" [personal communication].) These sorts of problems are not peculiar to the breast-preference test or Scodel's study; they are typical of attempts to test psychoanalytic hypotheses by correlating states of affairs that are thought identifiable independently of psychoanalytic hypotheses and clinical interpretation. Such studies tend to be systematically irrelevant to the claims they mean to test.

When a study (Beloff 1970 [1957]) of the etiology of anal character traits takes the time in infancy when toilet training had been completed as the measure of coerciveness, so that relatively early training is considered coercive and relatively late training permissive, this leaves out the character of the training in the child's experience—perhaps the training is completed later precisely because the child experienced it as peculiarly difficult and coercive. And the psychoanalytic claims are about the child's experience and the unconscious meaning of that experience. To be relevant to those claims, empirical psychologists would have to go beyond their favored operational definitions and statistical analyses. A person interested in the implications of oral dependency needs or anal erotism for later development would do better to read Karl Abraham's (1927) classic studies.

Freud himself suggested there might be a connection between the intensity of anal erotism and the lateness of overcoming "infantile *incontinentia alvi*" (1908b, 170). We don't know at what age Little Hans's toilet training was completed, but we do know that it was fraught with difficulty. There is the evidence of his problems with constipation (55–56, 65–66, 99, 112n.), the application of enemas (55) and the offering of raspberry syrup (99), and the "row" he would make with his feet when forced to go potty: "he used to stamp his feet in a rage, and kick about, and sometimes throw himself on the ground" (54). But it is really the role of anal themes in his thoughts and fantasies that reveals the psychological significance of those experiences in his life.

The Sexual Theories of Children

We learn very early in the case study of Little Hans's fascination with penises ("widdlers"—"*Wiwimacher*" in the German) and his attribution of a penis to all animate creatures, including his mother and his baby sister.[3] Freud writes here and elsewhere of the problems children have in understanding the differences between the sexes and the origin of babies (in particular, the father's role). He describes how children develop anal theories of birth and sadistic theories of intercourse (in which the male is thought to attack or beat up the female [122–23]).[4] Confronted with the idea of marriage, some children try to understand its nature by combining images of pleasure with disregard of modesty: for example, as a rite of urinating in front of each other, or of a man urinating into a woman's chamberpot, or of showing their behinds to one another without embarrassment (1908c). In all of these cases, the ideas about adult sexuality can be seen to be based on infantile sexuality, that is, the working of the child's own body. (Freud elaborates, for example, on the connection of anal theories of birth with anal erotism [107–8].)

But then, do little girls attribute penises to all? If so, do they do it on the model of the clitoris? Should that organ be presumed to have the same early importance for little girls as the penis has for Little Hans? One might imagine how Hans's anxiety about the possible loss of his widdler could make him want to attach them everywhere (see 34; and his fantasies about plumbers are also of interest in this connection—65, 98, 127–28, 131). But castration anxiety is supposed to work differently in the case of little girls (1924d). How are we to understand (how do children understand) the nature of the phallus in the supposedly universal "phallic" stage (110n.2; 1923e)? Even in the case of Hans himself, the attribution of a theory of phallic monism is questionable. His "symbolic phantasies of intercourse" (123) also may be read as premonitions or acknowledgments (on some level) of the existence of the vagina (see Janine Chasseguet-Smirgel [1984] and R. Horacio Etchegoyen [1988]). What of the importance of the vagina to little girls and of all children's awareness of their parents' sexual differences?

How universal are such theories? Their universality must be suspect on the basis of Hans's case, because we can see that he bases his theories (understood in Freud's sense) on lying information: for example, his mother, in response to his inquiry, asserts that she too has a widdler (7, 9–10). So it appears that the sexual theories of children may depend on social context, as well as on their own physiology and stage of development.

We should note that the mother's statement might be open to another interpretation (e.g., that she has an organ for widdling with, no claim being made that it is a penis), but that could not be Hans's interpretation if he is to use the statement to support his theory of the pervasiveness of widdlers/penises. If Hans's theory is not about widdlers understood as penises, Freud's theory of a universal phallic stage must look elsewhere for support (even in the case of boys). To put it slightly differently, what exactly Hans means by "widdler" is open to question—and interpretation. It can be taken ambiguously as a functionally or anatomically defined organ. It could mean, in some contexts of Hans's usage, "thing to widdle (urinate) with," as well as, more specifically, in some contexts, "a penis." "Why aren't udders and vaginas and, indeed, bottoms that widdle also widdlers?" (Lear 1990, 100).

Freud describes Hans's parents as enlightened (6, 103), yet they clearly fed their young son a number of lies, including the stork theory of birth. (On the distorted truth in the stork story, see Freud 1927c, 44–45.) Hans knew better than to accept that story, but that is no credit to the enlightenment of his parents. (Freud describes the box story as used for "revenge" by Hans [70, 129], and the knife in the doll as a symptomatic act to get at the truth [86].) Worse still, despite the parents' claimed commitment to avoiding coercion and intimidation (6, 143), Hans's mother actually threatens him with castration (when she finds him playing with his widdler at age three and a half [7–8, 24]). Is this universal? Here might seem a clear case of the overwhelming importance of social context and idiosyncratic experience, but Freud suggests children construct castration threats out of "the slightest hints" where they are not actually, literally, made (8n.). After all, every parent must make clear to his or her children that there are restrictions on showing, playing with, and using their genitals. Short of drastic threats, consider Little Hans's own mother's response to his invitation to touch his penis: "that'd be piggish" (19). And in our society, little girls often have to be told, whatever the temptation, not to lift their skirts before all and sundry. The matter calls for closer examination.

Primal Fantasies

Freud learned long before the case of Little Hans that many so-called memories could be understood as retrospective fantasies. That is, they are distortions projected back to early childhood or worked onto the experiences of early childhood. Freud regarded these structures as compounded out of elements of actual childhood experience, childhood impulse, and later impulse. This is clearest perhaps in the case of certain "primal fantasies." These occur almost universally, even in the absence of the appropriate precipitating circumstances. Impulse and experience are complementary: what is lacking in experience is supplied by the child's own impulses. Freud, in "Introductory Lecture 23," enumerates three primal fantasies:

> observation of parental intercourse, seduction by an adult and threat of being castrated. It would be a mistake to suppose that they are never

characterized by material reality . . . But it is highly improbable that children are threatened with castration as often as it appears in the analyses of neurotics. We shall be satisfied by realizing that the child puts a threat of this kind together in his imagination on the basis of hints, helped out by a knowledge that auto-erotic satisfaction is forbidden and under the impression of his discovery of the female genitals. (1916–17, 369)

In the case of Little Hans, for example, there is an actual threat "to cut off your widdler," but Freud notes:

Anyone who, in analyzing adults, has become convinced of the invariable presence of the castration complex, will of course find difficulty in ascribing its origin to a chance threat—of a kind which is not, after all, of such universal occurrence; he will be driven to assume that children construct this danger for themselves out of the slightest hints, which will never be wanting. (8n.)

The child's concern with the loss of his penis arises from his instinctually necessary interest in and "misuse" of it, combined with whatever forces lead him to regard acting on his interest as "misuse." A broader construal of "castration" broadens the range of things that can serve as models or "hints" for the construction of castration fantasies:

It has been urged that every time his mother's breast is withdrawn from a baby he is bound to feel it as castration (that is to say, as the loss of what he regards as an important part of his own body); that, further, he cannot fail to be similarly affected by the regular loss of his faeces; and finally, that the act of birth itself (consisting as it does in the separation of the child from his mother, with whom he has hitherto been united) is the prototype of all castration. (8n.)

In Hans's case, his mother's very specific castration threat ("If you do that, I shall send for Dr. A. to cut off your widdler" [7–8]) and later "warnings" (e.g., 24, 31) about putting his hand to his widdler may have been given deepened significance by the tonsillectomy he was subjected to shortly after the start of his phobia. As his father puts it, he "had his tonsils cut" (29). (We don't know whether Dr. A. was the surgeon.) (See Slap 1961; Silverman 1980, 105–7.) Around the same time as the castration threat, his mother gave birth to Hans's little sister, and Hans associated the blood he saw in basins in the delivery room with widdlers, saying, "But blood doesn't come out of *my* widdler" (10). This too may have deepened his concerns.

Ultimately, with loss of breast and feces and sight of the female genitals and perhaps other "hints" to back it, it is the fear of castration (of the non-metaphoric penis) that dissolves the male Oedipus complex at the end of the phallic phase (1924d). But if a "fantasy" of threat is to form a part of the castration complex, the generally plausible theory that fantasies are wish-fulfillments will require further explanation of how it is possible. (Freud later describes Hans's castration anxiety as "a realistic fear"—a warning [1926d, 108]. Cf. Freud's difficulties with punishment and anxiety dreams.) A distinction between unconscious fantasies and unconscious beliefs (provided the latter are not necessarily wish-fulfillments) might resolve part of the difficulty. The distinction between parts of the self, as with anxiety dreams, might also help. That is, it could be that the forces of repression, associated with the superego, might be satisfied while the individual as a whole is not. Freud's later theory of the death instinct and an associated wish for punishment might also be of value in this connection.

The case of primal seduction fantasies is (in some ways) more straightforward:

> A phantasy of being seduced when no seduction has occurred is usually employed by a child to screen the auto-erotic period of his sexual activity. He spares himself shame about masturbation by retrospectively phantasying a desired object into these earliest times. (1916–17, 370)

Since the desired object plays the active role in these fantasies, the child is further spared responsibility for its own impulses (let alone actions). That is, in one variant, the girl wishes to seduce the father, but in the fantasy it is the father who does the seducing.

Freud's account of observation of parental intercourse is similar to his account of castration fantasies:

> it is perfectly possible for a child, while he is not yet credited with possessing an understanding or a memory, to be a witness of the sexual act between his parents or other grown-up people; and the possibility cannot be rejected that he will be able to understand and react to the impression *in retrospect*. If, however, the intercourse is described with the most minute details, which would be difficult to observe, or if, as happens most frequently, it turns out to have been intercourse from behind, *more ferarum* [in the manner of animals], there can be no remaining doubt that the phantasy is based on an observation of intercourse between animals (such as dogs) and that its motive was the child's unsatisfied scopophilia during puberty. The extreme achievement on these lines is a phantasy of observing parental intercourse while one is still an unborn baby in the womb. (1916–17, 369–70)

This passage is a summary of one part of the extended discussion of the contrasting fantasy/experience interpretations in the case of the Wolf Man (see especially 1918b, 57–60, 95–97; see also Neu 1973 [chap. 11 here] and 1974.) If we add to the observation of parental intercourse the child's theory that it is an act of aggression by the father, it again becomes interesting to ask whether such "false theories" are fantasies, that is, wish-fulfillments.

Freud raises a further question about the universality of primal fantasies, that is, about their source:

> Whence comes the need for these phantasies and the material for them? There can be no doubt that their sources lie in the instincts; but it has still to be explained why the same phantasies with the same content are created on every occasion. I am prepared with an answer which I know will seem daring to you. I believe these *primal phantasies*, as I should like to call them, and no doubt a few others as well, are a phylogenetic endowment. In them the individual reaches beyond his own experience into primeval experience at points where his own experience has been too rudimentary. It seems to me quite possible that all the things that are told to us to-day in analysis as phantasy . . . were once real occurrences in the primeval times of the human family, and that children in their phantasies are simply filling in the gaps in individual truth with prehistoric truth. (1916–17, 370–71)

So the fantasies discussed are "primal" in time as well as in importance. But the question is as odd as the answer is "daring." First, because Freud had answered it long before in a note to the Rat Man case:

> The uniformity of the content of the sexual life of children, together with the unvarying character of the modifying tendencies which are later brought to bear upon it, will easily account for the constant sameness which as a rule characterizes the phantasies that are constructed around the period of childhood, irrespective of how greatly or how little real experiences have contributed towards them. (1909d, 208n.)

Second, because Freud seems to repeat this answer when he says that the need and material for the fantasies arise from "instincts." So there is no need of an appeal, even a "daring" appeal, to a discredited Lamarckianism. Or is there a further question? I think Freud is misleading when he suggests that "it has still to be explained why the same phantasies with the same content are created on every occasion." Instinct, on Freud's own account, can explain the content and uniformity of fantasy. If there is to be any further question, it must be about the source of the content and uniformity of instinct. Here the inheritance of acquired characteristics can be of no help, for the circumstances required are themselves even more implausible than the Lamarckian mechanism: to explain universality, an original single common ancestor must have acquired the trait, or all of many diverse ancestors must have, or the fantasies must somehow confer survival advantages on the descendants of those who did have the appropriate experiences. None of these is likely (Neu 1974). From my point of view, assuming that the contents of fantasy derive from the objects of instinct (or more properly, "the psychic representation of instincts"), the question becomes: where does instinct get its objects? If one were to develop an answer, I think one would need to refer to common infantile sexual development (especially the functioning of children's bodies) and common experience (especially restrictions on sexuality). Having raised the question, I must, for now, leave it. Children, in any case (whatever the source and whatever the degree of universality) do construct weird theories, and Little Hans offers insight into their character: both their actual content and possible sources.

Parental Analysis

A parent doing therapy heightens the risk of "suggestion." There are other risks. After all, parents are likely to be a part of any problem and so to have a stake in maintaining certain misunderstandings. And children may have a special stake in concealing things from them. The analysis itself can increase dependence, sexualize and aggressivize relations with the parents, reinforce parents' perceived omnipotence (including omniscience when interpretations are taken to be correct), and parents may use interpretations as a substitute for other forms of relationship and to control (Silverman 1980, 115). There are also advantages. Parents are likely to witness and so perhaps know and understand more. And children may be more likely to trust and so to reveal things to them. The result may be an alliance between the parent and child in therapy, an alliance that might actually serve to restructure the relationship usefully.

Freud reports on meeting Little Hans only once in the course of his treatment (41–42); the analysis in fact was carried out by the boy's father, even if Freud was very much a psychological presence for Little Hans: his all-knowing and authoritative pen-pal (38, 42, 48, 57, 61, 72, 97). Later the techniques and practice of child analysis would be developed considerably (notably by women followers of Freud, including Hermine von Hug-Hellmuth, Anna Freud, and Melanie Klein), but at this point Freud thought it hardly possible (just as earlier, before his understanding of infantile sexuality and psychosexual development, he had thought infantile neuroses themselves impossible). He believed it was the special circumstances in Hans's case, and in particular his relation with his father, that made the analysis possible. Freud writes:

> No one else, in my opinion, could possibly have prevailed on the child to
> make any such avowals; the special knowledge by means of which he
> was able to interpret the remarks made by his five-year-old son was indispensable, and without it the technical difficulties in the way of conducting a psycho-analysis upon so young a child would have been insuperable. It was only because the authority of a father and of a physician were united in a single person, and because in him both affectionate care and

scientific interest were combined, that it was possible in this one instance to apply the method to a use to which it would not otherwise have lent itself. (5; cf. 1918b, 8–9)

Freud may mislead when he describes Hans's father as a "physician." While this disguises the fact that he was a musicologist, and so helps conceal his identity, it also lends the father an authority that Freud plays with in the quoted passage. Max Graf was an early nonmedical follower of Freud. So he is accorded a false authority if his description as a "physician" is meant to imply he was a medical doctor. But then, the description may simply refer to the role he had assumed in the handling of his son's case (cf. 30). The problem here connects with a general difficulty in case histories: which facts should be disguised? In order to protect the privacy of patients, some facts must be concealed or altered. But in order not to mislead readers, it is crucial that the altered facts be of no significance in understanding the case. Freud added a note in 1924 to his case history of Katharina in *Studies on Hysteria* (1895d) to correct his original description of the person who sexually assaulted Katharina as her "uncle." It was in fact her father, which is an important point in light of Freud's early "seduction theory" of hysteria and his later views on the Oedipus complex and family structure and passions. As Freud lifted the "veil of discretion" in his note, he concluded, "From the point of view of understanding the case, a distortion of this kind is not, of course, a matter of such indifference as would be shifting the scene from one mountain to another" (1895d, 134n.2). But even the scene might have been crucial. In fact, in an example cited in the case of Miss Lucy R., reported just before that of Katharina in *Studies on Hysteria*, the identity of a street *is* crucial (1895d, 113n.). Thus, in order to know what facts may be altered safely for the sake of discretion, one needs a theory. And even then one must be aware that altered facts may matter in unforeseen ways, especially in the light of later theory and other facts.

Returning to the larger sphere, some parental analysis is inevitable even if parents are not psychoanalysts by profession and don't have the benefit of a supervising analyst such as Freud. After all, parents are always analyzing their children (as adults typically do each other). But what gets told, in what terms, and for whose benefit is constrained by the context of a psychoanalysis, and some of that protection may be lost when a child is psychoanalyzed by his or her parent—who cannot help but have an interest (both intense and in some ways independent) in the case and a powerful countertransference (if one may call it that). It is clear in Little Hans's case, for example, that his father was jealous of the attention his wife gave the boy, often blaming her excessive affection for the boy's problems (e.g., 22, 28, 39). That Freud psychoanalyzed (beating fantasies and all) his own daughter Anna (the "Annerl" of the 1897 letter cited at the start of this essay), albeit when she was in her twenties, was in every way extraordinary (Young-Bruehl 1988). While Freud certainly combined "the authority of a father and of a physician," he cannot be presumed to have been above the conflicts typical of fathers being asked to let go of their loving daughters.

The complications of parental authority and interests are not the only ones. Even more "objective" analysts can get things wrong. The right way to bring up a child is not obvious, even when aided by psychoanalytic understanding. In a discussion of sexual enlightenment at the Vienna Psychoanalytic Society in 1909, Freud said that not many mistakes were made in Hans's upbringing: "The boy should only have been refused permission to accompany his mother to the toilet. For the rest, neurosis is essentially a matter of constitution" (Nunberg & Federn 1967, 235). In his case study, Freud indicated that he also would have explained intercourse, including the existence of the vagina and the role of the father in procreation (145—Hans of course had been greatly curious about the role of the father, 92, 100, 122–23), and at the Vienna Society discussion Max Graf concurred that "the boy should have been told the last fact too" (Nunberg & Federn 1967, 234). As for accompanying his mother to the toilet, we know of Little Hans's fascination with children watching each other widdle (19–20, 61–63) and his intense interest in his mother's functions (57, 62–63), and these are not likely to have diminished in the face of external discouragement. (Freud notes in the Vienna discussion that suppression of physical masturbation does not result in the suppression of masturbation fantasies [Nunberg & Federn 1967, 229].) If actual parental nudity is regarded as seduction, we should remember that even if Hans had been kept out of the toilet, he slept in his parents' bedroom (and when he could, in his parents' bed) at least until the age of four (99) and is likely to have seen much. One also should note the aggressiveness of the parents' toilet-training ("aperients and enemas" [55–56], etc.) and the father's own anal account (fantasy?) of birth (87). Nor should one forget the mother's threats of castration and abandonment, which may well count as mistakes, even if one believes Hans might otherwise have constructed castration fears for himself out of "hints." (Freud seems to forget the evidence of coercion at the start of his case study when he says the parents let Hans "grow up and express himself without being intimidated" [6; and again at the end, 143].) But perhaps most telling was Freud's view that Hans was right in thinking "it was not right to be so very much preoccupied with widdlers, even with his own" (28) and the "enlightenment" he prescribed. As Freud concluded, "Doctor and patient, father and son, were therefore at one in ascribing the chief share in the pathogenesis of Hans's present condition to his habit of masturbating" (30). Freud seems to have shared their view.

Masturbation

Most modern thought agrees (given some complications) with Stekel's progressive view: masturbation does not make you blind, nor need it produce an "actual" or any other kind of neurosis (Reich 1951). But its psychological significance will vary from individual to individual, and it seems clear that whatever the effects or significance of masturbation itself, efforts to restrain impulses to masturbate can have deleterious effects—certainly they did in the case of Little Hans. Such efforts may be the result of societal (especially parental) pressure, but internal forces also play a role. Even without overt threats, without demands for absolute abstinence, castration anxiety can mount. And some social restraint may even be necessary, to the smooth functioning of society if not to mental health. Some restrictions are a matter of time and place, and must be regarded as reasonable. Others may ask too much. Little Hans shrewdly distinguishes thought and action ("wanting's not doing, and doing's not wanting" [31]) when discussing his masturbatory impulses, and understands that one need not suppress fantasies, even murderous ones (speaking of the wish for his sister's death: "But he may think it . . . If he thinks it, it is good all the same, because you can write it to the Professor" [72]). Of course masturbation fantasies are strongly tied to action, if not the action depicted and contained in the fantasy, the action of masturbation. But that action in itself does no harm. Nonetheless, Freud, in a discussion of masturbation at the Vienna Psychoanalytic Society in 1912, emphasized the underlying instinctual drives and spoke of the danger of "psychical infantilism" (1912f, 252). In his earlier essay on "'Civilized' Sexual Morality and Modern Nervous Illness," while in general attacking the excessive demands of society for repression ("surplus" repression), he expressed concern over establishing a pattern of avoidance of hardship in achieving satisfaction, avoidance of real relations (1908d, 198–200; cf. 1912f, 251–52)—after all, sexual desires are one of the main forces moving one out of the incestuous circle of the family, into the wider world, into civilization. At least that may be so for adults. Masturbation for them may be an easy way out, the path of least resistance. But to ask restraint of a five-year-old (in the privacy of his or her bed) may be to ask for too much. What after all are the social alternatives for a five-year-old? (This of course still leaves the underlying incestuous and other Oedipal fantasies, and their ensuing anxiety and guilt, to be dealt with.) When Freud reinforced Hans's parents' inclination to suppress his masturbatory tendencies (28), he may have been doing his little patient a disservice.

In the End

Freud did not work directly with children, and he was not infallible in his inferences about them, but the father of psychoanalysis—via subtle interpretation and theoretical insight—has taught us much about how to learn from and about them. The sort of evidence and argument he attended to offers a still unrivaled way into some at least of the mysteries of the mind.

Little Hans was amazed that Freud should have foreseen the Oedipal shape of his life in advance of his birth, wondering, "Does the Professor talk to God?" (42). But the persuasiveness of Freud's insights does not depend on a source in revelation. If Freud didn't talk to God, he nonetheless showed us how to listen to his Little Hans and our Little Hanses. A self-conscious appreciation of the importance of theory in perception, and of systematic power in providing confirmation for theory, can help us understand what we hear better than a self-deluded search for presuppositionless neutral data.

13

LÉVI-STRAUSS ON SHAMANISM

What is the role of thoughts or beliefs in Western and non-Western therapies? Why should thoughts have any role? What sort of thoughts must they be? Does it matter whether they are conscious or unconscious, fantasies or memories, true or false? What is the connection between the etiology of a disorder and the importance of the meanings or analyses provided in interpretative therapies?

Western therapies for psychological disorders can be ranged along a spectrum in accordance with the role they assign to thoughts. At the extreme ends can be placed drug and shock therapies, where no thoughts are involved, and Freudian psychoanalysis, where the patient's understanding of his suffering seems essential to "cure." In this context, shamanism is especially interesting because it seems to involve thoughts, but thoughts and a theory that need not be true. Is mere belief or a special form of faith enough? If so, why? And when? Claude Lévi-Strauss, in his two essays, "The Sorcerer and His Magic" (1963a) and "The Effectiveness of Symbols" (1963b), makes a number of suggestions. In the first essay, he suggests that what is essential to the effectiveness of shamanism is the provision of a theory or conceptual scheme that enables the patient to reintegrate an otherwise alien experience. It does not matter that the understanding provided is "mythical" or "symbolic." The shaman's theory need not be (literally) true, perhaps because his society accepts it, and in any case so long as the patient believes it and it is significant to him. When it comes to "The Effectiveness of Symbols," however, it seems that Lévi-Strauss would insist on at least "structural" correspondences, over and above coherence. It is these suggestions that I here wish to examine.

Quesalid

Lévi-Strauss tells the story of Quesalid. It is a fascinating and instructive story. Quesalid was an unbeliever in shamanistic powers, so he undertook training as a shaman in order to refute their claims. But, much to his amazement, his use of the bizarre procedures (especially the technique of extracting a concealed tuft of bloodied down from his own mouth and claiming he had sucked out the pathological foreign body in the form of a bloody worm [1963a, 175]) produced cures. And he became the most powerful shaman of all.

Now the initial undertaking, in so far as it was an effort to refute the shamans, is itself odd. What would Quesalid's failures contribute that a collection of the failures of established shamans would not? Indeed, on the face of it, such failures promise far less. A man who set out to refute astrology would gain nothing by himself mastering the techniques of astrology. It could be claimed that his failures counted only against him, not against the techniques. Similarly, if Quesalid had failed to cure, it would simply have shown that he had not mastered the techniques, that he was an inadequate shaman (not that shamanism was inadequate). This mode of defense would inevitably be open, and perhaps even more open for shamanism than astrology. Fellow astrologers might be sufficiently scientific in spirit to try to replicate the critic's procedures with greater precision and success. The principles might be sufficiently objective, so that their application by the believers yielded the same results: false predictions. The shamans have an extra out. It may be one of the principles of the practice, that only a believer in the principles can effectively use them. Or if not a "believer," someone infused with the proper "spirit," one with a "calling." Quesalid's failure would only reveal him as a failed shaman, not the failure of shamanism. Even if other shamans failed to succeed where he failed, they would have whatever outs would normally be available.

There is a problem about what distinguishes a routine failure from an "anomaly," a failure arising in the context of a challenge or test of their powers. (What makes something a problem in what Kuhn calls "normal science" rather than an anomaly leading to crisis and breakdown, and so revolution?) Two things to notice: nothing is added to the confirmation or falsification situation by Quesalid's becoming a shaman, or an unbeliever becoming an astrologer. The same difficulties arise for the theory from the failures of professionals. Second, if the usual outs used to explain failures seem *ad hoc* (and the juggling seems more *ad hoc* should Quesalid's failures receive special explanations: he lacks the spirit, etc.), one still has to explain what makes a change or adjustment in theory seem *ad hoc* rather than a natural development or articulation or elaboration. Every theory has to accommodate awkward facts. But sometimes the accommodations become more awkward than the facts. When there are too many epicycles and an alternative theory is available, a shift is possible. What exactly, however, makes a theoretical claim or shift in theory a "simplification" rather than *"ad hoc"* raises many of the deepest questions in the philosophy of science (and some of the hardest disputes within scientific argument itself). I will leave these issues here. Quesalid did not manage a successful refutation of the shamans through failure. His was a different success, and raises different issues.

We should note that Quesalid's undertaking would not be so odd if it were to *understand* rather than to *refute* the shamans. Indeed, many psychoanalysts claim that critics cannot understand the character of psychoanalytic claims or the nature of the evidence for them without themselves being psychoanalyzed. It is not, however, necessary that critics themselves become psychoanalysts. But Quesalid was dealing with a practice that depends on concealment: to appreciate the character of magic, it may well be necessary to practice it rather than simply experience its effects.

The Role of Belief

Lévi-Strauss tells the story of Quesalid mainly in order to emphasize the importance of belief by the community or group: cure by magic is a "consensual" phenomenon (1963a, 169). There are a number of separable claims which may get confused under this description. The point here is different from that made by saying that what counts as a "symptom" is a matter of the view of the society. Though that is (largely) true, once the character of sickness and health is fixed within a society, the transition from one to the other (cure) may not be achievable by change in public opinion (or anyone's beliefs). There are limits to the powers of consensus: a myth (of converging rivers, etc.) will not mend a broken bone, and faith will not turn an aspirin into a birth control pill. The point Lévi-Strauss wishes to make he puts as follows: "Quesalid did not become a great shaman because he cured his patients; he cured his patients because he had become a great shaman" (1963a, 180). Here, too, distinctions are necessary. We must distinguish group consensus in relation to the *status* of a sorcerer and in relation to the *power* of a sorcerer. Community belief may provide the criterion for a social role—this is a logical or conceptual connection. On the other hand, community belief may produce the power associated with a social role—this may be logical, but more interestingly may be an empirical connection. That social role and power can be separated is shown, in the cases of doctors and patients, by the fact that people may be able actually to heal or suffer independently of the opinion of their society. Confirmation by the community does, however, help determine who we are, whether doctor, shaman, or patient. In so far as this is a matter of social role, group consensus does indeed, meaning logically, determine who we are. This seems to be what is happening in the case of the Zuni boy who appears to become a witch in the course of his witchcraft trial (as his accusers and he too come to believe he is one). If the relevant community believes it, it is true. Their belief is part of what constitutes its being true. Who counts as a shaman, a doctor, a patient depends (in this way) on group consensus. But group consensus may also operate causally. It might be called the "Genet Effect." Told at the age of ten that he was "a thief," Genet (1967 [1949]) conceived himself in that way and decided he must become one, and did. He realized the label in his life. (Cf. the development of "patienthood" as an identity, e.g., in Dora. See Erikson 1964, 173.) In the case of shamanism and healing, the mechanisms may be more devious. The community's belief in the shaman's powers may help produce those powers. The ways in which this comes about may be quite various and complex. Before I proceed to look at some of those ways, let me try in another way to bring out the contrast I have been trying to make.

Consider the case of a "king." All believe x is the king and therefore he *is* (in a sense—not the sense that depends on bloodline) the king. But because there are some conditions that hold whether or not a community believes them to hold, and which a community cannot make hold by believing, the case of the "shaman" is importantly different from that of the king. If all accept x as a shaman he may therefore be a shaman, have the social role and have the social powers of the position. But unlike the king, all of whose powers are social, he may still lack the power to heal (though belief in that power may be what gave him community consensus to the role in the first place). That is, the doctor or shaman may not be the man who can heal. He is the man the community believes can heal. The title comes from belief in the power. The power, however, need not be a necessary condition of the belief, indeed, it may not exist prior to the belief. And it is possible that, in some cases, it arises as a result of the belief. If everyone believes "x is a king," he may have the power to rule *in virtue* of that belief. If everyone believes "x is a shaman," he may still lack the power to heal. The interesting question is whether the acceptance can produce the power (where this is an empirical connection) and how.

Lévi-Strauss cites Cannon on the physiology of voodoo; and one can understand how the withdrawal of the community, the isolation produced by a voodoo curse in virtue of the community's accepting it, might lead to physical collapse. (Consider models for self-fulfilling prophecies.) Freud himself recognizes the importance of acceptance by the community. (Consider the importance of the title "Professor" in Vienna.) Such recognition increases the "authority" of the physician, and may contribute to the effectiveness of his or her technique. But it is not by itself sufficient explanation of effectiveness. As late as 1910 Freud could write:

> Hitherto, this authority, with its enormous weight of suggestion, has been against us. All our therapeutic successes have been achieved in the face of this suggestion: it is surprising that any successes at all could be gained in such circumstances . . . I can only say that when I assured my patients that I knew how to relieve them permanently of their sufferings they looked round my modest abode, reflected on my lack of fame and title, and regarded me like the possessor of an infallible system at a gambling-resort, of whom people say that if he could do what he professes he would look very different himself. Nor was it really pleasant to

carry out a psychical operation while the colleagues whose duty it should have been to assist took pleasure in spitting into the field of operation, and while at the first signs of blood or restlessness in the patient his relatives began threatening the operating surgeon . . . Social suggestion is at present favourable to treating nervous patients by hydropathy, dieting and electrotherapy, but that does not enable such measures to get the better of neuroses. Time will show whether psycho-analytic treatment can accomplish more. (1910d, 146–47)

Certainly cooperation from surrounding family and community is helpful and perhaps even necessary. Their belief, faith, recognition, and so on, may yield such cooperation. But perhaps the essential element is the *patient's* acceptance of the doctor's authority. And belief by the community, consensus, may contribute to producing belief in the individual patient. But perhaps such belief can arise independently and still be effective. (Quesalid himself attributed his first success to the patient's faith. The treatment worked "because he [the sick person] believed strongly in his dream about me" [Lévi-Strauss 1963a, 176]. Freud says that the patient need not enter treatment with any initial belief [1913c, 126]. If it is necessary, it can develop in the course of treatment.) The question now becomes the relation of belief by the patient to the effectiveness of the therapy.

Lévi-Strauss, aside from emphasizing the consensual elements (without distinguishing the logical and causal) in shamanism, goes on to speculate about the mechanisms by which shamanistic ritual and magical symbols produce cures. And he extends his account of the effectiveness of symbols to psychoanalysis. This account requires that one pay attention to the content of the rituals and symbols (not just to their acceptance by the community).

Structuralist Explanation

There is ground for general suspicion of structuralist explanations: does being told that one thing we do not understand is similar in structure to another thing we do not understand help us understand either? The nature of the "similarities" must be specified. We must look to the details of each such explanation offered to see what, if any, enlightenment can be found. Lévi-Strauss offers parallels between the shaman and the psychoanalyst, and between the theories of both and physiological theory.

Quesalid effects cures by his technique of the bloody down despite the fact that he knows it to be bogus: it is not connected with any known or believed etiology ("sickness" is not really captured by bloodying a concealed tuft and Quesalid does not think that it is). But it works and even enables Quesalid to expose "imposters" (178). His success reveals that the therapist need not believe in order for the therapy to work. We should explore (though we can only begin to here) the natural implication of this: if belief by the practitioner is not necessary, then perhaps truth is not necessary either. Which is not to say that the *content* of rituals and symbols and inter-pretations is irrelevant—even if truth as literal correspondence to an objective reality is.

Lévi-Strauss, in his discussion of shamanistic therapies in non-Western cultures, suggests that they work because they provide a way of understanding problems and the world. The patient is given a theory, a set of terms and relationships, that enables him to fit his experience into an intelligible order:

> The system is valid precisely to the extent that it allows the coalescence or precipitation of these diffuse states, whose discontinuity also makes them painful . . . The song seems to have as its principal aim the description of these pains to the sick woman and the naming of them, that is, their presentation to her in a form accessible to conscious or unconscious thought . . . That the mythology of the shaman does not correspond to an objective reality does not matter. The sick woman believes in the myth and belongs to a society which believes in it. The tutelary spirits and malevolent spirits, the supernatural monsters and magical animals, are all part of a coherent system on which the native conception of the universe is founded. The sick woman accepts these mythical beings or, more accurately, she has never questioned their existence. What she does not accept are the incoherent and arbitrary pains, which are an alien element in her system but which the shaman, calling upon myth, will re-integrate within a whole where everything is meaningful. (182, 195, 197)

For Lévi-Strauss the beliefs need not be true, because in so far as the problem is *not understanding*, *any* coherent story or theory will solve that problem (though, of course, it must not fail to correspond at key points with known realities) and so end the suffering which is a *suffering from unintelligibility*. Psychoanalysis may be the new mythology of our culture (183). I think Lévi-Strauss's point sheds a certain light. Coherence matters because patients are partly suffering from incoherence, the alien unintelligibility of the experience. I think, however, that a Spinozist view of emotions and the mental would contribute much to a clearer understanding of the mechanisms, of how therapies that operate through beliefs can transform mental states. Rather than treating emotions as blind sensations or physiological responses, the Spinozist view emphasizes the importance of thought (of cognitive components) in the classification and discrimination of emotional states, and the consequent importance of reflexive knowledge in changing those states. If we follow Spinoza and accept that emotions essentially involve beliefs, we can begin to see how changing beliefs can transform emotions. In the realm of the mental, understanding of the state becomes part of the state, because it is identified or specified through the associated beliefs. Where knowledge is self-reflexive, knowing can transform the thing known. Following this line, we would begin to see why insight is important, and we might come to see why insight is not enough. But Lévi-Strauss develops his theory in a different direction.

Lévi-Strauss thinks symbols are effective, not because they are literally true and not because they change beliefs and so transform the associated mental state, but because they correspond with an underlying reality. (Consider Baudelaire on *"correspondances"* and Eliot on "objective correlatives.") The myth and the true account are similar in "structure." He speculates that the parallel in the case of a mythical incantation sung by the Cuna shaman to ease difficult childbirth is an underlying *physiological* reality. The myth is about a quest for the lost soul of the mother, a myth of passage through and over obstacles, and its elements correspond to or represent the vagina and uterus of the pregnant woman (188). He goes on to speculate that psychoanalysis too hooks onto the same physiological reality:

> Given this hypothesis or any other of the same type, the shamanistic cure and the psychoanalytic cure would become strictly parallel. It would be a matter, either way, of stimulating an organic transformation which would consist essentially in a structural reorganization, by inducing the patient intensively to live out a myth—either received or created by him—whose structure would be, at the unconscious level, analogous to the structure whose genesis is sought on the organic level. The effectiveness of symbols would consist precisely in this "inductive property," by which formally homologous structures, built out of different materials at different levels of life—organic processes, unconscious mind, rational thought—are related to one another. Poetic metaphor provides a familiar example of this inductive process, but as a rule it does not transcend the unconscious level. Thus we note the significance of Rimbaud's intuition that metaphor can change the world. (201)

But this pays too little attention to the elements on either side of the parallel, and to the nature of "induction" and of what he calls "reliving" or "abreaction." Again I would look to Spinoza for a better understanding of the power of metaphor, at least where the world changed is the mental world. But Lévi-Strauss means to explain how the myth can produce physical, organic, changes or cures.

He mentions that "Freud seems to have suggested . . . that the description in psychological terms of the structure of psychoses and neuroses must one day be replaced by physiological, or even biochemical concepts" (201). This is true, but as the *Project for a Scientific Psychology* shows, the sort of reduction Freud had in mind was neurophysiological. (To be fair, the *Project* was first published a year after the original publication of Lévi-Strauss's essay.) And neurophysiology is rather different from gross physiology: our mental states may be embodied, but they are not precisely "paralleled" on a gross level. Indeed, in the specific case of hysteria, no reduction to the physiological is possible. As Freud insists: "Hysteria behaves as though anatomy did not exist or as though it had no knowledge of it" (1893c, 169). And Lévi-Strauss does not notice the difference between "reduction" and "replacement." Modern biochemical theories about DNA and chromosomes *reduce* Mendel's genetic laws, leaving the truth of those laws basically unchallenged while explaining why they are true in terms of underlying biochemical laws. Modern biochemical theories of phenylketonuria (PKU) and various forms of schizophrenia *replace* competing double-bind and other psychological theories, displacing them and undermining their claims to truth. The sort of *reduction* Freud envisaged did involve precise parallels, preserving psychoanalytic laws in different terms.[1] But the sort of biochemical basis Lévi-Strauss mentions (a chemical basis for psychosis) would not provide parallels for psychoanalytic claims. Instead of reducing psychoanalytic theory, it would *replace* it. Indeed, it would leave the role of thoughts, their relevance, obscure. Why and in what way should ideas or thoughts provide a handle onto chemical forces? The term "induction" covers the obscurity without clarifying it. How does "inducing the patient intensively to live out a myth" help? Lévi-Strauss calls this "abreaction" (1963a, 182ff.; 1963b, 199), but this living or reliving is not the same as the early psychoanalytic notion (which involved "energy discharge" and hence relief). In relation to the shaman's bloody worm rituals, Lévi-Strauss actually speaks of the sorcerer abreacting *for* the silent patient (183), which is without sense in psychoanalytic terms. And again, he does not explain why symbolic thoughts should provide a lever for producing physiological changes, except that the thoughts run "parallel" to the physiology. But do they? And if they did, would that *explain* anything?

The difficulty may be brought out more clearly if we notice something Lévi-Strauss seems to notice but then neglects. He acknowledges at one point that the complicated itinerary of the Cuna song "is a true mythical anatomy, corresponding less to the real structure of the genital organs than to a kind of emotional geography, identifying each point of resistance and each thrust" (195). What he fails to emphasize is that this means that what is paralleled is not actual anatomy, but, as with hysteria, a fantasy anatomy. I am in fact inclined to think that the therapy will be effective only if the difficulties are hysterical, that is, ideogenic (Lévi-Strauss says the shaman cures "true organic disorders" [199]). But the deeper problem is that structuralist explanation will here, in any case, fail to explain. The general suspicion is here specifically realized: one process we do not understand is said to be similar to another process we do not understand, but this does not help us understand either of them. We cannot understand the process of psychoanalysis and the process of shamanism in terms of a third, underlying, process which they both parallel. We might begin *if* there were a third underlying physiological process common to them, but they each parallel fantasy physiologies, and there is no reason to expect that fantasy physiologies (unlike actual human physiology) will be the same for different cultures and individuals. Even if there were parallels to a common anatomy, how would this *explain* the effectiveness of either shamanism or psychoanalysis? Lévi-Strauss thinks these psychological treatments have direct physiological consequences, but does not explain how. He says, "In our view, the song constitutes a *psychological manipulation* of the sick organ, and it is precisely from this manipulation that a cure is expected" (192). Why should telling a story, even if parallel with actual anatomy, "work," e.g., make obstructions disappear? We can see how giving unintelligible physiological processes meaning may ease our psychological pain, but why should it alter the physiological processes themselves? The rhythm of the song may help (as a lullaby helps put a child to sleep) but this would not explain the relevance of the content of the song, of the meanings of the words or symbols.

Lévi-Strauss's account is inadequate. Mere parallels do not explain why changes in one branch should bring about changes in the other. Even if there were the claimed parallels, why should there be a necessity to *preserve* the parallel (through bodily changes as the song progresses)? His account should be restricted to shamanistic cures of hysterical disorders rather than of physical disorders in general. Indeed, the fact that a disorder was curable by shamanistic storytelling, and the like, might be part of what shows it to be "hysterical" (along with the absence of organic causes, dissimilarities in pattern of disorder, and so on). Nonhysterical disorders may lack even fantasy parallels (and hence lack symbolic meaning). Shamanistic

cures are of three types, which are not, however, mutually exclusive. The sick organ or member may be physically involved, through a manipulation or suction which aims at extracting the cause of the illness—usually a thorn, crystal, or feather made to appear at the opportune moment, as in tropical America, Australia, and Alaska. Curing may also revolve, as among the Araucanians, around a sham battle, waged in the hut and then outdoors, against harmful spirits. Or, as among the Navaho, the officiant may recite incantations and prescribe actions (such as placing the sick person on different parts of a painting traced on the ground with coloured sands and pollens) which bear *no direct relationship* to the specific disturbance to be cured. In all these cases, the therapeutic method (which as we know is often effective) is difficult to interpret. When it deals directly with the unhealthy organ, it is too grossly concrete (generally, pure deceit) to be granted intrinsic value. And when it consists in the repetition of often highly abstract ritual, it is difficult for us to understand its direct bearing on the illness. It would be convenient to dismiss these difficulties by declaring that we are dealing with psychological cures. But this term will remain meaningless unless we can explain how specific psychological representations are invoked to combat equally specific physiological disturbances. (191)

But Lévi-Strauss's attempt to generalize from the text he considers fails. The fantasy anatomy that a psychoanalyst may confront may be different from the fantasy anatomy a myth deals with. So psychoanalysis is not parallel to shamanism, (in this respect) for they are not parallel to the same third thing (actual anatomy). And many shamanistic cures are without "correspondences" or physiological parallels at all. So Lévi-Strauss's account cannot be extended to cures in general. Even the particular symbolic treatment he discusses lacks real physiological parallel (and even if it had it, the mechanism of change would not be clarified by merely pointing to the parallel). How relation to fantasy anatomy allows effects on actual anatomy depends, I think, on the original disturbances in anatomy being hysterical (i.e., also depending on fantasies of anatomy—though perhaps different ones). The importance of thought in therapy should be clarified by the importance of thoughts in etiology. Psychoanalysis tries to explain ideogenesis. Lévi-Strauss seems to deny or ignore it.

To summarize: Lévi-Strauss makes suggestions in terms of (social) consensus, (psychological) coherence, and (physiological) correspondence to explain the effectiveness of shamanistic symbols and magic, and extends his account to psychoanalytic treatment. Properly sorted out, I think the first two suggestions contain valuable insight, but that the third fails both for the particular case and in general.

14

"GETTING BEHIND THE DEMONS"

What makes room for a psychoanalytic account of a practice, especially where, as so often in anthropology, it involves setting aside or going behind (or below) alternative accounts? When are alternative explanations competing, when complementary, when merely incommensurable? This is an essay on psychoanalytic explanation in anthropology, on realism and relativism.

Explaining the Normal

There is a paradox about explaining the normal. For if, as Plato held, explanation essentially involves revealing the order behind apparent disorder, it becomes unclear how one can explain the normal; how is one to reveal the order behind apparent *order?*

There may, of course, be different levels of order, and there may also be a "larger" order. The normal can sometimes be explained as one of a range of alternatives. So, in explaining sexual perversion, Freud (1905d) exhibited it as involving variations along the dimensions (source, object, and aim) of a single underlying instinct. In explaining the abnormal, he also exhibited the normal (adult heterosexual genital intercourse) as just another constellation of variations along those same dimensions. And Lévi-Strauss (1963c), in accounting for one aspect of totemism, suggested that the choice of particular animal names for groups and individuals should be seen as a selection among alternative analogies, the significance of which is to be found in the range of alternatives, the sets of different contrasts available. This sort of explanation, in addition to leaving open the questions of how and why one particular constellation of variations is selected or emerges, calls into question the very notion of "the normal."

Explanation has to begin (and stop) somewhere. For that reason, theorists pick out certain circumstances, or aspects of circumstances, as normal—as given and unexplained, and not in need of explanation. Within Newtonian theory, that a body in motion continues in motion (in the absence of friction, etc.) does not need explanation. That is, according to the principle of inertia, how things are. The principle does not *explain* the continuing motion; it notes its place in the scheme of things as one not calling for explanation. In different theories (for example, Aristotelian dynamics) there are different starting points and different things will be taken as normal, as not in need of explanation. Now even if one is open-minded and wishes to judge a theory by its overall power, granting its assumptions, rather than by the plausibility or appeal of its initial assumptions, one may be driven to question the starting point, to want to explain the normal or at least see why *that* is selected as normal. This is inevitable in anthropology. In the social sciences, unlike the natural sciences, one is dealing with self-conscious agents who can, and typically do, have their own thoughts about why they do what they do. Such reflexive knowledge must be taken into account not because it must be correct—it need not be, people can suffer from false consciousness—but because people's views about why they are doing something may form an essential part of the full characterization of *what* they are doing. Where what one is explaining is the behavior of another—especially an alien other, a member of a different society—there are inevitably two points of view. An adequate anthropological theory, even if it never self-consciously questions its own notion of the normal, must seek to make intelligible the native's self-understanding. And in the course of doing this, the anthropologist may have to call into question both the native's explanations and his notion of what goes without saying, of what does not require explanation.

Moving to Another Level

In the second essay in *Totem and Taboo* (1912–13), Freud writes about the ambivalence that lies behind the treatment in many societies of dead enemies and dead loved ones. He cites rites of appeasement and mourning for slain enemies, restrictions upon the slayer, and ritual acts of expiation and purification and says, "The conclusion that we must draw from all these observances is that the impulses which they express towards an enemy are not solely hostile ones" (13: 38–39). On the other hand, dead loved ones, as can be seen in the consequences that follow contact with the dead and in the treatment of mourners in various societies, are often responded to as enemies. And Freud concludes, "Something other than mourning must be held responsible for the peculiarities of the taboo usages, something which has very different purposes in view" (13: 57). Freud's account brings in reference to unconscious hostility (a notion we will be returning to in relation to other rituals and other writers). The treatment of the dead, both enemies and loved ones, reveals ambivalence, a conflict between conscious attitudes and unconscious feelings. There is other evidence for unconscious feelings in natives (for example, the ambivalent treatment of rulers [13: 41–51]), but leaving that aside, why go beyond the native's point of view, why bring in another level of explanation?

After all, the natives have their own reasons to offer for their treatment of the dead, for they believe in ghosts and demons. Freud is well aware of this alternative account: "the savages openly admit their fear of the ghosts of dead enemies and themselves attribute to it the taboo usages [appeasement and other rites] which we are discussing" (13: 38). Dead enemies are one thing, dead loved ones—one would have thought—are another. But for loved ones, too, natives "make no disguise of the fact that they are *afraid* of the presence or of the return of the dead person's ghost; and they perform a great number of ceremonies to keep him at a distance or drive him off" (13: 57). Hence taboos, such as the one against uttering the name of the deceased loved one, stem from fear of demons. Freud points out that this, in relation to loved ones at least, involves a problematic shift: "This theory is based on a supposition so extraordinary that it seems at first sight incredible: the supposition, namely, that a dearly loved relative at the moment of his death changes into a demon, from whom his survivors can expect nothing but hostility and against whose evil desires they must protect themselves by every possible means" (13: 58).

This shift certainly seems to pose an internal problem for the theory of ghosts. And perhaps it is open to an internal answer, an answer that does not require movement to another level of explanation and reference to entities other than ghosts. Native fear of death may get extended to dead loved ones, who in the form of ghosts may be presumed to envy the living. (Freud quotes Westermarck's discussion of this approach [13: 59].) But Freud goes on to use what he has learned from the study of psychoneurotic disorders and mourning to offer a more comprehensive explanation (13: 57–63). There is every reason to believe that the psychological mechanisms behind obsessive self-reproach, ultimately involving unconscious feelings and ambivalence, are also what, with the addition of projection, lie behind native practices and native justifications of those practices. This explanation is more comprehensive than the native account, not only in connecting their lives with our lives—it enables us to understand how, despite differing beliefs and practices, they are like us—but also, in Freud's phrase, "in getting behind the demons."

The alternative native account is less adequate. It depends on belief in ghosts. And while the "belief" is real enough, "ghosts" are not. The native version fails to account for the mistaken belief. If ghosts were real, there would be no need for such an explanation: the existence of ghosts would provide sufficient support for belief in the existence of ghosts. But it seems clear (to us) that the native belief in ghosts is based more on emotional needs than evidence. As Freud concludes: "It is true that we have accepted the presence of demons, but not as something ultimate and psychologically unanalysable. We have succeeded, as it were, in getting behind the demons, for we have explained them as projections of hostile feelings harboured by the survivors against the dead" (13: 62).

Realism and Relativism

Does "getting behind the demons" involve epistemological imperialism (ethnocentrism), or does it simply reflect inescapable conditions for the intelligibility of others, including the fact that in understanding the beliefs of others we must start with what we believe? There is no problem in accepting mere analogies. To the extent that Freud's project is to use what he has learned from the study of obsessional neurosis to illuminate taboo by making comparisons (13: 26–36), the truth of beliefs need not come into question. Similarities may be merely formal (13: 26). But causal connections are different. If ambivalence provides the psychological basis of taboo practices, then native accounts may have to be set aside as false, or at best, wishful thinking. Psychoanalysis may displace demonology. In explaining beliefs, one is not always necessarily denying them; but if the reasons for belief are not connected with grounds of truth, independent support is required before it can be shown rational to go on believing. When Freud gets "behind" the demons, does he undermine them?

He says that he has "accepted the presence of demons." Has he? He seems to want to say that the natives are right, there are demons, *but* they are within them. Their recognition of hostile feelings is real enough, but their perception is distorted and they mislocate the feelings, projecting them outside themselves. But if the demons are within, are they "demons"? On the one hand, demons are supposed to be external, independent spirits of the departed. On the other hand, the unconscious may itself perhaps be regarded as an alien (external) part of the self.

Certainly it is sometimes plausible to suppose that others are saying the same thing that one is saying, but in different words. In the following passage, Erik Erikson sees the "same forces" being given recognition within very different conceptual schemes:

> In northern California I knew an old shaman woman who laughed merrily at my conception of mental disease, and then sincerely—to the point of ceremonial tears—told me of her way of sucking the "pains" out of her patients. She was as convinced of her ability to cure and to understand as I was of mine. While occupying extreme opposites in the history of American psychiatry we felt like colleagues. This feeling was based on some joint sense of the historical relativity of all psychotherapy: the relativity of the patient's outlook on his symptoms, of the role he assumes by dint of being a patient, of the kind of help which he seeks, and of the kinds of help which are eagerly offered or are available. The old shaman

woman and I disagreed about the locus of emotional sickness, what it "was," and what specific methods would cure it. Yet, when she related the origin of a child's illness to the familial tensions existing within her tribe, when she attributed the "pain" (which had got "under a child's skin") to his grandmother's sorcery (ambivalence) I knew she dealt with the same forces, and with the same kinds of conviction, as I did in my professional nook. This experience has been repeated in discussion with colleagues who, although not necessarily more "primitive," are oriented toward different psychiatric persuasions. (1958, 55; see also Neu 1977, 122–24)

Looking across conceptual schemes, we may find it very difficult to determine whether, despite inevitable differences, particular concepts such as "demons" and "unconscious hostility" refer to the same aspects of the world. Indeed, there may be limits on just how different separate conceptual schemes can be and still remain intelligible to each other—they all must somehow be anchored to the one world that there is (Davidson 1973–74). Our judgments about the significance of particular similarities and differences must depend on our general theory of reference and on what is at stake. And in judging, we must look from where we stand—that is, from within our conceptual scheme, our best understanding of the way the world is.

Quine argues effectively for what he calls the "indeterminacy of translation."[1] In general, theories are underdetermined by the data available. That is, alternative theories can cover any given set of experiences; moreover, the line between observation and theory is not as sharp as some might think, and one may always be saved by adjustments to the other. The Zande system of magic or any sufficiently complex demonology may appear able to answer any question our alternative theory may answer (Evans-Pritchard 1937; B. R. Wilson 1970). The psychological mechanism of projection is mirrored in the demonological notion of possession.

This takes one to large problems of realism versus relativism. It might seem that statements are true only relative to their theoretical context and that there is no independent (theory-neutral) way of choosing between theories—so that native views must always be regarded as true *for them*. But such relativism (attempting as it does to regard all theories as true on their own terms) seems to me an evasion. What in our society might be a superstitious belief might in another be a shared religious commitment; that does not make the belief *true* for them, although it certainly may change the significance we ascribe to the psychological state of the believer. We may want to distinguish literal or material truth and psychological truth, but that too does not make truth relative.[2] Theories sometimes conflict and cannot be simultaneously true. Magic is typically less effective than medicine: "'At Norwich in June 1902 a woman named Matilda Henry accidentally ran a nail into her foot. Without examining the wound, or even removing her stocking, she caused her daughter to grease the nail, saying that if this were done no harm would come of the hurt. A few days afterwards she died of lockjaw.'"[3]

While curing rituals are doubtless sometimes effective, the explanation of their effectiveness is not usually to be found in the magical gloss on the ritual (Neu 1975a [chap. 13 here]). The germ theory of disease is more powerful than witchcraft and other competing theories. It is an evasion to say that a theory remains true for someone else ("true for them") when it seems false to us, because when it comes to questions of truth we must use the best standards we know, namely ours (we make them ours precisely because we believe them best). Of course, others may go on using their standards and holding to their beliefs, and we must acknowledge that we may be wrong—*but recognizing fallibility is a part of realism, not relativism.* To admit the possibility of being wrong is also to admit the possibility of being right—which is all that realism requires.

The large problems of realism versus relativism can be seen in a more immediately pressing form if we focus on translation and the question of how we are to understand native views. Can we leave questions of truth-value aside? "Certain primitive Yoruba carry about with them boxes covered with cowrie shells, which they treat with special regard. When asked what they are doing, they apparently reply that the boxes are their heads or souls and they are protecting them against witchcraft. Is that an interesting fact or a bad translation?" (Hollis 1970, 221). There is always a potential choice between ascriptions of meanings to their words and ascriptions of beliefs to them. Suppose within our own society you had a conversation with someone in which you asked them to tell you what "dogs" are like, and the person said, "dogs meow, dogs chase mice, dogs climb trees," and so on. After a while, the "simplest" way to understand them would be to say they mean by "dog" what you and I mean by "cat." The alternative is to ascribe a rather weird set of beliefs about dogs to them. The more weird the beliefs become, the more plausible and the more "charitable" (one wants to maintain respect for their rationality) it will seem to take the first line, to treat what might be taken as a conflict of beliefs as a problem of translation.

Understanding of meanings is not totally separable from judgments about truth; and the pull of charity is toward the view that others must believe what we believe (after all, that is what we think is true), whatever they may say and however they may say it. If our beliefs are really beliefs, we are committed to a form of realism, and our judgment of alternative theories must be made from the point of view of the best theory we have (that is, what we believe). The criteria for choosing between alternative theories raise large questions we cannot pursue here, but the apparent coherence of a demonological system does not preserve it from psychoanalytic challenge. After all, some systems are delusional. Freud points out that coherence of systems, like the connectedness and intelligibility achieved in dreams, may be the product of "secondary revision." He writes: "Thus a system is best characterized by the fact that at least two reasons can be discovered for each of its products: a reason based upon the premises of the system (a reason, then, which may be delusional) and a concealed reason, which we must judge to be the truly operative and the real one" (1912–13, 7: 95–96). It is important to appreciate the character of the challenge provided by psychoanalysis. When psychoanalysis attributes belief in demons to projection and the denial of unconscious hostility, it does not *thereby* show that demons do not exist (even if what psychoanalysis says is correct). Psychoanalysis probes motives and can sometimes unmask reasons as rationalizations (that is, show that a belief would persist even if the putative reason for belief were admittedly refuted). But a theory may satisfy extraneous motives and still be true. (Acceptance of a belief may be overdetermined.) If demonology is false, the arguments that show it false are not psychoanalytic arguments (although psychoanalysis may show why it is believed despite its falsity). Psychoanalysis does not offer comprehensive grounds for choosing between theories (of disease, of physics, etc.). But once we suspect that a belief or system of beliefs does not support itself, that it is not grounded in evidences of truth, psychoanalysis can help us understand why belief persists, why individuals and groups—and the differences between these may be of great significance—cling to illusions. Natives outside our society do not, of course, have a monopoly on illusions. Psychoanalysis gets behind demonology, revealing motives for believing not connected with the (literal) truth of the beliefs, but Freud offered a similar challenge to Christianity (see Ricoeur 1970, 230–54, 531–51).

Couvade

In the first essay in *Ritual* (1976 [1931]), psychoanalyst Theodor Reik looks at various aspects of couvade, simulated childbirth by the father (putatively for the sake of the mother) and postnatal dietary and other restrictions on the father (putatively for the sake of the child), and sees behind the rituals and the restrictions the same unconscious ambivalences uncovered by Freud in relation to taboos in connection with the dead. Birth and death bring out the same hidden tendencies; universal feelings become manifest under extreme personal conditions, and unusual social practices may sometimes be better understood as helping to express or to respond to those otherwise unacknowledged feelings. Our concern here is with the relation of the psychoanalytic level of understanding to native self-understandings and to alternative accounts. For example, Reik goes on from Freud's discussion of belief in demons as projected hostility to interpret the simulation of childbirth by a father (pseudo-maternal couvade) as the product of the same feelings and mechanisms (49). This would seem to involve setting aside a number of alternative views, including native views that regard the ritual as for the sake of the mother (to protect her from demons or to transfer her pains [41–45]), Bachofen's view that it involves a pretense at maternity aimed at securing for the father rights over the children that had previously been enjoyed by the mother under a system of motherkin (37, 41), and Frazer's view that it is an attempt at sympathetic magic (46). Now these views are not in fact quite set aside, if that is taken to mean they are rejected as false; indeed, not all the views are themselves mutually incompatible. When Frazer classifies the customs as sympathetic *magic*, he is simultaneously taking up the native beliefs and stepping back from them. The native believes that his imitation, his conscious identification with the woman in childbed, is a loving and tender attempt to ease the woman's suffering, to transfer her pains; he also expects the attempt to be effective. Frazer, by calling the procedure magical, introduces doubt.

Reik accepts Frazer's classification, but he deepens it and goes beyond it. Imitative magic has itself to be understood in terms of the belief in "omnipotence of thought" discussed by Freud (1912–13, part 3) and illustrated by Reik (1931, 48, 52) with neurotic parallels. Native beliefs in relation to couvade are to be explained in terms of omnipotence of thought, just as native beliefs in relation to rituals to propitiate the dead are to be explained in terms of projection. As Reik concludes: "It is now clear why the men who carry out couvade allow themselves to be treated as though they were ill and miserable: it is as though they had actually suffered the pains which they had wished for their wives, making no distinction between wish and reality" (53). And again behind a ritual practice we find a denied emotion, unconscious hostility. The same concealed hostility against the woman is brought to light in Reik's analysis of the fear of demons (here they are again) involved in some couvade customs, such as those of the Tagals of the Philippines (44, 50). Women in childbed are thought to be particularly susceptible to the workings of demons, and the mock birth is sometimes supposed to draw them off. But other techniques are also used, and certain aspects of the measures taken for the supposed protection of the mother against demons provide further evidence for latent hostility, for motives that go beyond those recognized by Frazer and the natives. Reik reports:

> Among the Tagals confined women become seriously alarmed when their husbands lay fire round the huts and discharge firearms in their immediate vicinity. The unconscious hostile motivation of the protective measures against the demons comes out more clearly in that custom of the Turks where a sword is laid under the woman's bed. It seems like a re-emergence of the repressed in the repressive forces themselves when the same people beat the poor woman with a stick, ostensibly to ward off the demons, but really to gratify their own hostile impulses. (51)

And while Frazer's talk of imitative magic and the transfer of pains may be acceptable as far as it goes, it is incomplete; it does not account for

> why the man remains in bed and behaves like an invalid, while his wife goes calmly on with her daily work. Logically his magic action should

stop when her confinement is over. Here, again, psycho-analytic investigation helps us . . . The prohibition of the realisation of hostile wishes towards his wife, which the primitive man has imposed upon himself, exceeds the period of her confinement because his unconscious wishes continue to press towards active expression through the motor system. (54)

So the alternative accounts are in some ways true (there *are* demons to be wrestled with), but they are distorted and the level of motive is not adequately explored. The original meaning (let alone the hidden meaning) of ceremonies may also sometimes be lost, and some contemporary native accounts of the point of ancient customs may have to be dismissed as rationalizations (55). Reik concludes: "The social purpose of couvade is . . . twofold: primarily, to protect the woman against the latent hostility and sexual aggression of the man; secondarily, and fictitiously, to ease the woman's labour pains" (56).

Psychoanalytic Explanation and "Thick Description"

Freud and Reik and other psychoanalytic writers on anthropology often follow a typical pattern: first, ethnographic reports on totemism, couvade, and so forth ("the facts"), then alternative competing theories, then their own psychoanalytic theory. The question arises, in general, of why one should prefer or bother to go on to a psychoanalytic theory, especially if the alternatives are not manifestly false. An answer that is often given (I have just given it in relation to Reik's account of couvade) is that the psychoanalytic theory may better account for the facts. But it must be admitted that "the facts" as presented are often at several removes from the original (for example, Reik's reports of Frazer's reports of somebody else's ethnographic reports), and that "the facts," even in the original reports (for example, when the psychoanalyst is, like Géza Roheim, also an anthropologist, or when the anthropologist is, like Victor Turner, psychoanalytically informed), are inevitably already "interpreted"—if not, indeed, "translated" from native reports. Nonetheless, the psychoanalytic account may still be superior to competing alternatives. What this particular response does not do, however, is tell us anything about psychoanalytic accounts in general. After all, any account (any type of account) may, on a particular occasion, seem to cover the facts, such as they are, more comprehensively. Why should anthropologists, people trying to understand other cultures, look expectantly to psychoanalysis? The start of a general answer has already been suggested. Perhaps because it makes others seem more like us—that is, it finds the universal behind variations. Psychoanalysis has the advantage of speaking of what we know is real (look at children, look at neurotics), what we know has the power to motivate strange behavior. It has the disadvantage of leaving the variations without a specifically psychoanalytic explanation. Why, for example, does couvade sometimes rest with the identification involved in pseudo-maternal childbirth, and sometimes add projected demons? Between variations in natural endowments and in environments, these differences may well be accounted for. In accounting for the "choice of neurosis" in individuals, Freud often found himself appealing to such things as "the quantitative factor" in instinctual drives. The general advantage of a psychoanalytic approach to anthropological understanding may further be connected with general features of explanation and of ritual. I shall say something about the nature of ritual in a moment; first a word about explanation.

We have been considering a particular type of psychoanalytic explanation, a type that comes to rest, ultimately, on ascriptions of unconscious feelings (beliefs and desires). These feelings are manifested (in distorted form) in various rituals and practices, and the meaning of these practices, like the "meaning" of individual symptoms, can be understood in terms of the feelings that motivate them, the feelings that in one way or another are being dealt with. There may well be other types of psychoanalytic explanation that are of interest, but the movement to the level of motivation is illuminating precisely because it involves a shift in levels and because it involves motivation. It may be essential to explanation, as opposed to mere redescription, that there be a shift in levels. One problem with staying within native understandings is that while one may avoid ethnocentrism, one may come to feel that ethnographic description never ends and that *explanation* never begins. Even an anthropologist as methodologically sophisticated as Clifford Geertz in his essay "Deep Play: Notes on the Balinese Cockfight" (1973), where he is concerned with reading culture as a set of texts and with avoiding reductionism, makes us feel that he has *explained* the Balinese cockfight only when he enables us to see its role in the expression of feelings and the cultivation of feelings.

> To treat the cockfight as a text is to bring out . . . its use of emotion for cognitive ends . . . Attending cockfights and participating in them is, for the Balinese, a kind of sentimental education. What he learns there is what his culture's ethos and his private sensibility (or, anyway, certain aspects of them) look like when spelled out externally in a collective text; that the two are near enough alike to be articulated in the symbolics of a single such text: and—the disquieting part—that the text in which this revelation is accomplished consists of a chicken hacking another mindlessly to bits.
>
> Every people, the proverb has it, loves its own form of violence. The cockfight is the Balinese reflection on theirs: on its look, its uses, its force, its fascination. Drawing on almost every level of Balinese experience, it brings together themes—animal savagery, male narcissism, opponent gambling, status rivalry, mass excitement, blood sacrifice—whose main

connection is their involvement with rage and the fear of rage, and, binding them into a set of rules which at once contains them and allows them play, builds a symbolic structure in which, over and over again, the reality of their inner affiliation can be intelligibly felt. (449–50)

Geertz certainly provides a very rich (and "thick") description of the Balinese cockfight. But to enable us to see the order behind apparent disorder, he has to tell us things the Balinese did not tell him and would perhaps deny, and he has to move to another level—a level different from the descriptions of betting, gaming technique, and the like—in this case, a level of feeling. Perhaps explanation is thus, in a sense, essentially reductive. It involves moving to another level, a level using terms and principles different from those used to describe the thing to be explained. (What constitutes a difference in "level" is a further problem I cannot pursue here.) If his "thick description" (Geertz's preferred term for his method) is successful as *explanation*, rather than being merely redescription, perhaps it is because his descriptions are thick enough to include different levels and enable us to understand one in terms of the other—and so to see the order behind apparent disorder.

So the type of psychoanalytic explanation we have focused on has the advantage of offering an explanatorily promising shift of levels. The rituals considered can be understood as attempting to deal with (by expressing, by restraining, by cultivating, by denying, by projecting, etc.) emotions that might not be similarly mentioned in the description and explanation of the rituals offered by the participants themselves. Because the level is one of feeling (albeit unconscious feeling), the psychoanalytic explanation has the further promise of answering another "why" question. By exploring the level of motive, psychoanalysis suggests answers to the question, Why have any ritual or ceremonial? This is another question of meaning.

Ritual and Illusion:
Motives and Truth

Not every statement is a slip of the tongue. When what a person's words in fact mean (conventionally) and what they are meant (consciously) to mean coincide, there is no room for a psychoanalytic account—almost. On one level at least, the content of the statement is adequately conveyed and understood in terms of ordinary standards of interpretation. There is no surplus meaning, no hidden message between or under the words for a psychoanalytic interpretation to ferret out. But one can always move to another level. For any statement is, in addition to the content determined by the conventional symbols used in making it, an action in the world, and one can ask of the statement-as-action why it was made, why it was made then, why it was made to whom it was made, and why it was made in *that* way (with that emphasis, with that emotion, in those words). And the proper answer to these questions may sometimes, even when those words in that situation are not anomalous, call for psychoanalytic insight. Even when one knows what the words "mean," one may want to know what uttering those words "means."

Ritual performances, by virtue of being rituals, inevitably leave room for psychoanalytic speculation both at the level of action (repetition and compulsion are often puzzling) and at the level of content (rituals always carry a surplus meaning). Freud famously compared "Obsessive Actions and Religious Practices" (the title of a 1907 paper), pointing to the resemblances "between neurotic ceremonials and the sacred acts of religious ritual: in the qualms of conscience brought on by their neglect, in their complete isolation from all other actions (shown in the prohibition against interruption) and in the conscientiousness with which they are carried out in every detail" (9: 119). Are all rituals obsessive? One of the things that makes us regard an action as a ritual is that it is part of an individual or social practice that has a more or less formal structure. That is, ritual essentially involves the possibility of repetition. Even if a ritual is performed only once, it has a script that makes us think of it as repeatable, and repeatable in different ways. Some repetitions may of course be empty, making for "meaningless" ritual. Does meaningful repetition make ritual necessarily obsessive? In one sense, surely not. Since there are many reasons for doing things more than once (for example, sometimes we do things over and over because we are paid to), there need not be a repetition compulsion behind doing something again. Repetition need not be more problematic than a single occurrence, and doing something once may not be less problematic than repeated performances. Why something gets done, its motive and its meaning, may have something to do with its being done more than once, but it may not.[4] One has to distinguish between the content and the compulsive aspect of something that is repeated. That said, however, it may still be true that what makes us regard a repetition as *meaningful* may have something to do with its motivation, and the motives that matter may not be unconnected with criteria for compulsion and obsession. In any case, insofar as a ritual is compulsive, there is surely room for psychoanalytic illumination.

Further, rituals always carry a surplus meaning. That is, we would not regard an action, even a repeated action, as a ritual if its significance failed to go beyond its instrumental content. If everything a person does is adequately explained by acknowledged biological needs, without surrounding actions or thoughts that go beyond what accomplishing the task calls for, then we do not characterize that activity as "ritual." (Not *every* way of defecating constitutes a "defecating ritual"—which is not to say that there is only one "normal" way to defecate. And it should not be thought that every ritual need be tied to a biological point. Some initiation rituals, for example, may mark *social* transitions that might equally well occur without ceremony.) Freud describes a bedtime ceremonial which "seems to be no more than an exaggeration of an orderly procedure that is customary and justifiable," but it is the exaggeration that marks it as a ritual: "the special conscientiousness with which it is carried out and the anxiety which follows upon its neglect stamp the ceremonial as a 'sacred act.' Any interruption of it is for the most part badly tolerated, and the presence of other people during its performance is almost always ruled out" (1907b, 9: 118). The surplus meaning may thus be manifested in compulsive features of the acts, features that make us look for unconscious motivations. But the content of neurotic actions is also typically puzzling in itself, so that to find even an instrumental point one must uncover hidden purposes— ultimately, repressed instinctual impulses. And this marks an apparent difference between neurotic and religious ritual, for "the minutiae of religious ceremonial are full of significance and have a symbolic meaning" (1907b, 9: 119). While the neurotic's actions may be senseless even to him, religious ceremonial bears its meaning (at least, a meaning) on its face. So what makes room for a psychoanalytic account? Why go in search of further meanings? Because, as Freud points out, one can doubt the sense that religion makes of itself: "In all believers, however, the motives which impel them to religious practices are unknown to them or are represented in consciousness by others which are advanced in their place" (1907b, 9: 122–23). Freud is interested in getting behind God for the same reasons he is interested in getting behind the demons; he has a doubt that has two intertwining aspects: he doubts that the professed reasons for belief constitute the only motives for belief, and he doubts the truth of the belief. How do these intertwine?

In *The Future of an Illusion* (1927c), Freud explicitly detaches the status of a belief as illusion from the question of its truth-value (21: 30–33). An illusion may even turn out to be true. (That a belief turns out to be true may be the only thing that makes us call believing it, in retrospect, "having faith" rather than "self-deception.") What makes a belief illusory is the believer's motive for holding it: illusions derive from wishful thinking. The reasons put forward for illusions amount to "rationalizations" in the sense specified earlier: belief would persist even if the putative reasons were admittedly refuted; the reasons—be they good or bad—are not what move. Having detached questions of illusion from questions of truth-value, Freud goes on to consider religion as though he were not judging its truth. But on closer examination, I think it can be shown that his argument about motivation ultimately relies on arguments about truth. This can be seen if we first bring out two aspects of reasons. One aspect is causal: reasons move; they incline more or less powerfully toward belief. The second is evidential: reasons are good or bad; they are connected more or less rationally with grounds of truth. Corresponding with these two aspects of reasons, there are two approaches to showing that a particular belief is illusory, that the purported reasons are rationalizations. The first approach involves showing that the belief is supported by a wish (or something else), so that the belief would persist even if the purported reason were undermined. To show that a belief is supported by a wish, one must show that the content of the belief corresponds to the content of the wish, the existence of which is proven independently, *and* that the wish is what causes the belief. Note that this may leave the reason offered in evidence by the believer a *good* reason; it is just that the reason is not what supports (causally) the holding of the belief. So this approach might appear to avoid questions of truth-value. The second approach involves showing that the purported reason could not (evidentially) support the belief, that it is a *bad* reason.[5] This suggests that the person holding the belief, purportedly on the basis of that (bad) reason, is either self-deceived, stupid, or for some other reason (or no reason) mistaken. It is only in the case of self-deception that the reason is necessarily a "rationalization." Not all errors are motivated by or fulfill wishes, and it is only when they are that they involve rationalizations. So this second approach, while it looks to the evidential rather than the motivational aspect of the reason, must in the end include a consideration of motivation if it is to sustain charges of self-deception, rationalization, and illusory thinking. But if a number of people share a belief and the reasons they offer could not (evidentially) support it, that suggests (unless we think people uniformly stupid or prone to the same unaccountable errors) that something else does.

Freud runs both sorts of argument in relation to religion. Claims about motivation (causation) are important in both approaches, but so are claims about truth (evidence). In Freud's presentation of even the first argument, the sort that might appear to avoid issues of truth-value, the essential step of showing that a wish not only exists but plays a causal role heavily depends on suggesting that the purported reasons for belief *could not* play that supporting role because they are *bad* reasons. And this step cannot be left out. So after attacking arguments from revelation (revelation "is itself one of the doctrines whose authenticity is under examination, and no proposition can be a proof of itself" [1927c, 21: 27]) and other efforts at authentication, Freud speaks of the "incontrovertible lack of authentication" for religious ideas (1927c, 21: 29). His claims here are not particularly psychoanalytical. As Freud points out:

> Nothing that I have said here against the truth-value of religions needed the support of psycho-analysis; it had been said by others long before analysis came into existence. If the application of the psycho-analytic method makes it possible to find a new argument against the truths of religion, *tant pis* for religion; but defenders of religion will by the same right make use of psycho-analysis in order to give full value to the affective significance of religious doctrines. (1927c, 21: 37)

But again it must be emphasized that the psychoanalytic effort to get behind religious doctrines would seem less urgent if the content of religion could be shown to sustain belief. "We must ask where the inner force of those doctrines lies and to what it is that they owe their efficacy, independent as it is of recognition by reason" (1927c, 21: 29). It is the falsity of religious doctrine, or, more accurately, the absence of good reason for believing, that gives place to a search for another level of reasons, another level of meaning and motivation.

So questions of illusion and rationalization are not, in some ways at least, ultimately separable from arguments about truth-value. Similarly, earlier I suggested that questions of reference and meaning are also not ultimately separable from judgments about truth-value. But it is worth noting that in determining whether there is room for a psychoanalytic account, rather than whether there is a pressing need for one, questions of truth-value need not be *settled*. Because beliefs and actions may, after all, be overdetermined, a psychoanalytic account may always be appropriate. And the truth of a belief leaves room for other questions about it and related actions. The truth of a statement is not sufficient to explain why it was made when it was made, and we may wonder whether a person is glad or unhappy that what he or she believes to be so is so. But there will be a felt need for something like a psychoanalytic account whenever we discover that reasons are rationalizations—that they are not properly connected with grounds of truth or, even if they are, that the belief would persist even if they were not. When purported reasons are not what moves, we want to understand why the belief is held, or held with such unreasonable force.

Ndembu Ritual and Psychoanalytic Explanation

In *The Forest of Symbols* (1967) Victor Turner suggests a relatively restricted place for psychoanalytical interpretations. He argues that "the successive symbolic acts of many Ndembu rituals are given order and structure by the explicitly stated purposes of those rituals. We do not need to invoke the notion of underlying conflicts to account for their conspicuous regularity" (34). Similar things could of course be said for contemporary Christian ritual, but that does not keep Freud from dismissing religious doctrine as illusory and seeking to go behind it. While religion may tell the truth about itself, it may not tell the whole truth. While religious doctrine may give an intelligible meaning and order to religious ritual, that does not mean that it does not function as rationalization and that other levels of order need not be sought if we are to fully understand the content of religious ritual and its place in individual and social life. Native rituals may come with explanations, mythical or otherwise. Accepting the native glosses should not keep us from seeing that rituals may mean more than they say (indeed, that something is done or said via ritual forms may itself be revealing).

It is also worth remembering that even if a native gloss is attached, we face problems of translation. What is the relation of their language to ours? We have seen that this question is not independent of the question of the relation of their beliefs to ours. There is always the possibility of a choice between ascriptions of meaning to their words and ascriptions of beliefs to them. For example, could the Nuer mean, literally, that "a twin is a bird"?[6] The problem of how much charity to apply in interpreting what they say poses a dilemma: if their beliefs are too different from ours, we may find them incomprehensible; but if we assume they believe more or less what we believe, we may miss genuine differences, so that while we may understand something, it won't be *them* we understand. (Sometimes what looks like philosophical charity may be more like ordinary arrogance.) In addition, their beliefs may in fact be incoherent (Gellner 1970). But suppose that what we take them to say seems straightforward enough, leaving problems of the indeterminacy of translation aside; what is the place of psychoanalytical interpretation?

Certainly it must be acknowledged that forces may be operating of which the natives do not speak, indeed of which they are not aware, forces such as unconscious hostility. How can we know when they are operating? According to Turner, much of Ndembu ritual—especially "rituals of affliction," those related to misfortune in hunting, women's reproductive disorders, and various forms of illness—aims at propitiating and getting rid of "shades," the spirits of dead relatives thought to be behind the various afflictions (1967, 9). We need not doubt the stated purposes of these rituals, given what *we* believe about demons, in order to feel the need to get behind them. We have seen that psychoanalysis often finds unconscious hostility (along with projection and belief in the omnipotence of thoughts) behind belief in demons. But even in initiation ceremonies and other "life-crisis rituals" or rituals of transition, where shades or demons play a lesser role, unconscious hostility may arguably find symbolic expression. Turner himself says:

> at one phase in *Nkang'a* [the girl's puberty ritual], mother and daughter interchange portions of clothing. This may perhaps be related to the Ndembu custom whereby mourners wear small portions of a dead relative's clothing. Whatever the interchange of clothing may mean to a psychoanalyst . . . it seems not unlikely that Ndembu intend to symbolize the termination for both mother and daughter of an important aspect of their relationship. This is one of the symbolic actions—one of very few—about which I found it impossible to elicit any interpretation in the puberty ritual. Hence it is legitimate to infer, in my opinion, that powerful unconscious wishes, of a kind considered illicit by Ndembus, are expressed in it. (1967, 24)

Where native associations run out, outsider's views may carry special weight.

Even a brief acquaintance with depth psychology is enough to show the investigator that ritual symbols, with regard to their outward form, to their behavioral context, and to several of the indigenous interpretations set upon them, are partially shaped under the influence of unconscious motivations and ideas. The interchange of clothes between mother and daughter at the Nkang'a ritual; the belief that a novice would go mad if she saw the milk tree on the day of her separation ritual; the belief that if a novice lifts up the blanket with which she is covered during seclusion and sees her village her mother would die; all these are items of symbolic behavior for which the Ndembu themselves can give no satisfactory interpretation. For these beliefs suggest an element of mutual hostility in the mother-daughter relationship which runs counter to orthodox interpretations of the milk tree symbolism, in so far as it refers to the mother-daughter relationship. (1967, 33)

Sometimes one doesn't need to set aside a native account as rationalization or distortion in order to make room for a psychoanalytic account; sometimes there is no native account. Like the typical neurotic, the native may be bewildered by features of his or her own behavior. Here there may be a felt need for the meanings that psychoanalysis can supply—although, of course, the native, unlike the individual neurotic, may be able to accept the behavior required of him as a piece of social custom, accepting it as he does much else in his society that is unintelligible to him, even regarding it as normal and not raising questions of intelligibility. Turner is clearly right that one of the points where there is room for a psychoanalytic account in anthropology is where native associations run out before a bit of ritual has been made intelligible even by native standards. (One is reminded of Freud's admonition, in The Interpretation of Dreams, that one move to symbolic interpretations of dreams only after individual associations have failed.) The anthropologist, the outsider, may be able to see more, not just because he is more aware of the total social structure and is thus more readily able to offer "ideological" or social structural interpretations, but because he does not have the same motives for denying certain feelings and is thus more readily able to offer interpretations in terms of unconscious emotions.

The place this particular point gives to psychoanalytic approaches is rather limited; psychoanalysis is invited in to fill an explanatory void. Turner does not, however, insist that when the native does have something to say, the anthropologist has to take his word as final. After all, the anthropologist has a wider view than the lay native participant, or even the native ritual expert, whose "vision is circumscribed by his occupancy of a particular position, or even of a set of situationally conflicting positions, both in the persisting structure of his society, and also in the role structure of the given ritual" (1967, 27). And native perceptions may be limited in other ways, whereas the anthropologist who has previously made a structural analysis of Ndembu society, isolating its organizational principles, and distinguishing its groups and relationships, has no particular bias and can observe the real interconnections and conflicts between groups and persons, in so far as these receive ritual representation. What is meaningless for an actor playing a specific role may well be highly significant for an observer and analyst of the total system. (1967, 27)

Here greater objectivity amounts to taking a wider context into account, enabling the anthropologist to give ideological or social structural interpretations of ritual symbols that are less open to natives. It is not necessary to suppose that these interpretations have been repressed or would be resisted if made. Wider context need not be limited to social structure, and interpretations based on wider context need not be "ideological" as opposed to "sensory" or emotional (1967, 28). As an example Turner shows how looking at the use of a particular ritual symbol in the wider context of other rituals may reveal multiple meanings within the ritual being examined. So the red of the mukula tree in the *Nkula* ritual is ordinarily said to represent menstrual blood and the blood that accompanies the birth of a child, but Turner goes on to claim, "Although informants, when discussing this *Nkula* ritual specifically, tend to stress the positive, feminine aspects of parturition and reproduction, other meanings of the red symbols, stated explicitly in other ritual contexts, can be shown to make their influence felt in *Nkula*" (1967, 41). Turner goes on to argue persuasively that other meanings and their associated norms, while suppressed or submerged in *Nkula*, are indeed present—meanings connected with the blood of animals, the blood of homicide, the blood of circumcised boys, and the blood of witches' victims. While this goes beyond the explicit native interpretation of the particular ritual, it remains limited in that Turner remains within the society's own terms. Turner has us look to other rituals in their system to see the meaning of a single object, but Freud would have us look beyond the particular society to our own neurotics and children, to the universal. Is the move permissible?

Certainly Freud and other analysts bring out many persuasive parallels. But how much similarity is necessary before further parallels can be persuasive and before causal claims can be sustained? I think the answer must depend on the analysis of particular cases. The psychoanalytic system goes beyond the context of native ritual systems in ways that, sometimes at least, can illuminate that system and its particular symbolic elements. There is room for a psychoanalytic account wherever a native account is missing, but also wherever there is a native account that seems unbelievable or, although believable, seems to call for additional motives for belief. These possibilities cannot be denied in advance. We may feel the need to get behind the demons.

Turner thinks native accounts can never be dismissed as though they were the rationalizations of neurotics precisely because neurosis is individual and ritual social. He rightly points out that "those interpretations that show how a dominant symbol expresses important components of the social and moral order are by no means equivalent to the 'rationalizations,' and the 'secondary elaborations' of material deriving from endopsychic conflicts. They refer to social facts that have an empirical reality exterior to the psyches of individuals" (1967, 36). It must also be admitted that not all rituals are formal and rigid (like a compulsive neurotic's actions) and that psychoanalytic interpretations can conflict among themselves (1967, 34–35). But then, on the other hand, it must be wondered whether demons are also "social facts," and it must be said that explaining a rationalization is not necessarily the same as *dismissing* it. (The obsessive repeatedly cleaning his allegedly "dirty" hands, like the theologian talking of the "guilt" of original sin or the native talking of "demons," tells a truth, an incomplete and distorted truth.) And, more important, while the individual is different from the social, the social does not come from nowhere, and even social conflict needs to receive endopsychic representation before it can be given ritual expression. The separation Turner seeks to make between individual and social symbols, and the corresponding division of labor between anthropologist and psychoanalyst, seems to me too abrupt:

> In distinguishing between ritual symbols and individual psychic symbols, we may perhaps say that while ritual symbols are gross means of handling social and natural reality, psychic symbols are dominantly fashioned under the influence of inner drives. In analyzing the former, attention must mainly be paid to relations between data external to the psyche; in analyzing the latter, to endopsychic data. (1967, 37)[7]

Again, one wonders, are demons "external to the psyche"? And who is to judge (must one accept the native view as authoritative)?

In *Totem and Taboo* (1912–13), even while looking to the behavior of neurotics for parallels to illuminate social phenomena, Freud recognized the difference between individual and social and directly faced the questions it raises:

> In our analytical examination of the problems of taboo we have hitherto allowed ourselves to be led by the points of agreement that we have been able to show between it and obsessional neurosis. But after all taboo is not a neurosis but a social institution. We are therefore faced with the task of explaining what difference there is in principle between a neurosis and a cultural creation such as taboo. (13: 71).

In his subsequent discussion, Freud explored a number of differences, but the significant point remained that the individual and society may, in their different ways, be responding to the same underlying conflicts. As he put it elsewhere, his studies made it evident that individual forms of the neuroses showed a marked correspondence with the most highly valued products of our civilisation. The hysteric is undoubtedly a poet, though he represents his phantasies essentially by mimicry, without considering whether other people understand them or not. The ceremonials and prohibitions of obsessional patients force us to conclude that they have created a private religion for themselves; and even the delusions of the paranoiac show an unwelcome external similarity and inner relationship to the systems of our philosophers. We cannot get away from the impression that patients are making, in an asocial manner, the same attempts at a solution of their conflicts and an appeasement of their urgent desires which, when carried out in a manner acceptable to a large number of persons, are called poetry, religion and philosophy. (Preface to Reik 1976 [1931], 9–10)

The social solutions offer a number of obvious advantages, including the possibility of obviating the need for an individual solution. Freud occasionally suggests "that devout believers are safeguarded in a high degree against the risk of certain neurotic illnesses; their acceptance of the universal neurosis spares them the task of constructing a personal one" (1927c, 21: 44).

The same underlying conflicts may be dealt with individually or socially, more or less successfully or unsuccessfully, though it may not be given to an individual to choose which approach will be adopted. Freud says that because of the "similarities and analogies one might venture to regard obsessional neurosis as a pathological counterpart of the formation of a religion, and to describe that neurosis as an individual religiosity and religion as a universal obsessional neurosis" (1907b, 9: 126–27). Freud's formulation, while in some ways equating the two, leaves the sacred and profane different. The preferred solution shifts with changed conditions, especially with changes in conditions affecting what is believable, and the shift corresponds with the difference between the primitive and the civilized (which includes "modern nervous illness"). The instinctual problems remain the same. Are the social solutions ever totally successful? Do they ever get away from their instinctual roots to achieve independent status? This is the problem of "sublimation."[8]

Reduction and Meaning

Does bringing in reference to underlying instinctual conflicts "reduce" rituals to them? It must be remembered that explanations of the relation between a problem and its attempted solution may be very various. Freud related certain character traits—orderliness, parsimony, and obstinacy— to anal erotism. He laid down "a formula for the way in which character in its final shape is formed out of the constituent instincts: the permanent character-traits are either unchanged prolongations of the original instincts, or sublimations of those instincts, or reaction-formations against them" (1908b, 9: 175). Each of these types of connection requires its own appropriate type of evidence. For example, to show that miserliness can be understood in terms of sublimation, one needs to show the psychological equivalence of money and feces so that the hoarding of money can be seen as involving a displacement of the instinctual object (and perhaps a deflection in aim as well). It is equation of the substance (as shown by evidence from mythology, literature, and ordinary language), along with similarities of activity (infantile hoarding, retaining feces as a source of gratification—excrement as the body's property), that allows one to see the persisting similarities that establish the connection between the adult character trait and the infantile erotic interest. Establishing cleanliness as the product of reaction-formation requires a different sort of evidence. Now, the character traits that Freud discusses are distinctive; they come together in a constellation and may be pathologically exaggerated or fail to respond to changes in external conditions. But all character traits, including "normal" character traits, exhibit a certain order—that is what makes them character traits. Just as ritual inevitably has features that go beyond what can be explained by external instrumental requirements, so the character a person has will not be explained by the fact that he must have some character—it is not even clear that he must. (Recall that not every way of dealing with what must be dealt with repeatedly is a ritual.) Even normal character will have a history traceable to instinctual roots. This fact does not detach normal characteristics from their responsiveness to the world nor does it obliterate their differences from the exaggerated and otherwise pathological characteristics that also have instinctual roots. When Freud exhibited the larger order unifying "normal" and "perverse" sexuality, he did not thereby show they were the same (though he did show that they were less different than most had supposed).

Rituals may all carry a surplus meaning, and that meaning may often have to do with the expression of emotions (taking *expression* as shorthand for a variety of possible relations, and taking emotions to include both conscious and unconscious emotions). The significance of a ritual, its value, will depend in part on what gets done; but since its meaning always goes beyond its instrumental function, it will also depend on what emotion gets expressed and how. There are other ways to kill a sheep than by ritual slaughter. The sacrifice of a sheep has point and significance beyond the fact that in the end a sheep is dead (and its flesh eaten or wasted). That a death has occurred may have overriding importance—this is obvious where the object of sacrifice is a human rather than a sheep. (Geertz [1977] reports on how an incident of suttee in Bali looks from different points of view. Despite his appealingly sensitive, liberal, conscientious agonizing over the tensions within and among alternative perspectives, I do not see how we can avoid taking our own point of view. Just as beliefs we judge false cannot nonetheless be accepted as "true for them," so actions that we believe wrong cannot nonetheless be accepted as "right for them"—they remain wrong, even if they make a horrible sense. Ethical relativism seems as much an evasion as epistemological relativism.)

But apart from the intended or acknowledged practical consequences of a ritual, the emotions expressed and the manner of expression may give the ritual significance. Where a ritual manages to give fitting outward expression to an inner state or to expose feelings to the light of day, it may enhance those feelings and enhance life. In this way projection in ritual, as in art, can be valuable. But where projection functions as denial, it is less valuable. So by separating aggressive activity from its actual motives, a sacrifice (of a sheep or a woman) may in fact serve as a denial of the aggression that it nonetheless expresses.[9] By seeking to get behind native self-understanding, behind the demons, psychoanalytic inquiry can reveal such mismatches of public or intended meanings and unconscious motivations, and so better enable us to understand the true significance of a ritual to those who engage in it and to us who look on it and are moved or baffled or both.

The Critique of Culture

Psychoanalysis is more than just a therapeutic enterprise: it aims at truth. Freud sometimes waffled on this point. At the end of the case of Little Hans, in his eagerness to defend psychoanalytic treatment against charges of "suggestion," he became like the man, described in *The Interpretation of Dreams* (1900), "who was charged by one of his neighbours with having given him back a borrowed kettle in a damaged condition. The defendant asserted first, that he had given it back undamaged; secondly, that the kettle had a hole in it when he borrowed it; and thirdly, that he had never borrowed a kettle from his neighbour at all" (4:120). Each excuse might stand on its own, but when they are offered together, each undermines the others.

In discussing Little Hans, Freud first claimed that the effects of suggestion could be distinguished from evidentially valuable avowals; he then admitted that suggestion raises problems but claimed that they do not matter: "For a psycho-analysis is not an impartial scientific investigation, but a therapeutic measure. Its essence is not to prove anything, but merely to alter something" (1909b, 10: 103–4). In the end, however, he came back to the view that "therapeutic success . . . is not our primary aim; we endeavour rather to enable the patient to obtain a conscious grasp of his unconscious wishes" (10: 120). I think this final stance is the one that must prevail if psychoanalysis is to be of "scientific" interest and not a magical mystery cure. It is the faith of psychoanalysis. (Even psychoanalysis has its demons. Explanation has to begin, and stop, somewhere.) The theory behind the therapy is that it is the truth that will make one free, belief in illusions, however comforting, is not enough. Whatever one thinks of that claim (Neu 1977, part 3), certainly the theory behind psychoanalytic cultural explanations must aim at truth—for it is not clear that anything corresponding to therapeutic efficacy can be substituted for truth when explaining the normal (that is, the culture to which therapy supposedly helps individuals adapt). But then we have seen that there are problems in how there is room for anything like a psychoanalytic explanation of the normal, for the normal might appear to explain itself. We have also seen that an understanding of the normal necessarily (if one is to achieve explanatory understanding rather than mere redescription) takes one outside it, to other levels and wider contexts, so that the psychoanalytic understanding of cultures is also part of the critique of culture, a higher therapy.

15

LIFE-LIES AND PIPE DREAMS

Self-Deception in Ibsen's The Wild Duck *and*
O'Neill's The Iceman Cometh

Philosophers have a bias in favor of the truth; and we are not alone. That honesty is the best policy is supposed to be a truism. Certainly in our time sincerity and authenticity have assumed a place of unusual importance in the conduct of people's lives, the search for and the expression of the "true" self having become the central preoccupation of many: whether adolescents in quest of identity, or psychologists urging we heed the insights of schizophrenics, or philosophers contemplating the meaning of life and the possibilities for freedom. Amidst such assumptions, Ibsen and O'Neill provide disturbing arguments suggesting that self-deception may not always be bad, and that those who seek to undeceive others may not always be doing good. That these arguments take the form of plays is itself revealing: the position of the audience in a play provides an additional perspective on the lives portrayed, making for a contrast between what the audience knows and what the characters know, and it is perhaps only the fullness of characterization and of dramatization of circumstances that literature allows that can bring out the costs and benefits of knowledge and self-knowledge. The usual stark, isolated examples (often set on desert islands) of moral philosophers may leave out just those things which make a difference.

Ibsen's *The Wild Duck* (1978 [1884]) and O'Neill's *The Iceman Cometh* (1957 [1946]) make an argument worth attending to: the connections among truth and freedom and happiness may be more tenuous than we would like to think. Knowing the truth may ordinarily be adaptive, but it may not always or necessarily be so. Self-deception may not always be bad. It may sometimes be the best we can manage—however paradoxical and problematic the notion that it is an option we can choose. This is not to say that the unexamined or self-deceived life is more worth living than other types of life (or that it is more happy or free). Indeed, I would want to argue that the examined life should command allegiance despite what should be recognized as its limitations; what I want to focus on here, however, are some of the limitations. It all turns on particular cases.

Hjalmar's Deceptions

In *The Wild Duck* we enter into the world of Hjalmar Ekdal, an impecunious and somewhat pretentious photographer, and his family: his wife, Gina, his daughter, Hedvig, and his father, Old Lieutenant Ekdal. When we first meet him, he is in the company of Gregers Werle, an old friend who, on his return after a number of years' absence, makes it his business to undeceive Hjalmar about the circumstances of his life and confront him with a "Summons to the Ideal," especially the ideal of a "true marriage." In the course of the play it becomes clear that while Hjalmar is mistaken about many things, and that others have in different ways contributed to his condition, his most persistent and pervasive errors involve self-deception. It also becomes clear that in seeking to undeceive him, Gregers does no one any good, least of all Hjalmar, and indeed may himself be mistaken both about the truth and his own motives.

Right at the beginning of the play, we see Hjalmar take deceitful steps to protect his self-image. First we see him denying his father, pretending not to see him, when the broken old man walks through a dinner party at the elder Werle's (402–3). We next see him at home, misrepresenting his role at the party to his family, pretending to have been a commanding authority in conversation on vintages of Tokay and other matters, when in fact he had been a rather ignorant and reluctant discussant. But in these two cases he is attempting to deceive others. Of his more interesting deceptions he is not himself aware; they are self-deceptions, and they involve central features of his identity.

He tells Gregers at one point: "My lot is a poor one—but, you know, I'm an inventor. And I'm the family breadwinner, too. *That's* what sustains me through all the pettiness" (444). Hjalmar insists early (418) and often that he is the family breadwinner and an inventor. In fact, he is neither. That he is not really the family breadwinner is made manifest to the audience (at least) when, despite protests to the contrary, he takes any excuse to avoid work (419, 432) and it becomes clear that his wife and daughter in fact do the photography and retouching work that supports them all (434, 439, 441). Hjalmar should certainly know better, and he has even less excuse for thinking himself the family breadwinner once his wife, Gina, admits to him that his father, Old Ekdal, earns enough to cover his keep (456). Nonetheless, despite the revelation, Hjalmar persists in referring to himself as the family breadwinner (458, 464). It is worth noting that, here as elsewhere, others have colluded in Hjalmar's self-deception. When Gina admits under questioning that Old Ekdal earns "roughly what he costs us, with a little pocket money thrown in," Hjalmar complains: "What he costs us! That's something you've never told me before!" She responds: "No, I never could. You were always so happy thinking he got everything from you" (456). This gives the motive for the self-deception as well as for the collusion. As we shall see again, sometimes the having of a belief, rather than its truth, is what is essential to one's contentment. The main difficulty, of course, is that while the support of others may help sustain one in a false belief, the belief is always liable to be undermined either by counterevidence or by the withdrawal of support.

Hjalmar is also self-deceived in thinking himself an inventor. Indeed, it is his central "life-lie." Life-lies are what his friend, Dr. Relling, takes to be "the animating principle of life" (475), equating them with "ideals" (476). But they seem ideals with a difference. The life-lies the good doctor prescribes don't require much effort; the satisfaction they achieve through fantasy seems adequate—they seem designed for the weak, those defeated by reality. So Molvik, the drunken failed divinity student, is encouraged to think of himself as "demonic," because otherwise "the poor innocent mutt would have given in years ago to self-contempt and despair" (476). And Old Ekdal stalks rabbits in his dark loft as a satisfying substitute for the forest bear-hunting of his youth (477). According to Dr. Relling, "Deprive the average man of his life-lie and you've robbed him of happiness as well" (477). We shall explore the concept of a life-lie and its connection with happiness further when we come to consider O'Neill's *The Iceman Cometh*, where the concept of a pipe dream stands in its place. For the moment there seems in Dr. Relling's account an, in some ways cynical, in some ways soft, equation of life-lies, ideals, and delusions.

It turns out that the notion that Hjalmar might invent something useful in photography was originally Dr. Relling's idea (484), but Hjalmar has made it his own. The project is dubiously vague from the time we first hear about it (441), and it seems to involve a lot of naps (443). The invention is invoked by Hjalmar as the means to achieve his "mission in life" (430). Initially, that is described as "restoring the Ekdal name to dignity and honor" for the sake of his father (442). (The Old Lieutenant had been broken and disgraced by a criminal conviction involving business dealings with the elder Werle.) But the invention comes to bear the burden of multiple purposes (and so there are multiple motives for Hjalmar's belief in it): Hjalmar says his "one reward" is to be that they will let his father wear his uniform again (443), later he says "the poor inventor's sole reward" will be to secure his daughter's (Hedvig's) future (447), later still it is his wife's future it is meant to secure (458), and finally, when Gregers has persuaded Hjalmar that the elder Werle's generosity to his family is tainted, "the entire proceeds will be devoted to" paying his debt to the elder Werle (464). That the project is unreal, that Hjalmar has taken no steps toward its completion, is conclusively revealed to the audience when Hjalmar comes back for his books in the final act of the play and Gina asks, "Could I get Hedvig to cut the pages for you?" (479). Hjalmar's books, the technical journals he was supposed to be using for his invention, had obviously not yet been opened. Even Hjalmar finally (in effect) admits the sham in discussion with Gregers:

GREGERS: And don't forget you have your invention to live for, too.

HJALMAR: Oh, don't talk about the invention. That seems such a long way off.

GREGERS: Oh?

HJALMAR: Good Lord, yes. What would you really have me invent? Other people have invented so much already. It gets more difficult every day— (484)

Hjalmar then spells out another reason for his belief in the life-lie Relling had provided him: "I was so blissfully happy as a result. Not so much from the invention itself, but because Hedvig believed in it—believed in it with all the power and force of a child's mind" (484).

So Hjalmar has deceived others and he has deceived himself. It is true that others have contributed to his self-deception (e.g., Gina and Relling) and also that others have deceived him directly (most importantly, Gina has concealed her earlier affair with the elder Werle, and the elder Werle's possible parentage of Hedvig). The motive for deception and self-deception has typically included Hjalmar's happiness. But then, have the various deceptions achieved their goal? Could they? Is there at least one thing about which Hjalmar is not deceived, namely, the felt current happiness of his home? Answering this connects with interesting questions about the possibilities and limits of self-deception.

Happiness

Can a person be mistaken about his own happiness? Could a person believe himself happy and be wrong? Are feeling happy and being happy equivalent? Hjalmar believes himself happy, indeed, as a married man, "absolutely" happy (398). He declares, "I'm as well off as any man could wish to be" (444). But he comes to believe that he was mistaken: "I also thought this home was a good place to be. That was a pipe dream" (458). Should Hjalmar have given in so easily? Was he mistaken? *Could* he have been?

Some psychological states are arguably transparent in the way Descartes takes all psychological states to be: thinking you are in the state is both necessary and sufficient for actually being in it. If you think you are in pain, it follows that you are. If you don't feel any pain, you are not (it would seem) having any. Other states are more opaque; feeling x and being x are not so closely tied. One may not feel jealous, and yet nonetheless be jealous. Other people may be the first to know, and looking back on your own behavior, thoughts, and inclinations, you may come to admit that the fact that you were not aware of your jealousy did not mean you were not jealous. On the other hand, one may mistakenly admit to feelings that one does not in fact have. This happens when one mistakes one feeling for another (so you think you feel mere regret when it is in fact jealousy) or when the object is displaced (you think you are angry at your lover, when you are in fact angry at someone else, e.g., a parent or employer). It is in fact arguable that being in a state and feeling (or believing) that one is in that state are never as close together as Cartesians would have it, that even for sensations such as pain more errors are possible than is at first apparent. Descartes himself recognized the existence of phantom pains ascribed to amputated limbs, and offered a physiological account of the phenomenon (*Meditation* 6, 1984 [1641]). But while one must admit such experiences, one could insist that an error about the source of a pain (a causal hypothesis) does not amount to an error about pain—you feel what you feel even if you are mistaken about the source of the feeling. Perhaps this is the element of truth in the transparency thesis, though one must wonder whether the characterization of what one feels is properly so independent of one's beliefs about its sources or objects. (The description of a sensation as a "toothache" has a causal hypothesis built in; and whether one's state of mind is regret rather than remorse, or embarrassment rather than shame, depends more on beliefs about the situation to which it is a response than on fine differences in sensation; and it is difficult to imagine how one could be enjoying or angry without one's state having an object specified by one's beliefs about its cause.) In any case, the tie between feeling x and being x is even more questionable when looked at from the other direction, when a person denies a feeling he or she nonetheless has. Using "feeling" broadly, to cover emotions in general, it is certainly true that one can have a feeling (such as jealousy) one is not aware of having. Being in a psychological state does not necessarily depend on believing you are in it. And this may be true for feelings even in the narrow sense of bodily sensations. Unfelt feelings may not be as paradoxical as they sound. For sensations such as pain play relatively complex roles in our lives, and they are tied to various bodily states and dispositions to behavior as well as to bare feelings. What happens to the pain in a cut finger when we turn our attention away from it; must we say it goes out of existence? It is still there when we turn our attention back—or must we say *it* is no longer there, it is a *new* pain (we don't say that for chairs and tables, we don't think they cease to exist while they are not being attended to). A person in battle is wounded, during the fight feels nothing, but collapses in pain as soon as the immediate danger is past. Or less dramatically, a person sitting on a chair may not be aware of any sensations of contact on his rear end (he is too busy reading, or writing, or watching television) but if he turns his attention appropriately sensations of pressure are present. In these situations, signals are doubtless being sent along nerves even when we ultimately do not receive them. It is not obviously or necessarily nonsense to take sensation words to refer to the signals, or the bodily state, as well as the experienced feeling. (Is a warning a warning only if and when it is received?) Whether or not un-felt feelings arguably make sense, let us for the sake of argument grant the existence of the Cartesian end of the spectrum and suppose that pain is lo-cated there. The question I wish to pursue is whether happiness is, with re-spect to self-knowledge, more like a sensation (such as pain) or more like an emotion (such as jealousy and love)? Can one believe oneself happy and be mistaken?

Is happiness more like a sensation, and so transparent, or an emotion, and so sometimes at least potentially opaque? Certainly there are pleasant sensations. And some have assimilated the whole of happiness to pleasant sensations. Thus Bentham held that "quantity of pleasure being equal, push-pin is as good as poetry" (quoted in Mill 1961 [1838], 50). The source of the pleasant sensations is supposed to be irrelevant to the pleasure in them. But it would be a mistake to regard pleasure, which characterizes both activities and sensations, as though it were itself a separable sensa-tion. That might suggest that the pleasure of an activity could be detached from the activity and enjoyed in its absence. And that is not so. Sensations are, theoretically at least, detachable from their sources. The pleasure of an activity is not. The painful sensation normally induced by a pinprick might be induced by appropriate neurological stimulation or by a drug. And pleasant tingles and tickles might be similarly induced. But the pleasure of an activity is not separable from the activity. The pleasure of reading po-etry (or playing push-pin) cannot be obtained apart from the activity. Of course one might induce whatever pleasant sensations *accompany* an ac-tivity, and one might even enjoy those sensations, but that is not the same as the enjoyment of the activity. The enjoyment is inseparable from the ac-tivity. This is because the pleasure is thought-dependent. That is, the object of one's enjoyment or pleasure is specified in terms of its believed cause. Thus, in order for the pleasure of reading poetry to be produced by a pill, the pill would also have to produce the belief that whatever feelings one was having were induced by reading poetry. *What* one is enjoying depends, in part at least, on what one believes one is enjoying. Sensations, on the other hand, are characteristically independent of our beliefs about their causes (hence the phantom pains in severed limbs discussed by Descartes remain real pains).

Aristotle provides a much more plausible picture of pleasure (and hap-piness) than Bentham. He says that the pleasure of an activity supervenes on the activity like the bloom of youth. This suggests, rightly I think, that the pleasure of an activity is not like a separable sensation; the connection with the activity is more intimate. Modern writers (e.g., Ryle 1949 and 1954 and Williams 1959) have treated it as a form of attention. This ap-proach helps us understand certain special features of pleasure and en-joyment: why the enjoyment of an activity must cease with the activity (sensations can of course outlive their sources), why if one's attention is drawn from an activity one cannot be said to be enjoying *it*, and why in general one cannot have the pleasure of an activity without the activity (Neu 1977, 20–24). More broadly, Aristotle tells us that happiness is unimpeded rational "activity in accordance with virtue" (1098a). Without exploring this famous phrase further, we can note that it places an appropriate emphasis on activity. Anyone reading Aldous Huxley's *Brave New World*, with its soma-eating inhabitants, senses that something is wrong, something is missing. If Bentham were right, there would be no reason why a drug couldn't produce as much happiness as it is possible for humans to know. But while a drug such as soma might produce pleasant sensations in endless abundance, it should be clear that is not the same as producing human happiness. The inhabitants of Huxley's *Brave New World*, with their vacant grins, are more like contented cows than happy humans. A distinction between happiness and contentment is worth making.

When Mill insisted, against Bentham's doctrine, that it is better to be Socrates dissatisfied than a pig satisfied, he was making a point not fully captured by contrasting quantity and quality of pleasure, or higher and lower pleasures. Understanding the difference between needs and desires is the first step to a fuller appreciation of the point. Needs, particularly biological needs, are objective and given. What you need is in general independent of what you think you need. What an organism needs is revealed when one sees what is necessary for the organism to function. Failure to function is the surest sign of a need. The object of a need is whatever will in fact satisfy it. Of course people have different theories about what will satisfy their needs. The object of a desire is typically what a person believes will satisfy a need. Desires are thought-dependent, and in that sense subjective. It follows that one might get what one desires without getting what one needs. One can be mistaken about one's needs. Similarly, one might get what one needs without getting what one desires. In addition to the possibility of mistake, one's desires may go beyond one's basic needs. This contrast between needs and desires stands behind a useful distinction between contentment and happiness. I think it makes sense to understand contentment in terms of the satisfaction of acknowledged needs (i.e., conscious desires): if you get what you want, you are content.[1] But I have said that the satisfaction of desires may leave an organism malfunctioning, may leave needs unmet, and may leave other desires unacknowledged. So there is room for something more than mere contentment, and there is point to calling that something more "happiness." The person who gets what he wants (and so is content), may still be unhappy. Complete happiness may require, in addition to the satisfaction of acknowledged needs, the satisfaction of unacknowledged but nonetheless real needs, and also of desires that go beyond objectively given needs. And there may be a minimum. Perhaps a person cannot be happy if his or her basic needs are unmet and—a point we shall return to in a moment—there is room for argument about what the basic needs of human beings are, so a person might think he or she was happy when in fact some basic human need was going unmet. It is possible to mistake mere contentment for happiness. But the thought-dependence of desire introduces more than just the criticizability of desire (on the basis of the possibility of mistake about the objects of need); it makes possible the broadening of the range of objects of desire. Desires are not confined and bound to biological needs. Desires can be cultivated and educated as well as criticized. New dimensions of desirability become open. This is what lies behind Socrates's advantage over Mill's pig.

We are now in a better position to see what is wrong with the world in Huxley's *Brave New World*. If one fails to distinguish happiness and contentment, one might think one could produce happiness by satisfying acknowledged desires. And there are two ways of ensuring that no acknowledged desire remains unsatisfied: either by providing its object or by eliminating any desire for which the object cannot be provided. That is, if contentment depends only on getting what one wants, one can be made content if one can be made to want less. In which case pleasant sensations and soma might ultimately prove to be enough. What is wrong with *Brave New World*, among other things, is that in their passive contentment, the people want too little. The problem is much the same as with the slave who loves his chains. It is a form of happiness that depends on the truncation of human desire, the denial of possibilities for fulfillment. The denial remains real even when the objects missed are forgotten, when the loss ceases to be felt.

Hjalmar's Happiness

Such criticism ultimately requires a theory of real needs and desires, a theory of human nature. Such a theory would not be required if happiness were simply a matter of collecting pleasant sensations. But it is not. If we think of happiness in Aristotelian terms as involving unimpeded activity, then it can be understood as satisfaction of desires—suitably modified: the satisfaction of one's subjective desires of the moment should be described in terms of mere contentment, while happiness requires satisfaction of one's corrected or true desires. And specification of those requires a theory of human nature.

To make a persuasive case for saying someone is not happy even though they think they are, you need, in effect, a theory of human nature. There must be some gap between the desires they acknowledge, which are in fact satisfied, and their real needs. Something is missing of which they are not aware. This leaves room for a number of different types of error. The slave who loves his chains, who gets what he wants but does not want enough, makes one kind of error. He tends to mistake his contentedness for happiness. The person who pursues the objects of manufactured desires makes another type of error. He falsely believes he needs something he does not have, and so mistakenly thinks himself deprived and so unhappy. Marxists who attempt theories of false consciousness try to provide the sort of theory required in this area.

What of Hjalmar? I've tried to argue that he could think himself happy and be mistaken. Is he? He declares, "I'm as well off as any man could wish to be" (444). Gregers responds, "And your thinking so is part of the sickness" (444). Is Gregers right? Hjalmar comes to think so (458). I've said that if you wish to argue that someone who says he feels happy is not in fact happy, you need a theory of what is missing (and of why it is not missed), of the gap between fulfillment of acknowledged desires and happiness. What does Gregers think is missing? It is a fact that Hjalmar's wife, Gina, had an affair with Gregers's father, the elder Werle, before marrying Hjalmar. (Though Gregers mistakenly thinks the affair started before the death of his mother [456].) And it is also a fact that the elder Werle may have had multiple motives for bringing Gina and Hjalmar together, for helping them get set up in the photography business, and for the other things he did to help the family. (He may have made Gina pregnant, and he may have shifted the responsibility for certain illegal business dealings onto Old Ekdal, who was convicted and sent to jail.) Hjalmar is not aware of these facts, and Gregers concludes he is therefore "plunged in deception— living under the same roof with that creature, not knowing that what he calls his home is built on a lie" (409). And Gregers makes it his mission to undeceive Hjalmar, to lay the foundation of a "true marriage." But is the whole truth necessary to happiness? To a "true marriage"?

Gregers is surprised when his revelations don't produce happiness: "I was really positive that when I came through that door I'd be met by a transfigured light in both your faces. And what do I see instead but this gloomy, heavy, dismal—" (459). Of course, his notion of the highest happiness is rather eccentric: "there's nothing in the world that compares with showing mercy to a sinner and lifting her up in the arms of love" (459). But apart from that, Gina is clearly right in thinking that if she had told the whole truth at the beginning there would have been *no* marriage, let alone a "true marriage"; Hjalmar admits as much (457). Moreover, the pressing problem with happiness built on a lie is not that it is illusory, but that it is precarious. It is liable to collapse with the revelation of the deceit. But then it is not clear that undeceivers such as Gregers are doing anyone a favor: they would seem to be realizing the danger rather than obviating it. Gregers's attempts to provide a new foundation precipitate a collapse instead of preventing one. Even Hjalmar begins to suspect Gregers's ideals when he learns that Gregers's father and Mrs. Sorby have told each other the worst about themselves in preparation for what, by Gregers's definition, must be a true marriage. Hjalmar says to Gregers:

Your father and Mrs. Sorby are entering a marriage based on complete trust, one that's wholehearted and open on both sides. They haven't bottled up any secrets from each other; there isn't any reticence between them; they've declared—if you'll permit me—a mutual forgiveness of sins. (465)

Gregers refuses to admit that his hated father is achieving the good he has tried, and failed, to give his friend. That the truth in these circumstances contributes nothing to Hjalmar's happiness is made most clear by the further revelation that Hedvig may not be his daughter (467). (Gregers's one moment of considerate restraint comes when he tries to keep Mrs. Sorby from letting Hjalmar know that the elder Werle, like Hedvig, is going blind [463].) When he connects Hedvig's and Werle's eye problems and the deed of gift to her, the distraught Hjalmar in effect disowns her (469), and comes to doubt her love for him (485)—ultimately leading her to suicide in an effort to prove her love through sacrifice. Before that unhappy end, as difficulty at home mounts and Hjalmar seems to spurn her, Hedvig readily (with a child's confused insight) combines her father's actual worries with her own foundling fantasy: "I bet I know what it is. Perhaps I'm really not Daddy's child . . . Mother could have found me. And now maybe Daddy's found out. I've read about these things" (470). But her insight is in ways keener than her father's, she sees Hjalmar need not turn away: "Yes, I think he could love me even so. Or maybe more. The wild duck was sent us as a present too, and I'm terribly fond of it, all the same" (470). A biological connection is not necessary to love. Their mutual love was real whether or not Hedvig was Hjalmar's biological daughter. The truth (in this case a doubt about paternity) does not help. It does not make anyone either happier or more secure in happiness.[2]

So what was Gregers doing? We've seen what he thought he was doing. He thought of himself as having a mission of redemption, as presenting to people a "Summons to the Ideal" (446, 448, 476). At one point he compares himself to his father's clever dog, the dog that had fetched back the wounded wild duck: "If I could choose, above all else I'd like to be a clever dog . . . A really fantastic, clever dog, the kind that goes to the bottom after wild ducks when they dive under and bite fast into the weeds down in the mire" (428). Of course the wild duck, the chief object of rescue, is supposed to be Hjalmar.[3] His mission is "to open Hjalmar Ekdal's eyes" (449). But the efforts at rescue fail.

Dr. Relling sees that Gregers, with his "Summons to the Ideal," is a quack (459, 476). Gregers is in no position to help others. Relling provides a partial diagnosis (we should be aware that in seeking to open Gregers's eyes, Relling does not allow him the life-lie he suggests all may need):

you're a sick man, you are. You know that . . . Your case has complications. First there's this virulent moralistic fever; and then something worse—you keep going off in deliriums of hero worship; you always have to have something to admire that's outside of yourself. (476)

We must add to these problems a self-hatred that is revealed in Gregers's immediate response ("Yes, I certainly have to look for it outside myself" [476]), and earlier in his comments on his own name ("But when one carries the cross of a name like Gregers—'Gregers'—and then 'Werle' coming after—have you ever heard anything so disgusting? . . . Ugh! Phew! I feel I'd like to spit on any man with a name like that" [428]). And there is another problem that Gregers himself recognizes. He suffers from a relentless conscience. He complains to his father:

> You've spoiled my entire life. I'm not thinking of all that with Mother. But you're the one I can thank for my going around, whipped and driven by this guilt-ridden conscience . . . I should have taken a stand against you when the trap was laid for Lieutenant Ekdal. I should have warned him, for I had a pretty good idea what was coming off . . . The harm done to Old Ekdal, both by me and—others, can never be undone; but Hjalmar I can free from all the lies and evasions that are smothering him here . . . if I'm ever to go on living, I'll have to find a cure for my sick conscience. (449–50)

This might seem more than enough to explain Gregers's well-meaning actions. (He insists all along, both before to his father [449], and later to Gina after the tragedy has begun to unfold [470], that he meant for the best.) But his motives are in fact not all open to him and not all of his actions are well meant. Despite his denials of feeling about his father remarrying (408, 462), it is clear that Gregers acts as his mother's avenger for earlier infidelities. Gina was believed by her to be the last of her rivals before her death (406, 409). The situation was in fact more complex—as Gina spells out (456) and as Mrs. Sorby, the woman about to marry the elder Werle, understands (463). But Gregers sees the world through his mother's eyes, and won't have the matter discussed: "If you women are going to explore this subject, I'd better leave" (463). The identification with his mother is overwhelming. His father hears her voice in Gregers's reproaches (409). Gregers describes himself as looking like his mother (420). His grief at her death was profound (442). Even his moralistic fever can be traced to his mother. His father says, "Your conscience has been sickly from childhood. It's an inheritance from your mother, Gregers—the only inheritance she left you" (450). And Gina connects his behavior with his mother: "His mother, off and on, had those same conniption fits" (451). Gregers freely admits to hating his father (409, 449), and his feelings toward Gina are little warmer (409). He has taken on his mother's role of delivering sermons. While apparently trying to help Hjalmar, he can also be seen as acting as his mother's avenger: taking revenge on both his father and on Gina. Gregers, intent on opening Hjalmar's eyes, is blind to his own motives. He is self-deceived. (He is also doubtless a self-parody by Ibsen of his own attitude in his earlier didactic plays, presenting "Summonses to the Ideal.")

Gregers, the officious intermeddler, is repeatedly wrong about Hjalmar.

Moreover, he is arguably wrong about himself, in particular about his own motives in attempting to undeceive Hjalmar. It should be the first duty of people who wish to correct the understanding of others that they get the facts right. And it is an important step toward that end that they examine their own interests in a situation, that they make themselves sensitive to the possibilities of self-deception in themselves. (Training analysis and examination of countertransference are central aspects of the psychoanalyst's art.) That Gregers gets the facts about Hjalmar wrong is clear. Where he can see only a "poisonous swamp" (444), there is in fact a reasonably contented marriage. Gina's earlier relation with the elder Werle is irrelevant to the current state of Hjalmar's marriage with her (moreover, Gregers is wrong in thinking the affair was going on while his mother was still alive). When Hjalmar is persuaded (wrongly) to think of the contentment of his home as a delusion, he goes on thinking of himself as an inventor (458). That is a true delusion. Of Hjalmar's real self-deceptions, however, Gregers has little inkling. He misjudges Hjalmar's strength for reasons of his own. (Relling's diagnosis of a need for a hero to worship connects with Gregers's further need to salve his conscience—for to do that he must deny that Hjalmar is too weak to benefit from or thank him for his revelations.) He is also wrong about himself in another important way. No sooner does he tell Gina when renting a room from her, "I won't be any trouble to you; I do everything for myself" (429), than he proves himself wrong. Gina reports: "He wanted to do everything himself, he said. So he starts building a fire in the stove, and the next thing he's closed down the damper so the whole room is full of smoke. Phew! What a stink, enough to . . . But that's not the best part! So then he wants to put it out, so he empties his whole water pitcher into the stove and now the floor's swimming in the worst muck" (431). Others must clean up after him. He (like Hjalmar, the self-conceived breadwinner) is not as independent as he thinks. (Hjalmar in fact starts using Gregers's language of independence [454], just as he had earlier picked up his talk of poisons and swamps.) And most tragic of all, he is wrong about what people need. His notion of happiness is forgiveness of sinners. His notion of love is sacrifice. He is caught in a fog of religious ideals. He fails to distinguish between *necessary* sacrifice (which can truly be a sign of love) and pointless destruction. He urges Hedvig to sacrifice the wild duck to prove her love (471, 478). Hjalmar had earlier (454) inveighed against the duck, but only because it was associated with the newly hateful elder Werle (he was the one who had shot the duck that ultimately came into the caring hands of the Ekdals). He did not really wish to be rid of it. Hedvig in the end shoots herself instead of the foundling duck with which she had identified (470), and Gregers, self-deceived to the end, thinks himself vindicated: "Hedvig did not die in vain. Did you notice how grief freed the greatness in him [Hjalmar]?" (489). Dr. Relling has the final word: "go to hell" (490).

I have wanted to suggest at least three things. First, that happiness is not to be equated with pleasant sensations and so there is room for error about one's own happiness. But second, that to show someone is not happy when they think they are, other people must present a theory that explains the error and shows what is missing. And third, that Gregers's theory about Hjalmar, and his view of what is missing ("a true marriage"), is mistaken: that Hjalmar is not self-deceived about his contentment (at least), but Gregers is self-deceived about his mission, tragically self-deceived.

On Ibsen's telling it is overwhelmingly clear that, if Hjalmar is self-deceived about being the breadwinner and an inventor, and if others (such as Dr. Relling) collude, it harms no one, indeed if certain others (such as Gina) deceive him about other matters, this too (in his case) does no harm. It is not always better to know the truth, the whole truth, and nothing but the truth.

Pipe Dreams and Pity

The Iceman Cometh opens in a kind of hell, Harry Hope's Saloon, a dead-end bar, whose denizens support each other in maintaining their delusions about their pasts and futures. There are many echoes of the themes of *The Wild Duck* (subsequently cited as *WD* with page nos.), even of its language. Hickey, the Gregers of the play, speaks of "poison" (81) as he goes about his mission of opening other people's eyes. Gregers and Hedvig had referred to the place the wild duck had been before and the loft where it was now as "the depths of the sea" (*WD* 438, 440). Larry, the Dr. Relling of *The Iceman Cometh*, at one point refers to Hope's bar as "The Bottom of the Sea Rathskeller" (25); Hickey speaks of sinking "down to the bottom of the sea" (86; cf. 123). Finally, Larry transmutes the phrase when he says: "All I know is I'm sick of life! I'm through! I've forgotten myself! I'm drowned and contented on the bottom of a bottle" (128). The bottom of the sea serves as a place of refuge for those who cannot face reality and truth. Bars are likely places for self-deception. With critical faculties dulled and comradely support available, the demands of truth (the "Summons of the Ideal") can seem less pressing.

The first words (almost) are had by Larry, who like Dr. Relling (in Mrs. Sorby's characterization) has "wasted the best that's in him" (*WD* 462), and believes that the truth is less essential to life and happiness than the hopes embodied in life-lies or pipe dreams. He is as explicit at the beginning of this play as the good doctor was at the end of the other. He says to Rocky, the (at that moment) cynical bartender:

> Don't mock the faith! Have you no respect for religion, you unregenerate Wop? What's it matter if the truth is that their favoring breeze has the stink of nickel whiskey on its breath, and their sea is a growler of lager and ale, and their ships are long since looted and scuttled and sunk on

the bottom? To hell with the truth! As the history of the world proves, the truth has no bearing on anything. It's irrelevant and immaterial, as the lawyers say. The lie of a pipe dream is what gives life to the whole misbegotten mad lot of us, drunk or sober. And that's enough philosophic wisdom to give you for one drink of rot-gut. (9–10)

The doctrine of the play is spelled out right at the beginning, and much of what follows can be read as an argument in support. The various self-deceptions of the characters are made manifest to the audience. Hickey, like Gregers having problems of his own, enters the scene and seeks to undeceive them—clearly doing no one any good.

Are Ibsen and O'Neill saying happiness depends on self-deception always and for everyone? Larry seems to say as much, and Dr. Relling seemed to say so too: "Most of the world is sick, I'm afraid . . . Deprive the average man of his life-lie and you've robbed him of happiness as well" (WD 476–77). But note that his claim is actually restricted to "the average man." And it is part of Gregers's error in dealing with Hjalmar that he takes him for something more.[4] Our sympathy for the self-deceived in The Iceman Cometh (and against meddling truth-tellers in general) may depend on our sharing their own low estimate of their true powers. Which means that the burdens on those who would help others by enlightening them are complex.

There is a contrast between Gregers and Hickey, a contrast that might make Hickey seem worse. Gregers, as we have seen, because of his need for hero-worship (and other needs) thinks Hjalmar stronger than he is (WD 475–76) and expects his interference to yield a "true marriage" and happiness. But Hickey knows the weakness of those he undeceives. What then was he expecting? Like Gregers (WD 459, 470), he professes to be disappointed in the results of his efforts at enlightenment. He says the results are unexpected; looking at a dejected Harry Hope (who has just complained, "Bejees, what did you do to the booze, Hickey? There's no damned life left in it" [206]).

> You're beginning to worry me, Governor. Something's holding you up somewhere. I don't see why—You've faced the truth about yourself. You've done what you had to do to kill your nagging pipe dreams. Oh, I know it knocks you cold. But only for a minute. Then you see it was the only possible way to peace. And you feel happy. Like I did. That's what worries me about you, Governor. It's time you began to feel happy—(207)

But here Hickey is self-deceived. Larry suggests why when he says of the momentarily absent Hickey: "He'll come back. He'll keep on talking. He's got to. He's lost his confidence that the peace he's sold us is the real McCoy, and it's made him uneasy about his own" (223). And Hickey returns and confirms the point:

> I've got to tell you! Your being the way you are now gets my goat! It's all wrong! It puts things in my mind—about myself. It makes me think, if I

got balled up about you, how do I know I wasn't balled up about myself? And that's plain damned foolishness. When you know the story of me and Evelyn, you'll see there wasn't any other possible way out of it, for her sake. (231)

And he goes on to tell of how he came to murder his wife, Evelyn, revealing in the end the hatred he tries to deny even to himself. The murder was not done for her sake. So Hickey, like Gregers, is ridden by guilt, and he has his own motives for going around uncovering unhappy truths about others' lives, motives that have nothing to do with helping them. That Hickey in fact knew better all along (and this is the real point of contrast with Gregers), that he knew the others were weak and that he was not really helping them by undeceiving them, comes out in the fact that he sees death and indifference under the dreams he punctures:

> I swear I'd never act like I have if I wasn't absolutely sure it will be worth it to you in the end, after you're rid of the damned guilt that makes you lie to yourselves you're something you're not, and the remorse that nags at you and makes you hide behind lousy pipe dreams about tomorrow. You'll be in a today where there is no yesterday or tomorrow to worry you. You won't give a damn what you are any more . . . you can all see that I don't give a damn about anything now. And I promise you, by the time this day is over, I'll have every one of you feeling the same way! (147–48)

And later, as things develop, he says:

> I'm just worried about you, when you play dead on me like this. I was hoping by the time I got back you'd be like you ought to be! . . . And you've all done what you needed to do! By rights you should be contented now, without a single damned hope or lying dream left to torment you! But here you are, acting like a lot of stiffs cheating the undertaker! . . . Don't you know you're free now to be yourselves, without having to feel remorse or guilt, or lie to yourselves about reforming tomorrow? Can't you see there is no tomorrow now? You're rid of it forever! You've killed it! You don't have to care a damn about anything any more! You've finally got the game of life licked, don't you see that? (225)

He thinks dreams are a torment. Desire nothing and you should be content. But Larry seems closer to the truth about dreams: "The lie of a pipe dream is what gives life to the whole misbegotten mad lot of us, drunk or sober" (10). Note again that he does not restrict his claim for pipe dreams, like Relling's claim for life-lies, to "the average man." But at least he seems right when he tells Parritt not to waste his pity on the defeated inhabitants of the bar:

> They wouldn't thank you for it. They manage to get drunk, by hook or crook, and keep their pipe dreams, and that's all they ask of life. I've

never known more contented men. It isn't often that men attain the true goal of their heart's desire. (36)

"Contented" of course seems the right word. But some may not be capable of much more. Even Hickey comes in the end, as he is being arrested, to share Larry's view about the importance of pipe dreams: "God, you're a dumb dick! Do you suppose I give a damn about life now? Why, you bonehead, I haven't got a single damned lying hope or pipe dream left!" (245).

What then is the right attitude to pipe dreams—our own and others'? If we take Larry's view and think of them as necessary, at least for the weak, that tends to lead (despite Larry's earlier words to Parritt) to supportive pity. When Hickey attacks Hugo, the old revolutionary, Larry (according to the stage directions) *"gives Hugo a pitying glance"* and says, "Leave Hugo be! He's earned his dream! Have you no decency or pity?" But Hickey argues that is the wrong kind of pity:

> Of course, I have pity. But now I've seen the light, it isn't my old kind of pity—the kind yours is. It isn't the kind that lets itself off easy by encouraging some poor guy to go on kidding himself with a lie—the kind that leaves the poor slob worse off because it makes him feel guiltier than ever—the kind that makes his lying hopes nag at him and reproach him until he's a rotten skunk in his own eyes. I know all about that kind of pity. I've had a bellyful of it in my time, and it's all wrong! . . . No, sir. The kind of pity I feel now is after final results that will really save the poor guy, and make him contented with what he is, and quit battling himself, and find peace for the rest of his life. (115–16)

The pity Hickey got from his wife was destructive because it came tied with a package of guilt he connected with *her* pipe dream for his reform:

> I began to hate that pipe dream! I began to be afraid I was going bughouse, because sometimes I couldn't forgive her for forgiving me. I even caught myself hating her for making me hate myself so much. There's a limit to the guilt you can feel and the forgiveness and the pity you can take! (239)

So what is one to do? It would be too hasty to follow Hickey and Gregers and devote ourselves to spreading the truth, opening eyes, always and everywhere. First of all, we may not know the whole truth. And, as we have seen, we must be wary concerning our own motives. And even where our motives are clearly and only to help someone else, we must be careful about what lies hidden under the deceptions we lift: is it strength (which freed of delusions can now pursue a fuller happiness) or is it weakness (which requires the support of delusions to make existence bearable)? Gregers saw true marriage, happiness, and heroes. Hickey saw death and indifference under dreams. They were both wrong, in different ways.

Gregers saw only a web of deception by others—missing self-deception and weakness in Hjalmar and the importance of life-lies. Hickey was perhaps more culpably wrong, given what he believed, for he was wrong to think enlightenment was desirable if what it brings is deathly peace. Of course, he also failed to see his own guilty need to tell, or that he really hated his wife (241–42). But Gregers was just as limited in his understanding of his own motives. Even where pity may be out of place, there may be room for compassion.

The Ambiguities of Self-Deception

The term "pipe dream" is ambiguous. It may refer to ideals to be striven for. It may also refer to self-deceptive fantasies about one's actual powers. (This second interpretation is perhaps closer to the expression's presumptive origin in the delusions of opium smokers.) There is an easy transition from hoping to wishing to fantasizing, each of which involves different expectations about the future and/or different relations to desire. The differences may be covered over by the notion of a dream. When we listen to Larry's paean to pipe dreams, we may be lulled by the note of ideals the word can contain—despite the fact that he speaks of "the *lie* of a pipe dream" as "what gives life" (10). All of the characters in *The Iceman Cometh* self-consciously conceive of themselves and others in the language of pipe dreams, and the language slides easily between the poles of ideals and delusions, hopes and self-deceptive fantasies. The ambiguity is also present in Relling's equation of ideals and lies (*WD* 477). When he says that the two have as much in common as tetanus and lockjaw, he may be taken as saying that life-lies and ideals are the same (that is, all ideals are lies), or merely that life-lies are a type of ideal (suitable, in particular, for the weak). This sort of duality also appears in relation to the notion of integrity, which can function in at least two ways. In one sense, one may need to overcome self-deception in order to achieve integrity (here integrity means something like honesty). Or integrity (here meaning some sort of ideal unity) may function as a motive of self-deception, that is, a person may deny parts of himself in order to achieve integrity. But, of course, this involves distortion—the unity achieved by denial is hardly "ideal" and it is not even clear that it is unity (if that which is denied persists). Self-deception may be either the problem or the (distorting and inadequate) means to a valued goal.

Indeed, uneasy and complicating dualities are rife in this area. Hickey claims his kind of pity, the right kind, is aimed at making people contented with what they really are (116). But Larry, we have seen, claims that the people in the bar are already contented (36). Their pipe dreams require no actual effort, even though they fall short of "the true goal of their heart's desire." Are there two kinds of contentment? I think yes. Desires may be satisfied in reality or in imagination (Wollheim 1979). A desire is satisfied in reality by the actual attainment of its object. But it may be for an individual as if his desire is actually satisfied provided he believes the object has been attained and this produces the relevant pleasure. Such satisfaction is of course fantasy gratification; it does not change the world outside the mind, and only satisfies so long as the wish can be taken for the deed, fantasy for reality. Nonetheless, such wish-fulfillment, such pipe-dreaming, can offer a kind of contentment. It is the kind of contentment Larry advocates, and it has the advantage at least of not requiring of some the truncation of desire or the abandonment of hope. There is a further ambiguity here having to do with the role of guilt. I think Hickey's views about the importance of truth have less to do with achieving happiness than avoiding guilt. He thinks "encouraging some poor guy to go on kidding himself with a lie . . . leaves the poor slob worse off because it makes him feel guiltier than ever" (115). Does it? Does a pipe dream torment and produce guilt, or is it a way of avoiding guilt, and so, as Larry thinks, producing contentment? Both may be true. In fact, even Hickey notes that guilt can be a motive for self-deception as well as a consequence (147–48, 225). Guilt is certainly what drives both him and Gregers, but it is not necessarily behind others' self-deception. That guilt was also a consequence in Hickey's case has to do with his special circumstances: he was responding to pity from his wife rather than support from equally weak comrades. The role of such support in the maintenance of identity, and the ambiguous place of integrity in relation to self-deception and identity, is worth further consideration.

Consider Rocky, who denies he is a pimp, insisting he is a bartender and only a bartender:

Hell, yuh'd tink I wuz a pimp or somethin'. Everybody knows me knows I ain't. A pimp don't hold no job. I'm a bartender. Dem tarts, Margie and Poil, dy're just a side line to pick up some extra dough. Strictly business, like dey was fighters and I was deir manager, see? I fix the cops fer dem so's dey can hustle widout gettin' pinched. Hell, dey'd be on de Island most of de time if it wasn't fer me. And I don't beat dem up like a pimp would. I treat dem fine. Dey like me. We're pals, see? What if I do take deir dough? Dey'd on'y trow it away. Tarts can't hang on to dough. But I'm a bartender and I work hard for my livin' in dis dump. You know dat, Larry. (12)

Rocky uses a restrictive definition of "pimp" so that he can avoid accepting the natural implication of the central facts. His form of self-deception is rather like the bad faith of Sartre's homosexual. Sartre describes the example as follows:

A homosexual frequently has an intolerable feeling of guilt, and his whole existence is determined in relation to this feeling. One will readily foresee that he is in bad faith. In fact it frequently happens that this man, while recognizing his homosexual inclination, while avowing each and every particular misdeed which he has committed, refuses with all his strength to consider himself *"a paederast."* His case is always "different," peculiar; there enters into it something of a game, of chance, of bad luck; the mistakes are all in the past; they are explained by a certain conception of the beautiful which women can not satisfy; we should see in them the results of a restless search, rather than the manifestations of a deeply rooted tendency, etc., etc. Here is assuredly a man in bad faith who borders on the comic since, acknowledging all the facts which are imputed to him, he refuses to draw from them the conclusion which they impose. (1956 [1943], 63)

Sartre's homosexual is caught between facticity and transcendence, between his unalterable past and his open future. The truth in his self-understanding is that the fact that he has engaged in homosexual acts, that he has been a homosexual, does not mean he will always be a homosexual. The person who insists that he recognize he is a homosexual risks treating him as a thing, as though his past actions fully determine his future. He may act differently in the future and he is in that sense free. But the project of sincerity, that is, providing the whole truth, would also require him to acknowledge the implications of his past actions (that doing such actions *is* what being a "paederast" means). So his bad faith does not involve the unconscious and repression; it is a form of incompleteness. If we think of self-deception in general terms as motivated false belief in the face of the evidence, then Sartre's homosexual and Rocky the bartender-pimp exemplify one form of self-deception. The central conflict is not an inner one; instead it involves a comic contrast between self-perception and what an external, social, perspective would reveal. It is for this reason that the actual views of others can play a crucial role in this form of self-deception. It is for this reason also that the position of the audience at a play allows for ironic understanding, and that plays provide an especially revealing vehicle for the presentation of this form of self-deception.

Rocky's self-conception depends on a community of support, support which is mutual. By tracing out some of the developments in the play in relation to that community of support, we can see some of the social aspects of both identity and self-deception. In one scene, Rocky takes the money Margie and Pearl have earned, and despite some uneasy kidding, they support each other's self-understandings as tarts, not whores, and as honest bartender, not pimp (66–67). But Hickey enters into the situation and starts meddling with the community of mutual support. Rocky at first thinks he can except himself (97), but it isn't long before the community of support collapses, accusations of being a whore and a pimp are exchanged, and Rocky starts acting (more) like a pimp and slapping the girls (99–102). Pearl concludes: "Hickey's convoited him. He's give up his pipe dream!" (102). Hickey had deliberately used them against each other (147). Rocky makes a false start at recovery when he urges Larry to become a pimp.

Larry sees that Rocky, to be comfortable with himself, has to make everyone like himself (Hickey, of course, suffers from this same problem): "No, it doesn't look good, Rocky. I mean, the peace Hickey's brought you. It isn't contented enough, if you have to make everyone else a pimp, too" (222). But if a community of support was necessary to maintaining the various individual self-deceptions (their identities), and if Hickey was able to undermine the self-deceptions by undermining the community, in the end we can see that the suffering individuals can restore each other by restoring their community of support. As Hickey is arrested and about to leave, they clutch at the notion that Hickey was insane and they were just humoring him. Harry Hope spells it out and the others join in (244). The full process of restoration is well illustrated by the interaction of Harry Hope and Rocky (249–50), with Harry reaffirmed in relation to his claims about automobiles and other dangers outside the comfortable confines of the bar he really does not wish to leave, and with Rocky reaffirmed as a bartender (if not an honest bartender). The mutual aspect of the support has an additional implication. The reciprocity gives the support a motive other than guilt-inducing pity.

The social contribution to identity and self-conception is subject to certain complications. Whether one admits one is a pimp or denies it, what one believes may importantly depend on what others help or let one believe. But whether one is in fact a pimp depends less on what one and others believe than on what one does. On the other hand, some social roles are determined, in fact, by beliefs. It may, for example, be sufficient (and necessary) to make one count as "a leader" that others think you are. In such a case, their thinking is equivalent to your being. And sometimes the dependence on beliefs, while more indirect, may hold because the faith of others may causally produce certain powers (shamanism sometimes works this way). In any case, as Erik Erikson and others have argued, confirmation by others can be crucial to determining your identity. Both in fact and psychologically, you may become who others think you are.

It will be recalled that among Gregers's problems was that he stood outside any community of mutual recognition and support, that he was cut off from social life. He was pleased to think of himself as totally independent: "I won't be any trouble to you; I do everything for myself" (WD 429). After Hjalmar is subjected to Gregers's revelations and his "Summons to the Ideal," he starts to talk like Gregers and claims independence, telling Gina: "From now on, I'm doing everything myself; I just want to be left alone with all the work" (454). Gregers even pushes Hjalmar to reject further support from the elder Werle—he tells him that the deed of gift to Old Ekdal and Hedvig "is a trap that's been set for you" (468). Ultimately Hjalmar is pressed to become as alone and isolated as Gregers. Self-deception can be sustained by the collusion of others. When Gregers first starts to speak to Hjalmar as though he were like the wild duck ("you're wandering in a poisonous swamp, Hjalmar. You've got an insidious disease in your system, and so you've gone to the bottom to die in the dark"), Hjalmar does not want to hear of it: "don't talk any more about sickness and poison. I'm not used to that kind of conversation. In my house nobody talks to me about ugly things" (444). But while self-deception may sometimes depend on the collusion of others, it is not necessary, as the case of Gregers himself shows.

The form of self-deception we have just considered, the sort of denial engaged in by Rocky, is what introduces the ambiguous place of integrity in relation to identity. We can say both that the people in the bar lack integrity, that is, they live with lies; and that the people in the bar (perhaps self-defeatingly) seek dignity and integrity through lies. Of course, this is a shortcut to unity, and what is produced is at best a dubious unity. Getting rid of undesirable features of oneself is more difficult than simply denying those features. The situation is parallel with the situation in relation to self-deception and happiness. If happiness involves the satisfaction of desires, an apparent shortcut to happiness may be provided by getting rid of or denying certain desires. The (usually) more difficult path involves uncovering one's real needs and criticizing one's desires and then striving to actually satisfy the corrected desires. Self-deception may play a useful role in producing both happiness or contentedness (of a sort) and integrity (of a sort), at least for those who are weak, who are incapable of more strenuous achievement. This is part of the lesson of the plays. One must go beyond them to see that the sorts of happiness and integrity involved are limited and distorted, and that one does not really know in advance what one is capable of achieving.

The Paradoxes of Self-Deception

Can one "choose" the path of self-deception? There is a paradox in the suggestion that one might. For if one were intentionally to decide to deceive oneself, to deny what one knows to be true, that would seem to presuppose that one does already know that one knows it to be true. Of course one can simply forget something one once knew, but that is not the same as *intentionally* forgetting. The problem here is similar to that raised by a child's playful injunction: "Don't think of elephants!" Of course one can not think of elephants (one doesn't most of the time), but insofar as one is aware of the injunction (which includes reference to elephants) one *is* thinking of elephants while trying to follow it. Similarly, how can one intentionally forget? It would seem to require following a rule under conditions which do not allow one to follow it knowingly—in which case it is unclear in what sense one is actively following it rather than merely acting in accordance with it. So there is a paradox in the suggestion that one might intentionally deceive oneself. On the other hand, if one's false belief is not intentional, it is not clear why it should not be regarded as the result of simple ignorance or stupidity or something else other than self-deception. There is a paradox in the very possibility of self-deception.[5]

We do of course deceive ourselves. The problem is how we pull it off. One model of the mechanism is provided by the bad faith of Sartre's homosexual, a pattern also exemplified by Rocky the bartender-pimp. Here paradox is avoided because the sufferers from self-deception are at no point required to deny intentionally what they also acknowledge to be true. We need not say that they know better, or perhaps even that they should know better. What makes these cases recognizable as self-deception (rather than simple ignorance) is the disparity between self-perception and alternative perspectives available to others within their world, a disparity combined with a self-interested motive which explains it. The failure to draw the appropriate conclusions from the available and acknowledged evidence, the central incompleteness in their self-understanding, is no accident. And it is the special explanation of the incompleteness that differentiates this sort of self-deception from simple ignorance or stupidity. Note again that the conflict here is between the individual's perspective and other, external, perspectives. While the conflict may be comic, or tragic, or ironic, the mind itself remains undivided. (Indeed, the insularity of the mind, its self-enclosure, may contribute to the comic appearance of the dissonance.)

Self-deception as suppression or denial, as in the case of Rocky and Sartre's homosexual, is only one type of self-deception. One might be tempted to think it is the only type, or the only possible type. Paradox may seem inevitable if we attempt to understand self-deception on the model of other-deception. Other-deception, as in the case of lying, requires that the deceiver know the truth while keeping the deceived from knowing it. But in the case of self-deception, the two roles are collapsed into a single person and the problem arises of how one person can simultaneously know (as he must, if he is to be a deceiver) and not know (as he must, if he is to be deceived) a single thing. This is the paradox of knowing and not knowing, the paradox of knowledge in relation to self-deception. It is the paradox that drives Sartre to his models of bad faith.

If one takes a Cartesian view of self-knowledge, so that the mind is better known to us than any other thing—known to us directly and incorrigibly—then self-deception on the model of other-deception must seem impossible. For Descartes, psychological states are supposed to be transparent to the person having them. If one is in a psychological state, one must know that one is in it, and if one is not in a psychological state one cannot mistakenly think one is. In the realm of the mental, thinking makes it so. (This is a plausible view if one thinks of the realm of the mental as made up simply of one's thoughts, and restricts thoughts, by definition, to conscious thoughts.) There are supposed to be no hidden corners of the mind. In particular, for Descartes and for Sartre as a follower of Descartes, if I know something, I must necessarily be conscious that I know. Now, as we have discussed, while some psychological states (e.g., sensations such as pain) may well be transparent, as a general thesis applied to all mental states, the thesis of transparency is surely false. One is not an incorrigible authority on all one's psychological states.[6]

If the epistemological paradox of self-deception arises because a single mind must be in two incompatible states, it may be overcome if the mind is split, as by Freud, into the conscious and unconscious. Then one may on one level (the unconscious) know, while at another level (the conscious) one does not know. Because Sartre also believes in the Cartesian thesis of the unity of the mind, he rejects Freud's doctrine of the unconscious, arguing that the paradox of self-deception reemerges at the level of the censor. His argument against Freud involves many errors, including a false identification of the conscious with the ego and the unconscious with the id (Trilling 1972, chap. 6; see also Neu 1988a). But, most simply, Sartre does not see that the censor, even illegitimately personified, need not simultaneously know and not know. It (an unconscious aspect of the ego, functionally defined) must know what is to be repressed, but not in order to hide it from itself (a task as problematic as not thinking of elephants in obedience to a command of which one remains aware), but in order to hide the truth from another aspect of the self (the conscious aspect of the ego). This provides an alternative model of self-deception and raises further issues in connection with its treatment.

Unlike the conflict in suppression, which is between self-perception and what a social perspective would reveal, the conflict in repression is internal. There is a division of the mind, a denial of transparency, and forces of repression come into play. This sort of division is well illustrated by Freud's case of the Rat Man, in which we get a graphic picture of ambivalence between conscious love and unconscious hatred. The Rat Man's lady love (who had more than once rejected him) was about to leave a resort where they both had been: "On the day of her departure he knocked his foot against a stone lying in the road, and was *obliged* to put it out of the way by the side of the road, because the idea struck him that her carriage would be driving along the same road in a few hours' time and might come to grief against this stone. But a few minutes later it occurred to him that this was absurd, and he was *obliged* to go back and replace the stone in its original position in the middle of the road" (Freud 1909d, *SE* 10: 190). To explain that compulsive act (as well as the perhaps compulsive thought that led to his removing the stone in the first place), one must appeal to an unconscious but active hatred.

And Freud's case studies are not the only place where unconscious forces move. I have mentioned some of Gregers's Oedipal problems in *The Wild Duck*. In *The Iceman Cometh* too, some of the deepest self-deceptions seem to involve repression and not just suppression. One of the subthemes in *The Iceman Cometh* concerns Parritt, a young man who comes to Harry Hope's bar to seek out Larry. Larry was once the lover of Parritt's mother, and Parritt suspects that Larry is really his father; and he has come to tell him that his mother, a political radical, has been arrested. In fact, he has come for more. The thing he has most difficulty in acknowledging, even to himself, is his hatred. In this, as in much else, he has an affinity with Hickey.

Hickey spots the affinity ("We're members of the same lodge" [84]), as do Larry and Parritt himself (110, 159, 227, 239). Parritt suffers from the same need to tell (110, 117, 127), he too is driven by guilt. It was he who informed on his mother and, in effect, killed her. And while he confesses this, the reasons he puts forward (patriotism [127], money [160, 206]) are mere rationalizations. (Parritt's too many reasons for his betrayal are reminiscent of Hjalmar's too many purposes for his invention.) Like Hickey, he hated and ultimately destroyed the central woman in his life; and just as Hickey reveals his true motive, Parritt admits: "I may as well confess, Larry. There's no use lying any more. You know anyway. I didn't give a damn about the money. It was because I hated her" (241). We can't be sure how close to the surface this knowledge was, whether Parritt had been lying only to Larry or also to himself. So while we cannot be entirely sure we have here a case of self-deception (part of the problem with self-deception, aside from making clear how it is possible, is being clear that one has an example of it rather than something else), the divisions and confusions of mind, and their depth, are such that if we have a case of self-deception it is one involving repression. In the parallel case of Hickey there is no doubt about either the self-deception or its nature. And the existence of forces of repression helps make clearer the problems with Hickey's attempts to overcome self-deception in others through enlightenment.

Resistance

Simply telling a self-deceived person the truth is not enough to overcome their false beliefs. After all, their problem is not simple ignorance. Their false beliefs are motivated, and so they will resist any new enlightenment with the same energy that helped them maintain their ignorance in the face of contrary evidence in the first place. Freud recognized the resistance to the recovery of the repressed in his patients very early on:

> In one particular case the mother of a hysterical girl had confided to me the homosexual experience which had greatly contributed to the fixation of the girl's attacks. The mother had herself surprised the scene; but the patient had completely forgotten it, though it had occurred when she was already approaching puberty. I was now able to make a most instructive observation. Every time I repeated her mother's story to the girl she reacted with a hysterical attack, and after this she forgot the story once more. There is no doubt that the patient was expressing a violent resistance against the knowledge that was being forced upon her. Finally she simulated feeble-mindedness and a complete loss of memory in

order to protect herself against what I had told her. After this, there was no choice but to cease attributing to the fact of knowing, in itself, the importance that had previously been given to it and to place the emphasis on the resistances which had in the past brought about the state of not knowing and which were still ready to defend that state. Conscious knowledge, even if it was not subsequently driven out again, was powerless against those resistances.

The strange behaviour of patients, in being able to combine a conscious knowing with not knowing, remains inexplicable by what is called normal psychology. But to psycho-analysis, which recognizes the existence of the unconscious, it presents no difficulty. (1913c, *SE* 12: 141–42)

"Wild" psychoanalysts, and would-be enlighteners such as Gregers and Hickey, tend to ignore the forces of repression and their counterpart resistances. Of course, we've seen that Gregers was also (multiply) mistaken about the nature of Hjalmar's problems. So Hjalmar thinks himself undeceived when he says: "I also thought this home was a good place to be. That was a pipe dream. Now where can I find the buoyancy I need to carry my invention into reality? Maybe it'll die with me; and then it'll be your past, Gina, that killed it" (458).[7] But Hjalmar was right in thinking he had a happy (or at least reasonably contented) home and wrong (indeed, self-deceived) in thinking he was an inventor—yet he maintains that delusion. And we have seen that even after having been told that his father in fact supports himself, he persists in thinking of himself as the family breadwinner (456, 464).

Merely telling a troubled person the truth is not sufficient to improve their situation or produce a therapeutic cure. Freud recognized limits to even his sophisticated talking cure:

Various qualifications are required of anyone who is to be beneficially affected by psycho-analysis. To begin with, he must be capable of a psychically normal condition. (1904, *SE* 7: 254)

Let us remember, however, that our attitude to life ought not to be that of a fanatic for hygiene or therapy. We must admit that the ideal prevention of neurotic illnesses which we have in mind would not be of advantage to every individual. A good number of those who now take flight into illness would not, under the conditions we have assumed, support the conflict but would rapidly succumb or would cause a mischief greater than their own neurotic illness. Neuroses have in fact their biological function as a protective contrivance and they have their social justification: the 'gain from illness' they provide is not always a purely subjective one. (1910d, *SE* 11: 150)

For the denizens of Harry Hope's bar, Hickey's attempt to confront them with reality does them no good. That it doesn't has to do with the sources of their condition, and the limited possibilities they offered for change.

Forcing an unacceptable reality on someone or merely confronting them with the truth is not necessarily a better way to achieve internal balance or harmony with the external world—there may be both internal and external limits.

The inhabitants of Harry Hope's bar were being challenged to change in a way that denied their unconscious needs, and provided no way of overcoming the resistances they had—in addition to failing to better equip them to deal with the reality they were being asked to face. Hickey's confrontational tactics forced his friends to look objectively at their situation, but since they saw little hope of solving their problems in reality, they were left confused and uneasy, and, without the community of support previously available, became miserable where they had once been content. And of course Hickey suffers from illusions about himself. As Freud remarked,

> we have noticed that no psycho-analyst goes further than his own complexes and internal resistances permit; and we consequently require that he shall begin his activity with a self-analysis and continually carry it deeper while he is making his observations on his patients. (1910d, *SE* 11: 145)

> Since we demand strict truthfulness from our patients, we jeopardize our whole authority if we let ourselves be caught out by them in a departure from the truth. (1915a, *SE* 12: 164).

In the end, Hickey is unable to rejoin the community of support that had sustained him. Parritt, too close to Hickey in many ways, had never been a member of the community of support. Hickey goes off, presumably to die in the electric chair, no longer he says, giving a damn about life: "I haven't got a single damned lying hope or pipe dream left!" (245). (In truth, he clings to one, in his final words denying he hated his wife [246].) Parritt echoes Hickey's earlier words to his wife (241), revealing his denied hatred: "You know what you can do with your freedom pipe dream now, don't you, you damned old bitch!" (247). With no pipe dreams (and with Larry's assent), he goes off to commit suicide. Certainly Hickey was right in seeing the peace of death under the absence of pipe dreams. Living a lie and living a hope are not quite the same.

Illusions and Faith

A useful cover term that might do duty for what Ibsen's notion of a life-lie and O'Neill's notion of a pipe dream have in common is "illusion." The broad question of the plays then becomes: can humans live without illusions? And the broad answer is no. This is not because illusions are somehow inherent in human nature (they might be, but that is not the argument of the plays). It is because some people, at least, are too weak to live without them. Illusions seem a necessary condition of whatever happiness, or contentment, is open to them. But then, what sort of weakness is it that calls for illusions? And is it a defect, moral or otherwise, to suffer from such weakness? And what is the correct attitude toward the need for illusions? Is it the same whether the need is ours or someone else's? And there are further complications. I noted earlier an ambiguity in the notions of a life-lie and a pipe-dream, an ambiguity between ideals to be striven for and self-deceptive fantasies about one's actual powers. The notion of an illusion shares that ambiguity, it too floats in the space between ideal and delusion. And in judging the proper or necessary place of illusions in human life there is a further ambiguity of which one must take account—that between process and product. A belief may be regarded as an illusion either on the basis of the type of thinking that led to it (namely, "wishful thinking") or on the basis of its truth-value (illusions are typically regarded as false). But not every false belief counts as an illusion. So, while the role of a belief in one's life may also matter in this regard, the type of thinking that led to it must have a special importance in determining whether a belief is to count as an illusion. But then, are all beliefs that are the product of wishful thinking necessarily false? Indeed, might not a certain mechanism of belief-formation, a mechanism that does not attach the usual weight to evidence, sometimes be necessary to *make* something true? Is that not how "faith" often works?[8]

NOTES

1. Mill's Pig

This essay incorporates some material from Neu 1976a and 1993. Throughout this book, "they" and "their" are often used as (formally ungrammatical) singular pronouns to get around the intractable problems of potentially sexist uses of "he" and "his" versus arbitrary occasional use of "she" and "her" or awkward substitution of "he and she" and "his and hers" or "he/she," "s/he," and "his/her."

1. Mill writes: "It is better to be a human being dissatisfied, than a pig satisfied; better to be Socrates dissatisfied, than a fool satisfied. And if the fool or the pig are of a different opinion, it is because they only know their own side of the question. The other party to the comparison knows both sides" (1961 [1861], 333).

2. "A Tear Is an Intellectual Thing"

The initial version of this essay was written while I was a fellow at the Stanford Humanities Center in 1984–85. Later versions were prepared with assistance from Faculty Research Funds provided by the University of California, Santa Cruz.

1. Andrew Meister, personal communication.
2. In his poem, "The Grey Monk," which is also the source of the title of this essay and this book.
3. L. Borje Lofgren provides a decent catalogue, including tears of shame and tears at a happy ending (1966, 376–77).
4. Some evolutionary suggestions can be found in Andrew (1965).
5. The two observers who reported weeping in Indian elephants to Darwin both associated the weeping with grief, but they might have been projecting (Darwin 1965 [1872], 165–66). Writing in 1966, Lofgren reports: "Although lacrimation is widespread in the animal kingdom as a result of irritation of the eye or the nose, there now seems to be agreement that weeping as an emotional phenomenon is exclusively human" (376). Lofgren cites E. Treacher Collins (1932) and Ashley Montagu (1959). Montagu reaffirms the claim in a 1981 piece and William H. Frey surveys the literature as of 1985 in *Crying: The Mystery of Tears.*

The fullest discussion I am aware of is in the Collins article referred to by Lofgren. Collins argues that the observations of emotional weeping in animals reported by some of Darwin's informants have not been confirmed when further probed, and he concludes on a number of grounds that the notion that animals other than man weep, that is, express grief by shedding tears, is highly dubious (1932, 6–9). The crucial issue, in my view, is what thoughts, with what causal powers, one is prepared to ascribe to animals in certain contexts.

6. Frey denies the connection between squeezed orbiculars and stimulation of the lacrimal glands to secrete tears, but it is unclear why he denies it or how his alternative biochemical approach would explain laughing, coughing, and vomiting to tears (1985, 8).

7. See Paul Ekman (1984), esp. 324–28. The study is reported in Ekman, R. W. Levenson, and W. V. Frieson (1983).

8. See Wittgenstein's discussion of pointing and ostensive definition at the start of the *Philosophical Investigations* (1953). LaBarre talks of the misunderstanding of pointing by dogs and babies and his own misunderstanding of the American Indian style of pointing with the lips (1947, 51–52).

9. Ekman suggests they may be used to a blend: "The Fore failed to distinguish fear from surprise, perhaps because in this culture fearful events are usually also surprising" (1973, 212). But it would be at least mildly surprising if there were never pleasant surprises in this society and if some fearful events weren't familiar and even expected. Is more needed to learn to make the discrimination called for?

10. Actually, for the Fore the picture recognition test did not work at all. Ekman reports: "Our results, while similar to those found for literate cultures, were much weaker; agreement among members of these preliterate cultures was low on most emotions and totally absent on some" (1973, 210). Attributing this to special problems of the judgment procedure with preliterate peoples, Ekman and his colleagues went back to New Guinea and applied other tests. Instead of providing a contextless face in a photograph and asking the subjects to associate the expression with an emotion word on the short list, the investigators now provided a context in the form of an emotion story and asked the subjects to select a fitting expression from two or three photographed faces—with no emotion words used except sometimes in the telling of the story. In a related test, subjects were asked to make faces reflecting certain situations. It was in the results of these tests that the Fore failed to distinguish surprise and fear.

11. Carroll E. Izard (1980) reports much less agreement for the unstructured task of free-response descriptions of expressions. For example, "shame" was labeled correctly by as few as 7 percent of some groups in his study (206).

12. Otto Klineberg's (1935) summary of Lafcadio Hearn (1894, 656–83), as quoted in LaBarre (1947, 53).

13. But caution is needed: Hearn reports, "Cultivated from childhood as a duty, the smile soon becomes instinctive" (1894, 668). Is the situation really so different for other expressions or in our society? A mix of biology and convention may shape even "natural expressions." On the other hand, there may be a biological link of laughter with the pleasant that provides the anchor for the conventional, even though eventually instinctual, polite smile.

14. See Desmond Morris et al. (1979) and the works referred to in their extensive bibliography.

15. Arlie Russell Hochschild (1983) has written of the emotional labor ("the

management of feeling to create a publicly observable facial and bodily display" [7n.]) that flight attendants must engage in to produce the smiles that make passengers on airplanes feel comfortable and cared for. While much that she says is of interest, especially in terms of the costs in alienation from one's own feelings involved in such work, she tends simply to assume the professional smile of a flight attendant calls for "deep acting" of the kind advocated by Stanislavski. And she thinks deep acting involves self-deception. But need anger control involve self-deception? Changing one's perception (so irate passengers are seen as more like disturbed and frightened children) may *really* change anger. She also seems to think the commercial context of the flight attendant's acting makes it necessarily estranging. But the contrast with the (perhaps equally commercial) theater is not entirely clear, and Diderot suggests (in connection with the theater) that the best actors lack character to begin with, and so they do not lose it as a result of taking on other characters. As he puts it, "They are fit to play all characters because they have none" (1957 [1773], 48).

16. In crude parallel: the drunken actor is not necessarily the best portrayer of a drunken character in a play. Indeed, the actor might have trouble remembering the character's lines. The play risks collapsing into the actor's life. This is perhaps the inverse of the problem of alienation of feeling—where role takes over life instead of life taking over role—in the sort of commercialization of feeling described by Hochschild.

17. Deliberate smiles apparently tend more often to be asymmetric (Ekman 1984, 322).

18. "And if the boy have not a woman's gift / To rain a shower of commanded tears, / An onion will do well for such a shift," Shakespeare, *The Taming of the Shrew*, introduction, 1.124.

19. Lofgren 1966, 377. This may neglect mother's milk. But then, some patients are ambivalent about that.

20. The title of this section is a line from Alfred Lord Tennyson, "The Princess," part 4.

21. Recall Darwin's second question, and see his discussion in chapter 13 of *The Expression of the Emotions* (1965[1872]).

22. The very first cries, at birth, may not in fact communicate pain; they may just be a physiological response to the first inrush of air into the lungs.

3. Jealous Thoughts

This essay has benefited from the comments of a number of people, but especially Norman O. Brown, Ellen Hawkes, Robert Meister, and Amélie Rorty.

1. On communes, see Kanter (1972); on the Israeli experience, see Spiro (1975); on China, would there were something to let us know how it is going.

2. These points are elaborated in Neu (1974, 1976b [chap. 10 in this book] and 1995b [chap. 12 here]). Aristotle provides arguments (*Politics* 1260b–1264b) in favor of differentiation and diversity, and against the possibility of total "unity," in the course of his critique of Plato's scheme of communism.

3. According to Jerome Kagan (in conversation in 1976). It might be useful to consider a child's upset at another child's possession of an abandoned toy in connection with Freud's discussion of a child's game of disappearance and return ("*fort*" and "*da*"), where the need for active mastery and control comes to the fore (1920g, 18: 14–17).

4. Which is not to say that we are jealous only over relationships we have freely chosen. Again, the sources of our preferences are many and various, and often hidden (even from ourselves). And the fact that preferences may be socially prescribed or structurally dictated does not preclude jealousy. Indeed, as Amélie Rorty has put it: "After all, one doesn't choose parents, even to have them. But jealousy is rife there" (personal communication). On the relative contributions of social structure and emotional constellations to patterning relationships, anthropologists have much to say; see, for example: Claude Lévi-Strauss (1969 [1949]); George C. Homans and David M. Schneider (1955); Rodney Needham (1962); Lounsbury (1962). Again, it is to be remembered that whatever the sources of a particular relationship or patterns of relationship, one may develop a jealous concern to preserve it or them.

5. That is, Iago is envious where he is not merely vengeful (over Cassio's preferment, etc.). I am assuming that Iago himself did not especially desire Desdemona. At the least, his machinations were not aimed at winning her over (if he did desire her, he wanted even more that no one else have her if he did not). Essentially, he was a "spoiler" (in the language of Melanie Klein 1975 [1957]). See Auden's (1964) analysis of Iago in terms of the practical joker.

6. This corresponds, I think, to Aristotle's distinction, in the *Rhetoric* (1388ab), between *envy* and *emulation*.

7. Going back to the case of Iago, we can now see that even if Iago had himself desired Desdemona, his state would remain envy. The question that turns on whether Iago desired Desdemona—or only that Othello not have her or that Othello be lowered—is not whether his state was envy or jealousy, but whether his envy was malicious or admiring.

8. For parodies, see Hartley (1960) and Vonnegut (1970). For a beginning on some of the hard questions about equality (its meaning, which differences need remedy, which are remediable, how, etc.) see Bernard Williams (1973c).

9. Schoeck brings together much of this evidence, though he has a tendency to assimilate all forms of hostility and conflict and aggression to envy (an overcorrection of the frustration-aggression approach). In addition, there is George M. Foster's (1972) very helpful survey of ways societies cope with fear of envy. I have found Foster's subtle study useful at a number of points.

10. The skepticism emerges, for example in Schoeck (1970, 251–53). An empirical approach cannot dismiss the claims of socialists and egalitarians to moral (as opposed to envious) motivation without confronting their underlying conceptions of justice and perceptions of the social situation—for it is these that distinguish the moral emotions from envy.

11. I am indebted to Jay Cantor for raising the specter of Savonarola.

12. Erikson was responding to a presentation of an earlier version of this work at the Wellfleet Meetings in Summer 1976.

13. Comparative aspects of envy are discussed by (among others) Aristotle (*Rhetoric*, 1387b–88a), Hume (*A Treatise of Human Nature*, book 2, part 2, section 8), and Kant (*The Metaphysical Principles of Virtue*, §36). That self-esteem (unlike envy) is not *necessarily* comparative is part of the point of Nietzsche's contrast between the Ancients and the Horde. But, as Amélie Rorty points out, Nietzsche may have been mythologizing wildly, and dangerously ("because to set the ideal of a non-comparative self-esteem before us is to invent yet another way for us to fail" [personal communication]), and there may be features of language and self-imagery that force us to form our conceptions of ourselves initially (and therefore, to some extent, on some level, forever) through the eyes

of the other, so that comparison becomes a *psychological* necessity in self-conception and self-esteem.

For a perhaps helpful contrast between self-esteem and self-respect, see the final section of Neu 1998b (chap. 7 here). There remains a problem, the one we have been considering, of just how self-esteem depends on what one's society thinks and on what one thinks about others in one's society.

14. "If we assume *man* to be *man*, and his relation to the world to be a human one, then love can be exchanged only for love, trust for trust, and so on. If you wish to enjoy art you must be an artistically educated person; if you wish to exercise influence on other men you must be the sort of person who has a truly stimulating and encouraging effect on others. Each one of your relations to man—and to nature—must be a *particular expression*, corresponding to the object of your will, of your *real individual* life. If you love unrequitedly, i.e., if your love as love does not call forth love in return, if through the *vital expression* of yourself as a loving person you fail to become a *loved person*, then your love is impotent, it is a misfortune" (Karl Marx 1975 [1844], 379).

15. The importance of anger and resentment in jealousy, of the fear of loss as inimical, was usefully pressed on me in comments by Robert Solomon and Rogers Albritton. So long as the anger is understood as at loss or deprivation (or as a response to frustration rather than to violation of rights), it adds an important dimension to the component of fear emphasized throughout this discussion.

16. See Gregory Vlastos, "The Individual as an Object of Love in Plato" (1973, esp. 28–34). Professor Vlastos tells me that he would now prefer to get at the contrast between two types of love "by contrasting the attitudes of desire (which can be—though it needn't be—totally egoistic) and tenderness (which can be—though it needn't be—totally altruistic)"—that is, in terms of contrasting aims rather than objects. He points out that possessive love can be directed intensely and exclusively to an individual:

> when desire is deep and intense it *fixates* on the individual who instantiates the desirable qualities; the individual may then become irreplaceable. This is certainly what happens in the Odette-Swann case. Proust speaks of 'an anxious torturing desire, whose object is the creature herself,' that creature being the 'exclusive' object—the exclusivity of the desire being the most marked feature. (The quote is from p. 331 of The Modern Library translation.) The fungibility of the qualities X desires in Y characterizes an Epicurean or, better, sensualist, attitude that may be contrasted with what the novelists and even the philosophers (Lucretius, or Plato in the first two speeches in the *Phaedrus*) call 'love' even when speaking of love-desire rather than love-tenderness. The moment desire becomes deep, fungibility is lost: one is 'hooked' to a particular person. That is certainly the great point in the Odette episode. (Vlastos personal communication)

On this account, what I am calling "love of a particular person" is really tenderness for that person: "the sentiment which corresponds to the attitude of pure good will—desiring the good of that person ('for that person's sake, not for our own sake' in Aristotle's good phrase)." I think, however, that just as love-desire at its extreme can degenerate into exploitation, love-tenderness at its extreme can generalize into an unfocused goodwill (not directed toward any individual to the exclusion of any other)—so that to understand the most typical experiences of love we might have to acknowledge overlap in terms of aims (desires) as much as in objects. Since, however, as we shall see, jealousy can arise in relation to both types of object, it may appear that the more significant dividing line (in relation to the possibility of jealousy at least) depends on the types of desires involved rather than the objects. Genuinely and totally selfless desires for the good of the other may leave no room for jealousy. But then, sexual passion (arising in connection with instinctual needs) may leave no room for such purely selfless desires—a love without such passion, and so without mixed desires, if not an etiolated love, wins its distance from jealousy only at some cost. The need for mixed desires can also be seen from another direction: "It is the fate of sensual love to become extinguished when it is satisfied, for it to be able to last, it must from the beginning be mixed with purely affectionate components—with such, that is, as are inhibited in their aims—or it must itself undergo a transformation of this kind" (Freud 1921c, *SE* 18: 115). We should perhaps also note that there may be a level at which the distinctions in terms of attitudes, aims, and desires should themselves be understood in terms of differing objects, namely self and other (rather than particulars and bundles of qualities); so the multiple contrasts might in the end reduce to self-love versus love-of-other, egoism versus altruism, narcissism versus object-love.

Steve Kaye has also pointed out to me that "the fungibility factor may be given too much weight unless we take account of both the tendency to project qualities onto a lover and how much the nuances come to matter, i.e., how we come to see uniqueness in the ways our love object instantiates a desired quality." He also brings out another way in which love of a particular and love of a bundle of qualities may be seen to come together. He notes that my example uses physical qualities, and he suggests that we consider what happens when we turn our attention to other sorts of qualities, especially moral ones. If we leave our lover after discovering that he or she is not generous, or is, after all, insensitive, what does our leaving show? Was our love not true (while it lasted)? Is the ideal perhaps unobtainable? The whole matter of breaking-up is especially puzzling because, despite cases of leaving after discovering a mistake or a change in character, we *do* often forgive and accept faults of character in those we love—sometimes there are compensating factors and sometimes it is a part of the commitment we have made. (Cf.: "One of the important factors of a relationship is as a cushion for the jolts of bad fortune—we do not walk out on our spouse because he or she receives a pay cut, we comfort them.") Whether a change undermines a relationship is not determined, straightforwardly at least, by whether or not the change was in the person's control. While I am leaving out much of the subtle detail in Kaye's arguments, it is clear that one has to consider the question of which qualities (if any) are essential to identity, before one can be sure of a contrast (sharp or otherwise) between love directed at a particular person and love directed at a set of qualities.

17. This is part of the tragedy of the "legalization" and "commercialization" of our culture. "Family law" embodies the conflict in the very words used to designate it: the law disturbs personal relations when it intervenes, but if it fails to intervene it may leave the weak to be victimized by the strong, and when that happens personal relations have already been disturbed. But the *possibility* of the law intervening may itself have disturbing effects.

18. Since emotions are importantly constituted by beliefs and desires, much turns on the sources of belief and desire. Certainly we cannot choose our beliefs directly, but it does not follow that they are completely outside our control.

Certainly we can be overcome by desires, but it does not follow that they are not criticizable. The questions of the relation of belief and will, and of desire and belief, are as difficult as they are important. See H. H. Price (1954); Bernard Williams (1973a); Stuart Hampshire (1975); Harry G. Frankfurt (1971).

19. See Freud (1922b). The other great resource in this area is of course Proust. Among other things, Proust brings out how the freedom of the beloved can, by itself, become a ground for jealousy. The mere fact of freedom, the mere *possibility* of loss, gets experienced as a *probability* of loss. (Cf. how children may initially experience the mere fact of separateness as loss. Children have to *learn* that objects that can go away can also return.)

20. Which is not to say that because some love may have a selfish aspect, all love must be totally selfish. But it is to insist that that love which is the desire for the happiness of the other, perhaps the purest form of love, is not the only form or even the only valuable form. Indeed, mature sexual passion may always involve some variant of the desire to be desired. See Sartre (1956 [1943], part 3; and Thomas Nagel (1979d). See also Freud (1914c and 1921c, *SE* 18: 102–3, 112–13).

The wisdom of a fortune cookie (passed on to me by a friend knowing my research interests) has it that: "In jealousy there is more self-love than love." (The fortune cookie fails to credit La Rochefoucauld.) Life, including both love and self-love, is of course more complex than that. In regard to self-love, one ought to distinguish selfishness and self-esteem. One may be quite high while the other is quite low; indeed, the person suffering from jealousy will typically have very low self-esteem (lack of faith in own lovableness, etc.). In regard to love, one should note that the wisdom of the fortune cookie is tied to a very special, romantic, and as I have just said, pure conception of love: a view under which the true lover always puts the good of his beloved first (whether or not that good includes him). But we do not in general expect lovers to drive their beloved to the airport to help them go off with some other (better) lover. (Humphrey Bogart at the end of the film *Casablanca* is heroic—and his decision is made in the larger context of World War II: "Ilsa, I'm no good at being noble. But it doesn't take much to see that the problems of three little people don't amount to a hill o'beans in this crazy world.")

21. What may seem special about "my" case may be that when I am the one with multiple lovers I am sure of my control and that I won't desert anyone; or, again, I may be concerned about the shift of quantities in the case of others, while in my own case I have a sense of constant renewal of quantities, and so on.

4. Jealous Afterthoughts

1. I am grateful to Betty Sue Flowers for a conversation in July 1980 in Baca, Colorado, where she pressed this suggestion.

5. On Hating the Ones We Love

I was invited to participate in an American Philosophical Association symposium on "Hatred" in March 1989. I was also invited to participate in an American Academy of Psychoanalysis symposium on "Love" in May 1989. It seemed appropriate to present the same essay to both. I wish to express (unambivalent) thanks to Norman O. Brown and Lynn Luria-Sukenick.

1. Catullus (1962, 162–63, Poem 85), in Latin:

Odi et amo. quare id faciam, fortasse requiris.
nescio, sed fieri sentio et excrucior.

Louis Zukofsky (1969) offers a modern English play on the Latin:

O th'hate I move love. Quarry it fact I am, for that's so re queries.
Nescience, say th'fiery scent I owe whets crookeder.

2. See, for example, "He who imagines one he loves to be affected with hate toward him will be tormented by Love and Hate together. For insofar as he imagines that [the one he loves] hates him, he is determined to hate [that person] in return (by P40). But (by hypothesis) he nevertheless loves him. So he will be tormented by Love and Hate together" (*Ethics*, part 3, proposition 40, Cor. 1, trans. E. Curley).

3. Again Spinoza sees clearly. He writes of cases of "vacillation of mind" in which "two contrary affects" occur "at the same time," noting "we can easily conceive that one and the same object can be the cause of many and contrary affects" (*Ethics*, part 3, prop. 17 and Schol.).

Emotions in general should not be confused with fleeting sensations. Emotions, like beliefs, are typically dispositional states that occur over time. As Patricia Greenspan puts it, "we may be said to have or exhibit a particular emotion (and indeed, I might add, to exhibit it consciously) over a span of time which includes, but is not limited to, the times (supposing there are some) when we are actually experiencing it" (1980, 229). But the possibilities of ambivalence, of conflicting feelings toward a single object, do not depend on the feelings involved being extended over time. Philip J. Koch (1987, esp. 264–65) nicely brings out how the complexity of emotions, emotional components, and the self itself makes for the various common forms of ambivalence.

4. "Why does the lover want to be *loved*?" and "to love is to wish to be loved" (*Being and Nothingness*, 366, 377). If not the essence of love, as in Sartre, Spinoza makes the desire to be loved part of the logic of love: "When we love a thing like ourselves, we strive, as far as we can, to bring it about that it loves us in return" (*Ethics*, part 3, prop. 33). The proof, via prop. 29, involving as it does a reversal from active to passive, is obscure. It might be clearer if it went through props. 21 and 25.

5. Carol Gilligan (1982, 8). See also Nancy Chodorow (1978). The Hegelian dialectic of recognition, domination, and submission is most fruitfully explored in relation to psychological theory by Jessica Benjamin (1988).

6. Rivalry with those we love (and identify with) is a natural source of ambivalence. "If something like ourselves (another person, with whom we identify) causes us pain *by* gaining pleasure for itself—by getting something we would like to have ourselves, for instance—then according to Spinoza, it ought to cause us *both* pain and pleasure, and hence be an object of *both* hatred and love" (Greenspan 1980, 226).

Catullus's personal problems with rivalry are considered in Anne Vannan Rankin (1962).

The special intensity of infantile ambivalence is discussed by Freud in his lecture on "Femininity" (1933a, in *SE* 22): "A powerful tendency to aggressiveness is always present beside a powerful love, and the more passionately a child loves its object the more sensitive does it become to disappointments and frustrations from that object" (124); he speaks also of the child's "insatiable" needs

(122) and points out its "demands for love are immoderate, they make exclusive claims and tolerate no sharing" (123).

7. Norman O. Brown (1966, 142). "At the very beginning, it seems, the external world, objects, and what is hated are identical. If later on an object turns out to be a source of pleasure, it is loved, but it is also incorporated into the ego" (Freud 1915c, in *SE* 14: 136).

8. See Freud (1920g, *SE* 18: 53–54; 1923b, *SE* 19: part 4; 1930a, *SE* 21: part 6).

9. See Edward Bibring (1941); and "Editor's Note" to "Instincts and their Vicissitudes" (*SE* 14: 111–16).

10. Freud elsewhere connects doubt, as the repudiation of instincts for knowledge and mastery, with sadism (1913i, *SE* 12).

11. See Freud, "Mourning and Melancholia" (1917e, *SE* 14: esp 250–52, 256–58; "Taboo and Emotional Ambivalence," chap. 2 of *Totem and Taboo* 1912–13, *SE* 13). See also Neu (1981 [chap. 14 here]).

12. The paradoxes of erotic desire emerge as dilemmas of sensation, action, and value that are elegantly discussed in connection with ancient poetry by Anne Carson (1986). See also, Jon Elster (1979, chap. 4, "Irrationality: Contradictions of the Mind").

13. As Freud helpfully points out: "Loving admits not merely of one, but of three opposites. In addition to the antithesis 'loving-hating', there is the other one of 'loving-being loved', and, in addition to these, loving and hating taken together are the opposite of the condition of unconcern or indifference" (1915c, *SE* 14: 133). The Bible speaks of such neutrality: "So then because thou art lukewarm, and neither cold nor hot, I will spew thee out of my mouth" (Rev. 3: 16). Literature is full of talk of "nearest and dearest" enemies. Hume notes, "The connexion is in many respects closer betwixt any two passions, than betwixt any passion and indifference" (*A Treatise of Human Nature* 1888[1739], 420). Freud writes of himself in *The Interpretation of Dreams* (1900): "My emotional life has always insisted that I should have an intimate friend and a hated enemy. I have always been able to provide myself afresh with both, and it has not infrequently happened that the ideal situation of childhood has been so completely reproduced that friend and enemy have come together in a single individual—though not, of course, both at once or with constant oscillations, as may have been the case in my early childhood" (*SE* 5: 483).

14. The importance of splitting (and projection) in the psychology of am bivalence is emphasized by Melanie Klein and her followers. See Hanna Segal (1992).

15. We distinguish different kinds of love, but not different kinds of hate. Why not? Some might think because the objects of hatred are more uniform. This was Descartes's view though it is rather implausible; see *The Passions of the Soul* (1985 [1649], 1: 358, sect. 84).

16. See such surveys as Irving Singer (1984–87); Denis de Rougemont (1983); and C. S. Lewis (1936).

Even in my brief discussion of Sartre, one can discern two different conceptions of love. The first—taking its essence as the desire for the full possession of a free being—is what for him makes satisfactory love impossible. But while that definition relies on dubious notions of freedom and possession, he has a second definition—according to which love is equated with the desire to be loved— which seems to me to contain important psychological truth.

17. Given the vast literature on love, it should perhaps be emphasized that

hatred too is not to be understood as an isolated sensation. Its ascription similarly involves the summary of much. Even a Cartesian such as Sartre allows for error in relation to certain "states," notably including hatred, which extend over time (see 1936–37, 61–68; and 1943, 162.)

18. There are helpful thoughts on this in Jeffrie G. Murphy and Jean Hampton (1988). They start with hatred and ask how it should be modified by compassion—tempering justice with mercy, anger and resentment with forgiveness, hate with love. In this discussion I have been starting with love and asking how it is (in fact) modified by hatred, anger, and resentment.

6. Boring from Within

1. The extreme here is described in the literature of solitary confinement and of sensory deprivation experiments, where boredom may be the least of a person's problems. An early experiment in a rigidly monotonous environment, with resulting hallucinations, is reported in Heron (1957).

2. I owe this point to Bernard Williams.

3. I think it useful to regard boredom itself as an emotion, a psychological state with a characteristic structure. However, I do not think it useful to try here to work through the distinctions among emotions, moods, sensations, and other types of psychological states in order to set precise boundaries to the concept of emotion—this partly because I don't think those boundaries are precise: emotions are not natural kinds. We use emotion terms to interpret complexes of sensation, desire, behavior, and belief. I attach most importance to the cognitive element because I, like Spinoza, regard thought as the essential defining element in characterizing particular emotions and differentiating them one from another (Neu 1977).

"Interest" appears on many contemporary psychologists' lists of basic emotions (Oatley 1992, 59, 61), even if "boredom" does not. "Boring" has many possible opposites, including interesting, meaningful, and perhaps even wonderful. Descartes, strangely to modern eyes, treated "wonder" as the first of his six primitive passions in The Passions of the Soul. He there writes, wonder "has no opposite, for, if the object before us has no characteristics that surprise us, we are not moved by it at all and we consider it without passion" (1649, §53), but it seems clear that the novel and the unusual that provoke wonder (i.e., attentive intellectual interest [§70–71]) in Descartes's account are meant to be incompatible with boredom. Spinoza gives wonder no such importance, not regarding it as a distinct affect at all (1677, Ethics 3, Definitions of the Affects 4).

4. Much of that history is tellingly explored through its literary expressions by Reinhard Kuhn (1976). That emotions can have a history is a revealing fact about them, and that they have the particular histories they do is a revealing fact about us. Patricia Meyer Spacks, in a 1995 book that appeared after this essay was completed, also sees the vocabulary of boredom as reflecting and expressing historical shifts in sensibility and social categories.

5. Do animals suffer from boredom? How would we know if they did? And what kind of boredom would it be? A dog anxiously straining at its leash to go for a walk may manifest impatience. It would seem odd to call it bored. But a dog sinking into lassitude in the face of an uninviting training program may be recognizably bored. Still, we don't usually think of animals as suffering from directionless longing. We think of them as more simply driven by instinctual needs. Animals may lack the self-consciousness that is a necessary condition of

"boredom from within." But consider a caged monkey. Clearly it is agitated—is it bored? It knows it is missing something. It may not be disenchanted, but it is desperate. (How different is the monkey from humans fidgeting at a boring lecture?) Reactive boredom may make sense for animals, even if "boredom from within" has trouble getting a foothold.

8. *Plato's Homoerotic* Symposium

I wish to thank Norman O. Brown, David Halperin, Gregory Vlastos, and Carter Wilson for helpful critical discussion.

1. For example, Freud 1911c, *SE* 12: 61 (quoted in Neu 1987b [chap. 9 here], n.15). While the usual connection that Freud makes is between social feeling and sublimated homosexuality (rather than active homosexuality), he frequently points out the great social contributions of homosexuals in history, sometimes even tying the contributions to the sexual orientation itself, deriving social energies from homosexual inclinations (e.g., Freud 1922b, *SE* 18: 232, also quoted in Neu 1987b [chap. 9 here], n.15).

2. This goes with the importance attached to military prowess, the segregation of women of citizen families (women available outside of marriage were not likely to be "respectable"), attitudes toward sexual passivity, and other assumptions of the time. Plato's own rather mixed attitude toward women, expressed in *The Republic* and other works, is convincingly sorted out by Gregory Vlastos (1989). On Diotima's presence (and absence) in the *Symposium*, see David M. Halperin (1990).

3. Quoted by K. J. Dover in his authoritative work, *Greek Homosexuality* (1978, 52, cf. 76). Dover notes the dominance of intercrural frottage, as opposed to other physical interactions, and the absence of erections in the *eromenoi* ("even in circumstances to which one would expect the penis of any healthy adolescent to respond willy-nilly") in depictions on vases (91–109). See also Michel Foucault (1986, 215–25) and Halperin (1990, sec. 6). And despite the comment of the character Aristophanes in the *Symposium* (191E), in actual Aristophanic comedies, to assume a passive role in homosexual activity was to become the butt of jokes.

4. The normally highly reliable editors of the *The Standard Edition of the Complete Psychological Works of Sigmund Freud* claim in a footnote to the passage that it does (1905d, *SE* 7: 136); but one should note that there is an Indian version of the myth that may conform better to Freud's account, and Freud refers to it explicitly later in *Beyond the Pleasure Principle* (1920g, *SE* 18: 57–58).

5. See Dover (1978, 65–66) and Foucault (1986, 187–92). For a reading of the evidence that points to greater conflict in attitudes, see David Cohen (1987).

6. Freud makes this statement in the context of his later theorizing about the repetition compulsion and the death instinct, but the notion of a return to an earlier state is present even in the *Three Essays* (1905d), where Freud writes, "The finding of an object is in fact a refinding of it" (222). As Dover notes, in Aristophanes's myth, "as commonly in the folktale genre, the time-scale is ignored and the distinction between species and individual is blurred" (1978, 62); cf. Dover (1966, esp. 44).

7. On the complications in Plato's understanding of erotic object and aim, and especially on the contrast of physical appetite and value-laden desire, see Halperin (1985).

8. For Sappho's view, see C. M. Bowra (1961, 180).

9. "So each selects a fair one for his love after his disposition, and even as if the beloved himself were a god he fashions for himself as it were an image, and adorns it to be the object of his veneration and worship . . . But all this, mark you, they attribute to the beloved, and the draughts which they draw from Zeus they pour out, like Bacchants, into the soul of the beloved, thus creating in him the closest possible likeness to the god they worship" (*Phaedrus*, 252D and 253A, trans. Hackforth). While in this passage the lover may not risk mistaking the boy for the Form, he does seem (contra Vlastos 1973, 30 n.88) to idealize the boy by attributing to him virtues he does not have. (Cf. A. W. Price 1989, 215–22.)

10. See Freud (1914c, *SE* 14: 88ff.; 1921c, *SE* 18: 112–14). In addition to their relation to one's ego or ego ideal, both transcendental objects and idealized individuals may owe some of their overvaluation to their relation to those earlier objects of which they are a "refinding."

Narcissism is also at the center of Freud's later theorizing about the mechanism of sublimation, in which the ego "begins by changing sexual object-libido into narcissistic libido and then, perhaps, goes on to give it another aim" (1923b, *SE* 19: 30, 44–47).

11. Similarly, certain ancient authors argued that it was precisely the fleetingness of the bloom of youth that was part of its appeal, making desire directed at youthful beauty (particularly that of boys) more poignant and more intense (see Achilles Tatius, 2.33–38; cf. Foucault 1986, 199–201).

12. Diotima describes his interest, at the time of their meeting, in "beautiful boys and youths—who, if you see them now, strike you out of your senses, and make you, you and many others, eager to be with the boys you love and look at them forever, if there were any way to do that, forgetting food and drink, everything but looking at them and being with them" (211D). And Alcibiades, at the *Symposium* itself, describes Socrates as "crazy about beautiful boys; he constantly follows them around in a perpetual daze" (216D). Adding, in the course of their playful rivalry over Agathon, "when Socrates is around, nobody else can even get close to a good-looking man" (223A). The passages throughout Plato's writings describing Socrates's interest in beautiful youths are plentiful (e.g., *Charmides* 155C–E, *Meno* 76C), and in particular he is described at the start of the *Protagoras* as coming "from pursuit of the captivating Alcibiades" (309A, trans. Guthrie) and he describes himself in the *Gorgias* as "erastes of Alcibiades and of philosophy" (481D, trans. Dover 1980, 156).

13. Martha Nussbaum reads Alcibiades's speech as "a story of complex passion, both sexual and intellectual, for a particular individual" (1986a, 167). Less plausibly, she also presents it as an alternative ideal offered by Plato.

14. This may be Socrates's considered view (Vlastos 1991, 39, 245–47). In which case Socrates's objections to sexual relations with Alcibiades would ultimately be moral, not metaphysical.

15. There is some controversy about *Phaedrus* (250E). Vlastos argues that the passage, in context, should be read as critical only of homosexual intercourse (1973, 25 n.76). Dover and most other commentators do not accept that limited reading (1978, 163 n.15). Whatever the import of the particular passage, strictures against the body and restrictions on intercourse (though most often put in eugenic terms) pervade Plato's writings.

16. On "Sex in Platonic Love," see Vlastos (1973, 38–42), where he expands on the view that "Plato discovers a new form of pederastic love, fully sensual in

its resonance, but denying itself consummation, transmuting physical excitement into imaginative and intellectual energy" (22–23).

17. See, e.g., *Phaedo* (64D–67B) and passages cited in text. On Christianity, see Peter Brown (1988).

18. See Boswell (1980), Denniston (1980), Dover (1978, 167–70), Price (1989, 229–35), Slote (1975), and Winkler (1990).

19. Concern about exploitation emerges in *Charmides* 155D–E, *Phaedrus* 238E–41D (in Socrates's later repudiated speech), and can be seen in Pausanias's discussion of Common love (the superior lover, by contrast, is said not to "aim to deceive [the young man]—to take advantage of him while he is still young and inexperienced and then, after exposing him to ridicule, to move quickly on to someone else" [181D]) and the protections against it ("fathers hire attendants for their sons as soon as they're old enough to be attractive" [183C]). It is most explicit in Xenophon's portrayal of Socrates (*Memorabilia* 2.6, *Symposium* 8). And one should remember the special stigma that attached in ancient Greece to sexual passivity ("It is not only by assimilating himself to a woman in the sexual act that the submissive male rejects his role as a male citizen, but also by deliberately choosing to be the victim of what would be, if the victim were unwilling, hubris" [Dover 1978, 103–4]). See Vlastos (1991, 245–47).

20. J. M. E. Moravcsik (1971, 291) denies the link between Plato's theory of eros and Freud's theory of sublimation. But that offers no account for the call for abstinence from sexual intercourse illustrated in the relation of Alcibiades and Socrates in the *Symposium* and made explicit in the doctrine of love of the *Phaedrus*. Neither "unnaturalness" nor "sublimation" is mentioned in the *Symposium*, but both doctrines may be in play. E. R. Dodds, among others, does see the link between Platonic eros and Freudian libido and sublimation, and interestingly remarks that Plato never "fully integrated this line of thought with the rest of his philosophy; had he done so, the notion of the intellect as a self-sufficient entity independent of the body might have been imperiled, and Plato was not going to risk that" (1951, 218–19). Valuable discussion of the paradoxes and problems of sublimation can be found in Norman O. Brown (1959, pt. 4).

21. See Carson (1986, 23–25). "This erotic code is a social expression of the division within a lover's heart. Double standards of behavior reflect double or contradictory pressures within erotic emotion itself . . . Such societal and aesthetic sanction given at once to lover's pursuit and beloved's flight has its image on Greek vases as a moment of impasse in the ritual of courtship, its conceptual ground in the traditionally bittersweet character of desire" (24–25).

22. Halperin (1990, see 6, and 1986; cf. Foucault 1986, 229–46) claims to discern in Plato a move from hierarchy to reciprocity in eros, but the evidence is rather thin. There is none in the *Symposium* (unless one assumes Aristophanes's speech represents Plato's preferred view), and the import of the passage from the *Phaedrus* (255C–E) that Halperin emphasizes may be stretched. As Dover puts it, the conventional view allows that when the erastes succeeds in his aim, "there is indeed love on both sides, but eros on one side only" (1978, 53). The responsiveness of the eromenos is specifically not erotic, it is based on "affection, gratitude and admiration" (Dover 1980, 4). Even in the *Phaedrus* passage, which may go beyond the views of its time by allowing for mutuality of desire, if eros is returned, it is an eros that has been desexualized, dissociated

from the sexual activity (and passivity) of intercourse. And there is no notion at all in Plato of equality between lovers of the sort Aristotle (writing later) thinks necessary between persons capable of true friendship.

Plato's point about the lovers in *Phaedrus* (255C–E) may be that in loving each other, they love the same thing. On one reading, this same thing is the eromenos (his counter-eros is of himself reflected in the lover: "his lover is as it were a mirror in which he beholds himself"). On another, it is the Form, that is the ultimate object participated in or represented by the immediate object ("the stream of beauty turns back and re-enters the eyes of the fair beloved"). On no reading do the two become one (as in Aristophanes's account), nor does the eromenos see and so love his lover as instantiating the Form (in which case there *would* be reciprocity, each loving in the same way). In none of this, of course, is there a critique of double standards in courtship.

9. Freud and Perversion

1. While I here emphasize that the existence of some causal story does not render all evaluation out of place, I should perhaps also emphasize that some evaluations are almost always out of place. Whether homosexuality is the result of nature or nurture, it makes little sense to condemn homosexuality as "unnatural." For one thing, nature, or at least human nature, includes conditions of nurture: all humans must be somehow nurtured in order to survive and develop. The "somehow" of course allows for variations. The real point of the contrast of nature and nurture, two types of causes, may ultimately simply be in terms of uniformity versus variability. In terms of individual responsibility, nature and nurture may both be viewed as "external" causes (the individual does not choose them, and so does not control the result). For another thing, nature in general includes more than many would like to admit (one of the constant lessons of the Marquis de Sade). Insofar as charges of perversion are based on notions of unnaturalness, they may always be inapplicable. (See Slote 1975.) The various contrasts between the natural and the unnatural, and the historical development of the charge of unnaturalness against homosexuality, are interestingly traced by John Boswell (1980) in his *Christianity, Social Tolerance, and Homosexuality*. In the coroner's verdict, "death by natural causes," the contrast is with other types of causes, basically causes involving the intervention of human intentions. Whatever the causes of homosexuality and homosexual desires, they must be of the same *type* as the causes of heterosexuality and heterosexual desires. This point is reflected in Aristophanes's myth in Plato's *Symposium*. Incidentally, one might note that if Freud had this myth in mind in his discussion at the start of the *Three Essays* (1905d, 7: 136), as the normally highly reliable editors of the *Standard Edition* claim in a footnote, his account there is misleading. Freud speaks as if the "poetic fable" is supposed to explain only heterosexuality, and as if the existence of homosexuality and lesbianism therefore comes as a surprise. In fact, Aristophanes's story of the division of the original human beings into two halves, and their subsequent quest to reunite in love, allows for all three alternatives: Aristophanes starts with three original sexes: double-male, double-female, and "androgynous." Thus the myth offers an explanation (the same explanation) of homosexuality and lesbianism as well as heterosexuality. (One should perhaps also note that there is an Indian version of the myth that may conform better to Freud's account, and Freud refers to it explicitly later in *Beyond the Pleasure*

Principle [1920g, 18: 57–58].) From the point of view of psychoanalytic theory, heterosexual object-choice and homosexual object-choice are equally problematic, equally in need of explanation (1905d, 7: 146 n.).

Freud himself, in his published writings, only used the term "unnatural" three times in connection with perverse desires or practices. In each of the three instances (1898a, 3: 265; 1916–17, 16: 302; and 1920a, 18: 149), in context, the term refers to the views of others.

2. Freud spells out the content criterion for deviations in respect of source and aim: "Perversions are sexual activities which either (a) extend, in an anatomical sense, beyond the regions of the body that are designed for sexual union, or (b) linger over the intermediate relations to the sexual object which should normally be traversed rapidly on the path towards the final sexual aim" (1905d, 7: 150). The question remains, what is so objectionable about "extending" and "lingering"?

3. Freud summarizes his views on the child and feces in Introductory Lecture 20:

> To begin with . . . He feels no disgust at his faeces, values them as a portion of his own body with which he will not readily part, and makes use of them as his first "gift", to distinguish people whom he values especially highly. Even after education has succeeded in its aim of making these inclinations alien to him, he carries on his high valuation of faeces in his estimate of "gifts" and "money". On the other hand he seems to regard his achievements in urinating with peculiar pride. (1916–17, 16: 315)

4. "Not only the deviations from normal sexual life but its normal form as well are determined by the infantile manifestations of sexuality" (1905d, 7: 212).

5. Hence, as Erikson suggests, the infant is expelled from the oral paradise of an earlier stage (Erikson 1963, 79). Erikson is in general very helpful on the social contribution to and meaning of the psychosexual stages.

6. There has been some speculation on the possible evolutionary advantages of homosexuality in terms of altruistic and social impulses. See, for example, Wilson (1978, 142f.).

7. The multiplicity of ends and essences for sexuality, and the corresponding multiplicity of criteria for perversion, is amply evidenced in a growing philosophical literature on sexual perversion (much of it collected in two anthologies: Baker & Elliston [1975], and Soble [1980]). The authors tend to vacillate between, on the one hand, explicating the concept of perversion in a way that captures our ordinary classifications of particular practices and, on the other, providing a sustained rationale for a defensible ideal of sexuality (with its attendant, sometimes revisionary, implications for what counts as a perversion). Here, as elsewhere, a "reflective equilibrium" between our intuitions and principles may be desirable. Perhaps most interesting from the point of view of the issues considered in this essay are Thomas Nagel's "Sexual Perversion" (1979d) and Sara Ruddick's "Better Sex" (in Baker & Elliston 1975). Nagel finds the essence of sexuality in multi-leveled personal interaction and awareness, a dialectic of desire and embodiment that makes desires in response to desires central to sexuality. Hence the criterion for perversion that emerges is in terms of interactive incompleteness—according to which homosexuality need not be perverse, foot fetishism must be, and heterosexual intercourse with distract-

ing fantasies might be. While the form of incompleteness is different, the emphasis on incompleteness might be suggestively connected with the sort of unification or totalization of components in Freud's final genital organization of sexuality—in terms of which perversions might be understood as component (or "incomplete") instincts. (Cf. Freud's statement, echoed often elsewhere, that the perversions are "on the one hand inhibitions, and on the other hand dissociations, of normal development"—1905d, 7: 231.) In any case, Nagel's emphasis on a full theory of the nature of sexual desire seems to me right-headed. Also of special interest is Ruddick's "Better Sex," which, among other things, sorts out clearly the relation of reproduction to perversion in ordinary language and understanding.

Freud's emphasis on the role of pleasure (or discharge) in sexuality should be complicated by his emphasis on the psychological conditions of pleasure (thought-dependent conditions of discharge). Pleasure, as Freud well understood, is not itself simply bodily or otherwise simple. When the question shifts from sexuality and pleasure to the larger questions of love and falling in love, a whole range of additional factors has to be taken into account. Love and the family bring the Oedipus complex back to the center of the picture, and love relationships (whether the object is of the same or opposite gender) have to be understood in terms of transference, ego-ideals, and the splitting of the ego (Freud 1921c). The coming together of the sexual and affectionate currents in a mature love relationship raises all sorts of difficulties, but failures in this coming together tend to result in what might more properly be called "neurotic" love than "perverse" love (e.g., Oedipal dependence or triangles are recreated, or needs for degraded or forbidden objects with accompanying patterns of psychical impotence emerge—see 1905d, 7: 200 and 1912d, 11: 180–87).

8. It might for some purposes be helpful to maintain the distinction between inversion and perversion. For it then becomes easier to ask whether it is their inversion (in object) that makes some individuals perverse (in aim), or whether it is their perversion (in aim) that makes some individuals inverted (in their choice of object). Or, to put it slightly differently, the question of perversion may be relatively independent of the question of choice of object (of homosexuality or heterosexuality).

9. Indeed some analysts, such as Michael Balint, insist that many forms of homosexuality "are definitely not survivals of infantile forms of sexuality but later developments" (1965, 136). But it must be noted that many of Balint's views are insupportable, or at any rate not provided with support. In particular, he claims homosexuals "all know—that, without normal intercourse, there is no real contentment" (142). The development of psychoanlytic views of homosexuality from Freud onward is usefully traced in Lewes (1988).

The deeper problem raised by lesbianism (presuming that everyone starts with a female primary love object) may be how anyone (female or male) can love a man. Is it the sameness or the maleness of the object that matters for a homosexual? Again, how does maleness matter for women? For anyone?

10. When Mick Jagger married Bianca, a woman with some striking resemblances to him, some malicious wits claimed that Mick had finally succeeded in marrying himself.

11. Among the mechanisms of homosexual object-choice considered by Freud, the main one involves identification with the mother (1905d, 7: 145 n.; 1910c, 11: 98–101; 1921c, 18: 108; 1922b, 18: 230–31) and a secondary one involves reaction-formation against sibling rivalry (1922b, 18: 231–32). Freud

speaks elsewhere, in connection with a case of lesbianism, of "retiring in favour of someone else" (Freud 1920a, 18: 159n.). Lewes (1988) distinguises four main strands in Freud's theorizing about the etiology of homosexuality.

12. There is a difficult early passage in which Freud connects homosexuality with a transitional phase of narcissism (1911c, 12: 60–61). It is thoughtfully discussed by Laplanche and Pontalis (1973, 259).

13. The basic facts are recounted in Marmor (1980). A more detailed journalistic account is available in Bayer (1981). See also Lewes (1988, 213–29).

14. This may conflict with the APA's own general characterization of a mental disorder, which includes the following restriction: "When the disturbance is limited to a conflict between an individual and society, this may represent social deviance, which may or may not be commendable, but is not by itself a mental disorder" (APA, DSM-III, 1980, 363).

Culver and Gert (1982) raise difficulties of their own with the APA definitions and classifications of mental disorders, but they are less troubled than they ought to be about the category of "ego-dystonic homosexuality." They write:

> the primary reason why certain recurring sexual behaviors are maladies is that they are ego-dystonic. The person engaging in the behavior is distressed by it. Of course, such behavior is probably also a manifestation of a volitional disability, but even if it is not, the distress, if significant, is sufficient to make it count as a malady. Note that neither in the case of distress nor of a volitional disability is the sexual condition a malady because it is sexual, but rather because of some other characteristic attached to the condition. Thus, we believe that when homosexuality qualifies as a malady it is because of the distress the person experiences, not because of the person's homosexual phantasies or desires. (104)

But I believe that by their own criteria for what counts as a "malady" they should be more equivocal. They argue (Culver & Gert 1982, 95–98) that grief should not be regarded as a disease because it has a "distinct sustaining cause" (namely, an external loss—if the sufferer came to believe the loss was not real, grief and suffering would cease). And so it would seem that it is unclear whether "ego-dystonic homosexuality" is, in their terms, a "malady." Doesn't the suffering (and even the putative "volitional disability") have a "distinct sustaining cause"? After all, if society changed its attitude, the suffering might disappear and there might be no need to overcome desires. Culver and Gert at one point write: "If a person is suffering or at increased risk of suffering evils principally because of conflict with his social environment, then his social environment would be a distinct sustaining cause of his suffering and he would not have a malady" (1982, 94). A theory of the source of suffering is needed if suffering is to be the sign of a malady. Even supposing a change in social attitudes would not in a given case remove suffering, when a desire is ego-dystonic, it may be because the individual has internalized mistaken standards. Is the problem then in the desire or in the standards (it is the two together that produce the distress)? Which should be changed? An individual can suffer from an unjustified (but perhaps socially encouraged) self-loathing.

15. For example, Freud writes:

> It is well known that a good number of homosexuals are characterized by a special development of their social instinctual impulses and by their devotion to the interests of the community . . . the fact that homo-

sexual object-choice not infrequently proceeds from an early overcoming of rivalry with men cannot be without a bearing on the connection between homosexuality and social feeling. (1922b, 18: 232)

The more usual connection that Freud makes is, of course, between social feeling and sublimated homosexuality (rather than active homosexuality):

> After the stage of heterosexual object-choice has been reached, the homosexual tendencies are not, as might be supposed, done away with or brought to a stop; they are merely deflected from their sexual aim and applied to fresh uses. They now combine with portions of the ego-instincts and, as "attached" components, help to constitute the social instincts, thus contributing an erotic factor to friendship and comradeship, to *esprit de corps* and to the love of mankind in general. How large a contribution is in fact derived from erotic sources (with the sexual aim inhibited) could scarcely be guessed from the normal social relations of mankind. But it is not irrelevant to note that it is precisely manifest homosexuals, and among them again precisely those that set themselves against an indulgence in sensual acts, who are distinguished by taking a particularly active share in the general interests of humanity—interests which have themselves sprung from a sublimation of erotic instincts. (1911c, 12: 61)

16. In understanding why here, we also understand what it means to describe a desire or practice as "perverse." Foot fetishism is not generally regarded as disgusting. What is disturbing or troubling about it is the idea that someone might be (sexually) interested *only* in feet. However much such focus might simplify life, it does seem to leave out other valuable possibilities.

17. The problem here is rather like the problem with certain other behaviorist attempts to explain complex psychological phenomena. For example, Wolpe and Rachman suggest, in relation to Freud's case of Little Hans, "that the incident to which Freud refers as merely the exciting cause of Hans' phobia was in fact the cause of the entire disorder" (1963, 216). The incident involved was Hans's witnessing the fall of a horse that was drawing a bus. Aside from other problems with their account (see Neu 1977, 124–35, and 1995b [chap. 12 here]), Freud had pointed out fifty years before: "Chronological considerations make it impossible for us to attach any great importance to the actual precipitating cause of the outbreak of Hans's illness, for he had shown signs of apprehensiveness long before he saw the bus-horse fall down in the street" (1909b, 10: 136).

Later additions to the psychoanalytic theory of fetishism (including emphasis on phases of development earlier than the phallic stage) are traced in Greenacre (1979).

18. I, like Nagel (1979d), wish to give special emphasis to the role of desires in perversion. For whether a particular activity or practice as engaged in by a particular individual should be regarded as perverse typically depends on the desires that inform his practice (though the force of this point might vary with alternative criteria for perversion and for sexuality). Description, here as elsewhere, is theory-laden. Whether a particular observable action counts as "neurotic" depends on why it was done, on its meaning. A person who washes his hands fifteen times a day need not be obsessive-compulsive: he may be a surgeon. Similarly, a "golden shower" performed out of sexual interest has a very different signifi-

cance in respect to the question of "perversion" than one done as an emergency measure to treat a sea urchin wound. Of course, actions can be overdetermined, motives can be mixed, and motives can be hidden. In any case, the full description of what a person is doing typically depends on what he thinks (whether consciously or unconsciously) he is doing and why. Underlying thoughts and desires are essential in characterizing the nature of activities and practices.

And again, in understanding the nature of desires themselves, the role of thoughts can scarcely be overemphasized. As Stuart Hampshire concludes in the course of a discussion of the role of thought in desire:

> the traditional scheme, which distinguishes the lusts from thoughtful desires, may turn out to be much too simple, and to reflect too grossly simple moral ideas. Any study of sexuality shows that thought, usually in the form of fantasy, enters into a great variety of sexual desires, which are normally also associated with physical causes. The traditional equation of physical desire, or lust, with unthinking desire is not warranted by the evidence. Nor is it true that the more reflective and fully conscious desires, which are in this sense rational, are necessarily or always the most complex. On the contrary, there can be pre-conscious and unconscious desires which are shown to have developed from very complex processes of unreflective and imaginative thought. (1975, 137)

19. As Freud puts it in discussing the case of the Rat Man: "a man's attitude in sexual things has the force of a model to which the rest of his reactions tend to conform" (1909d, 10: 241). The thought also forms the basis for Freud's main doubt about masturbation: "injury may occur through the laying down of a *psychical pattern* according to which there is no necessity for trying to alter the external world in order to satisfy a great need" (1912f, 12: 251–52; cf. 1908d, 9: 198–200). I should perhaps note that he continues: "Where, however, a far-reaching reaction against this pattern develops, the most valuable character-traits may be initiated."

10. What Is Wrong with Incest?

A version of this essay was presented at the Pacific Division Meeting of the American Philosophical Association in March 1975. It has benefited from the comments of a number of people, but I am especially indebted to Robert Meister for criticism of an earlier draft. What is best in the essay is due to him.

1. This point is elaborated in Neu (1974).

2. Lévi-Strauss develops this idea (though perhaps confusing sex and marriage—incest and exogamy—in the process) in terms of women as tokens for exchange in his *The Elementary Structures of Kinship* (1949). See Leach (1970, chap 6).

3. What the role of the performance of plays such as *Oedipus Rex* and related rituals (e.g., the totemic feasts discussed by Freud, 1912–13) may be raises interesting questions. It may be that they provide occasions both for violating the taboo and for reaffirming its force (by repeating the feelings that led to its original institution).

4. On the place of absolute prohibitions in morality and ways of life, see Hampshire (1973).

11. Fantasy and Memory

1. Cf. Freud's "Lecture on Hysteria" of this period. He there argues that the memory is a "direct" rather than "releasing" cause by reversing the dictum "when the cause ceases the effect ceases" (1893h, 35; the passage is paralleled in Freud & Breuer 1895d, 7, where the memory is called a "directly releasing cause").

2. The editors of the *Standard Edition* note that the use of "intentionally" and "deliberately" to modify "repressed" "is expanded by Freud in one place (1894a) where he states that the act of repression is 'introduced by an effort of will, for which the motive can be assigned.' Thus the word 'intentionally' merely indicates the existence of a motive and carries no implication of conscious intention" (1895d, 10n.1). If this is so, what then is the "effort of will"?

There is further, indirect, evidence that Freud means conscious intention when he says "intentionally." He insists that conscious awareness of conflict (of incompatible ideas) must occur before the repression involved in "defense hysteria" can take place (1895d, 167). In the context of the statement about intentionally repressing, he speaks of the patient as "determined to forget" (1895d, 11). He also speaks of a patient's (Lucy's) "moral cowardice" ("the mechanism which produces hysteria represents on the one hand an act of moral cowardice and on the other a defensive measure which is at the disposal of the ego"), which seems inappropriate if the repression were not in the patient's control, i.e., "intentional" (1895d, 123). And at this stage, Freud's theory contains no notion of unconscious intentions, only unconscious memories.

3. There may be a question whether symptoms that are not in some way repetitions of elements in the originating thoughts and circumstances (e.g., Emmy's "Don't move!") should count as mnemic symbols. But if a connection by association or symbolism is sufficient to make for "repetition," it is not clear why a response (though not quite "mnemic" and certainly not a "symbol") should not be included. Mnemic symbols are basically substitutes for memories, and symptoms that are responses, associations, or directly symbolic all serve that function. (See Freud, 1910a, 16–17.)

4. I am indebted to Dr. Paul Myerson and Dr. John Maltsberger for providing clinical information.

5. The occurrence of a fantasy can, of course, itself be called a "real event," but I shall, for the moment, be using "reality" to refer to events as contrasted with fantasies of such events.

6. Dr. Stewart provides a detailed and careful account of the early theory of neurosis in chapters 3 and 4 of his book.

7. I am indebted to Gerald N. Izenberg for clarifying these developments, as well as other points.

8. Consider, for example, the Rat Man's transference rage against Freud (1909d). Is it infantile rage against his father continuing or is it a new rage? Is there distortion in perception and unconscious beliefs as a result of dispositions and character traits that cover (recurring) unconscious conflict? What is the status of such questions and their answers? Here one ought also to examine the nature of the more general psychoanalytic claim that later psychological failures are to be traced to disturbances in earlier development. Do empirical and statistical studies (e.g., of the connection between toilet-training and later "anal" characteristics) miss the point of the hypotheses they are meant to test? Do they necessarily miss the point? (See chap. 12 here.)

9. [Note added 1998.] During the twenty-five years since the original publication of this essay, there has been enormous controversy concerning fantasy and memory, in particular in terms of claimed "recovered memories" of sexual abuse. Freud has been accused of (among many other things) abandoning the horrible truths concerning child molestation confided to him by his women patients. Several points about the "recovered memory" controversy should be made based on the developments traced in this essay. First, Freud never denied that child molestation in fact sometimes takes place. His big discovery when he abandoned his *neurotica*, his seduction theory of hysteria, was that hysteria could emerge even in the absence of an actual sexual assault. Fantasy could have the same effects. Second, and theoretically of even greater significance, the major development in Freud's theory was the recognition that what was repressed was not *memories*, but *desires*. On the original theory, it had always been mysterious why it was that hysterical symptoms did not use up the (external) energy attached to traumatic childhood experiences, and so exhaust themselves and (in effect) cure themselves. The (internal) energy of unconscious desires solved that problem, among others. Recurring instinctual energy came to be seen as what fueled the repetition of symptoms. Third, some have charged that Freud abandoned his seduction theory out of "moral cowardice," that is, because of the unpopularity of the recognition of the sexual molestation of children in bourgeois Vienna. But that charge is simply ludicrous. For what Freud abandoned his seduction theory in favor of was his theory of infantile sexuality, which involved denial of the innocence of childhood—an even more unpopular view (perhaps especially at that time and place). The shift in theories is more than adequately explained by theoretical demands alone.

12. *"Does the Professor Talk to God?"*

The essay title comes from Freud (1909b), *Analysis of a Phobia in a Five-Year-Old Boy, Standard Edition* 10: 42. References to the case of Little Hans after this will occur as bare parenthetical page numbers in the text.

1. Especially in this section, but also elsewhere, I am indebted to lectures I heard Gerald N. Izenberg give many years ago. I am very grateful to him for the guidance provided by his remarkably clearheaded understanding of Freud.

2. Freud elaborates these points in his later discussion of the case of Little Hans in 1926: Hans fears his father because of his own hostile impulses toward his father (1926d, 102–3). The fear of the horse biting projects Hans's own oral aggression (1926d, 106) and can be understood as equivalent to castration (1926d, 108).

On Jonathan Lear's interesting reading, the displaced fear of horses is to be seen as an archaic (undeveloped, primary process) form of the fear of the father: "it is not that the conscious idea of a horse is substituted for the unconscious idea of the father. Rather for Hans's unconscious, there is no significant difference between fathers and horses" (1990, 109). This sheds light on the nature of primary process thinking, but it underemphasizes the evidence for a simultaneous, if not preexisting, independent fear of the father as such.

3. Freud adds a hilarious footnote on Wundt and the philosophy of science, in which he defends Little Hans against the charge of "the premature decay of a child's intellect" (11 n.3). On observing his baby sister being given a bath, Hans remarked, "'But her widdler's still quite small,' . . . and then added, as

though by way of consolation: 'When she grows up it'll get bigger all right'" (11: cf. 62). Freud points out that one does not surrender a well-confirmed theory simply on the basis of an isolated observation and in the absence of a plausible alternative theory. Little Hans appears an investigator in the spirit of Duhem and Kuhn (cf. 106). We are told that in the view of the school of Wundt "consciousness is the invariable characteristic of what is mental, just as in the view of little Hans a widdler is the indispensable criterion of what is animate." The unfortunate Wundt is charged with seeing (or, ambiguously, having) a "very small" widdler when he substitutes "semi-conscious" phenomena for the recognition of unconscious ones (12n).

4. Cf. certain modern feminist views of intercourse as rape. The tendency is to assimilate all heterosexual intercourse, in a society characterized by male power, to rape. While crucially based on the notion that general social inequality between the sexes makes free consent by subordinate or oppressed women to dominant men impossible, the view may be reinforced, if not otherwise influenced, by this infantile sexual theory. Indeed, the argument in terms of consent in an unequal society may itself in a sense infantilize women, regarding them like children who as a matter of law are held to be incapable of consent, in the case of children because "below the age of consent." (A contrast between structural incompetence and mental incompetence remains.) Andrea Dworkin starts her book *Intercourse* by crediting the Tolstoy of *The Kreutzer Sonata* with (what she takes to be) the insight that "intercourse was implicitly violent, predicated as it was on exploitation and objectification," that "sexual intercourse requires objectification and therefore is exploitation" (1987, 19), and concludes: "Perhaps incestuous rape is becoming a central paradigm for intercourse in our time" (1987, 194). Catherine MacKinnon, writing more subtly, criticizes feminist writers such as Susan Brownmiller who emphasize the element of violence in rape: "Never is it asked whether, under conditions of male supremacy, the notion of consent has any real meaning for women . . . Consent is not scrutinized to see whether it is a structural fiction to legitimize the real coercion built into the normal social definitions of heterosexual intercourse . . . They [readers] need never confront whether women have a chance, structurally speaking and as a normal matter, even to consider whether they want to have sex or not" (1979, 298 n.8). MacKinnon wants to question "the extent to which the institution of heterosexuality has defined force as a normal part of 'the preliminaries.'" She asks, "is ordinary sexuality, under conditions of gender inequality, to be presumed healthy?" (219).

13. Lévi-Strauss on Shamanism

The substance of this essay was originally included in a larger essay on "Thought, Theory, and Therapy," which was presented to a seminar on "Nosology" at the San Francisco Psychoanalytic Institute (March 1973) and a symposium on "Images of Body States" at the American Anthropological Association meeting (November 1973).

1. Whether such parallels exist we still do not know. And it is not clear, even if such parallels exist, whether "reductions" are possible. There is an enormous philosophical literature on the question of whether even "sensations" could be "brain processes." The importance of a distinction between "reduction" and "replacement" was first impressed on me by Alasdair MacIntyre.

14. *"Getting Behind the Demons"*

1. See Quine (1960, chap. 2); Harman (1967); B. R. Wilson (1970); Hookway and Pettit (1978).

2. At one point, Theodor Reik (1976 [1931], 83) concludes: "The people, therefore, are only apparently making an absurd statement when they say that the killing of an animal by the father will bring injuries and even death to the child, since this animal represents the child itself." Truth here is preserved by translation.

3. Freud, quoting Sir James C. Frazer, in *Totem and Taboo* (1912–13), 13: 82.

4. Think of the question of the meaningfulness of endless life, with its repeated patterns: length does not necessarily make life more meaningful (Nagel 1979a); indeed, it may make it boring (Williams 1973d).

5. Sometimes, in the face of nonsense, reasons are simply rejected rather than examined. Freud provides an interesting example at the start of his essay on "Dreams and Occultism":

> Let us suppose that the question at issue is the constitution of the interior of the earth . . . But suppose now that someone else comes along and seriously asserts that the core of the earth consists of jam. Our reaction to this will be quite different. We shall tell ourselves that jam does not occur in nature, that it is a product of human cooking, that, moreover, the existence of this material presupposes the presence of fruit-trees and their fruit, and that we cannot see how we can locate vegetation and human cookery in the interior of the earth. The result of these intellectual objections will be a switching of our interest: instead of starting upon an investigation of whether the core of the earth really consists of jam, we shall ask ourselves what sort of person this must be who can arrive at such a notion, or at most we shall ask him where he got it from. (1933a, 22: 32)

But then, as the inventor of psychoanalysis quickly adds, one should be wary of too quickly dismissing strange views as nonsense (22: 33).

6. See Gellner, MacIntyre, and Lukes in B. R. Wilson (1970); and Lévi-Strauss, *Totemism* (1963c).

7. Turner has elsewhere (while acknowledging the multivocality of symbols, the facts of cultural sublimation and suppression of meaning, the usefulness of notions such as "ambivalence" and "projection" and of procedures such as confession or making the unconscious conscious) reaffirmed his view of the limited power of psychoanalytic explanation: "I still think that it is theoretically inadmissible to explain social facts, such as ritual symbols, directly by the concepts of depth psychology" (1978, 576).

8. See N. O. Brown (1959), esp. parts 4 and 5.

9. These issues are intricately and compellingly explored by Richard Wollheim (1993 [1979]).

15. *Life-Lies and Pipe Dreams*

Parenthetical page references to *The Wild Duck* are to the translation by Rolf Fjelde in his *Ibsen: The Complete Major Prose Plays* (New York: Farrar, Straus & Giroux, 1978). Parenthetical page references to Eugene O'Neill's *The Iceman Cometh* are to the Vintage Books edition (New York, 1957).

1. More fully: if you think you have gotten what you think you need, you are content. Whether animals are capable of even contentment will depend on the degree of conscious thought one is prepared to ascribe to them. (I take the "acknowledgment" in this notion of contentment to require only consciousness, not self-consciousness.)

2. This does not settle the question of whether, before Gregers's meddling, Hjalmar was in fact happy. But with a distinction between happiness and contentment in hand, I think we are at least closer to a clear understanding. It is plausible to regard him as contented insofar as he at least believes his needs are met. It is harder to regard him as happy, though not for Gregers's reasons. In Hjalmar's case less than all arguable human needs are acknowledged and even the acknowledged ones may not in fact be met (he just believes they are). There are flaws in his situation and in him. Even his contentment is precarious.

Compare the situation of another of Ibsen's characters, Nora, at the end of *A Doll's House*:

HELMER: Haven't you been happy here?

NORA: No, never. I thought so—but I never have.

HELMER: Not—not happy!

NORA: No, only lighthearted. (191, Fjelde trans.)

3. The wild duck is the title character who never makes it onto the stage. Gregers twice likens Hjalmar to the wild duck: "My dear Hjalmar, I suspect you've got a bit of the wild duck in you . . . You've plunged to the bottom and clamped hold of the seaweed" (443). "You've *lots* of the wild duck in you Hjalmar" (459). Earlier, Gregers's father had likened Old Ekdal to the wild duck: "When Ekdal was let out, he was a broken man, beyond any help. There are people in this world who plunge to the bottom when they've hardly been winged, and they never come up again" (405). And later, Hedvig compares herself to the wild duck, not as giving up in defeat, but as a foundling (470).

4. One also has to distinguish questions about the truth in general and about self-deception in particular. Hjalmar may have been deceived about Gina's past, but that deception was due to others (Gina, the elder Werle). Gregers was not concerned to uncover Hjalmar's self-deceptions, which included the life-lie of the invention. Once Hjalmar admits the notion was a sham, he still realizes that he got much happiness out of it (484).

5. The problems and paradoxes of the intentionality of self-deception are fruitfully explored by Herbert Fingarette (1969). On the limits of decision in relation to belief see H. H. Price (1954).

6. One need not be a behaviorist in order to see this. To claim that one is not the final and incorrigible authority on one's own psychological states is not to say that one has no privileged access to one's states (after all, I can know I am in pain directly, by feeling it—you may also be aware that I am in pain, but you must know it by another route) or no special authority in relation to them (I may not need evidence in order to know I am in a certain state, say, that I am amused by your remark, even while I must be open to counterevidence, such as that of negative parallel instances, that would show I am mistaken). For more on a possible middle way between Cartesianism and behaviorism, see Stuart Hampshire (1972d).

7. The translator may be importing "pipe dream" back from O'Neill. The sentence is translated as "It was a delusion" by Michael Meyer, *The Wild Duck*

(London: Methuen, 1968), p. 93, and by R. F. Sharp, *Four Great Plays By Ibsen* (New York: Bantam, 1971), p. 276.

8. There may be another way of putting the point here, as a difficulty in distinguishing self-deception and faith. They both involve belief against the evidence. Ultimately I suspect the difference may be merely retrospective: that if one turns out to have been right in one's belief, then one had "faith" (what one had was faith). Those whose faith turns out misplaced turn out to be "self-deceived." As we live our lives, not knowing the outcome in advance, the governing notions may have to be those of chance, of a gamble, or (using Pascal) a wager. Often it is a wager one can never be sure one has won. ("Until he is dead, do not yet call a man happy, but only lucky"—Solon's words according to Herodotus, I. 32, a thought famously echoed in the final lines of Sophocles's *King Oedipus*.)

REFERENCES

Asterisks indicate chapters in this book.

Abraham, K. 1927. *Selected Papers on Psycho-Analysis*. Trans. D. Bryan and A. Strachey. London: Hogarth.

Achilles Tatius. 1917. *Achilles Tatius*. Trans. S. Gaselee. Loeb Classical Library. Cambridge: Harvard University Press.

American Psychiatric Association. 1980. *Diagnostic and Statistical Manual of Mental Disorders, Third Edition*. [DSM-III.] Washington, D.C.: APA.

Andersson, O. 1962. *Studies in the Prehistory of Psychoanalysis*. Stockholm: Norstedt.

Andrew, R. J. 1965. "The Origins of Facial Expressions." *Scientific American* 213 (October): 88–94.

Aquinas, St. Thomas. 1995 [1269]. *On Evil*. Trans. Jean Oesterle. Notre Dame, Ind.: University of Notre Dame Press.

Aristotle. 1984. *The Complete Works of Aristotle*, ed. Jonathan Barnes. Princeton, N.J.: Princeton University Press.

Auden, W. H. 1964. "The Joker in the Pack." *Selected Essays*. London: Faber and Faber.

Augustine, St. 1960 [401]. *The Confessions of St. Augustine*. Trans. John K. Ryan. Garden City, N.Y.: Doubleday Image Books.

Ayer, A. J. 1936. *Language, Truth and Logic*. London: Gollancz.

Baker, R., and F. Elliston, eds. 1975. *Philosophy and Sex*. Buffalo: Prometheus.

Balint, M. 1965. "Perversions and Genitality." In *Primary Love and Psychoanalytic Technique*. London: Tavistock.

Baudelaire, C. 1982 [1861]. *Les Fleurs du Mal*. Trans. Richard Howard. Boston: David R. Godine.

Bayer, R. 1981. *Homosexuality and American Psychiatry: The Politics of Diagnosis*. New York: Basic.

Beloff, H. 1970 [1957]. "The Structure and Origin of the Anal Character." In

Freud and Psychology, eds. S. G. M. Lee and M. Herbert, 121–47. Harmondsworth, England: Penguin.

Bellow, S. 1975. "On Boredom" (from *Humboldt's Gift*). *New York Review of Books* (August 7): 22.

Benjamin, J. 1988. *The Bonds of Love*. New York: Pantheon.

Berryman, J. 1969. *The Dream Songs*. New York: Farrar, Straus and Giroux.

Bersani, L. 1995. *Homos*. Cambridge: Harvard University Press.

Bibring, E. 1941. "The Development and Problems of the Theory of the Instincts." *International Journal of Psychoanalysis* 21: 102–31.

Blake, W. 1971. *The Poems of William Blake*. Ed. W. H. Stevenson. London: Longman.

Bloomfield, M. W. 1952. *The Seven Deadly Sins: An Introduction to the History of a Religious Concept, with Special Reference to Medieval English Literature*. East Lansing, Mich.: Michigan State College Press.

Bowlby, J. 1975 [1973]. *Separation (Attachment and Loss*, vol. 2). Harmondsworth, England: Penguin.

Bowra, C. M. 1961. *Greek Lyric Poetry from Alcman to Simonides*. 2nd rev. ed. Oxford: Clarendon Press.

Boswell, J. 1980. *Christianity, Social Tolerance, and Homosexuality*. Chicago: University of Chicago Press.

Brown, N. O. 1959. *Life against Death*. Middletown, Conn.: Wesleyan University Press.

Brown, N. O. 1966. *Love's Body*. New York: Vintage.

Brown, P. 1988. *The Body and Society: Men, Women and Sexual Renunciation in Early Christianity*. New York: Columbia University Press.

Camus, A. 1946. *The Stranger*. Trans. Stuart Gilbert. New York: Knopf.

Cannon, W. B. 1968 [1927]. "The James-Lange Theory of Emotion: A Critical Examination and an Alternative Theory." *American Journal of Psychology* (1927); reprinted in *The Nature of Emotion*, ed. M. B. Arnold, 43–51. Harmondsworth, England: Penguin.

Carson, A. 1986. *Eros the Bittersweet*. Princeton, N.J.: Princeton University Press.

Catullus, G. V. 1962. *The Poems of Gaius Valerius Catullus*. Trans. F. W. Cornish, Loeb Classical Library. Cambridge: Harvard University Press.

Chasseguet-Smirgel, J. 1984. "A Re-reading of 'Little Hans.'" In *Creativity and Perversion*, 35–43. New York: W. W. Norton.

Chodorow, N. 1978. *The Reproduction of Mothering*. Berkeley: University of California Press.

Cohen, D. 1987. "Law, Society and Homosexuality in Classical Athens." *Past and Present* 117 (Nov.): 3–21.

Collins, E. T. 1932. "The Physiology of Weeping." *British Journal of Opthalmology* 16: 1–20.

Culver, C., and B. Gert. 1982. *Philosophy in Medicine: Conceptual and Ethical Issues in Medicine*. Oxford: Oxford University Press.

Darwin, C. 1965 [1872]. *The Expression of the Emotions in Man and Animals*. Chicago: University of Chicago Press.

Davidson, D. 1973–74. "On the Very Idea of a Conceptual Scheme." *Proceedings and Addresses of the American Philosophical Association* 47: 5–20.

Davidson, D. 1980 [1976]. "Hume's Cognitive Theory of Pride." In *Essays on Actions and Events*, 277–90. Oxford: Oxford University Press.

Davidson, D. 1982. "Paradoxes of Irrationality." In *Philosophical Essays on Freud*, ed. R. Wollheim and J. Hopkins. Cambridge: Cambridge University Press.

Davis, K. 1936. "Jealousy and Sexual Property." *Social Forces* 14: 395–405.

Denniston, R. H. 1980. "Ambisexuality in Animals." In *Homosexual Behavior*, ed. J. Marmor, 25–40 . New York: Basic.

de Rougemont, D. 1983. *Love in the Western World*. Trans. M. Belgion, rev. ed. Princeton, N.J.: Princeton University Press.

Descartes, R. 1984 [1641]. *Meditations on First Philosophy*. Trans. J. Cottingham. In *The Philosophical Writings of Descartes*, ed. J. Cottingham, R. Stoothoff, and D. Murdoch, 2: 3–62. Cambridge: Cambridge University Press.

Descartes, R. 1985 [1649]. *The Passions of the Soul*. Trans. R. Stoothoff. In *The Philosophical Writings of Descartes*, ed. J. Cottingham, R. Stoothoff, and D. Murdoch, 1: 325–404. Cambridge: Cambridge University Press.

Diderot, D. 1957 [1773]. *The Paradox of Acting*. Trans. Walter Herries Pollock. New York: Hill and Wang.

Dodds, E. R. 1951. *The Greeks and the Irrational*. Berkeley: University of California Press.

Dover, K. J. 1964. "Eros and Nomos." *Bulletin of the Institute of Classical Studies* 11: 31–42.

Dover, K. J. 1965. "The Date of Plato's Symposium." *Phronesis* 10: 2–20.

Dover, K. J. 1966. "Aristophanes' Speech in Plato's Symposium." *Journal of Hellenic Studies* 86: 41–50.

Dover, K. J. 1978. *Greek Homosexuality*. London: Duckworth.

Dover, K. J., ed. 1980. *Plato: Symposium*. Cambridge: Cambridge University Press.

Duhem, P. 1954 [1905]. *The Aim and Structure of Physical Theory*. Trans. P. P. Wiener. Princeton, N.J.: Princeton University Press.

Durkheim, E. 1965 [1915]. *The Elementary Forms of the Religious Life*. Trans. Joseph Ward Swain. New York: Free Press.

Dworkin, A. 1987. *Intercourse*. New York: Free Press.

Ekman, P., R. W. Levenson, and W. V. Frieson. 1983. "Autonomic Nervous System Activity Distinguishes Between Emotions." *Science* 221: 1208–10.

Ekman, P. 1973. "Cross-Cultural Studies of Facial Expression." In *Darwin and Facial Expression*, ed. Paul Ekman, 169–222. New York: Academic.

Ekman, P. 1984. "Expression and the Nature of Emotion." In *Approaches to Emotion*, ed. Paul Ekman and Klaus R. Scherer, 319–43. Hillsdale, N.J.: Erlbaum.

Elster, J. 1979. *Ulysses and the Sirens*. Cambridge: Cambridge University Press.

Elster, J. 1983. "Sour Grapes." In *Sour Grapes: Studies in the Subversion of Rationality*, 109–40. Cambridge: Cambridge University Press.

Erikson, E. 1958. "The Nature of Clinical Evidence." In *Insight and Responsibility*. New York: Norton.

Erikson, E. 1963. *Childhood and Society*. 2nd ed. New York: W. W. Norton.

Erikson, E. 1964. "Psychological Reality and Historical Actuality." In *Insight and Responsibility*. New York: Norton.

Etchegoyen, R. H. 1988. "The Analysis of Little Hans and the Theory of Sexuality." *International Review of Psycho-Analysis* 15: 37–43.

Evans-Pritchard, E. 1937. *Witchcraft, Oracles, and Magic among the Azande*. New York: Oxford University Press.

Eysenck, H. J. 1965. *Fact and Fiction in Psychology*. Harmondsworth, England: Penguin.

Fairlie, Henry. 1978. "Pride or Superbia." In *The Seven Deadly Sins Today*, 39–58. Notre Dame, Ind.: University of Notre Dame Press.

Feldman, S. S. 1956. "Crying at the Happy Ending." *Journal of the American Psychoanalytic Association* 4: 477–85.

Fenichel, O. 1953 [1934]. "On the Psychology of Boredom." In *The Collected Papers of Otto Fenichel*, First Series, 292–302. New York: W. W. Norton.

Fine, A., and M. Forbes. 1986. "Grünbaum on Freud: Three Grounds for Dissent." *Behavioral and Brain Sciences* 9: 237–38.

Fingarette, H. 1969. *Self-Deception*. London. Routledge and Kegan Paul.

Foot, P. 1978 [1958–59]. "Moral Beliefs." In *Virtues and Vices and Other Essays in Moral Philosophy*, 110–31. Berkeley: University of California Press.

Ford, G. H. 1965. *Dickens and His Readers*. New York: W. W. Norton.

Forrester, J. 1996. "Psychoanalysis and the History of the Passions: The Strange Destiny of Envy." In *Freud and the Passions*, ed. J. O'Neill, 127–49. University Park, Pa.: Pennsylvania State University Press.

Foster, G. M. 1972. "The Anatomy of Envy: A Study in Symbolic Behavior." *Current Anthropology* 13: 165–202.

Foucault, M. 1986. *The Use of Pleasure*. Vol. 2. *The History of Sexuality*. New York: Vintage.

Frankfurt, H. G. 1971. "Freedom of the Will and the Concept of a Person." *Journal of Philosophy* 68: 5–20.

Freud, A. 1966 [1936]. "Identification with the Aggressor." In *The Ego and the Mechanisms of Defence*. London: Hogarth.

Freud, S. 1953–74 [1888–89]. "Preface to the Translation of Bernheim's *Suggestion*." In *Standard Edition of the Complete Psychological Works of Sigmund Freud*, vol. 1, ed. James Strachey. London: Hogarth.

Freud, S. [1889a]. "Review of August Forel's *Hypnotism*." In *SE* 1.

Freud, S. [1893c]. "Some Points for a Comparative Study of Organic and Hysterical Motor Paralyses." In *SE* 1.

Freud, S. [1893h]. "On the Psychical Mechanism of Hysterical Phenomena: A Lecture." Written with Josef Breuer. In *SE* 3.

Freud, S. [1894a]. "The Neuro-Psychoses of Defence." In *SE* 3.

Freud, S. [1895d]. *Studies in Hysteria*. Written with Josef Breuer. In *SE* 2.

Freud, S. [1896b]. "Further Remarks on the Neuro-Psychoses of Defence." In *SE* 3.

Freud, S. [1896c]. "The Aetiology of Hysteria." In *SE* 3.

Freud, S. [1898a]. "Sexuality in the Aetiology of the Neuroses." In *SE* 3.

Freud, S. [1899a]. "Screen Memories." In *SE* 3.

Freud, S. [1900]. *The Interpretation of Dreams*. In *SE* 4–5.

Freud, S. [1904]. "Freud's Psycho-Analytic Procedure." In *SE* 7.

Freud, S. [1905d]. *Three Essays on the Theory of Sexuality.* In *SE* 7.

Freud, S. [1905e]. *Fragment of an Analysis of a Case of Hysteria.* In *SE* 7.

Freud, S. [1907a]. *Delusions and Dreams in Jensen's "Gravida."* In *SE* 9.

Freud, S. [1907b]. "Obsessive Actions and Religious Practices." In *SE* 9.

Freud, S. [1908a]. "Hysterical Phantasies and Their Relation to Bisexuality." In *SE* 9.

Freud, S. [1908b]. "Character and Anal Erotism." In *SE* 9.

Freud, S. [1908c]. "On the Sexual Theories of Children." In *SE* 9.

Freud, S. [1908d]. "'Civilized' Sexual Morality and Modern Nervous Illness." In *SE* 9.

Freud, S. [1909b]. "Analysis of a Phobia in a Five-Year-Old Boy." In *SE* 10.

Freud, S. [1909d]. "Notes upon a Case of Obsessional Neurosis." In *SE* 10.

Freud, S. [1910a]. "Five Lectures on Psycho-Analysis." In *SE* 11.

Freud, S. [1910c]. *Leonardo da Vinci and a Memory of His Childhood.* In *SE* 11.

Freud, S. [1910d]. "The Future Prospects of Psycho-Analytic Therapy." In *SE* 11.

Freud, S. [1910e]. "The Antithetical Meaning of Primal Words." In *SE* 11.

Freud, S. [1910k]. "'Wild' Psycho-Analysis." In *SE* 11.

Freud, S. [1911c]. "Psycho-Analytic Notes on an Autobiographical Account of a Case of Paranoia." In *SE* 12.

Freud, S. [1912b]. "The Dynamics of Transference." In *SE* 12.

Freud, S. [1912c]. "Types of Onset of Neurosis." In *SE* 12.

Freud, S. [1912d]. "On the Universal Tendency to Debasement in the Sphere of Love." In *SE* 11.

Freud, S. [1912f]. "Contributions to a Discussion on Masturbation." In *SE* 12.

Freud, S. [1912–13]. *Totem and Taboo.* In *SE* 13.

Freud, S. [1913c]. "On Beginning the Treatment." In *SE* 12.

Freud, S. [1913i]. "The Disposition to Obsessional Neurosis." In *SE* 12.

Freud, S. [1914c]. "On Narcissism: An Introduction." In *SE* 14.

Freud, S. [1914g]. "Remembering, Repeating and Working-Through." In *SE* 12.

Freud, S. [1915a]. "Observations on Transference-Love." In *SE* 12.

Freud, S. [1915c]. "Instincts and Their Vicissitudes." In *SE* 14.

Freud, S. [1915d]. "Repression." In *SE* 14.

Freud, S. [1915e]. "The Unconscious." In *SE* 14.

Freud, S. [1916a]. "On Transience." In *SE* 14.

Freud, S. [1916–17]. *Introductory Lectures on Psycho-Analysis.* In *SE* 15–16.

Freud, S. [1917e]. "Mourning and Melancholia." In *SE* 14.

Freud, S. [1918a]. "The Taboo of Virginity." In *SE* 11.

Freud, S. [1918b]. "From the History of an Infantile Neurosis." In *SE* 17.

Freud, S. [1919e]. "'A Child is Being Beaten.'" In *SE* 17.

Freud, S. [1920a]. "The Psychogenesis of a Case of Female Homosexuality." In *SE* 18.

Freud, S. [1920g]. *Beyond the Pleasure Principle.* In *SE* 18.

Freud, S. [1921c]. *Group Psychology and the Analysis of the Ego.* In *SE* 18.

Freud, S. [1922b]. "Some Neurotic Mechanisms in Jealousy, Paranoia and Homosexuality." In *SE* 18.

Freud, S. [1923b]. *The Ego and the Id.* In *SE* 19.

Freud, S. [1923e]. "The Infantile Genital Organization." In *SE* 19.

Freud, S. [1924c]. "The Economic Problem of Masochism." In *SE* 19.

Freud, S. [1924d]. "The Dissolution of the Oedipus Complex." In *SE* 19.

Freud, S. [1925d]. *An Autobiographical Study.* In *SE* 20.

Freud, S. [1925h]. "Negation." In *SE* 19.

Freud, S. [1925i]. "Some Additional Notes on Dream-Interpretation as a Whole." In *SE* 19.

Freud, S. [1926d]. *Inhibitions, Symptoms and Anxiety.* In *SE* 20.

Freud, S. [1927c]. *The Future of an Illusion.* In *SE* 21.

Freud, S. [1927e]. "Fetishism." In *SE* 21.

Freud, S. [1930a]. *Civilization and its Discontents. SE* 21.

Freud, S. [1933a]. *New Introductory Lectures on Psycho-Analysis.* In *SE* 22.

Freud, S. [1939a]. *Moses and Monotheism.* In *SE* 23.

Freud, S. 1940a [1938]. *An Outline of Psycho-Analysis.* In *SE* 23.

Freud, S. 1940d [1892]. "On the Theory of Hysterical Attacks." Written with J. Breuer. In *SE* 1.

Freud, S. 1940e [1938]. "Splitting of the Ego in the Process of Defence." In *SE* 23.

Freud, S. 1950a [1887–1902]. *The Origins of Psycho-Analysis.* London: 1954. Partly, including *A Project for a Scientific Psychology,* in *SE* 1.

Freud, S. [1960a]. *Letters 1873–1939,* ed. Ernst L. Freud. Trans. Tania and James Stern. New York: Hogarth.

Freud, S. 1974. *The Freud/Jung Letters,* ed. W. McGuire. Trans. R. Manheim and R. F. C. Hull. Princeton, N.J.: Princeton University Press.

Freud, S. 1985 [1887–1904]. *The Complete Letters of Sigmund Freud to Wilhelm Fliess,* trans. and ed. J. M. Masson. Cambridge, Mass.: Harvard University Press.

Frey, W. H. 1985. *Crying: The Mystery of Tears.* Minneapolis: Winston.

Gagarin, M. 1977. "Socrates' Hybris and Alcibiades' Failure." *Phoenix* 31: 22–37

Geertz, C. 1973. "Deep Play: Notes on the Balinese Cockfight." In *The Interpretation of Cultures.* New York: Basic.

Geertz, C. 1977. "Found in Translation: On the Social History of the Moral Imagination." *Georgia Review* 31: 788–810.

Gellner, E. 1970. "Concepts and Society." In *Rationality,* ed. Bryan R. Wilson. New York: Harper and Row.

Genet, J. 1967 [1949]. *The Thief's Journal.* Trans. B. Frechtman. Harmondsworth, England: Penguin.

Gilligan, C. 1982. *In a Different Voice.* Cambridge, Mass.: Harvard University Press.

Glymour, C. 1980. *Theory and Evidence.* Princeton, N.J.: Princeton University Press.

Golding, W. 1954. *Lord of the Flies.* New York: Coward-McCann.

Graf, M. 1942. "Reminiscences of Prof. Sigmund Freud." *Psychoanalytic Quarterly* 11: 465–76.

Greenacre, P. 1979. "Fetishism." In *Sexual Deviation,* 2nd ed., ed. I. Rosen, 79–108. Oxford: Oxford University Press.

Greenson, R. R. 1953. "On Boredom." *American Psychoanalytic Association Journal* 1: 7–21.

Greenspan, P. 1980. "A Case of Mixed Feelings: Ambivalence and the Logic of Emotion." In *Explaining Emotions*, ed. Amélie Rorty. Berkeley: University of California Press.

Grünbaum, A. 1979. "Is Freudian Psychoanalytic Theory Pseudo-Scientific by Karl Popper's Criterion of Demarcation?" *American Philosophical Quarterly* 16: 131–41.

Grünbaum, A. 1984. *The Foundations of Psychoanalysis.* Berkeley: University of California Press.

Haight, M. R. 1980. *A Study of Self-Deception.* Sussex: Harvester.

Halperin, D. M. 1985. "Platonic Erôs and What Men Call Love." *Ancient Philosophy* 5: 161–204.

Halperin, D. M. 1986. "Plato and Erotic Reciprocity." *Classical Antiquity* 5: 60–80

Halperin, D. M. 1990. "Why Is Diotima a Woman?" In *One Hundred Years of Homosexuality and Other Essays on Greek Love*, 113–51. New York: Routledge.

Halperin, D. M. 1995. *Saint Foucault: Towards a Gay Hagiography.* Oxford: Oxford University Press.

Hampshire, S. 1972a. "Disposition and Memory." In *Freedom of Mind and Other Essays*, 160–82. Oxford: Oxford University Press.

Hampshire, S. 1972b. "Ethics: A Defense of Aristotle." In *Freedom of Mind and Other Essays*, 64–86. Oxford: Clarendon Press.

Hampshire, S. 1972c. "Feeling and Expression." In *Freedom of Mind and Other Essays*, 143–59. Oxford: Oxford University Press.

Hampshire, S. 1972d. "Sincerity and Single-mindedness." In *Freedom of Mind and Other Essays*, 232–56. Oxford: Oxford University Press.

Hampshire, S. 1973. "Morality and Pessimism." *New York Review of Books* 19, nos. 11–12 (January 25): 26–33. Reprinted in *Morality and Conflict* (Cambridge, Mass.: Harvard University Press, 1983), 82–100.

Hampshire, S. 1975. *Freedom of the Individual.* Princeton, N.J.: Princeton University Press.

Hampshire, S. 1996. "Justice Is Conflict: The Soul and the City." Tanner Lectures on Human Values, Harvard University, October 30–31, 1996. [unpublished ms]

Harman, G. 1967. "Quine on Meaning and Existence." *Review of Metaphysics* 21: 124–51.

Hart, H. L. A. 1968. "Responsibility." In *Punishment and Responsibility: Essays in the Philosophy of Law*, 211–30. Oxford: Clarendon Press.

Hartley, L. P. 1960. *Facial Justice.* London: Hamish Hamilton.

Hearn, L. 1894. "The Japanese Smile." In *Glimpses of Unfamiliar Japan.* New York: Houghton, Mifflin & Co.

Hegel, G. W. F. 1977 [1807]. *Phenomenology of Spirit.* Trans. A. V. Miller. Oxford: Oxford University Press.

Heron, W. 1957. "The Pathology of Boredom." *Scientific American* 196: 52–56.

Hill, T. E., Jr. 1991 [1973]. "Servility and Self-Respect." In *Autonomy and Self-Respect*, 4–18. Cambridge: Cambridge University Press.

Hirsch, F. 1976. *Social Limits to Growth.* Cambridge, Mass.: Harvard University Press.

Hochschild, A. R. 1983. *The Managed Heart: Commercialization of Human Feeling.* Berkeley: University of California Press.

Holland, N. N. 1985. *The I.* New Haven, Conn.: Yale University Press.

Hollis, M. 1970. "Reason and Ritual." In *Rationality,* ed. Bryan R. Wilson. New York: Harper and Row.

Homans, G. C., and D. M. Schneider. 1955. *Marriage, Authority, and Final Causes: A Study of Unilateral Cross-Cousin Marriage.* Glencoe, Ill.: Free Press.

Hookway, C., and P. Pettit, eds. 1978. *Action and Interpretation: Studies in the Philosophy of the Social Sciences.* New York: Cambridge University Press.

Hume, D. 1888 [1739]. *A Treatise of Human Nature,* ed. L. A. Selby-Bigge. Oxford: Oxford University Press.

Huxley, A. 1938. *Brave New World.* London: Chatto & Windus.

Ibsen, H. 1978 [1884]. *The Wild Duck.* In *Ibsen: The Complete Major Prose Plays.* Trans. Rolf Fjelde. New York: Farrar Straus & Giroux.

Ignatieff, M. 1993. *Blood and Belonging: Journeys into the New Nationalism.* New York: Farrar, Straus and Giroux.

Isenberg, A. 1980 [1949]. "Natural Pride and Natural Shame." In *Explaining Emotions,* ed. A. Rorty, 355–83. Berkeley: University of California Press.

Izard, C. E. 1980. "Cross-Cultural Perspectives on Emotion and Emotion Communication." In *Handbook of Cross-Cultural Psychology,* ed. H. Triandis, 185–221. Boston: Allyn and Bacon.

Izenberg, G. N. 1976. *The Existentialist Critique of Freud: The Crisis of Autonomy.* Princeton, N.J.: Princeton University Press.

Jackson, S. W. 1986. *Melancholia and Depression: From Hippocratic Times to Modern Times.* New Haven, Conn.: Yale University Press.

James, W. 1968 [1884]. "What Is an Emotion?" *Mind;* reprinted in *The Nature of Emotion,* ed. M. B. Arnold, 17–36. Harmondsworth, England: Penguin.

Joffe, W. C. 1969. "A Critical Review of the Status of the Envy Concept." *International Journal of Psychoanalysis* 50: 533–45.

Jones, E. 1953. *Sigmund Freud: Life and Work,* vol. 1. London: Hogarth.

Kant, I. 1964 [1797]. *The Metaphysical Principles of Virtue.* Trans. J. Ellington. Indianapolis: Bobbs-Merrill.

Kanter, R. M. 1972. *Commitment and Community.* Cambridge, Mass.: Harvard University Press.

Kaplan, M. 1997. *Sexual Justice: Democratic Citizenship and the Politics of Desire.* New York: Routledge.

Kierkegaard, S. 1959 [1843]. "The Rotation Method." In *Either/Or.* Trans. D. F. Swenson and L. M. Swenson, 1: 279–96. Princeton, N.J.: Princeton University Press.

Kierkegaard, S. 1983 [1843]. *Repetition,* ed. and trans. H. V. and E. H. Hong. Princeton, N.J.: Princeton University Press.

Klein, M. 1975 [1957]. "Envy and Gratitude." *Writings of Melanie Klein,* 3: 176–235. London: Hogarth.

Klineberg, O. 1935. *Race Differences.* New York: Harper.

Koch, P. J. 1987. "Emotional Ambivalence." In *Philosophy and Phenomenological Research* 48: 257–79.

Kuhn, R. 1976. *The Demon of Noontide: Ennui in Western Literature.* Princeton, N.J.: Princeton University Press.

Kuhn, T. S. 1962. *The Structure of Scientific Revolutions.* Chicago: University of Chicago Press.

LaBarre, W. 1947. "The Cultural Basis of Emotions and Gestures." *Journal of Personality* 16: 49–68.

Laplanche, J., and J.-B. Pontalis. 1973. *The Language of Psycho-Analysis.* London: Hogarth.

Leach, E. 1970. *Lévi-Strauss.* Glasgow/London: Fontana Modern Masters, Collins Publishers.

Lear, J. 1990. *Love and Its Place in Nature.* New York: Farrar, Straus & Giroux.

Lévi-Strauss, C. 1969 [1949]. *The Elementary Structures of Kinship.* Trans. from the French by J. H. Bell and J. R. von Sturmer; ed. R. Needham. London: Eyre and Spottiswoode.

Lévi-Strauss, C. 1963a. "The Sorcerer and His Magic." In *Structural Anthropology,* 167–85. New York: Basic.

Lévi-Strauss, C. 1963b. "The Effectiveness of Symbols." In *Structural Anthropology,* 186–205. New York: Basic.

Lévi-Strauss, C. 1963c. *Totemism.* Trans. R. Needham. Boston: Beacon.

Lewes, K. 1988. *The Psychoanalytic Theory of Male Homosexuality.* New York: Simon and Schuster.

Lewis, C. S. 1936. *The Allegory of Love.* Oxford: Oxford University Press.

Lofgren, L. B. 1966. "On Weeping." *International Journal of Psycho-Analysis* 47: 375–81.

Lounsbury, F. 1962. "Review of *Structure and Sentiment.*" *American Anthropologist* 44: 1302–10.

Lukes, S. 1970. "Some Problems about Rationality." In *Rationality,* ed. B. R. Wilson. New York: Harper and Row.

Lyman, S. M. 1978. *The Seven Deadly Sins: Society and Evil.* New York: St. Martin's.

MacIntyre, A. 1970. "Is Understanding Religion Compatible with Believing?" In *Rationality,* ed. B. R. Wilson. New York: Harper and Row.

MacIntyre, A. 1971. "Emotion, Behaviour and Belief." In *Against the Self-Images of the Age.* London: Duckworth.

MacKinnon, C. A. 1979. *Sexual Harassment of Working Women.* New Haven: Yale University Press.

Marmor, J. 1980. "Epilogue: Homosexuality and the Issue of Mental Illness." In *Homosexual Behavior: A Modern Reappraisal,* ed. J. Marmor. New York: Basic.

Marx, K. 1975 [1844]. "Economic and Philosophical Manuscripts." In *Early Writings.* Trans. R. Livingstone and G. Benton. New York: Vintage.

Meyer, M. 1968. *The Wild Duck.* London: Methuen.

Mill, J. S. 1961 [1838]. "Bentham." In *The Philosophy of John Stuart Mill,* ed. M. Cohen. New York: Modern Library.

Mill, J. S. 1961 [1861]. *Utilitarianism.* In *The Philosophy of John Stuart Mill,* ed. Marshall Cohen. New York: Modern Library.

Miller, W. I. 1993. *Humiliation.* Ithaca, N.Y.: Cornell University Press.

Montagu, A. 1959. "Natural Selection and the Origin and Evolution of Weeping in Man." *Science* 130: 1572–73.

Montagu, A. 1981. "The Evolution of Weeping." *Science Digest* (November): 32.

Montaigne, M. de. 1958 [1588]. "How We Cry and Laugh for the Same Thing." In *The Complete Works of Montaigne,* trans. D. M. Frame. Palo Alto: Stanford University Press.

Moore, G. E. 1903. *Principia Ethica.* Cambridge: Cambridge University Press.

Moravcsik, J. M. E. 1971. "Reason and Eros in the 'Ascent'-Passage of the *Symposium.*" In *Essays in Ancient Greek Philosophy,* ed. J. P. Anton and G. L. Kustas, 285–302. Albany: SUNY Press.

Morris, D. et al. 1979. *Gestures: Their Origins and Distribution.* New York: Stein & Day.

Murphy, J. G., and J. Hampton. 1988. *Forgiveness and Mercy.* Cambridge: Cambridge University Press.

Nagel, T. 1979a. "The Absurd." In *Mortal Questions,* 11–23. Cambridge: Cambridge University Press.

Nagel, T. 1979b. "Brain Bisection and the Unity of Consciousness." In *Mortal Questions,* 147–64. Cambridge: Cambridge University Press.

Nagel, T. 1979c. "Moral Luck." In *Mortal Questions,* 24–38. Cambridge: Cambridge University Press.

Nagel, T. 1979d. "Sexual Perversion." In *Mortal Questions,* 39–52. Cambridge: Cambridge University Press.

Needham, R. 1962. *Structure and Sentiment.* Chicago: University of Chicago Press.

Neu, J. 1967. "A Bibliography of Writings in English on Linguistic Method in Philosophy and Related Issues, 1930–1965." In *The Linguistic Turn,* ed. R. Rorty, 361–93. Chicago: University of Chicago Press.

Neu, J. 1971. "Plato's Analogy of State and Individual: *The Republic* and the Organic Theory of the State." *Philosophy: The Journal of the Royal Philosophical Institute* 46: 238–54.

*Neu, J. 1973. "Fantasy and Memory: The Aetiological Role of Thoughts According to Freud." *The International Journal of Psycho-Analysis.* 54: 383–98. [Chap. 11.]

Neu, J. 1974. "Genetic Explanation in *Totem and Taboo.*" In *Freud: A Collection of Critical Essays,* ed. R. Wollheim, 366–97. Garden City, N.Y.: Doubleday Anchor.

*Neu, J. 1975a. "Lévi-Strauss on Shamanism." *Man: The Journal of the Royal Anthropological Institute* 10: 285–92. [Chap. 13.]

Neu, J. 1975b. "Thought, Theory, and Therapy." *Psychoanalysis and Contemporary Science: An Annual of Integrative and Interdisciplinary Studies* 4: 103–43.

Neu, J. 1976a. "Unger's *Knowledge and Politics.*" *Texas Law Review* 54: 441–58.

*Neu, J. 1976b. "What Is Wrong with Incest?" *Inquiry* 19: 27–39. [Chap. 10.]

Neu, J. 1977. *Emotion, Thought, and Therapy.* London: Routledge & Kegan Paul.

*Neu, J. 1980a. "Jealous Thoughts." In *Explaining Emotions,* ed. A. Rorty, 425–63. Berkeley: University of California Press. [Chap. 3.]

Neu, J. 1980b. "Minds on Trial." In *Mental Illness: Law and Public Policy*, ed. B. Brody and H. T. Engelhardt, Jr., 73–105. Dordrecht: D. Reidel.

*Neu, J. 1981. "Getting Behind the Demons." *Humanities in Society* 4: 171–96. [Chap. 14.]

Neu, J. 1984a. "Looking All Around for Our Real Selves." *New York Times Book Review.* July 8: 24.

Neu, J. 1984b. "Mental Illness and Criminal Justice." *Criminal Justice Ethics* 3: 62–67.

*Neu, J. 1987a. "A Tear Is an Intellectual Thing." *Representations* 19: 35–61. [Chap. 2.]

*Neu, J. 1987b. "Freud and Perversion." In *Sexuality and Medicine, Vol. 1: Conceptual Roots*, ed. E. E. Shelp, 153–84. Dordrecht: D. Reidel. [Chap. 9.]

Neu, J. 1988a. "Divided Minds: Sartre's 'Bad Faith' Critique of Freud." *Review of Metaphysics* 42: 79–101.

*Neu, J. 1988b. "Life-Lies and Pipe Dreams: Self-Deception in Ibsen's *The Wild Duck* and O'Neill's *The Iceman Cometh.*" *Philosophical Forum* 19: 241–69. [Chap. 15.]

Neu, J., ed. 1991a. *The Cambridge Companion to Freud.* Cambridge: Cambridge University Press.

*Neu, J. 1991b. "Plato's Homoerotic *Symposium.*" In *The Philosophy of (Erotic) Love*, ed. R. C. Solomon and K. M. Higgins, 317–35. Lawrence, Kan.: University Press of Kansas. [Chap. 8.]

Neu, J. 1991c. "Hampshire's *Innocence and Experience.*" *Ethics* 102: 155–58.

Neu, J. 1993. "Emotion." In *Collier's Encyclopedia*, vol. 9: 131–34. New York: Macmillan.

Neu, J. 1995a. "Cavell's *The Psychoanalytic Mind: From Freud to Philosophy.*" *Philosophical Review* 104: 289–93.

*Neu, J. 1995b. "'Does the Professor Talk to God?': Learning from Little Hans." *Philosophy, Psychiatry, and Psychology* 2: 137–61. [Chap. 12.]

Neu, J. 1995c. "Freud." In *The Cambridge Dictionary of Philosophy*, ed. R. Audi, 285–87. Cambridge: Cambridge University Press.

*Neu, J. 1996. "*Odi et Amo*: On Hating the Ones We Love." In *Freud and the Passions*, ed. J. O'Neill, 53–72. University Park, Pa.: Pennsylvania State University Press. [Chap. 5.]

*Neu, J. 1998a. "Boring from Within: Endogenous versus Reactive Boredom." In *Emotions in Psychopathology: Theory and Research*, eds. W. F. Flack, Jr., and J. D. Laird, 158–70. Oxford: Oxford University Press. [Chap. 6.]

*Neu, J. 1998b. "Pride and Identity." *Midwest Studies in Philosophy* 22: 227–48. [Chap. 7.]

Neu, J. 1998c. "Sexual Identity and Sexual Justice." *Ethics* 108: 586–96.

Nietzsche, F. W. 1967 [1887]. *On the Genealogy of Morals.* Trans. W. Kaufmann and R. J. Hollingdale. New York: Vintage.

Nietzsche, F. W. 1974 [1882]. *The Gay Science.* Trans. W. Kaufmann. New York: Vintage.

Nozick, R. 1974. *Anarchy, State and Utopia.* New York: Basic.

Nunberg, H., and E. Federn, eds. 1967. *Minutes of the Vienna Psychoanalytic Society, Volume 2: 1908–1910.* New York: International Universities Press.

Nussbaum, M. C. 1986a. "The Speech of Alcibiades: A Reading of the *Symposium.*" In *The Fragility of Goodness*, 165–99. Cambridge: Cambridge University Press.

Nussbaum, M. C. 1986b. "'This Story Isn't True': Madness, Reason and Recantation in the *Phaedrus.*" In *The Fragility of Goodness*, 200–33. Cambridge: Cambridge University Press.

O'Neill, E. 1957 [1946]. *The Iceman Cometh.* New York: Vintage.

Oatley, K. 1992. *Best Laid Schemes: The Psychology of Emotions.* Cambridge: Cambridge University Press.

Payne, R. 1960. *Hubris: A Study of Pride.* New York: Harper Torchbooks.

Pears, D. 1984. *Motivated Irrationality.* Oxford: Oxford University Press.

Peyre, H. 1974. "Creative Boredom and French Literature." *Centerpoint* (Spring): 24–32.

Phillips, A. 1988. *Winnicott.* London: Fontana Press.

Phillips, A. 1993. "On Being Bored." In *On Kissing, Tickling, and Being Bored*, 68–78. Cambridge, Mass.: Harvard University Press.

Plato. 1997. *Apology, Charmides, Laws, Meno, Phaedrus, Protagoras, The Republic, Symposium.* In *Plato Complete Works*, ed. J. M. Cooper. Indianapolis: Hackett.

Price, A. W. 1989. *Love and Friendship in Plato and Aristotle.* Oxford: Oxford University Press.

Price, H. H. 1954. "Belief and Will." *Proceedings of the Aristotelian Society*, Suppl. 28.

Proust, M. 1981. *Remembrance of Things Past.* Trans. C. K. S. Moncrieff and T. Kilmartin. New York: Random House.

Quine, W. V. 1960. *Word and Object.* Cambridge, Mass.: Massachusetts Institute of Technology Press.

Quine, W. V. 1961. "Two Dogmas of Empiricism." In *From a Logical Point of View* (2nd ed.), 20–46. Cambridge, Mass.: Harvard University Press.

Rankin, A. V. 1962. "Odi et Amo: Gaius Valerius Catullus and Freud's Essay on 'A Special Type of Choice of Object Made by Men.'" *American Imago* 19: 437–48.

Rawls, J. 1971. *A Theory of Justice.* Cambridge, Mass.: Harvard University Press.

Reich, A. 1951. "The Discussion of 1912 on Masturbation and Our Present-Day Views." *Psychoanalytic Study of the Child* 6: 80–94.

Reik, T. 1976 [1931]. *Ritual.* New York: International Universities Press.

Reiman, J. H. 1976. "Privacy, Intimacy, and Personhood" *Philosophy & Public Affairs* 6: 26–44.

Ricoeur, P. 1970. *Freud and Philosophy: An Essay on Interpretation.* Trans. D. Savage. New Haven, Conn.: Yale University Press.

Rorty, A. 1980. "Jealousy, Attention, and Loss." In *Explaining Emotions*, ed. A. Rorty, 465–88. Berkeley: University of California Press, 1980. Reprinted in *Mind in Action: Essays in the Philosophy of Mind*, 135–54. Boston: Beacon Press, 1988.

Rousseau, J. J. 1950 [1755]. *Discourse on the Origin of Inequality.* Trans. G. D. H. Cole in *The Social Contract and Discourses.* London: Dent (Everyman's Library).

Rousseau. 1969 [1762]. *Émile.* Trans. B. Foxley. London: Dent (Everyman's Library).

Ryle, G. 1949. *The Concept of Mind.* London: Hutchinson.

Ryle, G. 1954. "Pleasure." *Proceedings of the Aristotelian Society,* Suppl. 28.

Sachs, D. 1981. "How to Distinguish Self-Respect from Self-Esteem." *Philosophy and Public Affairs* 10: 346–60.

Sachs, O. 1967. "Distinctions between Fantasy and Reality Elements in Memory and Reconstruction." *International Journal of Psycho-Analysis* 48: 416–23.

Sacks, O. 1990. *Seeing Voices: A Journey into the World of the Deaf.* New York: HarperPerennial.

Sartre, J-P. 1948. *The Emotions: Outline of a Theory.* Trans. B. Frechtman. New York: Philosophical Library.

Sartre, J-P. 1956 [1943]. *Being and Nothingness.* Trans. H. E. Barnes. New York: Philosophical Library.

Sartre, J-P. 1957 [1936–37]. *The Transcendence of the Ego.* Trans. F. Williams and R. Kirkpatrick. New York: NoonDay Press.

Scheler, M. 1972. *Ressentiment,* ed. L. A. Coser. Trans. W. W. Holdheim. New York: Schocken.

Schimmel, S. 1992. *The Seven Deadly Sins: Jewish, Christian, and Classical Reflections on Human Nature.* New York: Free Press.

Schoeck, H. 1970. *Envy: A Theory of Social Behaviour.* Trans. M. Glenny and B. Ross. New York: Harcourt, Brace & World.

Scodel, A. 1973 [1957]. "Heterosexual Somatic Preference and Fantasy Dependency." In *The Experimental Study of Freudian Theories,* eds. H. J. Eysenck and G. D. Wilson, 102–10. London: Methuen.

Segal, H. 1992. "The Achievement of Ambivalence." *Common Knowledge* 1: 92–103.

Sharp, R. F. 1971. *Four Great Plays by Ibsen.* New York: Bantam.

Silverman, M. A. 1980. "A Fresh Look at the Case of Little Hans." In *Freud and His Patients,* ed. M. Kanzer and J. Glenn. New York: Jason Aronson.

Singer, I. 1984–87. *The Nature of Love.* Chicago: University of Chicago Press.

Sitwell, E. 1962. "Pride." In *The Seven Deadly Sins,* ed. A. Wilson et al., 15–22. New York: William Morrow.

Slap, J. W. 1961. "Little Hans's Tonsillectomy." *Psychoanalytic Quarterly* 30: 259–61.

Slote, M. 1975. "Inapplicable Concepts." *Philosophical Studies* 28: 265–71.

Smith, A. 1969 [1759]. *The Theory of Moral Sentiments.* Indianapolis: Liberty Classics.

Soble, A., ed. 1980. *The Philosophy of Sex: Contemporary Readings.* Totowa, N.J.: Littlefield, Adams.

Solomon, R. 1978. "Emotions and Anthropology: The Logic of Emotional World Views." *Inquiry* 21: 181–99.

Spacks, P. M. 1995. *Boredom: The Literary History of a State of Mind.* Chicago: University of Chicago Press.

Spinoza, B. de. 1985 [1677]. *Ethics.* In *The Collected Works of Spinoza.* Trans. E. Curley, 1: 401–617. Princeton, N.J.: Princeton University Press.

Spiro, M. E. 1975. *Children of the Kibbutz.* Cambridge, Mass.: Harvard University Press.

Stanislavski, C. 1936. *An Actor Prepares.* Trans. E. R. Hapgood. New York: Theatre Arts.

Stendhal. 1975 [1822]. *On Love.* Trans. G. & S. Sale. Harmondsworth, England: Penguin.

Stewart, W. A. 1967. *Psychoanalysis: The First Ten Years 1888–1898.* New York: Macmillan.

Sulloway, F. J. 1991. "Reassessing Freud's Case Histories: The Social Construction of Psychoanalysis." *Isis* 82: 245–75.

Szasz, T. S. 1961. *The Myth of Mental Illness.* New York: Hoeber-Harper.

Taylor, C. 1964. *The Explanation of Behaviour.* London: Routledge & Kegan Paul.

Taylor, C. 1992. *The Ethics of Authenticity.* New Haven, Conn.: Harvard University Press.

Taylor, G. 1980. "Pride." In *Explaining Emotions,* ed. A. Rorty, 385–402. Berkeley: University of California Press.

Taylor, G. 1985. *Pride, Shame, and Guilt.* Oxford: Oxford University Press.

Trilling, L. 1972. *Sincerity and Authenticity.* Cambridge, Mass.: Harvard University Press.

Turner, V. 1967. *The Forest of Symbols: Aspects of Ndembu Ritual.* Ithaca, N.Y.: Cornell University Press.

Turner, V. 1978. "Encounter with Freud: The Making of a Comparative Symbologist." In *The Making of Psychological Anthropology,* ed. G. Spindler. Berkeley: University of California Press.

Twain, M. 1897. *Following the Equator: A Journey Around the World* (Vol. 1). New York: Harper & Brothers.

Vlastos, G. 1973. "The Individual as an Object of Love in Plato." *Platonic Studies,* 3–42. Princeton, N.J.: Princeton University Press.

Vlastos, G. 1980 [1958]. "The Paradox of Socrates." In *The Philosophy of Socrates,* ed. G. Vlastos. Notre Dame, Ind.: University of Notre Dame Press.

Vlastos, G. 1989. "Was Plato a Feminist?" *Times Literary Supplement* (March 17–23): 276, 288–89.

Vlastos, G. 1991. *Socrates: Ironist and Moral Philosopher.* Cambridge: Cambridge University Press.

Vonnegut, K., Jr. 1970. "Harrison Bergeron." *Welcome to the Monkey House.* New York: Dell.

Walsh, W. H. 1970. "Pride, Shame and Responsibility." *The Philosophical Quarterly* 20: 1–13.

Walton, K. 1978. "Fearing Fictions." *Journal of Philosophy* 75: 5–27.

Watson, J. B. 1924. *Behaviorism.* New York: W. W. Norton.

Wenzel, S. 1960. *The Sin of Sloth: Acedia in Medieval Thought and Literature.* Chapel Hill: University of North Carolina Press.

Williams, B. 1959. "Pleasure and Belief." *Proceedings of the Aristotelian Society,* Suppl. 33.

Williams, B. 1973a. "Deciding to Believe." In *Problems of the Self,* 136–51. Cambridge: Cambridge University Press.

Williams, B. 1973b. "Ethical Consistency." In *Problems of the Self*, 166–86. Cambridge: Cambridge University Press.

Williams, B. 1973c. "The Idea of Equality." In *Problems of the Self*, 230–49. Cambridge: Cambridge University Press.

Williams, B. 1973d. "The Makropulos Case: Reflections on the Tedium of Immortality." In *Problems of the Self*, 82–100. Cambridge: Cambridge University Press.

Williams, B. 1973e. "Personal Identity and Individuation." In *Problems of the Self*, 1–18. Cambridge: Cambridge University Press.

Williams, B. 1981. "Moral Luck." In *Moral Luck*, 20–39. Cambridge: Cambridge University Press.

Wilson, B. R., ed. 1970. *Rationality*. New York: Harper and Row.

Wilson, E. O. 1978. *On Human Nature*. Cambridge, Mass.: Harvard University Press.

Winkler, J. J. 1990. "Unnatural Acts." In *The Constraints of Desire: The Anthropology of Sex and Gender in Ancient Greece*. New York: Routledge.

Winnicott, D. W. 1958. "Transitional Objects and Transitional Phenomena." In *Collected Papers*, 229–42. London: Tavistock.

Winnicott, D. W. 1965. "The Capacity to be Alone." In *The Maturational Processes and the Facilitating Environment*, 29–36. London: Hogarth.

Winnicott, D. W. 1974a. "Mirror-role of Mother and Family in Child Development." In *Playing and Reality*, 130–38. Harmondsworth, England: Penguin.

Winnicott, D. W. 1974b. "The Use of an Object and Relating through Identifications." In *Playing and Reality*, 101–11. Harmondsworth, England: Penguin.

Wittgenstein, L. 1953. *Philosophical Investigations*. Trans. G. E. M. Anscombe. Oxford: B. Blackwell.

Wolff, P. H. 1969. "The Natural History of Crying and Other Vocalizations in Early Infancy." In *Determinants of Infant Behavior*, ed. B. M. Foss, 81–109. London: Methuen.

Wollheim, R. 1966. "Expression." *Royal Institute of Philosophy Lectures* 1: 227–44.

Wollheim, R. 1979. "Wish-fulfillment." In *Rational Action*, ed. R. Harrison. Cambridge: Cambridge University Press.

Wollheim, R. 1980. "On Persons and Their Lives." In *Explaining Emotions*, ed. A. Rorty, 299–321. Berkeley: University of California Press.

Wollheim, R. 1993. "Desire, Belief, and Professor Grünbaum's Freud." In *The Mind and Its Depths*, 91–111. Cambridge, Mass.: Harvard University Press.

Wollheim, R. 1993 [1979]. "The Sheep and the Ceremony." In *The Mind and Its Depths*, 1–21. Cambridge, Mass.: Harvard University Press.

Wolpe, J., and S. Rachman. 1963 [1960]. "Psychoanalytic Evidence: A Critique Based on Freud's Case of Little Hans." In *Critical Essays on Psychoanalysis*, ed. S. Rachman, 198–220. Oxford: Pergamon. Also reprinted in *The Experimental Study of Freudian Theories*, eds. H. J. Eysenck and G. D. Wilson, 317–41. London: Methuen, 1973; and in *Unauthorized Freud: Doubters Confront a Legend*, ed. F. C. Crews. New York: Viking, 1998.

Wood, E. C., and C. D. Wood. 1984. "Tearfulness: A Psychoanalytic Interpretation." *Journal of the American Psychoanalytic Association* 32: 117–36.

Wright, L. 1994. "One Drop of Blood." *The New Yorker* 70 (July 25): 46ff.

Xenophon. 1990. *Memorabilia, Symposium.* In *Conversations of Socrates.* Trans. H. Tredennick and R. Waterfield. Harmondsworth, England: Penguin.

Young-Bruehl, E. 1988. *Anna Freud.* New York: Summit.

Zukofsky, L. 1969. *Catullus fragmenta.* London: Turret.

INDEX

Emotions (*continued*)
emotions; Sensations, emotions not simply
Emotivism (in ethics), 102
Empathy, 21–22, 67, 75, 77, 160–63, 278, 280–81
Empire (Warhol film), 98
Emptiness, and boredom, 96, 103
Ennui, 102–3, 104, 105, 106
Envy, 47–54, 78, 127, 128, 241, 292 n.9; versus jealousy, 42–43, 47–49, 67; malicious versus admiring, 48, 53, 292 n.7; penis, 44, 157, 219; and self-esteem, 53–54.
Equality, 45, 115, 123, 141, 292 n.8; envy and, 49–54, 78; self-respect and, 116, 121, 126–29. *See also* Love, and reciprocity
Erikson, E., 53, 197, 208, 232, 242–43, 281, 292 n.12, 303 n.5
Erotogenic zones, 145, 193, 219. *See also* Anal erotism; Genital sexuality; Orality
Essence, 5–10, 113–14, 117–21, 294 n.16
Etchegoyen, R. H., 219
Etiquette, 24–25
Evagrius of Pontus, 128
Evans-Pritchard, E., 243
Evidence, 4, 19–20, 22, 60, 173, 179, 198, 200–1, 203–20, 228, 243–45, 247, 251–53, 288, 312 n.6
Evolution, 14–17, 37–38, 39, 153, 167, 223–24, 289 n.4, 303 n.6
Existentialism, 10
Exogamy and endogamy, 167, 168, 307 n.2
Explanation: of the normal, 239–40, 259, 261; psychoanalytic, 160–63, 164–65, 203–10, 211, 212–18, 239–61; structuralist, 233–37; and thick description, 247–49. *See also under* Object-choice; Reductive analysis
Expression of emotion, 14–40, 205–8, 214, 240–42, 245–47, 248–49, 254–55, 259–60; facial, 20–23, 34, 290 nn. 9–11; versus manifestation, 187–88; natural, 22–25, 30–31, 34–35, 39–40,

290 n.13; universal and local, 19–23, 33–36, 242–45, 247–49. *See also* Voluntariness
Eysenck, H. J., 212

Fainting, 26–27, 31
Fairlie, H., 110
Faith, 174, 231, 233, 251–53, 260, 287–88, 313 n.8
Fantasy, 70, 96, 107, 146, 159, 163, 168, 180, 191, 194–99, 205, 227, 236–38, 278–79, 309 n.9; and memory, 177–99, 222–23, 308 n.5; primal, 198, 207, 220–24; unconscious, 32, 74–75, 161, 171, 185, 193, 199, 309 n.9
Faust, 128
Fear, 20, 21, 24, 29–32, 34, 200–28, 241, 249, 309 n.2; of envy, 50–51, 292 n.9; of fictions, 29–32; and hatred, 84, 94, 115, 121–24; in jealousy, 48, 56–57, 62–63, 70. *See also* Paranoia; Phobias
Feldman, S. S., 33–36
Fellatio, 146, 149, 161, 194
Femininity, 83–84, 156–57, 217–18, 219, 256, 299 n.2. *See also* Activity and passivity, sexual
Fenichel, O., 96, 104
Fetishism, 146, 306 n.17; exclusiveness and fixation in, 151–52, 160, 162; foot, 156, 160–63, 306 n.16
Fiction, emotional responses to, 13, 16–17, 29–32
Fine, A., 212
Fingarette, H., 312 n.5
Flaubert, G., 102
Fliess, W., 149, 190, 191, 200
Foot, P., 114
Forbes, M., 212
Fore (of New Guinea), 21, 22, 34, 290 n.9
Forrester, J., 79
Foster, G. M., 292 n.9
Foucault, M., 117, 299 nn.3, 5, 300 n.11
Frazer, J., 246, 247
Freedom, 8, 11, 27, 83, 85, 94, 113, 122, 163, 173, 262, 280. *See also* Reflexive knowledge

Freud, A., 82, 150, 200, 224, 225–26

Freud, S., 4, 31, 34, 36, 51, 57, 61–62, 66, 70, 73–74, 76–77, 79, 82, 84–89, 92–93, 94, 99, 105, 106–7, 115, 121–23, 132–33, 134, 135, 136–37, 140, 142, 144–65, 168, 171–72, 177–99, 200–28, 229, 232–33, 235–36, 239–42, 245, 247–49, 250–53, 255, 256, 257–61, 284–87, 291 n.3, 296–7 n.6, 297 nn.7–11, 13, 299 nn.1, 4, 6, 300 n.10, 301 n.20, 302–3 n.1, 303 nn.2–4, 304 nn.7, 9, 11, 305–6 n.15, 306 n.17, 307 nn.3, 19, 308 nn.1–3, 8, 309 nn.2–3, 9

Frey, W. H., 28, 289 n.5, 290 n.6

Friendship, 47, 65, 69, 92, 302 n.22

Fungibility, 57–60

Geertz, C., 248–49, 259–60

Gellner, E., 254, 311 n.6

Genet, J., 231–32

Genital sexuality, 153–54, 214–15, 219

Gert, B., 305 n.14

Gilligan, C., 296 n.5

Glymour, C., 212

God and gods, 7, 73, 85, 99, 108, 110, 112–13, 128–29, 134, 138, 251. *See also* Religion

Golding, W., 8

Goodness, 4, 8–9, 92, 101–2, 107, 122, 134, 136, 141

Graf, M., 201, 206, 225–26

Gratitude, 49, 56, 187

Greenacre, P., 306 n.17

Greenson, R. R., 96–98, 99, 105

Greenspan, P., 296 nn.3, 6

Gregory the Great, 110, 112

Grief, 15, 17, 24–25, 30, 31, 33, 37, 42, 77, 87, 105, 172–3, 240–42, 289–90 n.5, 305 n.14

Grünbaum, A., 212, 217

Guilt, 19, 170–72, 189, 196, 227, 257, 272, 276, 277–78, 279, 281, 285. *See also* Shame

Halperin, D. M., 117–21, 299 nn.2–3, 7, 301–2 n.22

Hampshire, S., 23–25, 33, 40, 102, 122, 184, 307 nn.4, 18, 312 n.6

Hampton, J., 298 n.18

Handicaps, 57–58, 113, 115–16, 294 n.16

Happiness, 8–10, 20, 92, 105, 262, 264, 265–74, 282, 288, 312 nn.1–2; happy endings, 33, 36

Hart, H. L. A., 112

Hartley, L. P., 292 n.8

Hatred, 34–35, 41, 52, 56, 69, 77, 81–94, 111, 122, 207, 272, 276, 277, 284–85, 297–98 nn.15, 17–18

Hearn, L., 24–25, 290 nn.12–13

Hegel, G. W. F., 73, 76, 83, 91, 122, 125

Heidegger, 84

Herodotus, 313 n.8

Hill, T. E., Jr., 127

Hirsch, F., 50

Hobbes, T., 7–8

Hochschild, A. R., 290–91 nn.15–16

Hollis, M., 244

Homosexuality, 61, 62, 75, 116–21, 124, 130–43, 145, 146–48, 155–60, 166, 173, 218, 279–80, 300 nn.12, 15–16, 304 n.9, 305–6 nn.14–15

Hope, 274, 278, 279, 287. *See also* Faith

Hostility, unconscious 35, 205–8, 214, 240–42, 243, 245–47, 254–55, 275–76, 284. *See also* Aggression; Hatred; Rivalry

Hubris, 110, 128, 301 n.19

Hug-Hellmuth, H. Von, 224

Human nature, 5–10, 12, 94, 96, 105–7, 138, 141, 148–49, 165, 242–45, 265–70, 287–88. *See also* Instinct

Hume, D., 13, 34–35, 68–69, 79, 82, 91, 110, 114, 126, 198, 292 n.13, 297 n.13

Humility, 90, 110, 111, 124, 125, 127, 128

Huxley, A., 268–69

Hypnosis, 177–80, 183–84

Hysteria, 25, 92, 161, 177–99, 210, 235–38, 258